Biopolitical Ethics in Global Cinema

Biopolitical Ethics in Global Cinema

SEUNG-HOON JEONG

Oxford University Press is a department of the University of Oxford. It furthers
the University's objective of excellence in research, scholarship, and education
by publishing worldwide. Oxford is a registered trade mark of Oxford University
Press in the UK and certain other countries.

Published in the United States of America by Oxford University Press
198 Madison Avenue, New York, NY 10016, United States of America.

© Oxford University Press 2023

All rights reserved. No part of this publication may be reproduced, stored in
a retrieval system, or transmitted, in any form or by any means, without the
prior permission in writing of Oxford University Press, or as expressly permitted
by law, by license, or under terms agreed with the appropriate reproduction
rights organization. Inquiries concerning reproduction outside the scope of the
above should be sent to the Rights Department, Oxford University Press, at the
address above.

You must not circulate this work in any other form
and you must impose this same condition on any acquirer.

CIP data is on file at the Library of Congress

ISBN 978–0–19–009379–2 (pbk.)
ISBN 978–0–19–009378–5 (hbk.)

DOI: 10.1093/oso/9780190093785.001.0001

Paperback printed by Marquis Book Printing, Canada
Hardback printed by Bridgeport National Bindery, Inc., United States of America

In memory of Thomas Elsaesser

Contents

Preface	xi
Acknowledgments	xvii

Introduction: World Cinema in a Global Frame	1
The World as Global	1
A Microhistory of Globalization with the Ethical Turn of Politics	4
Subjectivity and Community in Crisis	8
Mapping Frames of World Cinema	12
A Matrix of Global Cinema	18

PART I: ABJECTION AND AGENCY

1. Multicultural Conflicts in Postpolitical Double Ethics	25
The Historic Falls and the Motif of 'Falling'	25
Multiculturalism from Multiple Angles	29
"Hate, a Last Sign of Life"	35
Theory of Abjection Reloaded with Agency	38
Paris and *Banlieues* in Post–*La haine* Mainstream French Cinema	44
Auteurist Responses to the Ethical Potential and Limitations of Abjection	49
2. The Narrative of Double Death with Abject Agency	58
Narratology and Ideology: Double Death and Abject Agency	58
Two East Asian Transnational Networks in Korean Cinema	61
The North-West Network: The 'Dog' and 'Thief' of Capital	64
The South-East Network: Cognitive, Financial, and Emotional Capitalism	72
3. Sovereign Agents' Biopolitical Abjection in the Spy Film	79
Biopolitical Abjection: Bare Life and Sovereign Power	79
The Bond Series: From the Cold War to the Global Millennium	81
Skyfall: The Self-Reaffirmation of the 'Dark Knight'	86
Abject Agency from Bond to Bourne	93

PART II: CATASTROPHE AND REVELATION

4. Law, Divine Violence, and the Sanctity of Life ... 101
   Violence as Power: Benjamin, Derrida, and Batman ... 101
   Divine Violence for the Sanctity of Life ... 109
   Divine Violence without God: Žižek and *The Act of Killing* ... 113
   (Pseudo-)Divine Violence and *Waltz with Bashir* ... 120

5. From the Disaster Genre to the Cinema of Catastrophe ... 124
   Global Catastrophes, Enforced Cosmopolitanism, and Cinematic Reflections ... 124
   Theorizing Disaster, Catastrophe, and the Sublime ... 130
   The Evolution of the Disaster Genre and the Cinema of Catastrophe ... 135

6. Human History in (Post)Apocalyptic Cinema ... 142
   Apocalypse between Revelation and Repetition ... 142
   Snowpiercer: A Global Allegory of Biopolitical Economy and Ecology ... 144
   Snowpiercer: Catastrophe as Breakthrough or Dead End ... 150
   The *Mad Max* Series: A Postapocalyptic 'Fury Road' of Historical Déjà Vu ... 157
   Preapocalyptic Yet Already Catastrophic ... 162

7. The Time Loop of Catastrophe in the Mind-Game Film ... 165
   Mind-Game Time Travel and Retroactive Causality ... 165
   Donnie Darko: An Indeterminate Text on Free Will ... 168
   Donnie Darko: "Time Is out of Joint" and Postapocalypse ... 173
   Source Code: Sci-Fi Mind Game and Video Game in Control Society ... 176
   Source Code: Time Travel, Performative Agency, and the Sacrifice of Sacrifice ... 183
   The Ideology of 'Undoing' in the Perpetual Present of Action ... 187

PART III: COMMUNITY AND NETWORK

8. Narrative Formations of Community and Network ... 193
   Global Society: Community or Network? ... 193
   Mapping Network Narratives; Global Community as a Totalized Network ... 195
   Theorizing Community and Global Network Narratives ... 200
   Pure Network Narratives with Free-Floating Agents ... 205
   Theorizing Network and the Shift from Community to Network ... 209

9. Nation, Transnationality, and Global Community as Totalized Network ... 214
   Community and Network in the National, Transnational, and Global Frames ... 214
   Islamic World: *Timbuktu, Taste of Cherry, Life and Nothing More*... 216

India's Nationalist Cinema and Beyond: *Roja, Rang de Basanti, Slumdog Millionaire*   225
Pan-Chinese Global Cinema: *Crouching Tiger, Hidden Dragon, Chungking Express, A Touch of Sin*   231

PART IV: GIFT AND ATOPIA

10. Alternative Ethics through the Paradox of the Gift   245
    Positive Modes of Abject Agency: Artistic Creativity and Ethical Gift-Giving   245
    Dogville: Being as a Gift beyond Gift Economy and Biopolitical Ethics   251
    Gran Torino: A Global Aporia of the Gift and the Birth of a (Multicultural) Nation   256
    Life of Pi: The Ontological Other as a Precarious Yet Precious Gift   263

11. The Abject as Neighbor beyond Cultural Mediation   269
    Ethical Philosophy on Abraham and Isaac   269
    The Promise: Walking Side by Side with the Abject Neighbor   273
    The Edge of Heaven: Relaying Gift-Giving in Zigzag as Atopian Ethics   279

12. Atopian Networking and Positive Nihilism   286
    Negative, Passive, and Active Nihilism in the Global Frame   286
    Children of Men: Atopian Networking in Global Dystopian Cinema   289
    Himizu: Existential *Amor Fati* in Positive Nihilism   294
    Cinema as an Ethical Art   299

References   303
Index   317

Preface

My idea of global cinema began a decade ago when I was still finalizing my first book, *Cinematic Interfaces: Film Theory after New Media* (Routledge, 2013). I had initially thought of writing a sequel to this book by expanding its film-based interface theory to new media works, but many changes redirected my focus. Among them, my experience living in the United Arab Emirates (UAE) while teaching at New York University Abu Dhabi may be worth noting. The oil-rich Gulf state was the epitome of globalization, with a nearly 90 percent expatriate population and an open attitude toward hot trends and cutting-edge trades, which transformed the endless desert into an ultra-urban landscape with marvelous skyscrapers. In addition, I found myself in a more transcultural and multiethnic society than anywhere else, a secular liberal Muslim country tolerant of other religions, unlike Western prejudices about the Middle East. A pioneering global liberal arts college, NYU Abu Dhabi was more colorful than NYU New York; in any given class of fifteen students there were typically about ten nationalities, including many Americans and Europeans. Teaching such a diverse, brilliant, and open-minded future generation was a sheer pleasure.

But soon I had to face the verso of globalization. The splendid surface of cosmopolitan metropolises barely covered up layered shadows cast from the relentless state-driven capitalist system, which was sustained by the massive influx of cheap labor and high-paid professionals from far away. The consequent labor exploitation, racial segregation, class disparity, and social hierarchy were palpable but seemingly taken for granted, as though they were public secrets everyone knew but despite which they should 'keep calm and carry on.' Admittedly, most foreigners had no public sphere, no access to the country's sociopolitical scene, and no need to engage in it. Poor immigrants endured harsh working conditions to pursue the Gulf dream of making money and sending it back home; upper-level expatriates lived an affluent lifestyle, comfortably confined within personal networks of professional interests or cultural tastes. Global citizens—and the 'global noncitizens' I discuss in this book—managed their globalized but atomized lives with no genuine sense or necessity of belonging to the nation. The state functioned just to facilitate the global flow of capital and human resources while operating all security measures to protect it from any risks. In truth, the region was undergoing various post–Arab Spring threats such as Islamic fundamentalism, terroristic attacks, and refuge crises, predicting a post-oil energy war along with global warming's effects on the already scorching land. Some people may have wondered if they weren't living inside a global bubble, glamorous yet vulnerable, like a mirage in the desert.

Crucially, the UAE is not exceptional, but representative of the current world order—and ever more countries will resemble it if globalization continues. Cultural liberalism and economic neoliberalism underlie this postpolitical order in which the state serves the market and the public dissolves into the private. Here, individuals directly float across the planetary net of limitless competition and connection with less and less mediation by political communities. Global society thus emerges as a matrix of ever-proliferating networks of the multitudes who enjoy multicultural hospitality, nomadic mobility, and borderless opportunities on the one hand and yet encounter uncontrollable catastrophes triggered by this system's structural contradictions and violent byproducts on the other. These two conflicting facets of globalization have been my existential condition and academic motivation. Building on critical theory, I have explored their various implications primarily through the lens of today's *soft* and *hard* ethics—inclusive tolerance and exclusive justice—while investigating significant changes in subjectivity and community in this double ethics. At the same time, I have designed a global frame of world cinema to elucidate even local films' reflections of such global phenomena by formulating *global cinema* beyond popular but vague usages of the term and exceeding the conventional frames of studying ghettoized national cinemas and their transnational interactions.

Not limited to film production and reception, this book thus thematically characterizes global cinema in the frame of globalism and its antinomies. Many films indeed stage the unresolvable antagonism between the inclusive global system and its excluded remnants, variants of catastrophe and nihilism, allegorizing the impossibility of political change for an alternative system. A global community often appears as a totalized network of sovereign violence and (counter)terror stuck in the impasse of utopian imagination. Nonetheless, some films open room for a new ethical potential irreducible to politics by shedding light on abject figures who, though deprived of social subjectivity and legal rights, turn into agents of existential gift-giving by fostering commonality without community, solidarity without unity. I here retheorize the psychoanalytic notion of *abjection* in postpolitical but biopolitical contexts, while also recharging it with the ethical agency that enables atopian, if not utopian, networking around the edge of the global regime and beyond the soft/hard ethics of problematic tolerance and justice. Highlighting this precarious yet precious *abject agency*, I affirm that it is immanent in cinema as an ethical art.

Throughout the book, I map a vast net of post-1990s films circulating globally in both the mainstream market and the festival circuit. They range from commercial genre films to independent art films beyond the biased dichotomy of Hollywood as global and world cinema as an alternative. I navigate them as compatibly embodying today's universal human conditions, especially illuminating the narrative of *double death*: the abject, symbolically dead, struggle to regain lost subjectivity or activate new agency until physical death. The book is also multimethodological, delving into critical discourses on crucial topics such as multiculturalism, terrorism, sovereignty, abjection, violence, catastrophe, community, network, nihilism, and the gift. I attempt not just to apply theories but to test and renew them face to face with existential situations on screen. It is my hope that this chemical interplay of film and theory will open new access points to film narratives, motifs, and genres, as well as political, ethical, and philosophical concerns, notably reinventing subjectivity as abject agency and community as gift-giving atopia. I couldn't desire more if the book thereby brings to readers fresh insights into global life through cinema and contributes to today's critical humanities, including film studies.

Far from being linear, the road to this monograph has been long and winding, with many interruptions and unexpected deviations. I have gradually developed a synthetic framework of diverse global themes while working on a variety of case studies and two related book-length side projects: *The Global Auteur: The Politics of Authorship in 21st Century Cinema*, which I coedited (Bloomsbury, 2016), and the "Global East Asian Cinema" special issue of *Studies in the Humanities*, which I guest edited (2019). Meanwhile, my global trajectory has led me to South Korea and then again to the United States after teaching back and forth, in a seemingly endless drift. On top of these relocations, the COVID-19 pandemic and other social or personal issues have further slowed the writing process, making me anxious as recent global events have seemingly challenged my framing of globalization. No wonder an anonymous manuscript reader wondered about my view of the world in the wake of the pandemic and the war in Ukraine. The global system might be transforming right now, the reader said, "with global economic integration no longer a sacrosanct feature of the world system, isolationist or nationalist political movements in the ascendancy, and 'hard' ethical positions crowding out the 'soft' human rights discourse." This book might then be read as focusing on "a potentially bounded historical era that may now be coming to an end," though the future of the current crises is unpredictable.

With appreciation of the reader's sincere comments,[1] let me briefly note that my global frame theoretically ranges up to the factionalism of the 2010s and the anticentrist populism featured by isolationist/nationalist backlashes against globalization, as seen in Brexit and Trumpism. In other words, these inner hard-ethical fractures of the already globalized world are not a postpandemic phenomenon but have occurred throughout the last decade, while the global system has continued to reinforce itself as Wall Street has never really been 'occupied' by its opponents. Likewise, despite the China-United States trade war and the Russia-NATO new cold war, economic crises like today's worldwide inflation and energy disaster caused by a series of US-driven sanctions against its enemies paradoxically indicate the impossibility of disentangling any part of the world from its economic interdependency. Doesn't the pandemic also prove that any local virus can instantly threaten the whole globe because of its networked integration? And doesn't it thus demand a genuinely global coalition for humankind's survival? Such global cooperation against global catastrophes is not a choice but a duty like 'enforced cosmopolitanism' for cohabitation, and separatist antiglobalism may only lead to co-destruction. We could not cope with the side effects of globalization without working in and through other potentialities of globalization. Now the global system may be its own poison and remedy.

Nonetheless, the last decade has indeed seen an increasingly strong trend of deglobalization. It provokes the territorial insiders' violent hatred toward their deterritorializing neighbors; they scramble to restore their crumbling privilege, as typified by the slogan, "Make America Great Again!" Feeling isolation from globalization and reverse discrimination against social

---

[1] The reader also offered a rich, inspiring observation of the abject character, wondering about a longer history that could align this figure with the outsider or antihero in the 1960s–1970s New Wave/New Hollywood up to "Maverick" in the *Top Gun* films (including the 2022 sequel). My simple response is that yes, the abject are found everywhere in film history, but I focus on their biopolitical nature in my global frame that should be specific enough. The maverick couldn't find a place here, though his peculiar status as integral to his institution deserves deeper discussion. I cannot go further in this book but could try a historical taxonomy of abject figures someday elsewhere.

minorities, the mainstream class employs hard-ethical terroristic violence and disrupts soft-ethical multicultural society from within. By extension, it is undeniable that just as the pandemic has forced a new normal in all domains of everyday life, contemporary hot issues—including big data, surveillance capitalism, artificial intelligence, climate change, and of course, infectious diseases—have simultaneously brought about new world visions and risks beyond the earlier paradigm of globalization. I thus feel some new 'urgency of now' to update this book's concerns, which were conceived with a similar urgency years ago. More recent films and books in the 2010s–2020s will inspire me to reshape my biopolitical and ethical points in a timelier frame of new topics and nuanced ideas. The future is always uncertain, but I will see when it is time to embark on this new project.

Acknowledgments

As in my first book, I would like to name my two former advisers and guiding lights at the top of this acknowledgment list. Dudley Andrew's class that I assisted as a teaching fellow at Yale University initiated me into studying world cinema as a concept, and his work later inspired me to reframe it from my own perspective. Offering me a few presentation opportunities and reading some chapters, he has always supported this book project, appreciated my approach as worth taking, and encouraged my perseverance during hard times. This was also the case with Thomas Elsaesser. Some films in his graduate seminar on world cinema sparked my initial ethical framework, and I later developed its core concepts, like abjection, in discussion with him while exchanging feedback on our similar works. He graciously invited me to give related talks in his classes at Columbia University, where I even had to take on his 2020 course left behind by his sudden, saddening death. With my never-fading memories of him, I dedicate to his spirit this book that should have come out when he was still alive.

My gratitude goes on to Fredric Jameson, Garrett Stewart, and Vivian Sobchack for their appreciation of my work and support for some other matters. Though my writing process has not involved their interventions, their longtime encouragement means a lot to me. Regarding the actual book writing, I am deeply indebted and grateful to William Brown and Madeleine Collier for their editorial work and enthusiastic support. William perused the first few chapter drafts while offering erudite comments with pointed questions and making minor corrections or suggestions to smoothen my language here and there. His advanced research on world cinema also impressed me, and I hope to update my scope via his material in the future. Similarly, Madeleine checked around the second half of the book chapter by chapter swiftly and effectively, sustaining my momentum for the final months and assisting some of my other jobs. Without her sincere help, I could not have juggled multiple tasks when extremely pressed by duties and deadlines.

Since my global cinema research has been growing for a decade, I owe a debt of gratitude to those who contributed to it in various ways, even if they are not fully aware. Thanks to Jeremi Szaniawski, my coeditor of *The Global Auteur*, I became clearer about how to map global cinema and rethink its auteurism critically. Reena Dube invited me to guest edit the special double issue of *Studies in the Humanities*, in which I enriched my conceptual scheme of abjection and agency through global East Asian cinema. In addition, many other people offered me precious opportunities to present or publish parts of the book content in different stages and forms. A significant portion of the book is based on my essays published in the journals or books edited by Jaap Verheul, George Dunn, Sangjoon Lee, Todd Comer and Isaac Vayo, Ju Young Jin and Jae H. Roe, Mirosław Przylipiak, and Temenuga Trifonova. Likewise, many ideas and case studies were globally presented in the conference panels or special events organized by Antonia Lant, Anita Starosta, Heike Harting, Robert Sinnerbrink and Lisa Trahair, Ella Shohat and Robert Stam, Richard Allen, Michelle Cho, Todd McGowan, Libby Saxton, Julia Alekseyeva, William Costanzo, and Manishita Dass and Samhita Sunya. In Korea, I was gratefully invited to speak, write, or teach, often multiple times, by Soyoung Kim, Miseong Woo, Moon Im Baek, Hye Jean Chung, Jeong-Hee Kim, Hyun Seon Park, and EunHyoung Kim. Many of these people are longtime colleagues and influential scholars for me. And so is Keith Wagner, whom I thank for his abiding collaborative passion for global cinema studies. Lúcia Nagib, Shohini Chaudhuri, Matthew Holtmeier, Julian Hanich, Martin Rossouw, and many others I couldn't list all helped advance my work at some point, too.

Thanks are due to some institutions as well. As a visiting fellow at Korea's Asia Culture Center and Yonsei University's Korean Studies Center, I worked and presented on some subjects around 'global Korean cinema'—which perhaps will be my immediate next book item to finalize my global cinema trilogy, which so far includes the global East Asian cinema journal issue and this global cinema book. It was also always productive to give invited talks and receive energizing feedback in many places across the globe, from Seoul National University to Harvard University. Three graduate courses I taught at NYU New York, partly via NYU Abu Dhabi's global fellowship, were vital to building and updating my overall research scope. Some graduate students I met at NYU, Columbia, SNU, Yonsei, and Korea National University of Arts are still in touch or are already my colleagues. Thanks to NYUAD's research support, I worked in Europe for several summers, often with student assistants, and participated in many events and conferences. I further note that it has been my great pleasure to teach global cinema even on the undergraduate level at NYUAD, SNU, K-Arts, and currently California State University Long Beach. I thank all my students and faculty members there.

This book could not have seen the world without the endless generosity of Norm Hirschy, executive editor of Oxford University Press. So many recent changes and events in my life, such as transcontinental relocations and unexpected projects, distracted my attention after making a book contract; he said the pandemic slowed down everything in OUP too. But even after we reset a new schedule last year, I had to shamefully push back the manuscript submission a few times over half a year while Norm patiently let me have more and more time. I cannot thank him enough for all his trust and support during this long delay. I am also thankful to other OUP staff in charge of every step toward the book publication. And special thanks go to a few anonymous proposal readers and a final manuscript reader for their favorable reviews, especially the admirably rich last one that motivated me to write a relatively long preface.

Finally, let me thank the copyright holders of my formerly published pieces for permitting me to reuse, reformat, and revise them to various degrees. The Introduction expands my article "Introduction—Global East Asian Cinema: Abjection and Agency," *Studies in the Humanities* 44, nos. 1–2 & 45, nos. 1–2 (2019): ii–xxii, and Chapter 2 includes "Dog and Thief: Two Modes of Abject Agency Crossing over East Asian Capital Networks in Global Korean Cinema" in the same journal issue (pp. 182–200) guest edited by myself. Chapter 3 is derived from "Global Agency between Bond and Bourne: *Skyfall* and James Bond in Comparison to the Jason Bourne Film Series," in *The Cultural Life of James Bond: Specters of 007*, ed. Jaap Verheul (Amsterdam: Amsterdam University Press, 2020), 207–25. Chapter 4 is based on "Sovereign Agents of Mythical and (Pseudo-)Divine Violence: Walter Benjamin and Global Biopolitical Cinema," *Philosophical Journal of Conflict and Violence* 4, no. 2 (2020): 81–98. Chapter 6 incorporates "*Snowpiercer* (2013): The Post-Historical Catastrophe of a Biopolitical Ecosystem," in *Rediscovering Korean Cinema*, ed. Sangjoon Lee (Ann Arbor: University of Michigan Press, 2019), 486–501. Chapter 7 includes material from "The Apocalyptic Sublime: Hollywood Disaster Films and *Donnie Darko*," in *Terror and the Cinematic Sublime: Essays on Violence and the Unpresentable in Post-9/11 Films*, ed. Todd Comer and Isaac Vayo (Jefferson, NC: McFarland, 2013), 72–87, and "A Thin Line between Sovereign and Abject Agents: Global Action Thrillers with Sci-Fi Mind-Game War on Terror," *CLCWeb: Comparative Literature and Culture* 21, no. 7 (2019). Chapter 8 readjusts "Network Narratives in Global Cinema: The Shift from Community to Network and Their Narrative Logics," *Panoptikum* 26 (2021): 131–52. And Chapter 11 includes much of "From 'Face-to-Face' to 'Side-by-Side': The Abject Neighbor in European Cinema," *Northern Lights: Film & Media Studies Yearbook* 18, no. 1 (2020): 53–67, published by Intellect Ltd (https://doi.org/10.1386/nl_00013_1). I put a citation note in the case of reusing a piece of mine only partially. All the images in the book are screenshots.

Notes: Throughout the book, I use open and close double quote marks (" ") for actual quotations and open and close single quote marks (' ') for my emphases (as well as coined and "defined" terms). Crucial concepts are italicized.

Introduction
World Cinema in a Global Frame

The World as Global

'Global,' a word that today can be used to modify anything in the world, is not always used without justification. Even the tautological idiom 'global world' implies more than just the world, namely a globally integrated world. Although we cannot visit all its corners and meet all people, we can imagine and cognitively map this global community to which we believe we belong more than to a mere world in which we remain ignorant of, detached from, or indifferent to most of its different parts. In short, the whole world is now an "imagined community" as Benedict Anderson (1991) would say, with the imaginary effect of global interconnectedness produced by globalizing apparatuses. Being 'global' means being 'globalized' from the nonglobal world.

Once globalization is settled in discourse, however, there have been attempts to expand its historical span retroactively. Peter Sloterdijk (2013), among others, formulates three grand phases of globalization: the ancient "cosmic-uranian globalization" as the metaphysical geometrization of an imagined globe; the modern "terrestrial globalization," nautically driven by the West's colonial expansion from 1492 to 1945; and the present "electronic globalization," characterized by decolonization and simultaneity. In each phase there emerged a certain cognitive paradigm of coordinating being and form, home and world, material and philosophical processes—a sort of Foucauldian episteme according to which a global community is imaginatively constructed. Notably, the terrestrial globalization led to the conquest of the world by a new type of subject: an autonomous "entrepreneur" who is rationally motivated to act beyond inhibitions by obeying only his internalized reason and sensible interests, practicing theory and progressing toward the new through self-advice and auto-persuasion. This action-man formed the "corporate identity" of being-in-the-world-of-capital and totalized the earth economically by circulating money (57–83).

Nonetheless, the total inclusion of the globe within a single capitalist empire turns out to be fiction because immune systems appear both to cope with the situation in which everyone becomes everyone else's friend or enemy and to generate global-scale apartheid. While capitalism continues to prevail, ideal cosmopolitanism pursued in the second, terrestrial globalization takes on "the provincialism of the pampered" in the third, most globalized phase. A third of the world's population living in the "World Interior" of capital consumes two-thirds of the world's resources and enjoys privately insured individualism, unlimited mobile freedom, better life chances, and more purchasing power. Capitalism has even newer contradictions that only indicate its magical invincible power: earning money without working, knowledge without learning, fame without performance, immunity without suffering, and security without warfare (Sloterdijk 2013, 193–222). Life without toxicity, I would say, intoxicates people who want to keep their exclusive, comfortable hothouse with a new subjectivity of narcissistic consumerism. It is a global "crystal palace" for the selected but also a fortress that towers over the rest of the world and operates militarized management to expel social minorities or exterminate external threats like terrorists. Noteworthy is Sloterdijk's reference to the globe as *globus*, that is, a complete round sphere with the enclosed inside like the ancient *sphaira*, a ball symbolizing perfect beauty with imperial power. Does the science fiction film *Elysium* (Neill Blomkamp, 2013) not show its most updated version in the form of a huge ring-shaped, eponymous space station whose inner surface is inhabited by the very wealthy, whereas the rest reside on overpopulated, ruined Earth?

Such diagnoses of current globalization with polarization abound (Appadurai 1996; Giddens 2001; Harvey 2006; Mignolo 2011; Pieterse 2017, to name a few). But without needing to recapitulate them, I make two points regarding Sloterdijk's inspiring approach. First, the mechanism of inclusion and exclusion may be immanent in any community as its sociopolitical foundation beyond the economic condition of today's globalization. Global or not, a community is essentially constituted on the communal basis of the power and sovereignty, law and violence, and discipline and control that affect and regulate people's lives and bodies, labor and production, and identity and collectivity. The matter of who is 'in/outside' our community, 'with/against' us, is biopolitical in this aspect, and so is the subjectivity of community members. Entrepreneurial autonomy or narcissistic consumerism could be seen as conditioning this fundamental biopolitical subjectivity in a certain historical mode of capitalism. Second, it may however be true that this biopolitics has become the most palpable in the third globalization, when unprecedented spatial contraction and enhanced proximity have brought about new global institutions and strategies for distanciation, distinction, detention, and dehumanization. The question, then, of how to treat biopolitical subjects and with how much dignity is not just political but even ethical, and it is all the more so because, as Sloterdijk (2013, 247) says, world politics is now nothing but "the administration of the crystal palace," its policing measures, security services, and disposal methods including military violence based on judgmental principles. Put simplistically, political ideologies have been replaced with the ethical mission of protecting a single-market global system as 'good' and eradicating the radical remainder as 'evil.' Given this historical specificity, I focus on the practical sense of globalization that colors our contemporaneity rather than speculatively extending or diluting it into a 'macrohistorical' span.

In sum, double attention should be paid to (1) the biopolitical universality of community and subjectivity formations that is susceptible but not subordinate to economic conditions; and (2) the ethical historicity of today's global governance, which betrays the lack of genuine political solutions. I intend to reframe (1) in (2) while differentiating biopolitics from politics and channeling various debates on globalization into its biopolitico-ethical dimension as the backdrop of this book on cinema. The periodization needs elaboration here. In effect, Sloterdijk's *spherology* philosophically updates the world-systems theory (developed notably by Immanuel Wallerstein) that illuminates long-term economic processes such as the postwar establishment of a capitalist order, which corresponds to Sloterdijk's third globalization in the age of "post-history" (2013, 165–68). But given the history of ideological politics continued during the Cold War and the 1960s–1970s revolutions, it is apt to view circa 1990 as the starting point of postpolitical globalization, the beginning of "the End of History" sensationally proclaimed by Francis Fukuyama (2006). Let's admit that Fukuyamaism may remain valid unless we have viable alternatives to capitalism, while the original Fukuyamaist partner of capitalism is now changing from democracy to authoritarianism, as seen in China and Russia, among other countries. This double bind of Fukuyaman globalization with its discontents marks a political dead end, the end of politics.

A Microhistory of Globalization with the Ethical Turn of Politics

In this context, it may be useful to examine postpolitics and its "ethical turn" as addressed by Jacques Rancière and the like by looking back on the past three decades, in which globalization has been literally realized with three 'microhistorical' waves that I will note. To begin with, for Rancière (2004), the core of politics is "dissensus": not a simple disagreement between different opinions or groups, but the structural division between different views on how to count a community's population and parts, or different ways of how to imagine the community as a whole. A political conflict occurs when those uncounted, whose voice is treated only as angry noise, speak out to those within the state by creating a common sphere of contestation, thereby redistributing "the sensible" in the sense of what is possible to see, say, hear, or do. A political "people" is thus born out of their sensible claim to rights that challenge the rights of other "peoples" inscribed in the law, restructuring the existing symbolic order of counting. Conversely, the ethical turn prioritizes "consensus": not a mere agreement, but the symbolic structuration of evacuating dissensus and reducing various peoples into a single people, the sum of the interests of a whole community (115). While everybody is to be counted here, the problem is that this inclusion deprives the excluded of their potential to be political subjects. The excluded exist as either mere vulnerable others for the community to grant rights to in order to re-establish a social bond or as radically threatening others to reject in order to maintain the established bond. Human rights, then, are less politically pursued by dissident subjects than ethically assumed as either the absolute right of the victimized Other, who should be saved through another party's humanitarian interference, or the self-protective right of this party's community to fight the fundamentalist Other who terrorizes it. Politics is therefore doubly ethicized: while the *soft* ethics of consensus on everyone's rights underlies the humanitarian community, the *hard* ethics of "infinite justice" is justified to defeat the "axis of evil" for the sake of security (116–17, 129–30).

We can trace these two ethical facets in light of the two decade-defining collapses that signaled the first two microhistorical waves of globalization. The first collapse, that of the Berlin Wall in 1989, ignited the fall of the communist bloc and integrated hostile halves into one world. Globalization then emerged as the postideological zeitgeist of the 1990s, driven by *systems of inclusion*: liberal democracy, transnational capitalism, network technology, and information industry. Cosmopolitan mobility and connectivity exponentially increased through cross-border departures and arrivals, free-trade imports and exports, massive immigration and emigration, and ever-faster transportation and communication. The entire globe, as well as each nation, took similar steps to become a capitalist multicultural society, including ever more racial, religious, and sexual identities. This democratic harmony of cultural differences was pursued in the name of the Third Way, which tried to reconcile socialism with the capitalist regime, not for economic Marxism but for the ethical values of diversity, tolerance, hospitality, and humanitarianism. 'Otherness' became worthy of absolute respect, to be accorded to all relative others. Insofar as such others were included in a global community, they were ideally supposed to have 'global citizenship,' as if it were a license, though not issued by any government, to access equal rights of universal education, health, and so forth. Human rights, a political goal difficult to achieve, then began to partake of an ethical 'default value' that should be taken for granted. The victims of human rights violations became not the subject of political struggle so much as the object of ethical responsibility. Political activism was more and more motivated by left-liberal 'political correctness' that tended to translate political complexity into moral activities like charity and moral policies like affirmative action. Correctness as institutionalized morality in multicultural identity politics underlay the postpolitical soft ethics.

Nevertheless, the Third Way ethical socialism was still capitalistic, incorporating diverse others and cultures neoliberally into the global market if they were profitable, enjoyable, or exploitable as commodity, service, or labor. That said, their genuine inconsumable otherness was filtered off, often fantasized as too excessive, dangerous, or fundamentalist to welcome. Some limits on admission to the World Interior, despite its empiric expansion, existed like a security check. Human rights were reappropriated here by global citizens as self-defensive power, the supreme right to not be harassed by others and even to remove the others' rights if they were harmful or useless—even the right to smoke was to be globally banned for the public right to health. Inclusive systems of multicultural globalization generated *symptoms of exclusion* in this manner: illegal migrants, precarious workers, refugees, and terrorists. Radical antagonism then occurred less and less between different yet integrated social groups and more and more between a whole global society and its remnants as either unqualified for global citizenship or resistant to the global order. On September 11, 2001, the world saw such antagonism hijacking the opening decade of the new millennium, causing the second historic collapse, that of the World Trade Center, which paradoxically revealed a new wall around the crystal palace. Those suicidal Islamists seemed proof that "the iron curtain of ideology" had been replaced with "the velvet curtain of culture," that the soft-ethical tolerance of diverse cultures as naturalized lifestyles left no room for political negotiation with intolerable cultures, just the "clash of civilizations" (Huntington 2011). In fact, there were not equivalent conflicting civilizations, but rather a handful of stateless guerrillas who attacked a single global civilization that pervaded most of the Islamic world as well, which thus backed the global war on terror. Global terrorism was like 'the return of the repressed' to the entire global regime, which in turn executed counterterrorism for self-protection. Moreover, both sides drew on religious fundamentalism and moralized their right to violence as sovereign, pseudo-divine justice against the evil other, only to end up stuck in a vicious cycle of retaliation. This harsh absolutism colored the postpolitical hard ethics, as seen in post-9/11 films about terror and counterterror.

In sum, the political dissensus that prompts passions and actions for dialectic change has globally shifted to the soft-ethical consensus that promotes pity and compassion for others on the one hand, and on the other hand the hard-ethical antagonism that provokes hate and apathy toward others. This double ethical turn underlies the age of globalization, its self-contradictory yet nondialectic operation: the softer a global community is, the harder its security and threats to it are; the more inclusive and expansive it is, the more exclusive and explosive it is. For glorious globalization entails unavoidable byproducts, the excluded as an exception to its universality who can strike back at its holistic system. Such risk, however locally triggered, is globally experienced in this networked world, as seen in the domino effects of terrorism and also debt crises, computer viruses, nuclear disasters, and climate anomalies—the more connection, the more contagion. These global catastrophes indicate the impossibility of complete globalization, its inevitable inconsistency and failure at suturing disruptive symptoms.

Notably, recent economic crises have ruptured the capitalist euphoria from within the crystal palace and caused complex socioethical repercussions. Cracks in Wall Street—another wall, one for the top 1 percent—devastated the bottom 99 percent upon the global financial meltdown in 2008. And a new worldwide free-for-all driven by neoliberal commerce has defoliated local industries and safety nets while accelerating polarization, unemployment, xenophobia, racism, anti-immigrationism, and hate crimes. A consequence, seen in Brexit and Trumpism, was a weird fusion of far-right and far-left mindsets against the integrated regime of global capitalism right at the core of it. A new exception to the Whole emerged not among dark outsiders excluded from it but among White insiders deprived of its benefits, the local losers of globalization, who then chose self-reclaiming self-exclusion from free trade and multicultural traffic. After the first microhistorical wave of globalization in the 1990s and the second wave with global (counter)terror in the 2000s, the third wave is therefore characterized by global factionalism in the 2010s. While the global system has still been growing—Wall Street bounced back without collapsing—it now sustains fractures caused by anticentrist populism that tries to build a new wall between nations. Which wall to choose, then? This uncomfortable question indicates today's stalemate. Like France's presidential choice of central globalist Emmanuel Macron over extreme nationalist Marine Le Pen, who beat the old rightists and leftists, the only alternative to the worst seems to be to remain in the status quo of the problematic global order.

Postpolitical globalization indeed marks our civilizational direction as difficult to change with all its side effects. Of course political struggles still exist, and multiculturalism is often (re)claimed as postcolonial emancipatory pluralism in ways of debunking its alleged complicity in apolitical globalization and challenging "unthinking Eurocentrism" to bring about a polycentric world (Shohat and Stam 1994). However, as seen variously in identity politics, does such resistance to hegemony not eventually envision an ideal equal society, namely a soft-ethical utopia? Political dissensus, if resolved consensually, inevitably brings with it the ethical turn of politics despite Rancière's critique. Politics is oriented not against but toward soft ethics in the end; it would otherwise turn into hard ethics like terror. Likewise, radical events like Occupy Wall Street, with no better world system entailed, make only a spasmodic impact on the current system, which reinforces itself flexibly by absorbing dissident power. Direct democratic actions of antiglobalization by the "multitude," far from opening a way out of global "Empire" in Michael Hardt and Antonio Negri's terms (2000), utilize its intranetworks, thereby conversely helping Empire's readjustment to schizophrenic desires. Here are two flows of (post)political activity: the "subpolitical" one from the decentered multitude's contingent participation in viral events, and the "hyperpolitical" one from the supranational Empire's institutional management of such events. These two correspond to globalizations "from below" and "from above," which in effect cooperate for inclusive capitalism (Beck

2013). Terrorism or factionalism would also end up as nothing more than a temporary break unless it develops into a paradigm-shifting revolution, which seems no longer possible in the postpolitical age. The end of the status quo then appears only fictionally in catastrophic imagination, and that is why, as we will see, cinema matters.

Subjectivity and Community in Crisis

Now let's note that the ethical turn of politics makes the biopolitical mechanism of inclusion and exclusion more palpable. While political subjectivity loses its dissensual power and nearly equates to sociocultural identity endowed with soft-ethical rights, the boundary between citizens who have such identity and 'subalterns' who are denied or deprived of it becomes all the more decisive. And it is on the latter that community exerts its hard-ethical sovereignty. Crucially, supreme sovereign power lies in suspending the rule of law if needed and creating a "state of exception" wherein one may be 'desubjectivized' without judicial process, not punished as criminal but expelled from the law itself and thus killed like an animal, a "bare life" or *"homo sacer"* as Giorgio Agamben (1998) says. Biopower works not only through Foucauldian apparatuses that subjugate people's bodies to the modern nation-state but primarily through this Agambenian sovereignty that can even throw these bodies out into a lawless state of nature. In truth, all nations transcend their normal law for the sake of security in a state of emergency that allows killing with impunity. Biopolitics in this sense has existed since long before the political utilization of modern biotechnology, just as *bios* meant "qualified life," in contrast with *zoe* as mere biological "naked life," in the polis of ancient Greece. The fact that ethics originated in ethology—the study of ethos as the set of beliefs and behaviors associated with a community—also suggests the relation of ethics to *police* (not *politics*), that is, the governance of the communal order by power that can put subjects under or outside the law, namely, in the soft- or hard-ethical way.

As already noted, my point is to historicize universal biopower from the perspective of globalization, or to 'biopoliticize' globally generated symptoms of exclusion. Various refugees, homeless diasporas, illegal migrants, and even suicide bombers are evident symptoms, but a wide range of subjects in crisis also deserve attention: those who are abandoned, rejected, fired, or unemployed by their community—family, school, workplace, institution, etc.—and pushed to the edge of the global system. It is also significant that if biopolitical violence occurs typically in an exceptional situation like war or dictatorship, today's terrorist attacks turn normal subjects into *homines sacri* like a blot out of the blue, without technically excluding them but by suddenly depriving them of self-reliance, as if to make the norm and the exception indistinct. And once the war on terror is prolonged, the state of emergency is normalized to the extent that democracy and human rights are regulated on a daily basis, that surveillance technology and security checks pervade both private and public spaces, and that anyone is treated as a potential terrorist who may be proactively detected and detained (or just destroyed) under the neoconservative politics of fear. No wonder Agamben asserts that "the camp" is "the nomos of the modern" from Auschwitz to Guantanamo Bay (1998, 166–80).

I propose to study this phenomenon of exclusion by revisiting the concept of *abjection*, the act of casting off or of being cast off, as widely known through Julia Kristeva's psychoanalysis; *abject* is thus used as both a verb and an adjective. Furthermore, as a noun, 'the abject' often refers to something disgusting or threatening like bodily fluids, detached organs, wastes, and corpses, separated from the subject (and its cultural domain) for self-protection or ego formation. The abject no longer belongs to the subject but is not an objective thing either, therefore lingering between subject and object, self and other, life and death. By extension, a subject as an individual can be an abject cast out of its core community, just like those people listed earlier. This biopolitical abjection has been investigated in the recent revision and expansion of the concept, as I later explore it. Then, if global citizens are normal subjects with guaranteed rights, the abject are global 'noncitizens' bereft of soft-ethical protection and exposed to hard-ethical threats. The point is that the abject are not identified as the lower classes so much as classless and are exploitable yet unqualified to be political subjects or blocked from being so. Community typically treats them with either soft-ethical pity and compassion or hard-ethical hatred and discrimination. In the latter case, they are debased and stigmatized as heterogenous, unnecessary, repulsive, or harmful, easily targeted by all sorts of sovereign violence from homophobia to genocide.

But more importantly, the ambivalent state of abjection implies its fluid nature with new potentialities for change. I claim that the abject differ from bare lives, social minorities, or political victims thanks to their *agency* as the causative force and capacity to act. That is, agency is the abject's mode of subjectivity, temporary and transitional yet also performative and modulable. By activating it, the abject become the *agent* of a mission to fulfill, mainly for recovering lost subjectivity. So the abject, symbolically dead, come back to their former community like the living dead, the 'undead' who never really die. However, this return does not always lead to resubjectivation (but often does lead to physical death), or rather it aims at vengeance or destruction (even at their own cost). Not to mention military terrorists, now cyber terrorists showcase the abject striking back at their nation or network all the more internally just as programmers can turn into hackers. Similarly, professional 'agents' like Edward Snowden and Chelsea Manning, by whistleblowing, undergo (self-)abjection from their sovereign 'agency' such as an institution like the National Security Agency, and they fight as exiled agents for cyber democracy while being pursued as traitors. In short, there is a thin line between subject and abject, between 'sovereign agents' and 'abject agents,' whose positions can quickly turn over; abject agents also reappropriate sovereign power when attacking people or communities extralegally. Sovereignty and abjection interlock tightly in this way.

That said, it should be noted that even terroristic agents now cannot help using skills obtained within the global system, such as connecting to its media platforms, and thereby acting on its immanent plane even as abject. The system allows no absolute outside or radical subversion. Imogen Tyler (2013) politicizes the abject compellingly as "revolting subjects" in some case studies, but the agency of revolt tends to disperse individually or dissipate like a collective relief of repressed desire without bringing a utopian alternative to the status quo. Suffice it to recall the riots of suburban 'losers' in France, the United Kingdom, and the United States as well as larger movements including the Arab Spring. What happens the day after is the restoration of global capitalism and racism with more technocracy and apathy to manage such riots or the change of a dictatorial regime into a worse, fundamentalist one. Of course, it is remarkable that the abjection of locals as in Gaza or even a photo of a Syrian baby refugee dead on the beach can attract global attention that goes viral like a butterfly effect through myriad social media, not because people around the world always look into local contexts but because they immediately share abjection and its agency for universal rights. Global networks indeed enable limitless connections and a new public sphere that is more flexible, irregular, and amorphous than any existing community. Nevertheless, the "deterritorializing" force of networking does not revolutionize but rather revitalizes the global system of inclusion, the machine of "reterritorialization" as Gilles Deleuze and Félix Guattari (1987) would say. No community is independent of this system.

What I have called 'global community' should then be reviewed regarding *community* and *network*, which differ theoretically. In my view, community forms a closed vertical 'totality' in which all are organically structured with the transcendent *desire* for utopian ideals oriented by an exceptional center of sovereignty, the big Other. However, network embodies open horizontal 'infinity' because of its *drive* to endless connections, which thus cannot demarcate all, yet leaves no outside since there is no center, boundary, or hierarchy. Here, just briefly because I elaborate on this later, Lacanian psychoanalysis could be linked to Nietzschean nihilism, which colors (post)modern subjectivity: desire, based on perpetually unfulfillable lack, underlies "negative" nihilists' pursuit of redemption beyond the meaningless earthly life, whereas drive is instantly satisfied and rapidly reborn, characterizing "passive" nihilists' indulgence in individual pleasures and security with no divine center, big cause, or transcendent Other. The turn of negative to passive nihilism then suggests the turn of the community as organized for a political utopia to the network as soft-ethically permissive with capitalistic hedonism. Moreover, it is "active" nihilists who try to overcome this decadent network even through suicidal activism, like hard-ethical terrorists. So, back to the double ethical bind, I redefine the global community contradictorily as a *totalized network* in that sovereignty and abjection are mechanized under many interfaces, communal causes give way to addictive connections, and extremist violence of the abject erupts internally.

The danger that this totalized network faces is not just a manageable disaster. It should be called *catastrophe*, the uncontrollable overturning that takes on the Kantian sublime in two facets: on the one hand, as aforementioned, endless connection is susceptible to 'immeasurable' contagious side effects, and on the other hand, the massive generation of the abject, their threatening return, and the system's counteraction are all entangled in 'insurmountable' violence. This catastrophe is often imagined to be stoppable only through a bigger catastrophe, the "divine violence" of annihilation that ends the world. Nonetheless, here is a turning point: we sometimes see unique solidarity formed among the abject in the middle of a catastrophe, which then works as a sort of positive *event* that opens up new possibilities to reshape subjectivity and community in crisis. Even a temporary agora of the abject appears with a spontaneous agency of direct democracy that is impossible in reality. I claim there is a third way between communal totality and networked anarchy, an alternative ethics irreducible to institutional politics, even if not on such a scale. It emerges when abjection brings liberation and creativity, while one becomes an existential *gift*. One can give one's abject being itself as retaining the potential sanctity of life to relay without return and closure. Often forming a contingent alternative family, this gift-giving makes a relationship of commonality without community, of solidarity without unity, through immediate connection to the other's very abjectness beyond cultural mediation or identity labels. It performs, so to speak, 'positive nihilism' by opening nonutopian yet nonsuicidal zigzag networking on the edge of the global regime. This is what I call an *atopian* movement, which continues without an anchor through the precarious yet precious *abject agency* of embracing the unknown and walking side by side with the other. It is the movement of displacing itself, abjected from the double ethical ideology of tolerance and violence.

Mapping Frames of World Cinema

Now let me bring cinema into this context, namely *global cinema*.[1] Undoubtedly cinema is the most synthetic cultural platform in which all the aforementioned issues can be concretized or allegorized in existential settings realistically and imaginatively, sensationally and philosophically. However, just as usages of 'global' have been trendy yet vague, global cinema is a popular yet unformulated term, often referring to Hollywood blockbusters or simply equated with 'world cinema' as such these days. It may then be vital to ask how world cinema is addressed and then related to global cinema if they imply different notions. In truth, world cinema has never meant the neutral totality of all films made in the world. Dudley Andrew (2010a) even relates it to just one of the following historical phases: the cosmopolitan phase (1895–1918), when early cinema spread over the world as a new medium; the national phase (1919–45), when classical cinema was established in each nation-state; the federated phase (1946–68), when film festivals and the French New Wave had international influences; the world cinema phase (1969–89), when New Waves hit not only Western but largely ignored non-Western countries; and the global phase (1990–present), when 'film' has

---

[1] A slightly different, longer version of this section was published elsewhere independently (Jeong 2021).

been replaced by digital spectacles that are consumed everywhere simultaneously. Inspired by this periodization, I suggest identifying *mapping frames* of world cinema as methodological rather than diachronic. World cinema is not gone as a phase but always growing as an audiovisual corpus while differently approached in different historical, geopolitical, and cultural conditions. Thus, the frames discussed in the following are about not world cinema but world cinema studies.[2]

First of all, in the most common and still dominant *national frame*, world cinema appears as a world map of national cinemas such as Italian cinema and Korean cinema. And each national cinema is studied in a broad sense of cinematic ethnography, referring to each nation's sociopolitical history, collective memory, and cultural contexts (Nowell-Smith 1997; Hjort and Mackenzie 2000; Hill et al. 2000; Chaudhuri 2005; Badley, Palmer, and Schneider 2006; Vitali and Willemen 2008; Nochimson 2010). The implication is that cinema plays a substantial role in building the imagery of a nation as an imagined community while becoming a national cinema that consists of selected films and their intertextual "coherencies or symptoms" in style, content, narrative, character, background, and so forth (Rosen 1984). However, it is the state, the legitimate agency of/over the nation, that institutionalizes national cinema, just as the government supports it against hegemonic Hollywood in many countries. Likewise, national cinema exists not only culturally as text or art but also economically for production, exhibition, and consumption. And its unique autonomy emerges in two paradoxical ways, as Andrew Higson (1989, 2000) suggests: in terms of outward-looking comparison, a national cinema tries to differ from other national cinemas but often adopts the international standard of Hollywood filmmaking; and in terms of inward-looking connection, it represents established national culture to the extent that nationhood, albeit constructed so, is passed off as natural. Nationalism is born in this way, naturalizing national identity and its boundary while (unconsciously) excluding heterogeneous elements. "Nationalist cinema," if not national cinema at large, performs this rightist repression of complexity (Willemen 1994). However, it is such essentialism

---

[2] For D. Andrew, the world implies variety while the global is a homogeneous entirety. World films promote the distinctive complexity of their place of origin, but global films entertain audiences everywhere, with remakes and byproducts converting all currency into a single value. From another noteworthy angle, he also proposes "an atlas of world cinema" (2006) including its political, demographic, linguistic, orientation, and topographical maps. In my terms, the political map fits in the 'national frame,' whereas the rest relate to the 'transnational frame.' I intend to add a map drawn in a 'global frame,' so to speak.

that constructivism debunks; there is no natural nation but only cultural production, and subjectivity, individual or national, is constituted in the system of power and knowledge (Hayward 2000).

For this reason, the *transnational frame* emphasizes difference and otherness excluded from national identity and sameness. It could apply to the "federated" and "world cinema" phases as previously mentioned on two levels. First, it works to map the New Wave phenomena, aesthetic or political movements of marginal, dissident, artistic filmmaking across different national cinemas, and a kind of leftist 'internationalism,' as seen in Third Cinema, against neocolonial capitalism (Nowell-Smith 2008; Betz 2009; Guneratne and Dissanayake 2003). Second, recent usages of the term 'transnational' imply the shift of ideological internationalism to deconstructive postcolonialism, but also more broadly to economic formations beyond nations, geopolitical regions sharing a cultural heritage, cosmopolitan nomadism and hybridity, postindustrial and cyber spaces, and so on. For example, European cinema is addressed as a whole from the supranational, translocal European Union (EU) perspective (Galt 2006; Rivi 2016; Bergfelder 2005). Here or elsewhere, both the top-down globalization driven by neoliberal corporations and the bottom-up transculturation of counterhegemonic minorities are transnational. While the former concerns the film industry—including production and reception, film policies and festivals, and transfers and exchanges of national cinemas and capital—the latter concerns identity politics of fragmented groups, polyphonic representations and cultural differences, directors' and characters' migration, diaspora, and exile (Ezra and Rowden 2006; Dennison and Lim 2006; Durovicová and Newman 2010; Higbee and Lim 2010; Hjort 2010). In both cases, however, the point is that the transnational does not purely negate the national but respects and transcends it. Multilayered heterogeneity within a nation is as important as borderless dynamism among nations in and beyond a region. Arab migrants' '*beur* cinema' in France, supranational pan-Chinese cinemas including Hong Kong's and Taiwan's, and such hybrids of Hollywood and local cinemas as Bollywood and Nollywood are all equally transnational beyond Third Worldism.

Nonetheless, the 'world' in these frames has been divisive rather than integrative. It has often been approached through the recognition of and passion for the 'others' of the world's cinematic empire, Hollywood, which assumes American exceptionalism. American cinema, though central to the cinema world, is not seen as part of world cinema. International film festivals have played the role of screen Olympics to stage all the 'rest' of the world as artistic, auteuristic, peripheral, postcolonial, or simply different from the missing center of Hollywood. Many scholars share this view of world cinema as a political alternative to Hollywood. However, as ever more cinematic 'subalterns' speak out with their distinct identities, this Olympic stadium has been displaying equivalent but exoticized, strange but benign minorities like world music or ethnic cuisine in metropolitan markets. World cinema then appears as a rainbow community of multicultural differences while its neoliberal implications are embedded at the empty center, which is taken unawares by film curators and researchers. Likewise, this inclusive cosmopolitanism has underlain the representation of the world in Hollywood that opens multiple access points to the world market by incorporating national, racial, and cultural diversity (Elsaesser 2012). Consequently, world cinema outside Hollywood and the world in Hollywood cinema share some 'softethical' tendencies despite their seemingly 'political' opposition. Both therefore reflect the postpolitical paradigm of globalization.

Sure enough, the Manichean dichotomy between 'bad' normative Hollywood and the 'good' alternative rest neglects their hybridity. But conversely, to view world cinema as only "polycentric," including Hollywood as "just another other" cinema, might reinforce the United Nations–style multiculturalism in "planetary consciousness" when this neutral position is taken as a backlash against the politically charged postcolonial theory (Nagib, Perriam, and Dudrah 2012; Pratt 2010). The point is that politicized cultural studies and critical 'post-' discourses have been the core of the transnational frame, centering on the old question of identity formation and representation to criticize bias or discrimination and promote diversity or pluralism. This approach is valid insofar as the power hierarchy remains between the First and the Third Worlds, the West and the East, and the North and the South (Shohat and Stam 1994, 2003). In this frame, however, new issues regarding today's globalized world and which are more comprehensive or fundamental than cultural identity might not be aptly and deftly detected. For the global milieu of unprecedented trade, traffic, and technology, as well as catastrophic risks—political, economic, or environmental—directly condition and impact local life without necessarily being mediated through the national/transnational dyad that is still based on the unit of nation. Indeed, if internationalism or transnationalism derives from state-centric discourses, globalization involves "non place-specific processes" that change local places, while its central system of neoliberal capitalism enables diverse cultural operations and entails instabilities and inequalities at the same time (K. B. Wagner 2015).

I therefore notice some 'urgency of now' to update the transnational frame on the new horizon of global-local relations reflected or refracted both 'in and outside' Hollywood, yet not wrapping them up reductively in 'apolitical polycentrism.' In this context, I propose a *global frame* of world cinema. It brings into relief not territorialized homogeneity or deterritorializing heterogeneity, but the reterritorialization of transnational forces onto the immanent plane of globalization and its antinomies, that is, a new universality and its cracks. For globalization has reunited a polycentric world into a 'totalized network' that has endless connections and crises that we experience more or less universally. My global frame thus hosts neither a world tour of distinct and even ghettoized national cinemas nor a transnational display of geopolitical and cultural exchanges, but instead critical engagement with global phenomena that contemporary films reveal or betray even in localized narrative space. My key backdrop is postpolitical double ethics, as the antagonism between the 'soft-ethical' systems of inclusion and the 'hard-ethical' symptoms of exclusion brings critical challenges to individual and collective life, subjectivity, and community. Therefore, I characterize *global cinema* as world cinema framed anew that thematically embodies today's globalism with its inconsistency. It often allegorizes the political impossibility of utopian change in various modes of catastrophe and nihilism, indicating the failure of imagining a better world system. However, some films suggest a new possibility of ethics when abject figures, deprived of subjectivity and rights, become contingent agents of existential gift-giving as common without community. Here abjection, as I discussed, implies both the biopolitical mode of bare life and its ethical potential for the agency that opens 'atopian' if not utopian networking beyond the problematic 'soft/hard' ethics of pity and hate.

In this global frame a sort of 'global narrative' with the motif of 'double death' is identified: the abject as the symbolically dead struggle for lost subjectivity or new agency until they physically die. Abject agency is then activated in various modes—sovereign, terroristic, gift-giving, and so on—while drawing our attention to such issues as multiculturalism, cosmopolitanism, fundamentalism, law, violence, catastrophe, community, network, desire, drive, utopia, gift, and nihilism. I investigate these issues with critical theory, drawing on a core cluster of political, ethical, and psychoanalytic philosophies. Theories here are not merely applied to films but tested and revamped in view of concrete existential situations depicted on screen.

Also, films are explored comparatively as representing less essentialist particularities than compatible localities. Indeed, the narrative of double death pervades global cinema, from Hollywood blockbusters and European art films to Middle Eastern dramas and Asian genre films. Locality then functions not as the basis of identity referring to a unique reality that both resists and requires the endorsement of a center, but as a contingent springboard for embodying a concrete universality of the world system including the very center. This is why Hollywood should be viewed as part of world cinema, which in turn should not be featured as marginal or exotic. Likewise, postcolonial emphasis on exilic subjectivity and ethics as in the "accented cinema" (Naficy 2001) could be reviewed in global terms of abjection and agency. Thanks to powerful visuality, world cinema globalizes locality much more vividly than world literature and enables its studies to not be entrapped in the logic of difference and the difficulty of its translation. We could thus 'go global' by recharging identity politics rooted in class, gender, and racial differences with a new theorization of global subjectivity and community.

Admittedly, there can be global frames other than mine. Some recent books on world cinema survey it through a specific theoretical lens, for instance, Deleuzian or realist, which offers a kind of global frame beyond the transnational one, not limited to the age of globalization (Martin-Jones 2011, 2018; Nagib 2011). Other notable books illuminate contemporary films with heated subjects such as globalization, neoliberalism, terror, and resistance (Kapur and Wagner 2013; Chaudhuri 2014; Holtmeier 2019; Lykidis 2020). Moreover, ever more monographs, anthologies, and textbooks include "global" in their (sub)titles, expanding 'global cinema' as a field (Hjort 2005; Galt and Schoonover 2010; Sinha and McSweeney 2012; Costanzo 2014; Stafford 2014; Gorfinkel and Williams 2018). But although the term is mentioned here and there, its nature and scope tend to be somewhat arbitrary or ambiguous, like 'world cinema,' involving a random variety of films around the topic of art, memory, genre, or industry. Against this background, I target a relatively clear range of issues and films. While the industrial base of film culture and technology should be noted wherever important, I focus on the thematic superstructure of biopolitical and ethical concerns on the postpolitical ground of troubled globalization.

In this regard, I map diverse constellations of local films across a vast net of post-1990 narrative cinema, both commercial and art films globally circulating in the mainstream market and the festival circuit, regardless of genre and style. This scope misses the so-called Fourth Cinema and noncinema, mostly indigenous, digital, or DIY-style film practices that are excluded from the institutional field of cinema although they are globally proliferating—in a sense, the 'abject cinema' per se (S. Murray 2009; Brown 2018). But conversely, my global frame intends to be efficiently limited to a selection of blockbusters and auteurist films as part of a global cinematic system mirroring the global system as such. This cinematic system is, as it were, a matrix of global cinema with unconscious symptoms, political dilemmas, and ethical potentialities, which I have related to current film authorship (Jeong and Szaniawski 2016). Now, in a consistent setting of agendas, I navigate around this matrix that includes both global Hollywood (Sam Mendes, Christopher Nolan, George Miller, Richard Kelly, Duncan Jones, Clint Eastwood, Ang Lee, Alfonso Cuarón, etc.) and global auteurs (Mathieu Kassovitz, Bruno Dumont, Na Hong-jin, Park Chan-wook, Ari Folman, Bong Joon-ho, Apichatpong Weerasethakul, Abderrahmane Sissako, Abbas Kiarostami, Rakeysh Omprakash Mehra, Wong Kar-wai, Jia Zhangke, Lars von Trier, the Dardenne brothers, Fatih Akin, Sono Sion, etc.).

A Matrix of Global Cinema

The overall flow of this book has a rough narrative arc in a clear conceptual framework. Four parts comprise a few chapters each and investigate diverse sets of films, with critical engagement in four pairs of pivotal concepts: abjection and agency, catastrophe and revelation, community and network, and gift and atopia. The terms in each pair are partially contradictory, but the second term turns out to be immanent to and derived from the first one. Moreover, while the core concept of abject agency traverses the entire book, the focus shifts broadly from its negative performance of violence and terror to its positive potential for atopian gift-giving.

In Part I ("Abjection and Agency"), to lay out the global framing of cinema, Chapter 1 begins with the cinematic motif of 'falling' that evokes the historic falls signaling two phases of globalization. It is in this context that the double ethical turn of politics takes place, with 'soft-ethical' tolerance and 'hard-ethical' violence. Chapter 1 delves into this pair in terms of 'multiculturalism' and 'hate,' reviewing related debates on French society, among others. The half-included, half-excluded people in the suburbs of global metropoles as depicted in *La haine*, then, are examined as 'the abject' in the process of tracing abjection theory, reloaded with the concept of 'agency.' The last two sections examine 'abject agency' with its ethical potential and limitations, exploring a series of post–*La haine* French films about multicultural conflicts that have globally circulated in the mainstream market and on the festival circuit.

Abject agency is further theorized in Chapter 2 as central to the 'double death' narrative of global cinema. Protagonists undergo sociopolitical abjection as symbolic death and then become agents to recover their subjectivity or fulfill other missions until real death. The chapter's case study moves the argument from Europe to Asia and highlights South Korean cinema while mapping its two transnational capital networks in narrative space. The North-West network depicts refugees or migrants whose mission renders them enslaved and abandoned like dogs (*Poongsan*, *The Yellow Sea*), whereas the South-East network stages professional outlaws like thieves as agents of neoliberal desires (*The Thieves*, *Thirst*). These 'dogs' and 'thieves' represent those circulated by capital and those circulating capital in the age of cognitive, financial, and emotional capitalism, leading to an ethical dilemma of today.

Biopolitically, abjection is the community's supralegal operation of hard-ethical sovereignty. The abject can for this reason become an agent to rejoin or resist the community. Chapter 3 explores this abject agency in global mainstream cinema, focusing on the spy genre, especially the James Bond series. *Skyfall*, for example, signals the crisis of the secret agent's identity against the post-9/11 backdrop of schizophrenic digital terror. Bond and his enemy here are both internally excluded from their agency, MI6, and this 'abjection' leads to terrorist revenge and sovereign reaffirmation respectively. Comparable is Jason Bourne, the ex-CIA agent in the *Bourne* series. He undergoes similar abjection yet becomes neither a terrorist nor a sovereign agent but a symptom of a perpetual mind game. This comparison enables a cognitive mapping of the contemporary spy genre regarding today's global system of sovereignty and abjection.

Opening Part II ("Catastrophe and Revelation"), Chapter 4 further investigates sovereignty through Walter Benjamin's critique of violence. While 'lawmaking' violence founds a biopolitical community and 'law-preserving' violence governs it, they interlock just as Batman and the police use supralegal and legal violence to restore law in the *Dark Knight* series. Meanwhile, 'divine violence' destroys law revolutionarily, but it often turns into 'pseudo-divine violence,' which sovereign killers justify for community-building without revolution, that is, into lawmaking violence. As *The Act of*

Killing shows, a global ethical dilemma appears here: that no absolute justice works as the basis of life's sacred value. The chapter then inquiries into true divine violence without any god-like sovereign and formulates the sanctity of life as a potential humanity yet to come.

Chapter 5 addresses the catastrophic effects of the global system that aggravate the political, economic, and natural environments of the world while mapping a myriad of related films. The discussion centers on biopolitical catastrophes and their cinematic reflections in the beginning and then develops into theorizing the notions of catastrophe and disaster, especially regarding the sublime in its aesthetic and ethical senses. Catastrophe overturns our frame of reference with its sublime power and scale, but it is often reduced to an amusing spectacle or a solvable problem in the disaster genre. The task is to elicit implications of catastrophe from the disaster genre and explore the 'cinema of catastrophe,' including films that challenge the genre's conventions.

Chapter 6 shifts our focus from disaster to catastrophe and further to apocalypse, reflecting on the complexity of (post)apocalyptic films. Among them, the chapter scrutinizes *Snowpiercer*, in which after a periodically programmed failed revolution, a postapocalyptic ecosystem of biopower leaves no exit but the divine violence of annihilation. The spectacular depiction of this second apocalypse betrays the failure of imagining a utopian alternative while opening a potential new beginning of humanity. The film's premise is integrated into an exploration of what would happen in just such a situation via the *Mad Max* series. A postapocalyptic time continues here in the way of revealing nothing but the same past without redemption. The saga's loop of historical déjà vu recycles primitive stages of human history in postmodern fusion. In this way, it reflects our posthistorical temporality, with revolutions recurring yet bringing no real change.

To enrich our study of catastrophe with another film trend, Chapter 7 explores time-travel mind-game films. Among others, *Donnie Darko* stages postcatastrophic redemption from a traumatic time loop through the abject hero's agency of retroactive causality and sublime self-sacrifice. Moreover, the catastrophe uncovers the hidden sides of the world, making room for a new beginning with unknown potentialities. *Source Code* uniquely updates and challenges this redemptive potential. Its protagonist, trapped in the loop of a traumatic counterterrorist mission, never finds an exit from the sovereign system of neoliberal productivity and pathological abjection. Even his sacrifice is 'undone,' and he ultimately embraces the perpetual present of 'redoing' this 'undoing' vis-à-vis repetitive disasters. This reinforced reaffirmation of sovereign agency underlies the transhuman ideology found in many post–*Source Code* films.

If Parts I and II centered on today's subjectivity under abjection and catastrophe, Parts III and IV shed more light on the nature of global society and ethical alternatives in the postpolitical age. As a transitional bridge in Part III ("Community and Network"), Chapter 8 begins with 'network films' to illuminate the mechanisms of community and network and their narrative formations in global cinema from biopolitical, psychoanalytic, and sociological perspectives. Community is characterized here as a closed set of subjects who may be 'abjected' from it, whereas a network is an open whole of endless links along which the subject-abject shift constantly occurs in the mode of being 'on/off' rather than 'in/out.' Building on an array of theories, the chapter maps a variety of films in this context and addresses network narratives as symptomatic of the paradigm shift from community to network with all potentials and limitations in our global age.

If Chapter 8 theorizes the community- and network-based narratives by mapping many Western films, Chapter 9 maps a series of globally recognized non-Western films, notably based in the Global South, including Arab, Indian, and Chinese regions: *Timbuktu, Taste of Cherry, Life and Nothing More . . ., Roja, Rang de Basanti, Slumdog Millionaire, Crouching Tiger, Hidden Dragon, Chungking Express, The World*, and *A Touch of Sin*. These films not only represent the community and network principles as perceptively as their Western counterparts but also call for further developments of formerly discussed topics such as law, violence, fundamentalism, multiculturalism, neoliberalism, and abject agency. Moreover, the paradigm shift from community to network is detailed along the frame shift from national to transitional to global in world cinema while enriching our view of the global community as a totalized network.

Part IV ("Gift and Atopia") proposes a third way between communal totality and networked anarchy, an alternative ethics beyond the postpolitical stalemate. Chapter 10 sheds light on positive modes of abject agency as liberated from fixed subjectivity, beginning with artistic creativity and extending to ethical gift-giving. The crux of the argument is that one's abject being itself can be an existential gift to the other, retaining the potential sanctity of life to relay without return, closure, or recognition as a gift. The chapter explores this paradoxical gift-giving beyond capitalist give and take through some gift theories and three notable films: *Dogville, Gran Torino*, and *Life of Pi*.

Building on the motif of the gift, these films inspire us to develop the ethics of the gift in global cinema and revisit the issues of multiculturalism, terrorism, divine violence, sacrifice, catastrophe, and redemption accordingly.

Chapter 11 further develops the ethics of the gift by comparatively reading *The Edge of Heaven* and *The Promise*, both of which are based on the Abraham-Isaac story. Abraham's sacrifice of Isaac epitomizes one's singular relationship with God beyond community, but the Abraham figures in the films (global Europeans) give themselves to the abject Isaac figures (migrant Muslims) through self-abjection. This becoming-abject as gift forms solidarity among the abject as 'faceless' strangers. And the self-other unit in Levinas's ethics of the other's face can be destabilized when the faceless third takes the other's place (repeatedly). The chapter addresses this new other, neither friend nor enemy, a 'neighbor' with whom one can walk side by side rather than face to face beyond cultural mediation or communal identity. Levinasian infinity is thus reframed in this network of neighboring as an alternative to the soft-ethical networking in the global system.

Finally, Chapter 12 elaborates on the ethics of atopia through the lens of nihilism. The argument first illuminates the negative, passive, and active phases of nihilism in the global frame of politics/postpolitics and community/network. *Children of Men*, here, signals a positively active mode of nihilism emerging through an atopian network of gift-giving abject agents. *Himizu* further draws our attention to the fundamental ground of this atopian ethics, where one can embrace the void of life with only life's self-transcending potential. The chapter derives 'positive nihilism' from this existentialist perspective and refines the new ethics of global cinema beyond the postpolitical framework of double ethics. Cinema sheds light on the abject inevitably generated in any political community, however utopian, and raises questions or possibilities irreducible to politics. This atopian nature of cinema makes it an ethical art.

PART I
ABJECTION AND AGENCY

1
Multicultural Conflicts in Postpolitical Double Ethics

The Historic Falls and the Motif of 'Falling'

In *The Double Life of Veronique* (Krzysztof Kieślowski, 1991), the eponymous doubles cross paths as follows. A Polish soprano, Weronika, is jostled by a protester in the main 'market' square in Kraków and 'falls.' Regaining her feet, she is transfixed by a woman who looks exactly like her and who is busy taking photos from a tourist bus, without returning her gaze. Later, Weronika 'falls' again, dying of a heart attack at a concert where her heavenly voice, singing a piece based on Dante's *Paradiso*, rises to the highest pitch in musical ecstasy. After that the story shifts to Weronika's double, Véronique, in France. She lives as a music teacher after giving up her singing career but feels a mysterious sense of loss. When making love to an enigmatic puppeteer, she happens to notice a woman who perfectly resembles her on a proof sheet of photos that she took in Poland. She breaks down in tears as if her other self had come back from the past, both alive and dead.

This uncanny art film, however, briefly indicates its historical context. In the beginning when a downpour causes Weronika's choir to rush for cover, a truck passes by, carrying a 'fallen' statue of Lenin, a signal that the protest in the square is part of the Solidarity movement that helped to end Poland's communist regime in 1990. The film can thus be read as a double allegory: Eastern Europe's (Weronika's) collapse opens it up to a Western Europe that can be understood as its more secular capitalist self, while Western Europe's (Véronique's) sense of melancholy suggests that the lost Eastern Europe is its more spiritual, transcendent self (music is Weronika's ideal but Véronique's livelihood). This identification of the two sides of Europe occurs through the doubles' double encounters, each time traumatically as intrusive yet impenetrable to each side. When the Iron Curtain is torn down, the 'other' beyond it turns out to be myself, and yet more than myself (she does not see me; we are different people). How could this other and I truly be One through this nonidentical identification? Eastern Europe dies. Then it returns like a specter (the photographic image of Weronika), posing the same question of identification to (the now integrated) Western Europe. But Véronique has no answer yet.

Meanwhile, no film could be more utopian about an integrated Europe than the tragicomic *Goodbye Lenin!* (Wolfgang Becker, 2003). In East Berlin in 1989, Alex's participation in an antigovernmental rally causes his loyal communist mother to 'fall' into a coma. After she wakes up, unaware of the 'fall' of the Berlin Wall, he tries to save her from any further cardiac arrest-inducing shock by making her room a time capsule of the East German products that are disappearing from the market. But when alone she happens to see a helicopter carrying a 'fallen' statue of Lenin, who stretches out his hand as if to say, "Welcome to the desert of the Real!"[1] The traumatic Real erupts onto the surface of her everyday reality embalmed in postmodern simulacra of the past. However, it is also the moment she recognizes Alex's sincere efforts to cover the very Real, which she then endures. After that, what they no longer believe but still perform like an empty ritual sustains their relationship: so as not to hurt each other, the son fakes the lost German Democratic Republic (GDR), and the mother fakes her belief in it.

Then, miraculously, this simulated belief becomes 'performative' in the sense that it performs content that is not planned: Alex becomes assimilated into the very fiction that he has created and begins to believe communist ideals as yet to be realized in the future. That is, his retroactive encounter with his mother's utopianism brings about his identification with her, the other. His final television show recoding the fall of the East as that of the West performs not a melancholic return to a paradisiac East that didn't exist but a deep mourning for the dead East and a new promise of saving its spirit to rectify capitalism's problems in the reunified Germany. The mother dies in peace while the transcendent vision depicted in the fake television show, although unrealized in her life, is transferred to her son as her other at this 'birth of a nation' moment. As Thomas Elsaesser (2005, 127–29) says, their "mutual interference" thus performs the "double occupancy" of a socialist dream and

---

[1] Quoting this line with which Neo is greeted in the real world in the Wachowski sisters' *The Matrix* (1999), Žižek (2002, 5–32) sees 9/11 as the attack of the Real on the safe, prosperous American reality. On the opposite side of capitalism, I say, the reality of Alex's mother sustained in a 'matrix' of anachronistic simulacra is shattered when she steps into the Real. The point is that reality is our fantastic subjective structure of beliefs, their symbolic constitution that conceals the Real only incompletely.

capitalist reality, and Alex ultimately steers not only his mother but himself and his generation, whose trauma is narrativized and therapized. This is perhaps the proper way of embracing the other's death and its postmortem life at the same time; its otherness is then relayed to and relived in the self without remaining lost melancholically as in *The Double Life of Veronique*.

The motif of 'falling' in these two films therefore opens room for redemption, suggesting that when the 'fallen' Eastern Europe turns into the uncanny undead other, Western Europe should internalize it in order to change into a genuine One Europe. However, this may not have happened in reality. The post–Cold War united Europe, institutionalized as the European Union, became less "postnational" than "supranational," mobilized and conditioned rather than threatened and impeded by the national. It was not "a Europe of citizens" constellated for universal democracy so much as "a Europe of nation-states" constituted with their competing sovereignties. Also, this supranational Europe embarked on a "supracolonial" undertaking, integrating the new nation-states of non–Western Europe by means of economic and financial assistance or debt (Rivi 2016, 113). Non–Western Europeans were then treated as second-rate Europeans—as "hicks" in a poet's expression—in the new, still West-centered Europe, especially when working in Western Europe (even today, Polish and Romanian immigrants in the United Kingdom feel unwelcome, all the more since Brexit). Half included, half excluded, they were (and still are) not that far from neocolonial others like non-European immigrants or refugees.

Goodbye Lenin! could then be reconsidered. As it is often criticized for doing, it shamelessly panders to *Ostalgie*, that is, nostalgia for the East, erasing the GDR's dark side full of repression, surveillance, and hypocrisy, as depicted in *The Lives of Others* (Florian Henckel von Donnersmarck, 2006). But more importantly, Alex's vision of 'socialism with a human face,' depicted in the fake news that West Berliners cross the border to escape capitalist pressure and inhuman competition, is an imaginary reversal of 'capitalism with a human face,' the motto of the 1990s postpolitical centrist Third Way. In other words, Alex's socialist humanism for revising pre-1990 capitalism secretly mirrors rather than subverts the post-1990 ethical flexibility of the capitalist market that even co-opts certain critiques of capitalism. What the screen screens out is not only the totalitarian past of the communist regime but also the liberal-democratic present of ever-adapting capitalism that welcomes all yet generates a new type of proletariat out of former communist nations. The film may thus be a neoliberal goodbye to Lenin (Cook 2007, 217–18).

As mentioned in the Introduction, the fall of the Berlin Wall was the historic collapse that opened the first decade of globalization. The second decade-defining collapse, that of the World Trade Center (WTC) in 2001, signaled an explosive backlash against the global system from its radical remnants. But this time the fall did not mean the end of an old order and the influx of others to accept. The global system instead reinforced sovereign power far beyond Europe. Let's briefly note two Jia Zhangke films with the motif of falling. When a rootless worker meets his lost wife at a run-down factory in *Still Life* (2006), we hear the noise of construction and see the sudden crumbling of a tall building in the background. This fall, though evoking 9/11, symbolizes the demolition of communist China but not of its Communist Party. Significantly, China was reborn as a global superpower amid the disintegration of the European communist bloc and as it crushed to death the protestors in Tiananmen Square. Ruling out liberal democracy, China's authoritarian central control has interdigitated with neoliberal capitalism more efficiently, with the dream of building a more invincible empire than the United States (Harvey 2006, 34–41). In *The World* (2004), the eponymous amusement park displays miniatures of the world's landmarks including the WTC, before which a visitor announces: "Ours is still there!" 9/11 is dehistoricized as if it had not happened, as if China desired to allow no terrorists. The only 'other' in the film is the internally generated migrant worker. Such workers wander over an ever-expanding territory where there is nothing but the perpetual present of development with the past submerged, or they are confined in a miniaturized global village with no time and money for escape. Such dream places as Mongolia and Belleville in Paris turn out to be another corner of the same empire that offers at best a similar life and familiar exoticism experienced in simulacra. The more global this empire is, the less of an outside it leaves.

In short, the end of the Cold War marks the birth of the global system and its 'others' as well. Communist regimes are either dissolved into the capitalist market, where their former citizens face degradation and deprivation, or like China, they are upgraded to a new center of that very market while putting some of their citizens under abjection. That is to say, near-neocolonial others appear from behind the fallen border or are produced within their national territory. In both cases, they are simultaneously included in and excluded from the system. This "internal exclusion," as Étienne Balibar (2005, 31) argues, characterizes new global ghettoes as "ubiquitous 'limbos' where those who are neither assimilated and integrated nor immediately eliminated, are forced to remain." Inevitably, inclusion entails exclusion insofar as one's rights to study, work, marry, and so on, which do not always coincide, are derivative of and conditional upon citizenship granted by the nation-state. Moreover, the reterritorializing power of the global system has only reinforced this mechanism. Of course globalization "liquidizes" the solid sense of territorial sovereignty and state boundaries, shifting power from local governments to the uncontrollable space of extra-territorial markets (Bauman 2006, 2–7), and cultural flows circulate among deterritorialized (land)"scapes" of ethnic groups, media, technology, finance, and ideas in flexible interplay and interconnection (Appadurai 1996, 33). Nonetheless, seemingly postnational phenomena do not contradict the operation of supranational institutions or nation-states whose sovereignty has never decreased, and which, while partly malfunctional, are still dominant while backing and benefiting from the market power for their territorial interests and security (Cazdyn and Szeman 2012, 7). Global exchanges are not free and equal, channeled along the center-periphery division and uneven development. From the historical viewpoint (Dussel and Ibarra-Colado 2006, 492–94), this asymmetry has been updated since Eurocentric colonization began and now takes the form of global integration that is violently exclusive, as we will see. This is why the postcolonial age is also neocolonial.

Multiculturalism from Multiple Angles

Given this backdrop, let me draw attention to Europe's troubled suburban populations—especially as reflected in the French cinema on which I focus in this chapter—since they typically represent both the neocolonial and internal others of globalized Europe: the *sans-papiers* including illegal immigrants, asylum seekers, refugees, and deprived citizens, including colorful diasporic settlers from ex-colonized *extracommunitari*. They knock on the door of metropoles and dream of entering mainstream society, only to encounter the ex-colonizers' pity for the disadvantaged or fear of a reversed invasion. They are stuck in poverty and discrimination, jobless or at best hired for casual, tough work, sometimes illegally but under the state's acquiescence. They exist in but do not belong to the very system whose economy they sustain from the bottom. Unemployment and exploitation are the double-binding means by which the system keeps them internally excluded without classifying them as a stable class. For this reason, it is often through noisy violence that they can receive social attention, as per a series of riots spreading over the French suburbs. When a revolt occurred in Chanteloup-les-Vignes in 1995, President Jacques Chirac even 'ordered' his cabinet to see Mathieu Kassovitz's *La haine* (1995), which was shot there, in order to grasp France's "social fracture."[2] Perhaps the film was a cinematic 'coming out' of the Parisian *banlieues*, which confronted the 'mainstream' French audience with the tough face of the peripheral ghettoes, a rude awakening that French society had failed to embrace those 'others' on screen as another self and that it had failed performatively to change itself into a true tricolor, or rather multicolor, republic.

Here, Chirac's order could be seen as a telling anecdote about *multiculturalism* as an ideology for administering cultural otherness. The term began to be officially used in the 1970s by anglophone leaders to cope with conflicting ethnic identities, and by the 1990s it had become a keyword for global society. Not an old universal viewpoint, it is thus a historically constructed policy to manage cultural tensions by accepting difference without discrimination and promoting diversity, tolerance, hospitality, and openness to others. That said, multiculturalism has not been developed primarily by colonial others themselves, even if it is aligned with postcolonialism. Just as colonized India, Algeria, and Korea received British, French, and Japanese imperial cultures, not in the name of multiculturalism but in the name of westernization and modernization by force, so it is not that Vietnamese refugees, Turkish migrants, and Aboriginal people in the United States, Germany, and Australia each directly demanded an equal cultural status. Instead, local governments, civil societies, and various intellectuals gradually recognized the need to formulate multicultural principles based on the liberal tradition of human rights and egalitarianism. However, there is a pitfall. The liberal ideal is to enable the coexistence of diverse lifestyles within a single polity, but it also tends to naturalize the liberal modus vivendi as "a way of life itself into which lesser peoples needed to be civilized" (Kundnani 2014, 285–87). Bhikhu Parekh (2002, 109–13) points out that democratic liberalists such as John Rawls, Joseph Raz, and Will Kymlicka tend to view nonliberal groups

---

[2] For details about the film, see Ginette Vincendeau (2005) among others. Unfortunately, the fracture continues and peaks around a 2005 massive riot when Chirac declares a state of emergency. In ten years again, a series of the Islamic State–led attacks on Paris indicates the global evolution of the fracture, and President François Hollande reenacts the state of emergency. It is extended upon the 2016 Nice terror and almost routinized, as though twenty years since *La haine* have seen nothing but the expansion of hate.

with nothing more than "tolerance" and continue to absolutize liberalism, which is thus paradoxically not entirely open and equal; that is, it is thus not liberal. Tolerance is indeed a problematic notion that assumes the hierarchy between its subject (self) and object (other), the former tolerating the latter as if to grant a certain dispensation. It also implies the intolerance of what violates the very boundary between self and other and thus preconditions the other's recognition and acceptance of the self's sovereign power to decide what is tolerable or not, what to include and exclude.

The limited notion of tolerance is the primary target of many critics when it comes to the postpolitical ethics defined in the Introduction. In Alain Badiou's (2012) view, this ethics updates Emmanuel Levinas's ethics while deviating from it. For Levinas, alterity as "Altogether-Other" evokes God, but in post-Levinasian ethics, this theological feature is decomposed into the secular right to difference. The "ethics of the other" then turns into the "ethics of human rights"; the singularity of absolute otherness is integrated into a set of relative differences that the multiculturalist can respect with his warm heart open to victimized cultural others. However, this respect presupposes his distance from those others, who should not invade his domain of rights and culture or challenge his status as the subject of 'liberal' tolerance or his power to let them in. The liberal defense of rights with cultural relativism and humanitarian individualism is thus underlain by a condescending attitude toward other cultures, with "pity for victims." The ethical doctrine of "consensual lawmaking" betrays the "self-satisfied egoism of the affluent West" (3–28).[3] In short, multiculturalism is a Eurocentric extension of colonialism and imperialism.

Slavoj Žižek (1997) expresses a similar critique but from a more socio-economic perspective. The multiculturalist's patronizing distance as respect implies "a disavowed, inverted, self-referential form of racism" since it is based on his "privileged *empty point of universality.*" Although this new racist no longer brutally says, 'I am superior to you,' his refined message 'I respect your culture' still asserts his superiority of being able to appreciate or depreciate it with a tacit guideline: 'insofar as you respect my very respect as well as my culture without bothering me.' His interest in other cultures might then be a euphemism for indifference. Here, tolerance only allows for

---

[3] This egotism culminates in everyone's slogan "Je suis Charlie," after the *Charlie Hebdo* attacks, recapping the double stance of France toward the Muslims supporting the national economy (Badiou 2005).

aseptic, benign cultural forms like world music, dance, and cuisine, and it denounces the "real Other" for its patriarchal, violent, fundamentalist core that is fantasized as too primitive, dangerous, and excessive to accept. What remains is "the Other of ethereal wisdom and charming customs" without the Other's toxic jouissance, just like the coffee without caffeine that postmodern hedonists safely enjoy. Cultural differences are easily consumed as exotic commodities or pleasurable services or, I would say, as a sort of 'orientalist simulacrum' in the global market. Updating Fredric Jameson's formulation of postmodernism, multiculturalism is thus "the cultural logic of multinational capitalism" (37–44).

This 'food-court multiculturalism' exposes the postpolitical mechanism of post–Cold War globalization. It suffices to recall how *Goodbye Lenin!*, movingly recuperating the GDR items obsolete in the new capitalist market, was inadvertently consumed as a well-made *Ostalgie* film thanks to its way of converting the formerly threatening communist nation into a set of enjoyable cultural products. The political difference that dominated the past was reduced to a mere cultural difference in the present. Ex-communists were integrated into multicultural Germany like Turkish immigrants. But as the latter still suffer from imperfect integration, multiculturalism still takes a double stance, as shown in the recent case of Mesut Özil, a German football star and yet a Muslim scapegoat who, after being hugely blamed by angry national fans in the wake of Germany's early exit from the 2018 World Cup, quit the national team, declaring: "When we win, I am German. When we lose, I am an immigrant." Complicating matters, the controversy was not just about his performance but more about his photo being taken with Turkish president Recep Tayyip Erdoğan, a dictator infamous for violating human rights, and whom Özil did not criticize as German fans expected. The point is that the liberal democratic standard of multicultural tolerance works harshly against cultural others when they fail to satisfy national interests. Their assimilation into a multicultural nation depends on the application of universal liberalism, which is highly nationalized and thus not purely universal. In truth, as David Harvey (2006, 52–53) points out, the appeal to the universalism of liberal values is a double-edged sword. Often progressively used in the history of humanism, human rights issues are also easily co-opted into "swords of empire," just as so-called liberal hawks justify imperialist interventions in lifestyles (e.g., banning the Muslim scarf) and other countries to spread democracy without carefully considering local particularities (the US military actions in Kosovo, East Timor, Iraq, etc.). In sum, the multiculturalist as a potential global imperialist does not care about otherness so much as his universal position from which to control and convert others.

Let's keep in mind, however, that there are positive projects of multiculturalism. Parekh (2002, 341–65), though critical of its liberal side, accepts cultural diversity and intercultural communication as inescapable and desirable in forming a dialogically constituted society that includes each culture's internal plurality, based on "operative public values" like "a shared commitment to political commitment." The point is that multiculturalism should still be 'political' by promoting pluralism rather than liberalism, thereby making Europe truly 'Europe' without being Eurocentric. Ella Shohat and Robert Stam (2014) have long been advocating multicultural identity politics since debunking "unthinking Eurocentrism." They fight against both the rightist critics of multiculturalism who say that "the CP (Communist Party) became PC (political correctness)" and the leftist ones who say that "campus quarrels" on culture dismiss class struggle in alliance with "corporate globalizers." They do this by claiming that culture and economy, university and society are inseparable and that to view multiculturalism as a universally disguised specific (American) discourse is myopic. Far from being apolitical, multiculturalism is a "champion of subversion" that has politically expanded deconstruction to the battleground of culture wars (2012, 95–117). Above all, Shohat and Stam trenchantly criticize Žižek. Tolerance is not central to radical multiculturalists, they argue, who have already rejected it as moralistically and paternalistically premised on a prior normativity as well as the social division of major and minor elements. And while attacking co-optive forms of multiculturalism, Žižek overlooks multiethnic counterhegemonic formations such as the modernity project, Black radicalism, indigenous activism, and transnational feminism. Žižek's criticism of Eurocentric multiculturalism then proves his own Eurocentric "white solipsism" that only the West can be historically dynamic and revolutionarily universal, as seen in his (and Badiou's) leftist adaptation of Paulinism, which repeats the Christian/pagan dichotomy (118–26).

Nevertheless, it should be noted that the boundary of tolerance still firmly works like that of normativity in every society while stigmatizing the excluded from normalized identities. This hegemonic power of exclusion is immanent to inclusive tolerance and even grows into the rightist suspension of multicultural reality through the "reactionary passion for the Real" in Žižek's (1997, 46–50) expression: the pursuit for the good of the nation, the superpower's self-righteous retribution for evil, the sovereign power that generates and defeats its own violent excess as the Central Intelligence Agency (CIA) treats Osama bin Laden. However, this fascistic refusal of multiculturalism does not resolve but rather repeats the vicious cycle of terror and war on terror between "Jihad and McWorld" (Barber 1996). Conversely, the "progressive passion for the Real" is the leftist suspension of the symbolic order of global capitalism, through the identification with its symptom of exclusion: the internally excluded "rabble" who may retain the antagonistic potential of revolution. Not limited to Europe and to economy, Žižek's emphasis on the universality of the rabble's struggles for equality and justice—often noted with not only Christ/Paul but also with Mahatma Gandhi, Malcolm X, Frantz Fanon, Nelson Mandela, and the Haitian Revolution—is furthermore not far from what Shohat and Stam (2012, 127) argue: "Multiple subalternizations in terms of class, race, sexuality . . . grant this social category more claims on the universal [. . .] the social creativity of resistant knowledge and code-switching survival strategies."[4] Despite their oppositional usages of multiculturalism, the question mediating between Žižek and Shohat and Stam would thus be how to activate political practices that overcome the capitalistic reduction of class antagonism to multicultural difference and the 'class-over-race' doctrine of economic reductionism.

A more delicate question might also be about what effects this political struggle causes, and in what direction. It ultimately demands the excluded and underrepresented be included and represented more authentically in a more equal and diverse society beyond the dubious logic of multiculturalism. However, this progress has historically occurred little by little up to today in the way in which the universal ideals of liberty, equality, and fraternity have become ever more absorbed into laws and norms, institutions and policies, common senses, and codes of conduct. Ideal political values have gradually become default ethical values accordingly. Human rights are less and less to be attained by political subjects and more and more to be granted by ethical societies to deprived others. Hence the turn of human rights to humanitarian duties. This is the ethical turn of the political as elaborated in the Introduction via Rancière (2004); the paradox is that political "dissensus," if resolved, leads to ethical "consensus," and thus hypothetically politics would aim at its own end: a postpolitical utopia where no one is excluded and no struggle is needed. The system of inclusion tries to be more inclusive

---

[4] For Shohat and Stam, Žižek also decolonizes Eurocentrism, as do postcolonial scholars, but ignores or takes the latter as no other than the multiculturalists he criticizes. That said, Shohat and Stam's "radical multiculturalism" also criticizes the "naïve multiculturalism" that Žižek criticizes.

in this direction while remaining imperfect all the same. We thus fall into a trap: political practices against the problematic multiculturalism are destined toward perfect multiculturalism, which would, however, still unavoidably cause problems like exclusion, as already discussed. In this way, the *soft ethics* of pity and hospitality cannot help entailing the *hard ethics* of infinite justice against the others beyond its limited tolerance, which is ready to turn into hate, hostility, discrimination, and expulsion. Political principles are co-opted not only into soft-ethical but also economic principles: liberty is thus reduced to free choice, equality to cultural harmony, and fraternity to social networking, all contributing to universal global capitalism. But when it comes to security and self-interest, this system of inclusion (soft ethics) is ready to wield its sovereign power of exclusion (hard ethics) with the aforesaid reactionary passion for the Real. The democratic and fascistic facets of the global system are thus its recto and verso. The postpolitical double ethics is its Janus-faced universality.

"Hate, a Last Sign of Life"

With the preceding in mind, let us return to *La haine*. Against the backdrop of the 1990s riots in the suburbs of Paris, the film follows a day in the lives of three angry young men from immigrant families who happen to find a handgun left by the police. But rather than exploding social fracture, the film exposes multiple signs of the postpolitical age. The three musketeers' teamwork based on their old friendship despite their ethnic difference—Jewish, Arab, African—partakes of some multicultural soft ethics. They fight extreme-right skinheads, a racist enemy of multiculturalism, while their resistance to the police, though seemingly fiery, is quite scrappy, just as the leading character, who mimics the hero of *Taxi Driver* with a handgun, ends up being killed by the police. In fact, *La haine* is inclined toward a stylized ideational radicalism: in the surrealist opening shot, a firebomb is thrown to earth from outer space; in the realist ending scene, Charles Baudelaire painted on a wall looks at us ambiguously as if to exude "the Spleen of Paris" or to cast a vicious gaze of a cultural gestapo co-opted by the ruling class. As Bob Marley's "Burnin' and Lootin'" plays over a newsreel on uprisings and Edith Piaf's "Non, je ne regrette rien" is remixed with techno beats in a helicopter shot, the 1990s postmodern style decorates this 'breathless' subcultural film in a way that rivets metropolitan moviegoers. Sure enough, the box office success and the 1996 Cannes Film Festival best director award made the film a commercialized icon of subversive culture à la *Trainspotting* (Danny Boyle, 1996), a contemporary British hit that rode the global wave of youth culture infiltrated by modern rock and drug addiction. It is noteworthy that the protagonists of *La haine* sleep in a shopping mall after wandering and making petty disturbances in Paris without using the weapon. In a sense, they take no more than a picnic of resistance into the center of global capitalism, with no political repercussions.[5]

For this reason, *La haine* literally signals the turn of political subversion into ethical hate and the linking of multicultural soft ethics to terrorist hard ethics. Let me rephrase this double ethical turn via Jean Baudrillard's (2015) idea of the postmodern turn. If the modern era was driven by the "passion" for freedom with political action that enables the dialectic reconciliation or negotiation to resolve conflicts, then the postmodern era first sees the universal consensus on human rights based on happiness, especially on "compassion" for others' unhappiness, and second sees the explosion of retaliatory "hate" by the excluded from the very (supposedly) universal order (132–42). Political strife thus gives way to the soft and hard ethics of compassion and hate. In other words, hate is a refusal of politics itself, a violent reaction to the situation in which social problems cannot be resolved politically. This hard ethics indicates the crisis of otherness despite the soft-ethical embrace of it. On the one hand, alterity is lost as too much information about unhappy others in media causes indifference and incredulity; on the other hand, alterity is radicalized as this apathy aggravates the antagonism between the inconsistently universal global system and its remnants that singularly pursue total reversion or revenge. Hate, then, works in both directions between the whole and the rest, each of which forms and protects its identity by desperately producing and expulsing the other as the object of aversion and abhorrence. However, this fascistic nature is ever more complicated. As the political division of friend and enemy is dissolved into the single plane of inclusive networking, it is all the more difficult to specify a central target of/for antagonism. With no clear subject to act on, hate only "acts out" its expression, dispersed over global viral networks that rather facilitate a chain reaction of virulent events like contingent depredation, contagious arson, and

---

[5] In *Nocturama* (Bertrand Bonello, 2016), too, a multiethnic gang of youths escapes into a department store after enjoying a rave party and planting bombs on the streets of Paris. Their resistance unfolds less as a radical political act than as symbolic terror in the face of capitalist consumerism.

objectless self-destruction. Only in this sense does hate paradoxically prove aliveness as if it were "a last sign of life" (137–39).

Hate is therefore a vengeful resentment that may return infinitely and a deviational spasm that may explode indiscriminately. In *La haine*, violence against the police who killed a civilian brings back violence by the police; the last scene ends only with the sound of firing between a protagonist and a policeman without showing who kills whom, suggesting a vicious cycle of violent retaliation to come. Just like the loop of terror and war on terror, hate bursts into a hard-ethical affection of vengeance, rejecting and removing the other. And as at a gallery opening during the trio's visit to Paris, hate also provokes random insults to the masses instead of having any focus. It blows up repressed rage like masturbation in the circuit of its drive with no political cause, process, and goal, as if the trip to Paris were to vent stress with no meaningful revolt. If "anomie" temporarily rejects order to reshape it, hate provokes "anomaly," an irrecuperable breakdown of order without dialectic sublation (141–42). Further, the destruction of the globe envisioned in the opening of *La haine* exhibits a potential self-annihilation immanent to the libido of violence. Such catastrophic imagination often leads in cinema to an apocalyptic conclusion, which is thus the only solution to the impossibility of politically changing the hopeless world, while the spectacle of destruction lets us forget the failure of imaging a better world (see Chapter 5).

Likewise, the 2005 suburban uprisings, dubbed the French Intifada, brought less a political struggle than a domino effect of hate triggered by taking revenge on the police. We could here think about the root of the Arab word *intifada* ('tremor' or 'shuddering'), which is *nafada*, meaning 'to shake off' or 'get rid of,' in two directions. While the rioters wanted to shake off the world by incendiary violence as though they were infected with the virus of hate, governmental power also threw them off as if they were human trash. In fact, given the history of the governmental power, the term French Intifada might better fit the French state's modus operandi of segregating and degrading the immigrants while hosting and using them for labor, thereby keeping French identity pure. The suburban residents have been 'othered' as a sort of second-rate citizen, as postcolonial subalterns whose sociopolitical subjectivity and human rights are precarious and easily forfeited in a state of exception such as a riot. Without this 'othering,' there is no self-identification because "The Self is nothing but *the Other's Other*"; in France, a common self of "the Western-Christian-Democratic-Universalist identity" keeps itself away from all that is other than itself (Balibar 2005, 30). However, the universality modified in this way is already exclusive, although its multicultural ideal includes the Other in the same name of humanity. The Other is thus the Self's uncanny double, neither purely exterior nor interior—again internally excluded. This internal exclusion is the key to the modern biopower that sustains the nation-state on two levels. As Hannah Arendt (1973) typically analyzes, a totalitarian "war of races" can be conducted against stateless individuals like Jews, who are singled out as "superfluous" by an imperialist nation-state like Nazi Germany. Also, as Michel Foucault (1995) influentially argues, the "micro-fascisms" of the institutions systematically discipline subjects and rule out the "abnormal" that can damage the quality of the population. Biopolitics, then, embodies its reverse, namely what Achille Mbembe (2003) calls "necropolitics": it produces those legally, normally, rationally stigmatized 'others' and leaves them in the path of being debased into, as it were, "living corpses."

Theory of Abjection Reloaded with Agency

I call this 'nonpart' of a biopolitical community *the abject* because *abjection* is at the core of the internal exclusion that I have identified in identity formation. The abject as a concept can thus be revitalized better to account for the crises of subjectivity in the postpolitical, or more severely the biopolitical, age. Let me develop it while tracing crucial theories of abjection. As noted in the Introduction, *abject* can be both a verb ('cast off/out') and an adjective ('humiliating, servile, despicable'), so *abjection* means both making abject and being abject. Julia Kristeva (1982) highlights this double aspect in her seminal psychoanalytic intervention in Jacques Lacan's model of subjectivation. For Lacan, first, in the Imaginary (capital I) mirror stage, the child identifies itself with its unitary form reflected in the mirror as 'other,' whose function is primarily performed by the mother who says 'my lovely baby!'; the child's ideal ego is thus united with the mother. This euphoric bond is broken in the Symbolic (capital S) order represented by the law of the father; imaginary identification gives way to linguistic communication, and the primordial object of desire is lost then sought only indirectly and imperfectly through different objects or others under social norms. Then, what is excluded from this reality returns as what could not be called other than the Real (capital R), the traumatic Thing or repressed jouissance.

Kristeva introduces in this triad IRS a pre-Imaginary phase termed the Semiotic. Relating it to Plato's notion of *chora*, a space of interval between being and nonbeing, she argues that a newborn child is still in a sort of uterine receptacle, a boundless state of "the bottomless 'primacy'" (1982, 18) like being embraced within the mother's breast. Here the child experiences a chaotic mix of prelinguistic signifiers like fluid demarcations, rhythms, and tones (not yet distinct images) that cause material sensations. Abjection, then, occurs as the child's separation from the mother, the act of abjecting her to gain autonomy out of her hold. Only after this narcissistic individuation can the child undergo socialization in the Symbolic as a speaking subject. This primary repression of the mother before the father's intervention is therefore essential to establish a stable identity with the self/other boundary, implying a symbolic matricide, not the typical Oedipal patricide. The maternal body, domineering and suffocating, must be cut off. However, not reduced to a mere thing, it appears as the abject between inner and outer worlds, disturbing the (super)ego in the Symbolic yet also provoking uncanny nostalgia for the lost oneness with the other in the Semiotic (conceptually close to the Real). Likewise, all sorts of the filthy, nauseous, hateful, and horrible abject— from menstrual blood and milk cream to ghosts and zombies—terrorize and fascinate the subject at the same time, lingering in the limbo state of being neither subject nor object, in between life and death. Put poetically, the abject is: "Not me. Not that. But not nothing, either. A 'something' that I do not recognize as a thing. A weight of meaninglessness, about which there is nothing insignificant, and which crushes me. On the edge of non-existence and hallucination, of a reality that, if I acknowledge it, annihilates me" (2).

Kristeva's influence has been widely palpable in the arts and humanities (see Fletcher and Benjamin 1990; Lotringer 2002; Reader 2006; and Arya 2014 for a recent overview). While "Abject art," above all, experimented during the 1990s with the aesthetics of disgust by both threatening and attracting spectators with body images of distortion, excretion, or castration, its precursors were traced back in century-long avant-garde challenges to norms and taboos (Houser et al. 1993; Foster et al. 1994; Krauss 1996).[6] And just as Kristeva explores "perverse" literary figures who neither obey nor deny religion, morality, and law, but who instead corrupt and transgress

---

[6] Remarkable artists include surrealist Hans Bellmers, blasphemous Andre Serranos, feminists from Valie Export to Cindy Sherman, and Kiki Smith. Also notable are performance artists (Carolee Schneemann, Sterlac, Zhu Yu) as well as great painters in art history (Hieronymus Bosch, Caravaggio, Francisco Goya). Also, see Chapter 10.

them,[7] so have studies emerged on ambivalent abjection in diverse topics beyond abject bodies: the "abject hero" in modern literature (Bernstein 1992), the motif of "beheading" in visual arts (Civitarese 2015), "play" as a castaway in Western philosophy (Nagel 2002), "makeovers" in medicine and popular culture (Covino 2004), "Asian Americans" in drama and performance art (Shimakawa 2002), and so on. In film studies, Barbara Creed (1993) and Carol Clover (1993) sharply critiqued the misogynistic tropes of the "monstrous-feminine" and the "final girl" in horror cinema regarding abject female bodies. Horror has since been scrutinized from classic creature features to postmodern gory terrors (Magistrale 2005), inspiring other genre studies too—for example, such institutions as prisons and hospitals in thriller and sports films are seen as abject spaces of Foucauldian control (see Pheasant-Kelly 2013). However, the expansion of 'abjection criticism' also involves its own critical turns. Tina Chanter (2008, 6–23) claims that it tends to fetishize the abject 'others,' including the maternal body, as primitive, animalistic, and ugly, thereby reifying hegemonic sexist or racist categories despite the critics' feminist, liberal stance. Kristeva's introduction of the "loving father" into the Semiotic or Imaginary does not disrupt the phallocentric myth of castration because the abjection of the mother as the precondition of ego formation is already misogynistic (45–52). In a notable attempt to overcome this limitation, Elsaesser (2018b, 129–61) maps a comprehensive range of cases and discourses along with European auteur films on abjection beyond the psychoanalytic focus and draws attention away from the "substantive" abject provoking material disgust to "structural" abjection as radical rupture and disorder (to which I return later).[8]

Broader studies on social abjection deserve a spotlight in this context. While the abject in art and film becomes a clichéd trope or a catch-all term for "yucky" stuff (Jay 2012), the term is increasingly explored as an allegory or economy for social identity. In this shift lie two facets of Kristeva's theory. The "structuralist" facet is indebted to Mary Douglas's (2002) *Purity and Danger*, whose anthropological approach to pollution and taboo inspires Kristeva to

---

[7] Kristeva's focus falls much more on social characters and modern writers (Dostoyevsky, Lautréamont, Proust, Artaud, Kafka, Céline) than on material abjection and ego development.

[8] Elsaesser's rich list of European abject films includes *Vagabond* (Agnès Varda, 1986), *Enter the Void* (Gaspar Noé, 2009), *Fat Girl* (Catherine Breillat, 2001), *Barbara* (Christian Petzold, 2012), *Head-On* (Faith Akin, 2005), *I, Daniel Blake* (Ken Loach, 2016), *Naked* (Mike Leigh, 1993), *The Turin Horse* (Béla Tarr, 2012), *In Vanda's Room* (Pedro Costa, 2000), *The Man without a Past* (Aki Kaurismäki, 2003), *Nymphomaniac* (Lars von Trier, 2013), *The Death of Mr Lazarescu* (Cristi Puiu, 2006), *The Skin I Live in* (Pedro Almodóvar, 2011), and such Dardenne films as *Rosetta* (1999).

address the impure abject's horrible threats to the categories of life/death, man/woman, and human/animal. However, the less illuminated "poststructuralist" facet suggests that the pure/impure opposition has no universal archetype, varying among cultures instead, and that the abject thus serves as the constitutive outside of identity in situated practices (Goodnow 2010, 28; Duschinsky 2013). Identity, the integral unity of the intentional self, is stabilized through a "coding" of the culturally specific "differentiation" of the self from the other (Kristeva 1982, 82). That is, abjection is a performative act of making boundaries as the "primers of my culture" (2), not always entailing horror for transgressive impurity. It performs the repulsion to and expulsion of social minorities, thereby building and keeping dominant identities.

Notably, the first theoretical usage of abjection appears in Georges Bataille's (2002) short essay on "the miserable": "the wretched population, exploited for production and cut off from life" no longer cause pity but aversion—this signals the 1930s fascist turn from soft to hard ethics. To exclude these human "dregs" like abject things "constitutes the foundation of collective existence." The imperative power of abjection thus partakes of "sovereignty" over "bestiality," as if the abject could be killed like animals.[9] The abject are the rabble as a classless class that is required by the system but not represented in it, thus included through their exclusion. The abject are the populace in the gutter who are, like invisible men, not sensed except as an abomination. When abjected with no room for resistance, they even internalize stigmatization to the point of having self-contempt and self-loathing. Hatred for them generates their self-hatred and a total loss of political subjectivity.

Tyler (2013) impressively updates this sociological approach to biopolitical abjection. Tyler points out that Kristeva (1994) posits the psychoanalytic matricidal abjection as the universal root of all hatreds while condemning xenophobia as a form of abjection. As an alternative, Kristeva claims, we should recognize ourselves as strange and accept foreigners within us (just as any subject and its mother, the first abject, were not two separate beings). But contradictorily, Kristeva privileges the "abstract" advantages of French universalism over the "concrete" benefits of a Muslim scarf (47) and signs a 2003 petition for the ban of the scarf in France, in this way fetishizing the veiled woman as a threat to the tricolor republican values despite her legal

---

[9] Thus psychoanalytically, for Bataille, abjection is associated not with the development of the ego but with "anal eroticism" in excluding excreta and "sadism" in sovereign cruelty exercised on people (12–13).

entitlement to equality. In Tyler's view (2013, 27–35), Kristeva's universalist demand for enlightened pan-European subjectivity thus implies a cosmopolitan disguise of Eurocentrism. This psychoanalytic and ethical universalism ideologically veils its historical contingency. To forget its colonialist backdrop makes a "memory hole" and causes "collective amnesia" about the imperial past and an "epistemic violence" on the historically produced abjects.

Against Kristevan 'abject studies,' Tyler takes an emphatic cultural studies position by proposing a "situated psychoanalysis" of politicized abjection, focusing not on a universal law but on norms forged through cultivated practices and mediated performances in concrete contexts (2013, 35–38). The maternal body, then, is explored not as the ahistorical abjected *chora* but as a biopolitical object historically constituted to produce labor power for the capitalist patriarchal state. It is this maternal norm that is challenged by such "naked protests" as that of abject Nigerian mothers in 2002 against global oil corporations devastating their environment (104–24). Likewise, the first step to address the riots in French suburbs should be a historical look into the "hygienic governmentality" by which Muslim youths have long been pushed out to ghettoes and humiliated as *racaille* (scum, riff-raff). The postcolonial mourning for the past, if only expressed with a soft-ethical gesture of pity, would end up being the double denial of unhealed colonial traumas and increasing neocolonial inequalities (38–46). Now the neoliberal system demands every citizen-subject be an entrepreneurial, competitive worker, privatizing public sectors, cutting the welfare budget, and inevitably generating the loser-abject. This underclass, the lumpenproletariat and not the proletariat, is even seen as an inferior race from the standpoint of economic Darwinism. When looting shops, the abject are depicted as "verminous waste" that causes a "Hobbesian dystopia of chaos and brutality," and which must be cleaned up. No politics works here; only a moral panic, a "penal pornography," and a hard-ethical vigilantism over outlaws (179–97).

Tyler's ultimate point is, however, that the abject have the political potential to revolt. The suburban looters exhibit nothing but aimless hate in Baudrillard's view, but their brutal "shopping" might be the only way of gaining visibility and entering the public sphere of the sensible in a society where consumption determines one's social dignity, which in turn is reduced to a capitalistic citizenship. Moreover, their violence momentarily makes the law obey them and gives them a sense of control, "a feeling of standing up straight against an institution." They enjoy a euphoric carnival of reversing power, a flash mob that at least exposes structural inequalities. Eventually the punishment is also inflicted unequally between these 'poor looters' and 'rich looters' such as politicians and bankers guilty of expenses fraud and economic crimes (2013, 201–6). Tyler's several case studies on neoliberal Britain illuminate this turn of the abject to "revolting subjects."

Similarly, discussing cinema if not real issues, Elsaesser (2018b, 142–52) differentiates the abject from mere victims, highlighting "the uncanny effects of the excluded over those that exclude them." The abject is "not a recipient of philanthropy, nor the object of pity or compassion," but can make a positive relation to the other in "a freedom outside the law." This emancipation evokes a new "universality" that such leftist thinkers as Balibar, Badiou, and Rancière—notably a trio of former students of Louis Althusser—detect and desire (along with Žižek) in history and revolutions to come. To rephrase Balibar (2002), this universality is neither that of "globalization" realized into a disappointing cosmopolis nor that of multiculturalism recognizing "otherness-within-the-limits-of-citizenship." It is rather the universality of abjection, the universal struggle and solidarity of the abject whose internal exclusion from the global, multicultural system symptomatizes its inescapable inconsistency, and whose absolute infinite claims for ideal "equaliberty" should bring the collective emancipation of the oppressed to the whole of society (146–75). Their insurrection thus aims at affirmative autonomy for a counter-construction of the world—a Badiouan "event" for a new communism, or the Rancièrian "politics" for a real democracy (see Chapter 5).

I formulate such potentialities of the abject in terms of *agency*. Losing subjectivity can make one try to regain any subjectivity if not the lost one. Agency, philosophically meaning the causative force to act, works in this transitional, temporary, tentative mode of being-in-action. It activates the performativity of 'becoming-other,' challenging fixed identity categories while also underlying the constructivist notion of identity, that is, not an a priori entity but an effect produced through abjection (which itself is an agentic act). Construction is indeed "the necessary scene of agency" in which the latter is culturally articulated while also immanently contesting preconstructed forms of identity (Butler 2006, 201).[10] The abject, reloaded with agency, is then the 'abject agent' who acts to fulfill a mission of resubjectivation. Its most

---

[10] In this Foucauldian constructivism, the subject is not the "doer" so much as the vehicle of language, norms, and power. With no internal essence, it is formed through individual performances and circumstantial practices. Agency indicates this contingent, precarious potentiality of nontranscendent self-construction. Judith Butler (1995a, 46–47; 1995b, 137; 2006, 141) further deconstructs gender identity, highlighting its "strategic provisionality" and "operational constitutivism."

utopian case would be the collective restoration of political subjectivity that I explored earlier, and which has been lost since the ethical turn of politics. However, this political rupture of the status quo is not only rare but all the more difficult since the reterritorializing global system leaves no real outside for total liberation. Agency thus cannot help being hybrid, appropriating the system's toolbox and becoming something new and other within the system. However, again, multicultural capitalism also recruits ever-borderless agents to reappropriate hybrid cultures, rendering radical utopianism unfeasible as well as safely consumable in the global market of ideas. This dilemma makes me grope for a new ethical if not political direction that the abject could take on the existential ground of individual life if not directly oriented to a collective movement of revolting subjects. Cinema matters in this regard, making us encounter the abject concretely and even violently beyond our symbolic, fantasized construction of their otherness. Cinema has agency to interface us with them, to abject us from ourselves, and to ask us to be virtual agents in exile who walk or work with them even if nothing utopian is promised.

Paris and *Banlieues* in Post–*La haine* Mainstream French Cinema

In short, it is what I call 'abject agency' that this book explores in cinema. How can the abject be an agent at the crossroads of global inclusion and exclusion? Is utopian politics still possible through abject agency? If not, is there any alternative to the postpolitical double ethics of multiculturalism and terrorism, pity and hate? In the rest of this chapter, I concisely survey a series of post–*La haine* French films—and '(post-)*beur* cinema'[11]—that respond to these questions in the mainstream market and on the festival circuit.

Let me begin with *Banlieue 13* (Pierre Morel, 2004), a Luc Besson-produced action blockbuster with a setting evoking *La haine*. The eponymous imaginary suburb of Paris—hereafter called B13—is an extralegal

---

[11] Beur cinema refers to the 1980s–1990s films about people of North African origin called *beur* (slang for *arabe*), focusing on their hybrid identity and (failed) assimilation into French society. Fusing post–New Wave and Third Cinema styles, its underground attitude is gradually mainstreamed along with the emergence of the '*beur-geosie*'; around this turning point is *La haine* seen as a 'beur' film despite the director's 'non-beur' identity. The 2000s sees the post-beur cinema of Maghrebi-French second-generation immigrants in a wide range of genres and styles. Key figures include Mehdi Charef, Djamel Bensalah, and Abdellatif Kechiche (see Tarr 2005; Higbee 2014; Bloom 2006).

ghetto autonomously ruled by a gang. Here, policeman Damien assumes the mission to deactivate a nuclear bomb taken by the gang, assisted by Leïto, an imprisoned guerrilla fighter against the gang. They collaborate like two different cops in a buddy film, only to realize that the given code for deactivation is rather for activation and that they were used and abjected in the state's plot to wipe out the troublesome B13. The duo then find the government official in charge and force him to take democratic actions. In the sequel *Banlieue 13: Ultimatum* (Patrick Alessandrin, 2009), corrupt government officials fake the B13 gangs' murder of two policemen, whom they killed to create a pretext for destroying B13 and gentrifying it while colluding with construction companies to further their interests. Damien, now wrongly accused and imprisoned, escapes with Leïto's help, and after finding out that the policemen were murdered by the government, the duo rally five ethnic gangs—African, Arab, Chinese, Hispanic, and neo-Nazi—to thwart the state's dirty business. At the end, they ask the president to demolish B13 and to build a new community.

This film franchise, though seemingly political, brings to light the exertion of biopolitical power and the hard-ethical antagonism between the whole and the exception. The supralegal power of life and death is wielded on multiple levels: between the state and the ghetto, between the sovereign and the abject within the ghetto, and between the officials and the police abjected within the state. Those officials claim to declare a state of emergency as "the standard procedure necessary to protect democracy" and exterminate the ghetto that threatens the safety of the Republic (Figure 1.1). In Walter Benjamin's terms

Figure 1.1. Corrupt state officials plot to demolish the gang-ridden ghetto near Paris, perceiving it to be a safety threat, in *Banlieue 13* and its sequel.

(1996; see Chapter 4), the claim justifies "lawmaking violence" that suspends the law itself and transcends the "law-preserving violence" of the police (like the supralegal violence of superheroes with the 'license to kill' and immunity). The abject is none other than the defenseless body vulnerable to this violence. Nonetheless, unlike in *La haine*, the abject figures in B13 challenge power in solidarity without being trapped into the closed circuit of hate. Communing with the abject Leïto, the abjected Damien even performs the self-imposed mission of whistleblowing by digging out corruption in the government. This resistance exemplifies abject agency. Not only Leïto and Damien but also the five tribes of gangs are abject agents who contribute their talent to making a 'dream team' for saving their community beyond their cultural differences. Although their cause is political concerning fighting for independence, this solidarity among the abject suggests an ethical direction irreducible to the double ethics of sympathy and hatred.

What deserves attention, then, is the team's final decision to destroy B13. It is made to build a utopia out of the ghetto, unlike the officials' destructive plan to privatize the public sphere through the corrupt cartel of neoliberalism and power. But this utopianism implies the impulse to devastate the status quo and to restart from ground zero—a system reset like the Flood or the Last Judgment. Historically, such "divine violence" for absolute justice has brought about political revolutions as well as fundamentalist destruction. However, the epilogue of the second film shows not the unknown future of B13 but a fantasy of primordial democracy: a 'happy hour' of the abject agents with the president, drinking wine and chatting about architect Jean Nouvel. The idea of political utopia dissolves into a happy ending with no vision of real struggle. In the end, spectators conventionally consume the heroic individuals' spectacular resolution of social conflicts with no collective, structural approach to them. What we see is a cool French touch added to the trend in today's action cinema to stage disastrous polarization and solidarity among the abject in the global age (see Chapter 6). In particular, the spatial montage of the ghetto used to introduce multiracial gangs in a deft music video style displays the rainbow community of the abject with multicultural clichés. We also see a poster of Bruce Lee and rising Chinese power, while Damien does a drag queen dance and has a Black girlfriend. Meanwhile, Leïto's parkour running over rooftops like Spider-Man thrillingly grafts the extreme sport—formerly shown in *Yamakasi* (Julien Seri and Ariel Zeitoun, 2001) and *Ong-Bak* (Prachya Pinkaew, 2003), both of which Besson re-edited and wrote—onto urban chase scenes. This aestheticization stylizes a postmodern punk rebellion, updating *La haine*. Consequently, the abject's solidarity as a new ethics turns into attractive content viable in the mainstream film market.

If such solidarity typically brings the collaboration of abject agents into the action genre, it takes more subtle, quotidian forms in human dramas. *The Intouchables* (Olivier Nakache and Éric Toledano, 2011), a global box office smash, is a buddy dramedy that stages a rare friendship between a superrich quadriplegic, Philippe, and a poor Black ex-convict, Driss, who is hired as his caretaker. Philippe's palace-like Parisian mansion and Driss's suburban apartment with a near-open toilet epitomize their class difference. The distinction of cultural tastes is more explicit: the millionaire buys a painting extempore at a gallery, cites Guillaume Apollinaire in a love letter, and brings home a chamber orchestra on his birthday. This modern aristocrat opens his mind to the straightforward, hot-tempered abject figure who sincerely treats him like a normal person and not as a disabled person, with pity. Without the asymmetric hierarchy between the subject and the object of soft-ethical compassion, the physical abject and the social abject shake hands and make a human-to-human connection undiminished by any abjecting gaze. This solidarity on the horizon of equal abjecthood offsets the distance immanent in multiculturalist respect through the experience of the other's culture to transform the self: Philippe is fascinated by Driss's magic of filling his 'classical' birthday party with hip-hop music and dance; Driss tries painting, inspired by modern art he peeks at over Philippe's shoulder. The abject are resubjectivated in this sensorial manner by performatively rediscovering their potentialities through the other, beyond their sedimented identity.

Nevertheless, *The Intouchables* also stops short at subordinating the issues of race and class to singular individuals' humanism, as in *Driving Miss Daisy* (Bruce Beresford, 1989), an elegant story of an elderly Jewish widow and a Black driver set in the 1950s American South. As Philippe flies to the Alps with Driss just to get refreshed by enjoying paragliding, cinematic attractions often come from Driss's initiation into upper-class culture à la Cinderella. It is Philippe's wealth that enables their free, equal fraternity, which is less an eternal friendship between the top 1 percent and the bottom 1 percent than a temporary one that depends on the former's conditions and contract. Surely he is not a condescending multiculturalist. Thanks to Driss's active mediation, Philippe indeed goes beyond writing love letters and tries actually to meet his love interest, eventually marrying her and in the process overcoming both his physical and mental disabilities—in the way of performing an act beyond the sterile 'courtly love' that idealizes the unobtainable object of desire with resignation. But as soon as his lover takes the place of Philippe's lost wife, Driss disappears as if his final mission has been accomplished. Driss is replaced by the lover and thus no more than an agent who enables Philippe to enjoy a free vacation away from his cultural world until he can recover his masculine subjectivity and marital status. Just as Rose, stifled by her high-class culture in *Titanic* (James Cameron, 1997), is revitalized through her romantic adventure with penniless artist Jack before ultimately living a long, rich life ("I'll never leave you," says Rose to Jack, even though she lets go of him, and he is submerged in the Atlantic ocean), so the multicultural cordiality in *The Intouchables* is an ideological veil of the top-class liberal's self-empowerment with the help of the caretaker, who remains socially abject in the end. But the film defuses this critical viewpoint with the charm of the bourgeoisie. In sum, the Real of racial and class complications dissipates into the slick surface of commercialized multicultural imagery.

Such a moderate solidarity of the abject is prevalent in human dramas with the motif of cultural conflict, such as Nakache and Tolédano's next film, *Samba* (2014), about a Senegalese immigrant and a caseworker; Alain Gomis's *As a Man* (2001), about a Senegalese student in Paris; and Merzak Allouache's *Salut, cousin!* (1996), about two Algerian cousins. Also notable are works by female directors, including Coline Serreau's *Chaos* (2001), about feminist solidarity between an Algerian immigrant and a rich Parisian; Julie Bertuccelli's *Since Otar Left* (2003), about three generations of a Georgian family; and Houda Benyamina's *Divines* (2016), about a poor suburban girl's friendship with a dancer. However, when it comes to films sprinkled with comic cultural codes, the genre tends to fall into the trap of representation. For instance, in *Serial (Bad) Weddings* (Philippe de Chauveron, 2014), an elderly White bourgeois Catholic couple, whose three daughters are married off to Arab, Jewish, and Chinese men, are shocked when the last daughter introduces a Black boyfriend—the French title means: "What did we do to God?" Facing this national identity crisis, the multicultural sons-in-law incorporated into mainstream France first object to, but later collaborate to forward, their youngest sister-in-law's marriage. But here too, the point is that humanistic racial harmony would work out because the family has no lack of money, jobs, or whatever. To help the Jewish son-in-law open an ethnic food restaurant, the Arab husband, a lawyer, offers legal assistance, and the Chinese one, a banker, facilitates capital investment; it is as if this collaboration exemplifies the cultural logic of multinational capitalism. The process of making a rainbow France, with funny unharmful squabbles, embodies the global practice of a multicultural market economy. And racial and cultural diversity is stereotyped into only consumable jokes and comfortable satires. This limited sphere of the French bourgeoisie's openness to others exhibits a sweet fantasy of multiculturalism in the form of a romantic comedy that flattens out all serious problems on the surface of customary representations.

Auteurist Responses to the Ethical Potential and Limitations of Abjection

The 'too easy' communion of the mainstream White with the racial abject in 'politically correct' films eventually betrays the hollowness of multiculturalism. Most of today's auteurs do not compromise with such a cure-all happy ending in a problem-solving narrative. Laurent Cantet, whose authentic realism is palpable in *Human Resources* (1999), *Time Out* (2001), and *Heading South* (2005), spotlights in *The Class* (2008), for example, a suburban site of French public education from the perspective of François, a high school teacher. The winner of the 2008 Palme d'Or and shot in the documentary mode of cinéma vérité, the film depicts François's class, full of distracted, ungoverned, and rebellious teenagers, as a miniature of multiethnic France in identity crisis. Students complain about impractical conjugations, question the exclusive use of White names in sample sentences, seek clarification of François's alleged gayness, and take the assignment of writing on "respect" as "discipline." In truth the school is an Althusserian "ideological state apparatus" in which Foucauldian biopolitical discipline starts national subjectivation, but where its traditional authority no longer works: teachers say that teaching Voltaire today is hard, François is brought to book for shouting an insult, and Black students squabble over whether they root for French or African football teams. When students ask the meaning of "condescendence," François's response suggests that the patronizing attitude of mainstream French society toward sociocultural minorities underlies the proud republican values of respect and tolerance. But as students prioritize "electricity" over "liberty, equality, and fraternity," the universality of the tricolor ideology seems to be fiction to the abject in the ghetto, whose mere base for survival is unstable. As already discussed, multiculturalism in this liberal democracy is a disguised form of a still-Eurocentric global capitalist sovereignty.

The Class lets us look at daily cultural conflicts in the institutional and ethical dimension rather than reductively judging them in the theoretical dimension. In fact, the teachers here, though all White, work hard for the educational equality and integration of multicultural students. Their eye-level approach to impolite, aggressive students enables bidirectional discussion beyond the transfer of knowledge; their meeting with both students and parents to decide on grading and punishment could not be more democratic; their dialogue with immigrant parents via translation is patient and sincere; and their concerns over the possible deportation of a Chinese student's family arrested for illegal residency are not fake and hypocritical. Nevertheless, their peril point is tested when the student representatives leak grades to the class after the aforementioned meeting, and François in anger calls them *"pétasses"* (whores), which causes Souleyman, a student who is upset by this swear word, to storm out of the classroom, accidentally hurting another student. Souleyman is then summoned to the disciplinary committee and expelled from school despite his mother's appeal.

We could wonder if this expulsion, though democratically voted on, is right or desirable, given Souleyman's momentary act and François's own wish to keep him. This immigrant student, whose artistic talent is seen in his photos of his poor mother, might be tempted into wrong ways or even deported to Africa after expulsion. However, the multicultural community resorts to the law to protect it from any contingent violence that goes beyond the limit of tolerance. In this order of soft and hard ethics, interlocked inclusion and exclusion, the inevitable punishment does not fully suture ethical conflict in people's mind, nor does it leave room for ethical alternatives to anyone, be they student or teacher. The last scene, in which students and teachers play football together, celebrating the end of the year, shows the restoration of daily life as if the traumatic memory about Souleyman is healed or consigned to oblivion. Nonetheless, the final shot of the empty classroom evokes the absent abject, like a visual symptom of ethical emptiness or fracture. When a student confesses that she understood nothing throughout the school year and that all thought of the future causes anxiety, we cannot help but imagine a more anxious future for Souleyman, who now does not even have the chance to be encouraged by his teacher.

No wonder many realist films deal with the abjection of suburban youth stuck in a double bind: either they fall into crime and punishment, or they remain unable to regain proper subjectivity even after leaving prison. The former includes *Girlhood* (Céline Sciamma, 2014), about a poor girl joining a gang, and *Learn by Heart* (Mathieu Vadepied, 2015), about a Black kid becoming a drug dealer. The latter, meanwhile, includes Rabah Ameur-Zaïmeche's films such as *Wesh Wesh, qu'est-ce qui se passe?* (2001), about an Algerian French person's harsh life in a ghetto after incarceration and release, and *Bled Number One* (2006), about the same character's deportation to Algeria and involvement in fundamentalist violence and retaliation. By extension, and evoking *La haine*, some films capture a predicament between crime and punishment or a prelude to riots. Ghetto buddies in *Ma 6-T va crack-er* (Jean-François Richet, 1997), a Marxist version of *La haine*, show the vicious cycle of hatred between rival gangs in the suburban slums of Paris while asking if a riot could have political potential beyond the hard ethics of hate, per the communist revolution. In $13m^2$ (Barthélémy Grossmann, 2007), friendship is tested as burglars find themselves confined in a small bunker. In *The Disintegration* (Philippe Faucon, 2011), Arab French youths are exposed to Islamic radicalization against a backdrop of social discontent and increasing inequality.

Jacques Audiard's Cannes winners *A Prophet* (2009) and *Dheepan* (2015) also need to be revisited critically. *A Prophet* minutely depicts how Malik, a delinquent young Franco-Arab, kills an Arab prisoner on trial in order to be taken under the wing of a Corsican mob boss in prison, where he grows powerful by fulfilling a series of criminal tasks, to the point of eliminating the very boss and taking his place. In other words, Malik undergoes double abjection: being abjected into the prison, then abjecting his own racial identity there, he becomes an agent of the Mafia and even its sovereign (subject). Here, the prison as a 'microsociety' driven by power struggles between the abject inmates is also a model of the Hobbesian 'state of nature,' in which the inmates directly use violence outside social regulations, unfolding a "war of all against all." This extralegal state is of course not a prelegal natural state (as it takes place in a prison), but rather a state of exception in which the abject community under the law is split into the sovereign and the rest. The latter use bloody fighting to usurp sovereignty, that is, the supralegal power that makes of the rest *homines sacri*, whose bare life can be removed with impunity; Chapter 3 highlights this Agambenian biopolitics. Moreover, the prison authorities represent not only antihuman sovereignty over bare life, as seen in the inspection of naked bodies, but also bureaucratic corruption, as seen in their connivance with, and even subjection to, the Mafia power. The prison is doubly exceptional to the law, which is enforced in both supralegal and extralegal manners. In a sense, *A Prophet* is a coming-of-age story about an abject's growth into a sovereign. The problem is that the violent process of conspiracy, murder, and betrayal does not pose ethical questions about sovereignty and abjection, which take a back seat to the inevitable portrayal of jungle law as viewers are sutured into a heroic saga of the abject individual's survival and conquest of a dominant group. This is not far from a Mafia myth à la *The Godfather* (Francis Ford Coppola, 1972), shedding little light on multicultural conflicts in a larger sociostructural context. The solidarity of the abject is then rigidified as the Mafia familism of fascistic bonding and Oedipal renewal, making no ethical breakthrough.

Likewise, *Dheepan* absorbs the social dimension of the refugee crisis into an individual drama. A man who was a member of the Tamil Liberation Army defeated in the Sri Lankan Civil War (1983–2009) seeks refuge in France with an unknown woman and an orphaned girl, using a deceased family's passports (thereby taking the name Dheepan). Pretending to be a family until acquiring citizenship is notably like experimenting on the new ethical solidarity of making an alternative family. However, the Parisian housing project they settle in turns out to be an extralegal battlefield of gangs, much like the prison in *A Prophet*. Here Dheepan, who shouts "The war ended!" to his former Tamil superior, reencounters violence like that in Sri Lanka. Again, the film focuses not on the systemic controversy of French multiculturalism but on the conflict over microsovereignty among the abject and the inescapable choice of violence as the only survival/escape strategy. The woman's increasingly cordial relationship with a gang member beyond cultural barriers is broken when Dheepan rushes to save her from that very gang. That is, the alternative family is consolidated in exclusive familism, and any larger solidarity of the abject is blocked. The ending shows a happy day as the Dheepan family has remigrated to the United Kingdom, but this abruptly utopian epilogue feels empty, as if it were a fake suture of abjection. For if such brutal chaos as has taken place in Sri Lanka repeats itself in even a small district of France, then the abject's new ethical potential is lost in the double ethics of pity and hate and the antagonism between self and other that allows nothing more social than a family.

Why does solidarity fail even among the abject? Because their pursuit of microsovereignty to become a subject and to abject the others enables no real equality experienced on the same level of abjecthood. Only renouncing one's sovereign subjectivity would bring about solidarity. But how could one do so? Michael Haneke, though widely analyzed, may help us ponder this specific question. He considers France's affected parts in the omnibus-style *Code Unknown* (2000), in which a White boy throws trash at a beggar from Eastern Europe, but the police arrest a Black young man who is upset by this behavior and deport the beggar, who is identified as an illegal alien. Meanwhile, a French woman uninterested in social issues is insulted by an Arab bully, and nobody but an old Arab man intervenes. Such apathy and antagonism inherent in multiculturalism also pervade *Hidden* (2005) in the most ordinary but persistent manner. Television show host Georges receives videos showing just his daily surroundings, which he later believes to have been sent by Majid, his former Algerian French adopted brother. It turns out that young jealous Georges mischievously told his parents about being threatened by Majid, who then was expelled to an orphanage. This 'petty' past event, erased from Georges's memory, might have been a life-changing trauma to Majid who, deprived of all the benefits offered to Georges, might have had to survive like a semi-abject. Those puzzling videos thus arrive like 'uncanny letters' sent from Georges's forgotten past, which might not have been past for Majid.

Interestingly, Majid not only denies any connection with the videos but appears more gentlemanly than Georges, who is a nervous, menacing, bourgeois intellectual. Majid's cutting his throat upon pleading innocence in the presence of Georges, who visits his shabby apartment, is shocking. This suicide, captured in a static long shot and long take just like some of the previous video images, looks as though it could be and will be the content of another video, but we spectators have already seen that the apartment has neither cameramen nor a place to install a hidden camera. Instead, what is hidden would be the Lacanian "gaze" of the Real that intrudes into reality from a realistically inexplicable position. The video works not as a practical medium for transparent face-to-face communication but as what elsewhere I have called an ontological "interface" that connects reality with the Real, only asymmetrically. Reality disintegrates in the Real, the unconscious realm, from which the abject past, repressed yet undead, returns to shake stable reality. All enigmas around Majid indicate that the Real can never be linguistically signified and socially communicated in the symbolic order (Jeong 2013b, 19–31). Georges is only demanded to face a certain calm but insistent otherness abjected from him, which he hardly grasps or controls. Right before the ending, young Majid is seen being expelled from home in another lengthy long shot taken by the gaze of a "hidden" camera fixed afar. It is unsure whether we see Georges's dream or recollection.

Unlike suicide bombing, Majid's suicide implodes such codestructive hard-ethical aggression into himself. By doing this, he issues an unavoidable ethical order ('Look at me!') while causing Georges to pose an unanswerable question ('But why?'). This question is also a hint given to Georges ('I know what you did in the past'), which is nothing but a message ('Look into the abyss of your memory!'). The ethical awakening that Georges should receive from this is not multiculturalist tolerance or pity but guilt. More precisely, he is brought to justice not because of his puerile past action as objectively guilty but because of his present lack of subjective guilty feelings. If heroes in Greek tragedies take responsibility even for unintended fateful actions, Georges avoids feeling responsible for Majid's abjection even though he triggered it by self-defensively rationalizing his vested rights. From his position, Majid is nothing but a shameful stain on his confident, wealthy, and sophisticated life. "Shame" is experienced as something to be avoided, a self-oriented psychological feeling that causes the shift of blame from the self to the other and the destructive desire to remove the other, as seen in Georges's rage against Majid. Conversely, "guilt" is to be accepted, an other-oriented ethical principle that enables participation in social relations through the assumption of responsibility for the other (Wheatley 2009, 164–71). *Hidden* suggests that shame should turn into guilt even before attempting solidarity or reconciliation.

Remembering and recognizing uncured past traumas is the first step toward this ethical responsibility. Conversely, given that Majid's birth parents were among the Algerian protesters massacred in Paris in 1961, Georges's unethical attitude recalls the French government's denial of that event for thirty-seven years. More than two hundred Arabs were dumped in the Seine due to the severe repression of a pro–National Liberation Front demonstration, but the state admitted this massacre only in 1998, reducing the number of the dead to forty.[12] Such collective amnesia suppresses and dissipates the French history of colonialization like a black hole of memory. Furthermore, Majid's son represents second-generation Arab immigrants, whose social abjection and revolt ruptures the postcolonial fantasy of global multiculturalism, which pretends that both the traumatic colonial past and the unequal

---

[12] *The Colonel* (Laurent Herbiet, 2006) is a reportage-like drama about the belated return of such a historical trauma and its problematic resolution. A lieutenant is eliminated by a colonel after resisting the latter's antihuman violence against Algerian people in the 1950s, but later, in 1993, the colonel is assassinated by the lieutenant's father—as if Majid in *Hidden* committed murder instead of suicide. The private judgment and punishment imply a deep distrust of public jurisdiction while foreboding retaliation that is also based on subjectively executed justice.

neoliberal present are overcome—although this is not the case according to Tyler, as discussed earlier. Likewise, the reckless suture of traumas with the hurried mourning for the dead might end up with a sympathetic charity to integrate the abject into the symbolic order of the subject. This soft ethics instead speeds up oblivion in a symbolic gesture of remembering the past while keeping a distance from it. The reason only self-reflexive guilt, and not self-protective shame, can bring about a genuine apology and reconciliation is that the subject of guilt comes down to the ground of the abject and looks back on its acts from the abject's perspective. Only then can genuine solidarity with the abject take place.

Finally, however, let me devote attention to a pitfall that can appear even right in the middle of seemingly authentic guilt and solidarity. Bruno Dumont's *Hadewijch* (2009) inquires into religious and existential ethics related to identity crises. Here, the eponymous aspirant nun pursues ecstatic absolute faith, only to be thrown out of her convent owing to her self-injurious anorexia, which is not allowed. This abjection initially brings her back home to her former social identity as the daughter of a wealthy French diplomat, but then it also leads to further abjection from her busy, apathetic parents, who neglect her. Deviating from her bourgeois White family, she happens to meet a Muslim boy and follows the sermon of his jihadist brother concerning abject Muslims suffering in a bombed Arab country. Awakened to this dark side of reality, Hadewijch accepts Islamic fundamentalism with a deep conviction that the way to God is to become a martyr and soldier of God. She decides to act in a mission of divine justice, as if to atone for the guilt of the West for devastating the Arab world. Like committing divine violence, she bombs a subway station.

What we see is not that different from the typical process in which a lone wolf becomes a terrorist: preradicalization, self-identification, indoctrination, and jihadization (Kundnani 2014, 134). But unlike the suburban abject, Hadewijch's radicalization occurs in the way that a subject of high society abjects herself, by encountering, embracing, and embodying the abject other. This passionate solidarity develops into devotion to the most fundamental level of otherness, contrary to multiculturalist integration by absorption. She performs ethical self-transcendence to supreme supralegal justice like following a divine revelation, just as Antigone ethically insists on holding the funeral of her abject brother in the name of divine law, even though the action is banned under state law. The problem is not that Hadewijch converts from Christianity to Islam, but that she, still praying in a Christian pose beside the Muslim priest, takes God—Christian or Islamic—as the still ultimate big Other who should offer ethical solutions (see Figure 1.2). That is, the same God only converts her obsessive self-harming faith into terrorist aggression. The solidarity with the abject then takes on the hard ethics of abstract hate for the entire world to which she used to belong. After the bombing, however, she comes back to the convent and, evading the police, asks God, "Why do you draw me and flee?"—a question about the existential void that she can never fill with any religious commitment. Here is what she calls "sadness as a human," the subject's tragedy of being subject to the absolute big Other that inspires self-transcendence while never being reachable. Hadewijch, named after a medieval mystic, ultimately fails in belonging to God and throws herself into a brook like the abject girl in *Mouchette* (Robert Bresson, 1967). Though a Jesus-evoking carpenter saves her, we cannot but critically revisit the self-abjecting connection to the abject other through whom she wanted to be guided and saved by the transcendent Other.

In sum, Hadewijch epitomizes the performative agency of becoming an abject. That agency's potential is first activated contingently by the abject, before changing her identity with her self-determination to go down to and stand on the same horizon as the abject. However, her unique abject agency to fulfill what she believes is God's order makes her a 'sovereign agent,' not

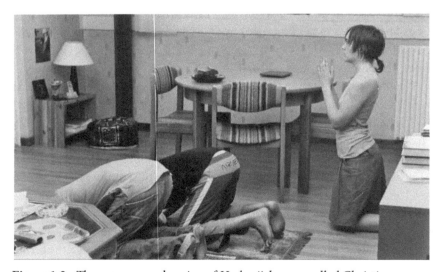

Figure 1.2. The eponymous heroine of *Hadewijch*, an expelled Christian, pursues divinity in Islamic fundamentalism to become a radical terrorist.

persevering with her void of Being as the existential opening to a new subjectivity without any Other to resort to, but blindly filling it in with the same old Other. Her self-abjection for true solidarity with the other abject thus resubjectivates her as a divine soldier, who in reality is simply a criminal pursued by the police. Admittedly, it is difficult to make an ethical breakthrough between the soft and hard ethical traps. A positive alternative would be sensed only when the abjected subject faces and embraces the abject other with no transcendent Other—be it religious, political, or social—that institutes a sovereign community abjecting such others. Only then could the abject be freed from any identity and relationship regulated in the community and appear to retain the potential sanctity of (bare) life, not to abject but to relay to each other in the way of Being itself becoming an existential gift. Their solidarity would perform this gift-giving as commonality without community on the edge of the global system even if it promises no land to reach, no divine providence to follow. It would be precarious, but all the more precious as it has 'life and nothing more' (see Part IV). With this potential in mind, we continue to navigate our way through different constellations of films and agendas in global cinema.

2
The Narrative of Double Death with Abject Agency

Narratology and Ideology: Double Death and Abject Agency

Global cinema in this book is none other than the global cinema of abjection. It has a typical narrative arc. Main characters die symbolically at the beginning by being lost, cast, detached, or expelled out of their community, while often encountering (this experience as) a traumatic event; on a daily level, it may appear as being abandoned, rejected, suspended, or fired from their family, school, workplace, or institution. This symbolic death makes them the abject, deprived of their sociopolitical subjectivity and even homeless, jobless, or moneyless. The rest of the story shows their survival in this symbolic postmortem state of being, a state of limbo between life and death, subject and object. Most of the abject then struggle to rejoin their community and regain their subjectivity, succeeding or failing toward the end, often at the cost of their biological life; this means they are often redeemed paradoxically through their real death. The two deaths, symbolic and real, bracket and shape the narrative of abjection and redemption in this way.

We could trace this narrative far back to the Bible. The Fall of Man—the primeval instance of 'falling' sketched in Chapter 1—is nothing but abjection from the Garden of Eden. Man would return to it only in the hereafter through the grace of God. The life of all of humanity including Adam on Earth is thus already a second-rate life, a mortal one as conditioned, contaminated by death, and each one's salvation to eternal life in the Paradise Lost will ultimately be determined on the Judgment Day upon the Second Coming of Christ. As a human being, Christ in his First Coming also undergoes double death: his symbolic death occurs as his triple abjection by the Jewish priests, the Roman empire, and even the Father—hence his shouts on the cross, "My God, my God, why have you forsaken me?" Then his real death leads to his resurrection and redemption to heaven. In sum, the cycle of abjection and redemption in the vertical movement of descent and ascent, advent and ascension, characterizes Judeo-Christian life on both the individual and collective levels. When it comes to collective humanity's eschatology, abjection on Earth (after the Fall) is experienced through "catastrophe"—political, economic, natural, religious, or moral (world wars, revolutions, epidemics, famine, apostasy)—which is believed to presage not only the end of the world but also redemption by the Messiah. The treatment of catastrophe as "a sign of a promised redemption" is found in diverse sorts of utopianism including even antireligious Marxism, which sees the collapse of capitalism as the necessary step toward a communist ideal world (Whyte 2013, 6).

In this regard the *cinema of catastrophe* deserves special attention, as we will see in detail in Part II. A catastrophe devastates everyday reality, causing protagonists' abjection and action for postcatastrophic redemption, and the original state is restored mostly at the expense of their lives or with some changes in the end. This narrative structure perfectly realizes what Deleuze (1986, 141–59) calls the large form of the "action-image," namely situation-action-situation modified (SAS': "from the situation to the transformed situation via the intermediary of the action"). Indeed, I claim that SAS' is the formula of the catastrophe-redemption narrative in its broadest sense found in many action-driven genres such as the western, thriller, war, and adventure. The 'action genre' as such, which is the umbrella term for all these, could thus be defined better concerning this 'action-image' as a universal narrative form than concerning spectacle. Notable here is the motif of 'last-minute rescue' whose prototype was set up as early as in D. W. Griffith's silent films, from *The Lonely Villa* (1909) to *The Birth of a Nation* (1915): there is a peaceful (white) family or community (S); it or its members are endangered by (black) villains, who are defeated by (white) heroes (A); the endangered are barely rescued and brought back into the original state, if slightly modified (S'). The rescue at the last minute maximizes the dramatic effect of redemption especially when (super)heroes save people like a messianic deus ex machina while demolishing 'axes of evil.' Not to mention this is the nation-(re)building narrative that American cinema has been updating through time, staging the rescue of Americans endangered by Nazi Germany, the Vietcong, the USSR, various terrorists, and the like—suffice it to recall *Saving Private Ryan* (Steven Spielberg, 1998), *Argo* (Ben Affleck, 2012), and other such war/action films and franchises, like the *Rambo*, *Die Hard*, and *Mission Impossible* series. Rooted in the goal-oriented problem-solving classical

Hollywood cinema, this narrative further embodies American imperialism by depicting America not only as the world police but also as the guardian of the entire world facing global disasters or alien attacks. In short, America as/and the world (S) overcomes the enemy/other (A) to be reintegrated and reinforced (S'). The narrative is deeply ideological.

The double death structure that I formulate in global cinema, however, has significant differences to note. First, unlike the biblical Fall and rise, abjection does not occur as the punishment for the original sin or any wrongdoing, nor does redemption mean the compensation for penitence or any good deed. What is questionable is not the subject but often the community, whose sovereign power to abject the subject is unjustly executed; as it were, not the son of God, but God himself is ethically problematic. The pursuit of salvation then does not always stand for the post-fall vertical rise back to the original normality. Even if the abject act to fulfill the mission of this return at first, that action might instead turn into resisting or debunking the sovereign community. Second, what matters in the SAS' narrative is the extent of modifying the original situation through action. This modification may go beyond the restoration of the same with minor changes, as the abject can revolt against the divine sovereignty that destroyed their very original situation. The potential of such modification implies multiple directions that the abject can take and their change as well, their self-empowerment or self-redemption if not resubjectivation into their past and lost identity. The abject's mission is thus not limited to or does not merely last as regaining their 'normal' state. They might take revenge, terrorize those who abjected them, or even destroy their former community. But in positive directions, they might also make a new relationship or form certain solidarity outside the biopolitical mechanism of abjection. Global cinema could be 'postclassical' given such ideological deviations and their narratological impact on the classical SAS' structure.

Psychoanalytically speaking, the abject thrown out of their community have all the more potential to challenge the existing social order or liberate themselves from it toward the Real that is not representable in the Symbolic. Abjection as symbolic death can thus be understood as death from the Symbolic perspective while embracing the Real if not yet real death, the Real as still very real outside ordinary reality. Perhaps Antigone is the most critical mythical abject in this sense. She desires to bury her dead brother, the abject whose funeral is banned for betraying the country—namely, a *homo sacer* not to be sacrificed to the gods—at the risk of being imprisoned and abjected, which leads to her suicide in the end. Against the Symbolic of the state laws, she pursues the chthonic laws, the laws of the earth (blood relations) that are genuinely divine for her. Her mission is thus to directly sacrifice/dedicate her brother to the gods without the sanction of the state. By doing so, as Jacques Lacan (1997, 270–83) notes, she enters "the zone between life and death" or "two deaths" (symbolic and real, as I define), the zone that is none other than the Real. Lacanian ethics lies in this transgression of the Symbolic, "not giving way on one's desire," the desire taking on the "death instinct" that runs blindly till its extinction in the paradoxical mode of being "dead in life" on the blurred boundary between life and death. This ethics of the Real that Antigone embodies through her self-abjecting sacrifice to a significant cause is what I called the *hard ethics* at its purest, prefiguring terrorism with neither fear nor pity from the viewpoint of the state power. Antigone might be the first hard-ethical terrorist.

Tragically this radical ethics tends to be suicidal, and we must think about alternatives, but the point to re-emphasize is that the abject do not remain victimized once they cultivate agency, the causative power to activate actions for a mission, though the effects are uncertain and might be negative. As noted in the Introduction, agency is the abject mode of subjectivity. This subjectivity is not preformed but performed only at the moment of action, and it can be constantly reperformed through temporary modulation and flexible adaptation to changing circumstances. Agency in this performativity, not predestined toward any lost origin or subservient to the Symbolic order, accounts better for the (re)assemblage of subjectivity confronting unpredictable crises in the global age than does the traditional notion of identity or any a priori essence. So the abject with this agency are literally 'agents' including, but not limited to, genre-specific professional (secret) agents in spy, crime, or disaster films, who are often abjected from their institutional agency, such as the CIA. Professional or not, the abject agents in general play the role of action heroes in the narrative of double death, with the potential for modifying their original mission itself as well as themselves.

Two East Asian Transnational Networks in Korean Cinema

Although the double death narrative has been elicited from the Western culture and cinema, its universality may be better tested in a non-Western setting.[1] South Korean cinema then serves as a vibrant platform that deserves spotlighting, given its remarkable growth in the global age.[2] But to what does the so-called global Korean cinema refer? Is it Korean films shot in a "Gangnam style" or Hollywood movies made by Korean directors, such as *Stoker* (Park Chan-wook, 2012) and *The Last Stand* (Kim Ji-woon, 2012)? Unmistakably all these testify to the globalization of Korean cinema, the ongoing global expansion of its production and reception, like the K-pop-driven *Hallyu* (Korean wave). Against this industrial backdrop, however, I address global Korean cinema as no other than a part of global cinema, with our key issues localized in/around Korea. Korean cinema thus concerns 'systems of inclusion' generating the neoliberal milieu and multicultural traffic as well as 'symptoms of exclusion' generated by these whole systems, involving illegal migration, casual labor, and various catastrophes. Like other cinemas in the global frame, global Korean cinema reflects this two-sided self-contradictory global condition of life in which both subjectivity and community undergo new crises and changes. What we encounter locally are Korean variations of abject agency. Locality works here not so much as the root of identification with a unique untranslatable reality, national or regional, but as a contingent springboard for embodying the concrete universality of the global system and precarious life in it.

To map global Korean cinema, then, I locate in narrative space two transnational East Asian networks of capital around the Korean peninsula—two networks in which global systems of inclusion are localized, and symptoms of exclusion appear in the form of the agents of capital abjected from the very networks. The first network is the 'North-West network,' which ranges over North Korea; northeastern China, including provinces populated with ethnic Koreans such as Liaoning, Heilongjiang, and Jilin (where the Yanbian Korean Autonomous Prefecture is located); and Mongolia/Russia. The second is the 'South-East network,' which spreads over Japan, Chinese metropolises such as Shanghai and Hong Kong, and Southeast Asia. The North-West network has emerged against the background of the former communist big brothers, China and Russia, rapidly joining global capitalism since the end of the Cold War. The South-East network has long been the backbone of the East Asian economic and cultural markets, significantly established in the world system. Korea has the tradition of film coproduction and distribution, including

---

[1] This and the next sections include a substantial revision of my previous essay on the subject (Jeong 2014).
[2] 'Korea' refers to South Korea hereafter unless South Korea and North Korea need to be specified.

both importing and exporting films over the South-East network, and now the North-West network appears as a new channel for such exchanges. These two networks, with their differences, could be seen as Korea's main routes for what Jungbong Choi calls "cultural regionalization" through geohistorical, ethnolinguistic, and emotive-aesthetic correlatives shared in the East Asian cultural sphere (2010), and also for the "transnational-Korean cinematrix," including not only film but diverse media and other public cultures (2012). But while Choi emphasizes the distinctive value of the term 'transnational' in this regional context, I further recontextualize it in the 'global' frame.

The point is how these networks are cinematically represented as harsh existential conditions of film characters and their frantic survival strategies, indicating their abjection and agency in the narrative of double death. The notion of network is scrutinized in Part III, but for now, let's take it as a geocultural web of connections that subjugate the characters to the system of capital and power, from which they often try in vain to draw Deleuzian "lines of flight," to flee, flow, or break through the cracks in the system toward a plane of exteriority (Deleuze and Guattari 1987, 9–10). However, before delving into films in the two networks, it is worth mentioning a few films that are precursors of this theme and unfold dramas in the Korean demilitarized zone (DMZ) or similar places near the border, thereby touching on the origin of the division between the two networks, that is to say the division of Korea into South and North. In Park Chan-wook's *Joint Security Area* (2000), a South Korean soldier, lagging behind the line, strikes a mine but is saved by two North Korean soldiers. They then deepen a dangerous yet utopian friendship, exchanging gifts in a DMZ checkpoint until they are exposed by the authorities and involved in tragic incidents. In *Welcome to Dongmakgol* (Park Gwang-hyun, 2005), the eponymous virtual village appears as a fantastic haven of lost soldiers from two Koreas and the United Nations during the Korean War. Touched by innocent golden-hearted villagers, these former 'enemies' team up to protect the peaceful village from the attacking armies to which they belonged. *Underground Rendezvous* (Kim Jong-jin, 2007) shows another imaginary place in a demilitarized village, a secret place that was built for the reunion of families and friends separated by the truce line and has been kept until the 1980s as a time capsule, evoking Emir Kusturica's *Underground* (1995). *On the Pitch* (Kye Yoon-shik, 2010) is a comic fantasy about some North Korean guards of the DMZ who fall into the fever of the Korea-Japan 2002 World Cup through radio, melt down the national division, and join the imagined community of reunified Korea.

All these films have common points. (1) Protagonists are lost or separated from their family or army, so their social subjectivity or national identity is suspended, though they could recover it by returning to their community. (2) These abject figures encounter other abjects or subjects on the edge of borders and laws, and they experience unexpected friendship, unlimited hospitality, or unthinkable solidarity by exchanging various sorts of gifts beyond economic calculation. (3) This positive potential for a utopian community is threatened by their original community, which represents and monopolizes the sovereign power of the nation. We end up seeing either a realistic tragedy of failure to keep anarchic relations or a fantastic comedy that compensates for such failure. In sum, the DMZ is the dramatic place of the double death narrative in which subjects become the abject and then the agents of an alternative community that is hardly imaginable or sustainable in reality. This narrative is both liberating and traumatic. The DMZ, the crossroads of different national identities and ideologies that are literally if temporarily disarmed, indeed stands for the networked topos (place) of abjection and agency and is thus figuratively locatable in broader contexts—especially over the North-West network where North Koreans wander. That is, there are more scattered DMZs, not limited to the zone around the truce line, where more different cases of abjection draw our attention to global Korean issues. While the aforementioned films approach the national division in nationalist humanism, the following films cast more cool-headed, critical perspectives on abjection in the world of global capitalism and migration. The DMZ, in this expanded sense, becomes a symptom of globally networked Korea.

The North-West Network: The 'Dog' and 'Thief' of Capital

Including the actual DMZ, narrative space in the background of the North-West network is the main stage of North Korean defectors and (Korean) Chinese migrants.[3] When they come to South Korea for a new life away from oppression or poverty, they mostly end up in total abjection, like the poor Chinese woman in *Failan* (Song Hae-sung, 2001). She, orphaned, enters into

---

[3] Though the global facet of the North-West network is new, its geographic area has long been present in Korean film history (Jeong 2014). However, the recent flood of North Koreans (partly due to famine in the late 1990s) and Korean Chinese (illegal) workers into South Korea is reflected only in global Korean cinema.

a paper marriage with a South Korean hood to remain in Korea, but barely escapes human trafficking and dies of tuberculosis. She leaves a love letter to the near-imaginary husband she never met. He has completely forgotten about the marriage, which he entered into to make pocket money, but bursts into tears while reading her letter, too late to save her. *Failan* is perhaps the first major Korean film that brought to the screen hitherto unseen immigrant workers and their imagined but failed integration into the Korean society that was increasingly rich and multicultural yet still harsh to strangers. But as the film is a commercial melodrama that centers on the Korean abject hero and his spiritual redemption through the ethnic Chinese woman, it remains exceptional to the North-West network films, which mostly consist of trendy action thriller films showing Sino-Koreans on the one hand and dry, realist, independent films about North Koreans on the other hand. In the latter case, for instance, *Dance Town* (Jeon Kyu-whan, 2010)—a third of the director's "town trilogy" including *Mozart Town* (2008) and *Animal Town* (2009)—highlights a North Korean woman who flees from totalitarian oppression toward Seoul only to face a pitiless capitalist reality that promises no better tomorrow.

More notable is the North Korean defector in *The Journals of Musan* (Park Jung-bum, 2010). Musan, the name of his impoverished hometown—let's call the defector Musan also, for convenience—also means the 'proletariat' in Korean. But in truth, Musan is a subproletarian subaltern whose resident registration number (which is given to all South Korean citizens) starts with "125," a social stigma that hinders him from finding employment in Seoul. He belongs to nothing but the class below the class system, with no secure job and wage. Typical realism is manifested in both theme and style, mainly when the camera follows him wandering in a dingy urban landscape. The only object of his self-identification is his beloved dog, found abandoned toward the beginning of the story and dead at the end on the street—an animal abject undergoing double death—evoking the retired old man's dog in the neorealist classic *Umberto D* (Vittorio De Sica, 1952). Coincidentally or not, *The Journals of Musan* shows the abject protagonist changing from a precarious day worker posting fliers to a thief stealing his only friend's (escape broker) money (which itself is illegally taken from poor North Korean escapees), like the poster-becoming-a-thief in De Sica's other masterpiece *Bicycle Thieves* (1948). In effect Musan is a dog of his friend too, who shelters him and asks him to bring the money left in his room; it is in the middle of carrying out this task like an agent that Musan turns into the thief. Here, I would like to present the 'dog' and the 'thief' as a crucial pair of figures that represent two modes of abject agency in the circuit of the capitalist network: either slaving and straying like a dog or stealing and seizing capital like a thief. As if these are two sides of the same coin, a dog becomes a thief when its repressed desire or oppressed rights are not sublimated into social subjectivity. Moving from under the law to outside the law, a 'sub-law slave' becomes an 'out-law stealer' and struggles for survival between symbolic and real death.

No doubt realism in the North-West network is the most consistent and palpable in Korean Chinese auteur Zhang Lu. *Grain in Ear* (2005), *Desert Dream* (2007), and *Dooman River* (2009)—all with the character names Soon-hee and Chang-ho—make up his trilogy about Joseonjok in China (Korean Chinese people whose ancestors moved to China mostly in the period of the late Joseon dynasty) and North Koreans who escape to China and even Mongolia (not to South Korea). Their entrance into hardly globalized local communities nonetheless causes universal conflicts over 'the others.' These abject figures barely live, barely acquiring living necessities, like the animals that often appear beside them and symbolize their state of 'bare life.' Local communities treat these strangers in different ways. The Chinese policeman in *Grain in Ear* is like an 'obscene superego,' harshly punishing illegal immigration and prostitution while secretly desiring the body of the lonely Joseonjok woman Soon-hee. In *Dooman River* it is the Joseonjok village in Yanbian that hosts North Koreans, but under the authorities of both China and North Korea, the autonomy of the village, with its traditional familism, works ambivalently as its hospitality turns into hostility against any threat from the outsiders. Not a legal community, the Mongolian man's house welcoming the North Korean refugees in *Desert Dream* is a primitive "non-place," a space of transience like a hotel or an airport that is always open and serves only for a temporary stay (Augé 2009; Chapters 3 and 9 further explore this notion). The three films thus unfold the spectrum of the sovereign community's attitude to the abject, resonating with the double ethics of global societies regarding multicultural migrants: the 'soft-ethical' pity/tolerance and the 'hard-ethical' hate/violence (see Chapter 1).

On the 'soft-ethical' side, the most basic and generous hospitality is expressed in the form of offering accommodation and meals. This warm gesture always leads to a quasi-family relationship. The Mongolian man in *Desert Dream* plays the role of husband and father for Soon-hee and Chang-ho from North Korea, who in turn take the places of his absent wife and daughter. North Korean kids in *Dooman River* receive food from Joseonjok kids while joining the latter's football team, and Chang-ho sacrifices himself to save from being deported a North Korean friend who has become no other than his sworn brother. Crucially, hospitality is not limited to a one-way dispensation but develops into a virtuous cycle of gift exchange like an accelerating potlatch unrestrained by capitalist calculation. The hosts and the guests give and take not only material objects (a model missile, a crayon set, a hat) but also immaterial service and labor (playing, farming, cooking, cleaning). Not just giving something extra that is good, this reciprocal gift-giving enables the giving of oneself to the other in the way of filling in the other's gap, left by something absent yet necessary. Conversely, the other can be given to me, enter into my life deeply to the extent of becoming the kernel of myself, without which my subjectivity would disintegrate. The 'being' itself is then a sort of existential gift even without being recognized as a gift in the economic sense of the term. At this point, gift-giving goes beyond the soft-ethical tolerance and pity offered from the privileged position of subjects in their sovereign community; I develop this ethics of the gift in Part IV.

The tragedy occurs when gift-giving is put into the capitalist logic combined with the hard-ethical sovereignty. In *Grain in Ear*, Soon-hee's well-wishers—a factory owner, a policeman, and a compatriot—all enjoy her body by force and then abandon her like a dog. Whenever sex is traded and enforced as compensation for hospitality or damage, the abject other is reduced to an expendable thing under the self-interested sovereign power. Conversely, then, the other-as-gift can turn into 'poison' (which the German word *Gift* means), a lethal weapon terrorizing the sovereign figure or community by way of reprisal for exploitation and abjection. Soon-hee, as the male subjects treat her only as the other to expel, becomes a kind of terrorist by offering poisoned kimchi, a gift-as-poison, so to speak, for a community event. This radical retaliation conducted by the abject who turns into an agent of terror is as liberating as it is catastrophic, though such antagonism might fall into the vicious cycle of hard-ethical violence between the community and the abject in reality. In *Dooman River*, Soon-hee aborts her fetus, conceived through rape, and Chang-ho resists the authorities who exclude his gift-like friend by shockingly killing himself, that is, by giving his community the gift of his own death as if he were killed by them. This alternative of 'killing or being killed' is a biopolitical double bind of the abject. The only exit is to leave the community, to draw a desperate 'line of flight' as seen at the end of each film, but it has nothing to do with the romantic nomadism that global jet-setters enjoy. With no promised land to reach, this abject flight is not utopian but rather 'atopian,' abjected from any topos, any place fixed within a community (see Chapter 12). It has the potential agency to form a gift-giving relationship on the edge of the community and to poison this community at the same time.

If the ambivalent notion of gift-poison indicates the (im)possibility of exiting the system of power and capital, the similarly ambivalent agency of dog and thief concerns how to live within it. Keeping this topology in mind, let's explore more (dog and thief) abject agents that abound in mainstream genre films beyond the realistic auteur cinema. Among others, the spy/espionage genre with secret agents—the agent as a profession—has rapidly evolved in the post–Cold War period since the first Korean blockbuster *Swiri* (Kang Je-kyu, 1999). Typically, North Korean secret agents are abjected from their agency, build excellent rapport with South Koreans (agents), and yet have to take the antagonistic position in the end. With a touch of the dramatic thriller, this narrative line penetrates films set in South Korea, such as *Secret Reunion* (Jang Hun, 2009) and *Alumni* (Park Hong-soo, 2012), and films showing global locations, such as *Typhoon* (Kwak Kyung-taek, 2005) and *Double Agent* (Kim Hyeon-jeong, 2003). The abject agents here are relentlessly subordinated to the sovereign system and desperately struggle to survive in its closed circuit.[4]

Remarkable is *Poongsan* (Jeon Jae-hong, 2011), written and produced by Kim Ki-duk. The title role is a kind of double agent who secretly delivers anything for families separated between the two Koreas while belonging to neither of them, like a maverick mercenary. His social identity is suspended in self-abjection, and as 'Poongsan' means a North Korean breed of dog, he embodies animality when passing through the DMZ with his naked body all plastered with mud. This border crossing in camouflage, I argue, makes an ontological shift to the deterritorialized zone of being. His animal body incorporates the environment like a "phasmid," a stick insect indistinguishable from a leaf or twig, and even looks like a ghost, apparent yet not appearing, just as the phasmid etymologically relates to the phantasm or apparition (see Didi-Huberman 1998). However, this desubjective, inhuman state does not mean liberation from society, since the agent is also a dog of

---

[4] On the other hand, there have been many comedies that depict traditionally demonized North Korean spies in a daily setting with humor, sympathy, and humanism and thus liberate them from South Korea's 'Red complex': *The Spy* (Jang Jin, 1999), *Man from the South, Woman from the North* (Zeong Cho-sin, 2003), *Spy Girl* (Park Han-jun, 2003), *Secretly Greatly* (Jang Cheol-soo, 2012), and so on.

capital and power. The National Intelligence Service asks Poongsan to bring back the lover of a former North Korean senior official who has defected to South Korea, but once the mission is accomplished, the government agency tortures and uses Poongsan without paying him. He is indeed treated like an animal, stripped of human dignity, a *homo sacer* that they can kill with impunity outside the law.

This betrayal by the authorities provokes the 'dog' into becoming a sort of 'thief' of sovereignty. Poongsan traps both the South and North Korean agents who pursue him in a private prison, where they are now forced to become *homines sacri* who should kill each other as enemies. He watches this extralegal jungle without being seen, like an invisible hand pulling strings from behind. In sum, Poongsan as an autonomous phasmid becomes an enslaved dog and then a divine ghost, a sovereign-like terrorist; the turn of a nomadic abject into a ghostly agent of terror is typical in Kim Ki-duk's films, including *Bin-Jip* (2004) and *Time* (2006). Interestingly, for Poongsan this turn involves the new self-imposed task of debunking the two Koreas' ideological regimes and their agents, who, like the obscene superego, turn out to be ridiculously driven by the desires for money and pleasure—which is also manifest in another Kim-produced spy film, *Red Family* (Lee Joo-hyung, 2013). It is of note that Poongsan's earlier task commissioned by the government was due to the impellent desire of the North Korean defector, a possessive, jealous lover whom South Korea wants to use for digging up secret information. Capital circulates through a kind of 'black market' of such selfish desires, and the regime politically exploits this extralegal market against the other regime.

Though not a spy film, *The Yellow Sea* (Na Hong-jin, 2010) is a seminal action thriller driven by just such a unique abject agent as Poongsan. It touched off the noir trend of highlighting Joseonjok illegal immigrants and cruel villains in Korea, as seen in *Traffickers* (Kim Hong-sun, 2012), *New World* (Park Hong-jung, 2013), *Sea Fog* (Shim Sung-bo, 2014), *Coin Locker Girl* (Han Jun-hee, 2015), *Asura* (Kim Sung-su, 2016), *The Outlaws* (Kang Yoon-sung, 2017), and the comedy *Midnight Runners* (Jason Kim, 2017).[5] In *The Yellow Sea*, a black market of capital and crimes takes multiple forms

---

[5] This trend reflects the ongoing influx of Joseonjok, up to over a million (accounting for over 40 percent of all foreigners in Korea) since the 1992 establishment of diplomatic ties between Korea and China and the consequent increase in their crimes. But it must be noted that the Joseonjoks' crime rate is about average despite some sensational cases, and the stereotypical xenophobic demonization of them on screen has been criticized.

between China and Korea. At the origin of the complex narrative are, again, very personal desires. A bank manager steals a married woman from her husband, a professor, who steals the lover of another man, a bus company president. All these owners and thieves of the women officially represent fame and power in the mainstream capitalist society. However, to kill the professor, the bank manager and the company president resort respectively to the underground economy of contract killings via Joseonjok killers. This black market of violence then unfolds two transnational chains of gangs, brokers, and hit men in the chaotic way that their (dis)connections are made as accidentally as pervasively beyond anybody's control, where anybody can betray or erase anybody else.

It is in this lawless network that the Joseonjok protagonist Gu-nam has to carry his bare life. A poor taxi driver in Yanbian, he anxiously waits to hear from his wife, who went to Korea to make money, and suffers from huge debts incurred for sending her there illegally. In this crisis, Gu-nam accepts a job of contract murder offered by Myun-ga, a gang boss, monstrous dog trader, and smuggler of Joseonjok, only to become a dog-like slave to him (see Figure 2.1). But Gu-nam, sent across the Yellow Sea to Korea (where he also hopes to find his wife), is shocked to see the target of the murder plot (the professor) being killed by someone else; his mission turns out to be

Figure 2.1. In *The Yellow Sea*, a poor taxi driver (middle) takes on a job of contract murder, only to be enslaved like a dog by a dog trader (right).

impossible to fulfill. Then, misunderstanding the situation, the two groups of black market agents want to kill Gu-nam in pursuit of money. Gu-nam runs away madly while at the same time embarking on a new task of finding and taking revenge on the invisible hand who initially requested the murder and triggered this whole chaos. The film thus develops into a whodunit with an abject agent who replaces the given mission of serving the sovereign network of capital with the self-set mission of revealing and attacking it. What draws our attention is that, as if to drive his taxi, Gu-nam must quickly map unknown places to visit following contingent clues with no linear itinerary, transnationally from China to Korea and nationally to many cities and the sea on all three sides of the Korean peninsula. In this tough journey, he endlessly fights, hurts, bleeds, and heals himself. His subjectivity is nothing but this abject agency that continually adjusts and re-adapts to the threatening contingency of the world. Moreover, he trains these cognitive and corporeal faculties in himself through the skillful 'bricolage,' the deft creation of tools from randomly available, mostly abandoned materials, as also seen in *Poongsan*. That way, the enslaved docile dog of the capital network changes into an independent wild dog hunting for the truth.

Soyoung Kim (2013, 258–61) argues that Gu-nam's struggle allegorizes the pressure on precarious migrant workers in the global system of "cognitive capitalism": the post-Fordist late capitalism in the age of information technology and information as capital. This new capitalist regime depends less and less on full-time jobs, long-term specialization, material means, and products, instead requiring quick instincts, flexible actions, multitasking skills to handle immaterial assets, unpredictable situations, casual labor, and so forth. Of course *The Yellow Sea* and *Poongsan* end with the abject heroes' real death between China and Korea and between two Koreas, so they do not represent any success in that neoliberal system. They rather come to resist it through their self-changing abject agency. Nonetheless, it is true that they cannot help appropriating cognitive capacities and qualities required by the system in order to complete their missions within it and even to fight against it. Their subjection and resistance to the system are each other's flip sides. Also, their quest for the truth is accompanied by extreme physical suffering and self-healing mechanisms as their bare bodies are broken into bare bones and yet restored, as if in an auto-rebooting system. Such heroically idealized yet utterly abject bodies float over the global network of capital like its embodied antibodies—like its parasitic terrorists, ghost hackers, or drifting guerrillas in 'atopian' trajectories.

The South-East Network: Cognitive, Financial, and Emotional Capitalism

As we will see in Chapter 3, the Jason Bourne series presented such an abject agent adapted to cognitive capitalism and global networking well before *The Yellow Sea*. The series has since influenced the spy genre not only in Hollywood but also in Korea, as seen in *The Berlin File* (Ryoo Seung-wan, 2012) and *The Suspect* (Won Shin-yun, 2013), where North Korean agents go through abjection in a labyrinth of conspiracies and fights between North and South. In another fashion, such films as the *Iris* series (2010) and *The Spy: Undercover Operation* (Lee Seung-joon, 2013) imitate the typical James Bond theme and style, depicting South Korean agents who wield and maintain their sovereignty in global settings. These two trends represent global agency differently, yet they are not opposite in fleshing out the globalized look of Korean cinema. Likewise, historical action films such as *The Good, the Bad, and the Weird* (Kim Jee-woon, 2008), *War of the Arrows* (Kim Han-min, 2011), and *Gabi* (Chang Yoon-hyun, 2011) fantasize some moments of the past national crises related to the North-West network (Manchuria, China, Russia), with near abject agents fighting in splendid style. Here we can detect a certain nationalism of global Korea cinema itself rather than of its content, an industrial ambition enveloped in various genre fantasies of the state of emergency and new heroes as abject.

By extension, there is a case in which abject agency stands not for migrant labor but global capitalism as such, and a dog-like character becomes not a terrorist agent but a capitalist agent. In this direction let's now move onto the South-East network. For example, the Korean outlaws in Choi Dong-hoon's *The Thieves* (2012) form a group of abject agents who are not dogs but thieves of capital from the beginning. They are seemingly antisocial rebels, but they manifest the values and abilities that the global capitalist system demands and represents while acting spectacularly in the project of stealing a big diamond. Their cognitive mapping is excellent for obtaining systematic information about places to intrude; their bricolage is the professional operation of high-tech equipment and not the ad hoc recycling of wastes; and their physical assets include not only power and flexibility but also attractive style, fashion, and sex appeal (see Figure 2.2). Linked in a small network of fluid connections, they also form a more extensive network with their transnational peers in Hong Kong, Macao, and Japan. Though they are thieves, their fascinating intellectual, physical, and social qualities bring up the image of

Figure 2.2. The criminal heroes of *The Thieves* display the professional qualities that today's capitalist system demands and represents.

jet-setting professionals or businesspeople who circulate capital rather than the image of migrant workers circulated by capital. Interestingly, nobody notices their secret illegal work in public places, not because they become ghostly agents like Poongsan but merely because they look and behave just like ordinary people around them. Similarly, their black market of theft exists as a double of the legitimate market of exchange, so it is virtually impossible to distinguish the two. Far from resisting global capitalism or fleeing from it, the ultimate desire of these thieves is to acquire the freedom to enjoy all pleasures in a luxurious lifestyle that money can provide from within the mainstream capital network without working like a dog. The film ends with a scene in which they take a happy rest in an upscale hotel in Hong Kong, perhaps enjoying a sense of superiority over the public who do not notice their identity.

The enormous commercial success of *The Thieves*, which overlaps with the success of the thieves in it, indicates that global Korean cinema co-opts the alternative potential of the abject agency to resist the capital networks. If the agent of *Poongsan* exposes the gap between the ideological regimes and personal desires, the agent of *The Yellow Sea* reveals the gap between the black market and the legitimate market, the gap that capitalist individuals make but want to hide. Conversely, the agents of *The Thieves* take this capitalist position while merging the underground and mainstream lifestyles. Whereas *The Journals of Musan* shows the dog-like agent becoming not a terrorist but a thief of capital, this abject North Korean refugee is upgraded to the cool South Korean capitalist offenders in *The Thieves*. That they are the social abject only makes their bourgeois characteristics more bohemian. The danger they risk in being chased by the police rather causes a visual thrill as they cross the boundary of the system with confidence in the takeover of money and pleasures. In some sense, abjection is now an attractive motif, and abject agents are appealing heroes. This co-option of the abject is a smart strategy of mainstream global cinema. It refreshes the cultural face of global capitalism by flexibly absorbing into cinematic entertainment some deviant imagination that could appeal to global audiences. In this process, all the qualities celebrated in the capitalist system are displayed by its outsiders, freed from being exploited, and the critical capacity of abject agency is packaged in the hedonistic fantasy of acquiring capital without being bound by law and labor. The masses buy and enjoy this fantasy. Then does the film ultimately suggest that the capitalist is the most desired thief?

Here let me briefly refer to Choi Dong-hoon's hit *Tazza: The High Rollers* (2006). As its poor protagonist steals his sister's money to gamble on *hwatu* (games with "flower cards" popular in Korea), this film also begins with the motif of theft. However, the money, which he hopes to return later, is not just loot but a debt to repay and an investment to make more money for this repayment. The gambling scene then appears as a black market for capital growth rather than as a one-time playground, and the film—along with the sequel *Tazza: The Hidden Card* (Gang Hyung Chul, 2014)—appears as a commercial film about (pseudo)commerce. This reflexivity is multiple. First of all, the rules of gambling lay down a commercial platform for the 'noncommercial nature' of gambling, that is, luck, but hustlers called *tazza* who manipulate luck continue to break them. The rules exist as far as the hustlers can violate them and because the opponents must follow them in order for the hustlers to win the game by violating them. If the opponents break the rules, the hustlers overturn the gambling table immediately, as if the natural power struggle is always ready to explode as the state of exception to the social contract of the rules. Gambling is thus a special noncommercial variant of general commerce. However, the implication is that this variant is the very core of commerce at large. The film depicts the gambling scene like a miniature of society, displaying the raising of capital acquired by fraud instead of labor as though it is the natural way capitalism works. When a pushover is tricked by the hustlers, they send his money to the gambling hostess confederated with them, and she lends money to the very same pushover at high interest; he loses it and borrows money again in the same way, while they receive interest. This loop captures the process in which capital increases itself only by circulating itself, while belonging to nobody and yet drowning somebody in debt. This underground economy shows the ABC of financial capitalism based on debt.

Of course cinematically audiences are induced to enjoy this commercial film as a fantasy and not to confront the commercial reality reflected there. Toward the end the protagonist's money is blown away in the wind, but it is also intimated that despite the vanity of gambling, he will return to it, just as money always circulates in the world and life goes on—hence the sequel follows conventionally. Nevertheless, without gambling he would have been no other than a dog of capital who slaves away but hardly escapes from a vicious cycle of debt and poverty. Thus his desire to live in "Tower Palace"—a symbol of wealth in Seoul—is no different from the desire of the world itself, wherein speculative capital takes over the value of labor, the return on capital based on money-making-money is greater than the rate of economic growth based on production, and class structure changes into the 'winner-takes-all' system of the 1 percent versus the 99 percent. A hustler's line, "How could we make a living if the world is beautiful and equal?" is beyond a joke. For the fulfillment of desire, it is necessary to embody "capitalist concepts, not human emotions." In this society, where abnormalities are normalized, to train the gambling skill for the change of life is suggested as not only a necessary survival strategy for the have-nots but also an active and enthusiastic self-development to realize their dreams beyond survival. This wonderful self-realization occurs as the cognitive-capitalist stealing in *The Thieves* and develops into the financial-capitalist speculation in the *Tazza* series. As a result, the black market and the legitimate economy intermingle ever more indistinguishably into predatory capitalism.

Last but not least, global Korean auteur Park Chan-wook's *Thirst* (2009) can be seen in this context, though it is a very different film.[6] While the *Tazza* series is quite local despite evoking globalized speculative capital, *Thirst* has a widespread global network in the backdrop. On the one hand, the film's main stage, a store of *hanbok* (traditional Korean clothes), is located in a Japanese-style house where popular 'trot' genre songs from the colonial period flow

---

[6] This part of *Thirst* expands my brief comments on it made elsewhere (Jeong 2016, 372–73).

out from an antique phonograph, and people play Chinese mahjong while drinking Russian vodka. On the other hand, *Thirst* is a rare Korean vampire film loosely based on the French novel *Thérèse Raquin*, with Bach's cantata playing and a Catholic priest, Sang-hyun, appearing as the hero who even visits Africa. This cultural mixture, though critiqued as stateless, indicates that other cultures are already deeply rooted in Korea as natural simulacra that would not stick out except on screen. Given that *hanbok* is so otherized that it is no longer a daily dress, the narrative space looks like a sample of the global, multicultural environment in which internalized otherness and otherized selfhood fuse. There is also a Filipina who married a Korean man for money, and in a similar social position Tae-ju, the heroine, appears as a quasi-abject figure who has to work like a live-in slave under the owner of the *hanbok* store—her foster mother and hysterical mother-in-law—and take care of her foster brother and impotent husband, in a sort of incestuous marriage. The shelter and the unpaid job that Tae-ju gets in return for her physical and emotional labor imply no more than oppression and abuse.

In this respect, as bloodsucking is a (Marxist) metaphor for exploitation, Tae-ju's change into a vampire can be seen as her change into a subject of exploitation; that is, the dog-like worker becomes a capitalist. The catalyst is Sang-hyun. He volunteers to be infected with a virus that is devastating Africa in order to help find a cure, but he dies; he then resurrects as a vampire after receiving unidentified blood and lives as an abject priest who fails to achieve religious devotion and salvation. However, this abjection unexpectedly brings him some superhuman power and libido liberated from the ascetic ministry and emotional labor in religion, including helping and praying to God for dying people. From the economic perspective, he now craves only the capital as blood for the maintenance and strengthening of this new capacity and desire. His affair with married Tae-ju is like the plundering of private property from the bourgeois family system. Furthermore, the scene of Sang-hyun and Tae-ju's mutual transfusion in an erotic '69' pose looks as though they become the doubles while multiplying their blood-capital by circulating it, as in *Tazza*. After that, Tae-ju commits serial killings for more and more blood in ecstasy, just as financial capital infinitely monopolizes ordinary people's blood-like assets. The emotional laborer who served her family with care and intimacy, a dog of emotional capitalism, is now a financial capitalist, a neoliberal thief full of greed. Killing is part of the natural economy for Tae-ju, as she retorts, "Is it a sin for a fox to eat a chicken?" This law of the jungle works in the state of exception to the law of society that she suspends as a "man-eating beast" or a sovereign agent of blood. Humans are none other than bare lives, weak animals to devour. Animality and sovereignty become one, as do the thief and the capitalist.

This vibrant, unfettered blood hunt might look like an affective performance liberated from emotional labor, a positive play (*Spiel*) like games or gambling that Walter Benjamin sees has some emancipatory potential in a capitalist society (Kim 2013, 267). But just as information processing in cognitive capitalism and deceptive speculation in financial capitalism also partake of the nature of play, as seen in *The Thieves* and *Tazza*, so deviation from the system is co-opted into the system itself today. Interestingly, Sang-hyun, who liberated Tae-ju from her house, tries to break her bloody desire and avoid killing people after he kills a senior priest, a father figure to him, as if he wants to tell her, "Let's not become monsters even if we cannot become humans."[7] This difference between the two vampires implies the self-division that a singular being undergoes between desire and ethics when losing or leaving their parental figures or God as the big Other. Sang-hyun says, "Not to suck up the entire blood of those killed is to devalue life"; this weird joke suggests his instinctive pursuit of ethical values that he cannot abandon even after quitting the church. For him, it is unethical to exploit and consume humans by abusing vampiric sovereignty, as he may believe the potential sanctity of life is immanent in the bare lives. He becomes a sort of abject agent who imposes an ethical if not religious mission on himself. This mission turns out to be to renounce his transcendent power, thereby finding sacredness after the death of God not in the transcendent reign of animalistic desire but in the transcendent value of life, which could be killed by that very desire. Divinity is neither in God nor in sovereign animality but in human bare life, to be believed as potentially self-transcendent because man would otherwise be nothing but an animal *homo sacer*.

In the last scene, Sang-hyun goes to see the sunrise with Tae-ju to welcome their demise. This drive toward death also implies his ethical desire for self-transcendence, for transcending his sovereign animality by choosing to die of his own free will against that very sovereign animality. Something that is in him more than himself is realized through this paradoxical abject agency. His self-salvific sacrifice, delayed after the first death, is rendered possible upon this second death. Allegorically, *Thirst* tells a story in which the abject,

---

[7] It is a famous line from Hong Sang-soo's *On the Occasion of Remembering the Turning Gate* (2002).

freed from the religious and family systems of emotional labor, seeks the pleasure of neoliberal capital growth and then performs ethical resistance to this infinite greed through self-destruction. Here is another direction of realizing abject agency.

In conclusion, today's global Korean cinema is full of abject agents who traverse the dual East Asian networks of the neoliberal trinity: cognitive, financial, and emotional capitalism. These agents range from dog-like workers to capitalists like thieves, from ghostly terrorists attacking the system to transnational professionals embodying the system. And there is a penitent choice of ethical suicide away from the vicious circle of slaving and stealing, of attacking the system and appropriating the system. That being said, all of these cases imply conformity or conflict with the global system, or at best a self-destructive rejection of it. What is absent is the imagination for a better world, and this absence is covered with artistic achievements and commercial fantasies. But as global Korea cinema has never ceased to be dynamic, we may hope that it will experiment with more alternative potentialities of abject agency.

3
Sovereign Agents' Biopolitical Abjection in the Spy Film

Biopolitical Abjection: Bare Life and Sovereign Power

The two cases of abject agency explored in Chapter 2, the 'dog' and 'thief' of capital, indicate two ways of being outside a legal society: below or above it. That is, one may either literally be 'abjected' from one's community, deprived of one's social subjectivity, or transcend the legal system, depriving others of their subjectivity. If the former is the abject per se, the latter is close to someone who has the power to abject others. In this sense, Kristeva's psychoanalytic opposition between the abject and the superego overlaps with Agamben's (1998) biopolitical opposition between "bare life" and "sovereign power." Abjection occurs when a community exerts its sovereignty by suspending the law in a "state of exception," wherein one may be desubjectivated without judicial process and thus killed like an animal, a bare life stripped of human rights—namely *homo sacer*, who is expunged from society and cast out of law, and whose murder is thus no longer a crime to punish. In truth, any nation can transcend its law for the sake of security, the right of self-defense, as in war, which allows lethal violence with impunity. Any constitutional government is ready to realize this state of exception to the rule of law. That is, supralegal sovereignty is integral to the constitution of law. Sovereignty as this self-transcending potential of law literally embodies the power of the 'sovereign,' the monarch who can both make and break the law, and who can make anyone a *homo sacer* by breaking it. Two structural limits of the order are represented here: "The sovereign is the one with respect to whom all men are potentially *homines sacri*, and *homo sacer* is the one with respect to whom all men act as sovereigns" (84). The point is that while there is a stark hierarchy between these two, a subject's status is never absolutely fixed as she or he may turn into *homo sacer* at any time—just as ordinary people are temporarily presumed to be potential terrorists when passing an airport security checkpoint. Citizens, who are legal subjects "at the level of Law," are treated as *homines sacri* "at the level of its obscene superego supplement, of this empty unconditional law," which can suspend and transcend itself (Žižek 2010, 124).

Chapter 4 elaborates on the complexity of law and violence through Benjamin and Agamben, among political philosophers. But the point I wish to emphasize here is that while abjection is the universal mechanism of biopower, the age of globalization sees the globalization of sovereignty. The latter directly affects biological lives beyond political and juridical mediation in the state of emergency, in the same way that across the globe it judges people's eligibility for citizenship, detecting, detaining, deporting, and/or dehumanizing people considered to be dangerous or useless (illegal migrants, refugees, terrorists, and the like). The war against terrorism has been the salient operation of the global system's 'hard-ethical' sovereignty to expel and eradicate the so-called fundamentalist axis of evil in the name of 'infinite justice.' However, as we have seen, the abject do not remain mere passively victimized bare lives but can become agents to recover subjectivity or even resist the sovereign system. Terrorists are also 'abject agents' in that they aim to attack the system by appropriating sovereignty in their self-proclaimed state of exception to the law, even at the cost of their lives. The endless loop of terror and war on terror implies the global struggle for sovereign power between the system and the abject.

Hollywood-driven mainstream global cinema presents this loop and struggle, above all, through 'professional' agents of 'institutional' agencies like military or secret agents in state organizations. They are 'sovereign agents' who exert supralegal sovereignty with the 'license to kill' for the cause of global policing as well as patriotic service. Post-9/11 action thrillers are full of such agents, who not only are loaded with counterterror missions but undergo transformative challenges and (self-)abjection from their agencies. In this context, I will draw attention to the post-9/11 spy genre and delve into new relations between sovereign agency and the abject in the global age by comparing recent segments of the James Bond series—especially *Skyfall* (Sam Mendes, 2012)—and the Jason Bourne films, a twenty-first-century game changer in the genre. This study will later connect (via a few chapters on the cinema of catastrophe) with Chapter 7, wherein I investigate the cutting-edge trend of sci-fi time travel films staging the transhuman war on terror.

The Bond Series: From the Cold War to the Global Millennium

If the success of *Skyfall* celebrated the fiftieth anniversary of the James Bond series and revitalized it for another half century, this longevity could be viewed on two axes. First, synchronically, its brand power has already become 'too big to fail' despite the ups and downs of individual entries in the series. Audiences know and repeatedly enjoy what they can expect from this longest film franchise. The Bondian narrative follows the flowchart of "moves" with archetypal characters: M's assignment of a mission to Bond, the Villain's threat, Bond's reactions, the Woman's seduction, the Villain's capture and torture of Bond, Bond's escape and victory, and his convalescence with the Woman. Along this syntactic line, the semantic Manichean oppositions between characters, ideologies, and values are arranged in a quasi-mythical, structuralist fashion, with sexist, imperialist, and phallic codes crossing hermeneutically (Eco 1966, 37–39). Second, diachronically, the Bond series has never ceased evolving through the Cold War against the larger backdrop of the British Empire's decline and its global Anglo-American remodeling. As a "militainment" that meets societal expectations about war, media, and popular culture (Stahl 2009), it has flexibly adapted to the ages of the nuclear crisis, the Iraq War, 9/11, and communist and postcommunist militancy. Moreover, the agent with the license to kill has incarnated a modern fantasy of sovereign masculinity, stylish and high living as well as fast shooting and sexually liberated, while having been played by six actors. In short, 007 has been viable as "a variable and mobile signifier rather than one that can be fixed as unitary and constant in its signifying functions and effects" (Bennet and Woollacott 2003, 31).

Skyfall, however, leaves room for revisiting this general account in light of new challenges brought about by both today's globalized world and the spy genre. Bond here, in the beginning, undergoes the symbolic death of being inadvertently but unsympathetically abandoned by M and MI6, whose role with its murky methods is questioned in its turn and which is almost cast out of the government. The rest of the narrative unfolds the struggle of Bond, M, and MI6 at the same time to restore their endangered identity before their possible real death—thus all happens between the double death, symbolic and real. The mission given to Bond by M after his return is not just another countervillain operation but a sort of 'qualifying exam' to test their necessity in order to reconfirm their value. This self-reaffirmation is all the more tough yet urgent as the antagonist turns out to be a former MI6 agent, so to speak, an ex-child of M and a deserted brother of Bond. Moreover, this villain hacks the agency like an externalized insider who exposes its dirty business. In sum, the sovereign system generates its abject remnant, who may then become either a sovereign agent or a terrorist one, either rejoining or rejecting that very system. The post–Cold War enemy of the digitally globalized agency is nothing but its double, and one's subjectivity precariously oscillates between sovereignty and abjection. Bond's unusually aging body materializes this vulnerability, with little leisure for pleasure while trying to escape immaterial informatics and fight the enemy behind it physically in his Scottish childhood home to reclaim his identity as an MI6 agent.

Indeed, Bond's self-reflection in this global backdrop is as desperate as it is timely. Now given the Brexit vote that revealed Britain's internal and external schisms, the final scene of Bond's return to London as a nationally reintegrated global hero may provoke all the more questions about his agency, nationality, and cosmopolitanism. However, these questions have been raised and addressed throughout the Bond series. What I propose then is to trace how Bond's sociopolitical subjectivity has resonated with the series' historically global nature and to highlight the line between sovereignty and abjection that has become ever more blurred since Daniel Craig's introduction in *Casino Royale* (Martin Campbell, 2006). Importantly, Craig's tenure has been influenced by the contemporary spy genre, which has challenged 007 to renew its name value and differentiate its direction, too. This interaction may tell us much about today's global *agency* in both senses of the term: the sovereign organization and subjectivity in action for a mission.

It is noteworthy that although Ian Fleming's early 1950s Bond novels emerged right in the wake of the Cold War, his 1960s sequels introduced the swift shift to an imaginary post–Cold War world with sprouting effects of globalization. Hinting at a thaw in the Cold War, the source of enemies changed from SMERSH (Smiert Spionam [Death to Spies]), the most secret department of the Soviet Union, to SPECTRE (Special Executive for Counter-Intelligence, Terror, Revenge, and Extortion), an international criminal and terrorist syndicate. The latter is a nongovernmental organization unaligned with any nation or political ideology, a borderless assembly of freelance villains only aiming to acquire power and wealth through terrorism. Exploiting the fragile relations between the East and the West, it holds them to ransom for private gain and carries out its threat to cause global catastrophes (Bennet and Woollacott 2003, 19–23). In a Marxist sense,

SPECTRE then appears like the "spectre" of neoliberal terrorism or terrorist neoliberalism haunting the world, as explicitly shown in *Spectre* (Sam Mendes, 2015). This fictional fusion of two oppositional facets of globalization, that is, neoliberalism and terrorism, even betrays their real proximity in their pursuit of private greed through their supralegal modus operandi. In effect, the globally operating MI6 transcends the law in order to protect the order of neoliberal globalism. SPECTRE is thus like the mirror image of MI6 reflected from the outside of the latter's system.

Interestingly, the Bond film series adopts the SPECTRE formula from the inception with *Dr. No* (Terence Young, 1962), under the pressure of the film industry to depoliticize Bond, thereby maximizing worldwide profits. This widens the cultural spectrum of the Bond character with multiple access points, without ideologically pigeonholing him as the guardian of a big cause like freedom or equality. Above all, he appears as a traditional upper-class English gentleman: White, chivalrous, courteous, humorous, sporting, and patriotic. However, he is also a transatlantic hero whose British origins are offset by American classlessness and openness, leading "the first truly global media phenomena of the modern age, crossing boundaries of language, social background, ethnicity, and culture," comparable to Coca-colonization or McDonaldization (Chapman 2005, 138–40). While this "international Mr. Fix-It who just happens to be British" is still "a protector of Western interests" (141), the Westernized global hegemony seems to indicate not so much contradiction as mutual reinforcement between the national and cosmopolitan Bond, his Britishness, and his global appeal.

To amplify further, on the one hand, his Britishness lingers nostalgically in the conservative imagery of an elitist, nationalistic England: in Fleming's words, "a world of tennis courts and lily ponds, and kings and queens, of London, of people being photographed with pigeons on their heads in Trafalgar Square," and of people who "still climb Everest and beat plenty of sports and win Nobel Prizes" (Chapman 2008, 29). But on the other hand, Bond embodies an emerging fantasy of luxurious consumption in the society of the spectacle after the United Kingdom's imperial decline, breaking free from austerity and moving toward moral fluidity. He is a walking department store, displaying tasty food, nice clothes, brand-name goods, and technological gadgetry. He is a jet-setting free trader of sexual encounters and erotic adventures with multinational beauties in exotic locations. As if to watch a series of commercials or soft-core porn, spectators are titillated to experience by proxy his capitalistic hedonism, which is endlessly explored in a single global market of material splendor and sexual drives. That both Bond and *Playboy* were created in 1953 is coincidental yet convincing evidence of the cutting-edge "ethos of easy, free, open sexuality" in the backdrop of such easy, free, open consumerism (31). In a nutshell, Bond is a playboy spy who transgresses laws and taboos while protecting the world as a global pleasure dome, which represents his mindset and lifestyle, shared or envied by his contemporaries.

The point is that Bond seamlessly mingles local anachronism with the global zeitgeist. Not rendered obsolete, his British legacy is updated as Anglo-American hegemony that sustains the global frame of transnational mobility and multicultural consumption. And yet it also underlies a new privileged place taken by the happy few in this classless frame. Capable but cruel in work and attractive but unattached in love, Bond is a winner in the modernity of meritocratic professionalism and sexual liberation. His hegemonic power typifies the collective spirit of the age precisely because it is desired by many but realized by few. Moreover, his "rebellious streak and less deferential attitude toward his chief" (Chapman 2005, 138) does not imply serious dissidence but just his free spirit, independence, and individualism, which are allowed and even valued within the liberal democratic system—he is like "a cocky star student irritating his stuffy teachers" (Smith 2016, 153). His supralegal sovereignty for the cause of patriotic service and global policing—the essential motif of the spy genre—may then function as an umbrella for individual desires and gratifications, which he can pursue at liberty insofar as this capitalistic world system is defended from its spectral attackers. In this sense, the Bond films of the Cold War era prefigure the post–Cold War tendency toward apolitical globalism. The global agent is already posthistorical, with ideological seriousness left behind a capitalistic world of thrilling actions and teasing sensations.

In the 1990s, Pierce Brosnan as Bond accelerates this 'end-of-history' tendency after the real end of the Cold War. While a major threat still comes from Russia, it takes the form of the postcommunist Russian mafia, which exploits a flourishing black market as well as unstable local governments transitioning into global capitalism. Also, although China as the world's leading communist power is in conflict with Taiwan in *Tomorrow Never Dies* (Roger Spottiswoode, 1997), Bond teams up with a Chinese agent against the global villain, who is a Western, power-mad media mogul. In short, the line between old friends and foes is blurred as ideological politics hardly matters. Enemies appear as the invisible hand of a global market for crimes, a power-controlling, extralegal Big Brother. And while Bond's patriotic and global sovereignty resonates with Tom Clancy's high-tech novels and films, such as *Patriot Games* (Phillip Noyce, 1992) and *Clear and Present Danger* (Philip Noyce, 1994), global blockbusters that flexibly use the motif of espionage, even a comedy like *True Lies* (James Cameron, 1994), trigger 007's depoliticization further in a spectacular fashion of media entertainment (Chapman 2008, 249). Bond's world now shows bungee jumping, computer hacking, new sports cars, and a female M, who even calls him "a sexist, misogynist dinosaur, a relic of the Cold War" as a way of recognizing the critiques of the Bond series from the liberal democratic perspective of 'political correctness.' In other words, the series has long been developed to the point of reflecting creative and critical challenges to it and co-opting them for its survival. To leave a self-critical room is even a marketing strategy, as shown in advertising copy (Chapman 2008, 252): "Is there still a place in the modern world for a Secret Agent like 007?"

In the era of Craig's new millennial Bond, this self-reflexivity is not jokingly sprinkled but seriously embedded in the series' engagement with global terrorism. *Casino Royale* highlights the linked issues of global security and economy, showing that an international cabal led by stateless paymaster Le Chiffre (Mads Mikkelsen) finances terrorist organizations and African freedom fighters. So, while he is implied to have conspired with al-Qaeda in engineering 9/11, what matters is not just a single bomb maker but a big picture of terrorist networking backed by wealthy sponsors with connections to the world of high finance. This picture is all the more shadowy because the black market of terrorism is no longer detached from the official financial sector that prospers through dynamic globalization. Sure enough, Le Chiffre means the cipher or the number, "a stand-in variable, a system of encoding that signifies meaning, but meaning that remains absent and undecipherable" (Omry 2010, 170). This spectral evil reflects the verso of globalization and its internalized external surplus, raising hysterical anxieties about the invisible complexity of the millennial world's operating system.

Bond's body is reformulated accordingly. He can cope with these anxieties technologically, but once stripped of tech gear, his body is all the more natural and raw, tough and gritty, showing off hegemonic masculinity realistically. Conversely, he is exposed to globally erupting danger, with the scar of technology inscribed on his flesh and its masculinity becoming vulnerable. Le Chiffre's sadistic torture poses a castration threat to Bond's well-trained male body, which is taken out of the law as if it were abandoned like "waste," in

Le Chiffre's word, by his agency and country, which might consider him expendable. Bond is degraded, as Agamben would say, to the animal-like bare life that is deprived of the right to protect biopolitical subjectivity and thus can be killed with impunity in the state of exception to normal law, which is suspended. His body is no longer the slick, classy, unharmed container of a stable identity secured by state sovereignty, but a 'precarious life,' disposable any time. If Bond's law-bound submission to M's authority is masochistic in a socially acceptable way, his law-escaping surrender to Vesper is masochistic in the opposite manner of opting out of that social structure, which does not necessarily guard him (Johnson 2010). He loves her enough to quit his precarious job and social subjectivity when he says, "I have no armor left. You've stripped it from me. Whatever is left of me, whatever I am, I'm yours." Of course, after her death, all this self-skeptical deviation turns back into the reconfirmation of his name as "Bond, James Bond," but this reaffirmation itself draws delicate attention.

Skyfall: The Self-Reaffirmation of the 'Dark Knight'

Now let us get back to *Skyfall*. Ironically, it is in this most successful Bond film that Bond undergoes the most existential crisis, along with M and the entire MI6. The motif of falling suggested in the title is manifested at the beginning when Bond's colleague Moneypenny obeys M's ruthless order to shoot from a long range Patrice, a villain fighting with Bond on the roof of a train, but Bond is hit instead and falls into the river below (Bond's revenge is achieved later by making Patrice fall from a building). Accidentally abandoned by his agency, Bond is then presumed dead; M writes his obituary later. This symbolic death happens in a 'teaser sequence,' which conventionally shows Bond's climactic action and resolution of an undetailed mission before the opening credits with title music, followed by the main narrative. Moreover, *Skyfall*'s title sequence does not titillate with the usual exhibition of girls, guns, and travels, but instead unfolds an experimental perspective of the camera falling into the abyss of expressionist, partly animated imagery as if it dug inside 007's dying mind, ending up with a vertiginous zoom into Bond's iris. The implication is his social *abjection*, cast off from subjectivity yet not dead like an object, and thus stuck between life and death. After this prologue, Bond reappears as an aging, grudged alcoholic, spending a time of depravity in a tropical town, no longer as the hegemonic agent but as an abject whose loss of belongingness leads to physical and moral dilapidation. This period is brief, as he soon returns to London after receiving the news of a terrorist attack on MI6, but his full resubjectivation is completed only at the end of a whole new mission. Meanwhile, M's weakened operational edge and moral authority confronts her with the pressure to retire as well as the criticism of the entire agency for lacking democratic transparency and strategic capability. So the film will be about the quasi-postmortem redemption of both the agent and the agency.

Such an identity crisis becomes all the bigger as globalization renders global systems and subjects increasingly precarious. The posthistorical systems of inclusion based on liberal democracy, multicultural commerce, and social networking inevitably generate symptoms of exclusion, the abject in various forms who are deprived of global citizenship and whose vengeful return to the systems may be catastrophic. Also, due to the collapse of political barriers like the Iron Curtain, which separated ideological oppositions, enemies are difficult to detect, germinating in the systems as internally excluded byproducts. Criminal and financial forces mingle; schizophrenic terrorism and transnational neoliberalism mirror each other in their expansion. *Skyfall* updates this situation, staging the hacking of MI6's global network by its former agent as cyberterrorist. The post-9/11 globalism is more complicated in the backdrop of the digital revolution. The World Wide Web is ubiquitous, and information flows omnidirectionally. Warfare is net-centric, and satellite cartography casts an inescapable web of global surveillance. The leaks of computer data and the loss of network control are riskier than any physical military action, the information technology (IT) infrastructure of daily life offers a broad platform for hostile attacks, and global networks of opportunities are those of threats. The more connection, the more contagion. Not the gun but the computer as weapon renders Bond's physical action anachronistic, while the civilian overseers' demand for clear accountability harshly questions the dysfunctional role of MI6.

Raoul Silva, the ex-agent terrorist connected to SPECTRE, is an up-to-date villain in this regard, a master computer hacker who steals and leaks MI6's agent identities on YouTube. While hacktivists and whistleblowers such as Julian Assange and Edward Snowden are even revered as freedom fighters for the public right to know about the suspicious power mechanism, Silva, though evoking these digital heroes, is nothing but a public enemy engaging in a renegade activity (Smith 2016, 147–50). The conservative logic of stigmatizing displacement works here: civil protest is externalized as a national security threat, and the inner problems of the state apparatus are singularized into an individual's abnormality. Silva appears like a sadistic monster when torturing Bond and killing Bond girl Sévérine, a psychopathic predator when caged in his turn, and an insane warmonger when flying to the last battlefield in a military helicopter while loudly playing The Animals' rock number "Boom Boom." In short, he is a subject of jouissance who enjoys surplus pleasure beyond normalcy, obsessed with "a maniacal desire for revenge rather than any higher notions of transparency or democratic duty" (147–50).

This revenge results from Silva's backstory. An MI6 agent in Hong Kong, he was caught for hacking China beyond his brief (another sign of excessiveness), then tortured by the Chinese when M gave him up and got six agents in return upon Hong Kong's retrocession to China. That said, his hatred for M's complicity with the Chinese in torturing him appears too traumatically twisted when it turns out that M made an inevitable decision, which is aligned with her justification of some "reasonable" cases of torture. Consequently, on the one hand Silva's message to M ("Think of your sins") signals the return of the repressed, the punishment by the 'undead' abject who cannot die since "life clung to me like a disease" after the torture as symbolic death. He recalls the horrors committed for imperial interests and mocks Bond's patriotic loyalty to M. On the other hand, Silva's resentment only turns into the active nihilism of pure destruction without any alternative idea, ideal, or ideology. He is oriented to no future but to the past, just as his island kingdom is nostalgically associated with a ruined empire: a counterpart to Bond's Scottish home. The cyber war entailing actual torture and terror characterizes the dystopian closed circuit of posthistorical globalism and abjection.

The dilemma of Bond's body is intensified accordingly. To upgrade it as a human interface with an embedded positioning device and info-processing capabilities is crucial for countering new enemies. When Silva escapes capture into the London Underground in the disguise of a policeman—the visualization of his ghostliness as a hacker—Bond chases him, with the live guide of the control tower mapping their changing routes. However, as Silva still causes a massive train accident, recalling the 2005 London terror, such risks literally make Bond bare life: vulnerable, suffering, bloody, and sweaty, unlike earlier incarnations of Bond who fought without dirtying his suit. Now he must survive with technical proficiency for intelligent tasks as well as the self-healing power of body recovery (pulling out heart-screwing pins), flexibly adapting to volatile situations that test his superhero-like status, to be retained despite its disposability by and in the system. From the socioeconomic standpoint, this new working condition of Bond reflects the nature of postindustrial late-capitalist labor. One is required to acquire technical skills for handling knowledge and information as immaterial assets that overwhelm physical assets in cognitive capitalism, along with corporeal tenacity, mapping ability, flexible mobility, and useful adaptability in a globally expanded workspace and limitless competitive market. Work is relational, communicative, boundless, and continuous, and workers become easily hurt, casualized, fired, and dehumanized in an economic war of all against all—a new Hobbesian state of Nature in which the social safety net to protect precarious labor from aggressive capitalization disintegrates to the extent that social abjection is no longer exceptional but normalized.

Likewise, Bond is put into the war on terror during the state of emergency, which is now all the more normalized as aggressive terrorization is omnipresent, even invisibly networked and internally generated. The Bond series indicates a historical shift in this regard. In the past, as described in Fleming's *Moonraker* (1955), Bond would venture out only two to three times a year and was basically "an easy-going senior civil servant" who would enjoy a routine of "elastic office hours from around ten to six" with "evenings spent playing cards in the company of a few close friends" and "weekends playing golf for high stakes at one of the clubs near London" (Smith 2016, 153). That is, disciplined work and pleasurable leisure were separated in his normal life, while risky missions were assigned only exceptionally. The state of exception in which he worked as a secret agent was, like the 'dark knight,' hidden under the surface of his official life as 'white knight' (mirroring Christopher Nolan's *Dark Knight* trilogy, which I explore in Chapter 4). This distinction is blurred in Daniel Craig's impersonation of Bond, whose status and environment are continuously unstable and modulable due to the infernal fusion of belongingness and abjection, loyalty and betrayal, peace and crisis, sovereign and terroristic agencies, and normal and bare lives. His world tour is no longer hedonistic but breathless, with unpredictable, widespread threats; the only sexual moment, of taking a shower with Séverine, who is soon to be killed, is very short. Even M is nothing but a replaceable boss; her desk is cleaned for a successor right after her death, which receives no official acknowledgment.

This precarious condition of life and work may underlie Bond's bitterness over M and her would-be successor Mallory, the "bureaucrat." Bond is no longer a loyal servant of the state with some rebellious attitude, but a twin of Silva, who says that they are M's two kids, two caged rats tested to survive cannibalism. Their bifurcation into the opposite sides seems contingent and thus reversible; it suggests Bond as a seeming renegade antagonistic to the state. However, skepticism about the system also appears as the official interrogation of MI6 by civil servants and government ministers in parliamentary committees, who stand for the very system more comprehensively and so require more democratic transparency, global efficiency, and neoliberal competitiveness in operation. For them, MI6 is a "bunch of antiquated bloody idiots fighting a war [they] don't understand and can't possibly win," and M is responsible for the "monumental security breaches and dead operatives" (*Skyfall*). No longer a denied or obscured taboo, the agency is asked to be a collective 'white knight,' publicly named and openly advertised on the web with official histories.

For M, however, those civilians and noncombatant bureaucrats are too naïve, because new enemies are no longer nations but unknown individuals without a face, uniform, or flag. M says in *Skyfall*, "Our world is not more transparent now. It's more opaque. It's in the shadows. That's where we must do battle. So, before you declare us irrelevant, ask yourselves, how safe do you feel?" This logic renews the Cold War rhetoric of fearmongering politics in the posthistorical (and post-9/11) age, in which global networks generate the schizophrenic multitude of stateless hackers and ghostlike terrorists. In this world, which itself lacks transparency, secret agencies would become more vulnerable and ineffective under open scrutiny and public interference. M thus advocates for the secrecy of MI6, with 'dark knight' elite agents as inevitable and even invaluable in the global fight against dark enemies. The terms of criticism are then inverted; it is not the citizen or politician but the agency that is "the true defender of democracy" against ubiquitous threats (Smith 2016, 156). The agency is not oppositional to, but rather protective of, the open democratic system from behind. It works like a hidden underlying principle of the system, like the dark Real of the symbolic order. The transparent efficacy of legitimate reality does not function without this bloody invisible hand for dirty yet necessary businesses. The ideological effect is the conservative perpetuation of supralegal sovereignty, which enables the justified perpetuation of panoptic surveillance, unrestrained violence, and state-sponsored crimes. Now MI6's headquarters are moved to one of Churchill's war bunkers; there, M quotes Tennyson's "Ulysses": "One equal temper of heroic hearts / Made weak by time and fate but strong in will / To strive, to seek, to find, and not to yield."

Bond's excursion with M in an old car—the canonical Aston Martin from *Goldfinger* (Guy Hamilton, 1964)—to his family estate of Skyfall, following Silva's brutal attack on M's inquiry hearing, is no other than Ulysses's homecoming, a journey to reclaim their identity with "heroic hearts" as well as the identity of the spy genre (see Figure 3.1). The itinerary from London to the Scottish Highlands, recalling Alfred Hitchcock's *39 Steps* (1935), suggests a nostalgic return to the origin and heyday of the spy thriller in the way of escaping from the tech-web of digital networks and surveillance apparatuses. Skyfall is in the middle of nowhere, of nearly sublime Scottish nature. It is a dark old place for traditional physical actions of bare lives. Bond uses conventional firearms with no computer; he fights, hurts, and 'falls into water' (again), almost dying, before finally killing Silva with a knife. Only after this experience of going down to the bottom of life does he resurge and reconfirm himself. The entire sequence indeed indicates Bond's self-recovery. It is revealed that he was orphaned very young—his parents' tombstone shows their names, Andrew and Monica Delacroix Bond—and now M and Kincade, the estate gamekeeper, symbolically take the place of his parents. This quasi-family triangle forms a minimal unit of agency temporarily bonded for the mission of action, grounding Bond's pseudo-Oedipal quest to protect the matriarchal M from Silva. But the death of both Silva and M, for whom he

Figure 3.1. James Bond journeys to his family estate in Scotland to reclaim his sovereign identity and the series' genre identity, in *Skyfall*.

mourns in a chapel, alludes to Bond's final overcoming of his revisited past. In fact, he expresses his hatred of his childhood, and Skyfall is destroyed, while he escapes the explosion through a tunnel. Like these repetitions of falling and escaping, Bond lives his past again as if to work through the trauma of being in an orphanage that led him to MI6, whose recruiting target was "maladjusted young men who give little thought to sacrificing others in order to protect Queen and country" (*Casino Royale*, film version). In other words, this past in which he became an adult as an agent, is relived in order to reaffirm the sublimation from the lost primary identification with his concrete family to the higher secondary identification with the abstract nation. It is the classical double step of identity formation.

Back in London, the iconic rooftop scene of Bond contemplating the skyline dominated by Union Jacks repositions him as an adult son of the Queen and a loyal servant of the country. By extension, he is a heroic guardian of its imperial nostalgias; the locations of Shanghai, Macau, and some islands evoke the sunset-less empire and its loss of colonies like Hong Kong. J. M. W. Turner's painting *The Fighting Temeraire*, on display in the National Gallery where Bond meets Q, shows a gunship that led the Trafalgar victory being tugged to its last berth, to be broken up upon the British navy's transition from sail to steam. Silva hits the spot: "England. The Empire. MI6. You're living in a ruin. It's over. Finished. What are you doing clinging to this notion of nation?" The recovery of MI6 therefore operates as a reassuring fantasy of the national empire's postmortem resurrection as a global empire in which London is (again) the center, maintaining the imperial legacy—Bond's victory over Silva valorizes traditional physical and mental strength over postmodern techy smartness. However, this fantasy is not smoothly sutured. The problem is not simply that the nostalgia of shadowy antiterrorism may involve "the use of unaccountable and extreme violence in our battles with cyberterrorists" (Hasian 2014, 585). More profoundly, the new global empire is like the British Empire without an emperor in Hardt and Negri's (2000) terms, full of posthistorical symptoms related to cognitive capitalism and precarious labor, already cyber-networked and ready to abject its own agents. Bond's coolness barely hides insecurity and terror, and his harsh actions infinitely inscribe fatigue and pain on his body. The agency's self-reclamation of its raison d'être is the desperate attempt to find an ideological frame in which what is lost is self-illusively retrieved. Bond's traumatic past is called for back here, not to be affirmed in itself so much as to reaffirm his present identity in crisis. Abject subjectivity regains agential sovereignty in this way.

In *Spectre*, Sam Mendes again stages the United Kingdom's political hazard and physical insecurity in central London and on British soil, where the state appears as a significant threat to itself. But again, it is noteworthy to read global symptoms in the national framework, as the title explicitly designates SPECTRE. Bond is networked into a collective working unit as never before, while his and MI6's relevance to the new world order is critiqued again within the government—hence Bond's realization that "the best way to protect the country is to protect oneself from the country's government." Leading the sinister global SPECTRE, Ernst Stavro Blofeld taunts Bond about his one-person show, telling him, as Silva had: "Everything you stood for . . . is a ruin." His torture, using computer-controlled micro-drills to penetrate Bond's skull, looks almost like a psychotic play for sadistic jouissance, again evoking Silva. Facing this bodily pain as bare life in abjection, Bond performs his mission against SPECTRE as his self-imposed mission of identity reaffirmation, too. The doubly Proustian name of Madeleine Swann, his love interest, suggests that the Craig films are an "ostentatious and extended *Remembrance of Things Past*": *Skyfall* goes back to the time "before Bond" and *Casino Royal* to the time of "becoming Bond" (J. Murray 2016, 6). The ironic opening intertitle "The dead are alive" is then not only about SPECTRE but also about Bond himself. The Self finds himself through the encounter with the Other, while both are floating around the world like undead phantoms of the past and intermingled shadows of the present. Of course, the film ends up with the neat separation between them and the Self's triumphant elimination of the Other. This separation is reaffirmed every time the franchise struggles to reposition itself.

Abject Agency from Bond to Bourne

At this point, Bond's self-reaffirmation can be seen as the series' survival strategy in the contemporary context of the action spy genre and the global film market. The new millennial reflections of post-9/11 espionage, surveillance, security, and precarity have blossomed in the Jason Bourne (2002–present) and *Mission: Impossible* (1996–present) franchises; political thrillers such as *Syriana* (Stephen Gaghan, 2005) and *Rendition* (Gavin Hood, 2007); and high-budget TV serials including *24* (Joel Surnow, 2001–14), *The Wire* (David Simon, 2002–8), *Spooks* (David Wolstencroft, 2002–11), and *Homeland* (Howard Gordon, 2011). For example, *Ghost Protocol* (Brad Bird,

2011), the most successful *Mission: Impossible* film, maximizes the crisis of secret agencies during the post–Cold War disintegration of the distinction between friends and foes, the Self and the Other. In the Fox television series *24*, a counterterrorism agent must cope with an enemy's ticking-time-bomb scenario as well as inner critics' disapproval of his ruthless methods. Typically, global agents undergo the symbolic death of abjection, then restore or transform their suspended subjectivity before their probable biological death by carrying out a traumatically (self-)imposed mission. It is often fulfilled through a double cognitive-corporal mapping under lethal threat: the temporal reconstruction of their pathological mind/memory and the spatial reorientation of a disastrous and apocalyptic territory. In this narrative bracketed by double death, global abject-subjectivity emerges as both reflecting and performing cognitive capitalism as well as its catastrophic imagination. However, the forking point appears here. Although the Bond series rebooted to reflect the sociophysical vulnerability of agency beyond its old fantastical luxurious escapism, Bond is sutured back into the system as a sovereign agent like the Dark Knight. By contrast, Jason Bourne, among others, has become a new type of terroristic agent who refuses this reterritorialization of old subjectivity and leaves open the gap between the global system and its inherent inconsistency.

Undoubtedly 'Jason Bourne' intends to reconfigure 'James Bond' in a continuous saga up to the latest segment, titled just *Jason Bourne* (Paul Greengrass, 2016). The only enemy of the CIA is its own ex-agent Bourne, who thus fights with his former agency. However, unlike Silva's pure revenge or SPECTRE's terror for capital and power, Bourne becomes a terroristic agent only to discover who he is and why the agency threatens him. The beginning marks his failure in a mission of assassination, after which he is shot and presumably becomes amnesiac. The rest of the film chronicles his nomadic struggle to recover his memory, under attack from unknown assassins, whom he defeats while discovering secret CIA operations that involve and target him. As in the Bond series, the beginning is the end of the hero's normal life, his symbolic death as traumatic abjection from his psychological, sociopolitical subjectivity. His quasi-dead body floating in the sea visualizes a rootless bare life deprived of identity in Agamben's sense of *homo sacer*, whose murder by sovereign CIA agents is to be done in the state of exception with no due regard for any legal system.

Indeed, the CIA functions as a supralegal global network agency. The US headquarters connect to international branches; local agents carry out remotely delivered missions in global metropolises. Using private planes and satellite surveillance, they intervene in the entire world under the Geographic Information System (GIS). Moreover, information is corruptly capitalized and traded by senior CIA officials with Russian magnates in the global black market of private greed. This dirty business implies 'disaster capitalism' on the level of power elites who monopolize control over security and industry, taking benefits from real or potential crises. They are enemies within who suppress uncomfortable truths and engineer illicit execution for "our" security at the cost of bare lives, including their own former agents who might debunk the system. That is why Bourne is trained and then threatened by them, treated like a potential terrorist, "a known unknown," as Donald Rumsfeld posited, in the sense that we know we don't know his location, which is a security risk. The CIA is a global ideological apparatus of neoliberal information capitalism and neoconservative patriotic vigilantism.

Bourne is defined in this system as "government property" but also as "a malfunctioning $30 million weapon" and therefore "a total goddamn catastrophe." He is a corporeal program that merits high investment by removing threats from the info-market, but he would otherwise turn into the system's own disaster. Bourne is therefore both a product and byproduct of the global system, embodying its cognitive capitalism and precarious labor, terror and war on terror at the same time. His pistol, money, and multiple passports symbolize his physical, financial, and intellectual qualifications for working like a global freelancer. He is an all-around professional with neoliberal abilities for success: quick decision, swift movement, high intelligence, and risk-taking. His cognition perfectly maps new places at first sight, while a traumatic sense of déjà vu brings him some lost memory. His action is fast enough for flexible adjustment to unstable situations, particularly during acrobatic chases. This competitive worker, however, suffers from endless labor without leisure and from constant insecurity without protection in a perpetual state of emergency. Far from Bond's bourgeois bohemian lifestyle, Bourne enjoys no consumerist relaxation, no exotic tourism, no hedonistic liberation. His only sexual partner becomes his romantic girlfriend, who is subsequently killed. All this precarity, worse than in *Skyfall*, characterizes Bourne's body, which is shot, left drifting, strangled, wounded, and stabbed. However, this bare life equips itself with the endurable agency, the causative force to act for a mission, the self-imposed task of self-rediscovery through his continual self-recovery.

The Bourne series indeed combines James Bond's efficiency with Noam Chomsky's politics, renewing the 1970s paranoid thriller—such as *The Conversation* (Francis Ford Coppola, 1974) and *The Parallax View* (Alan J. Pakula, 1974)—which reflected cynically on the US government and articulated conspiracy theories about the Vietnam War and the Watergate scandal. The Iraq War and the war on terror provoke a new paranoiac view in which our corrupt elites might create terrorists who could be internalized more dangerously. The sovereign system intensifies global surveillance and supralegal violence while violating democratic procedures, wreaking havoc on civilians, and convoluting terror and counterterror. Suggestive are Bourne's chases, as well as Bond's, in "non-places" (Augé 2009) as spaces of transition without identities, like a motorway and a supermarket. The Waterloo Station scene in *The Bourne Ultimatum* (Paul Greengrass, 2007) particularly shows how a public place becomes claustrophobic under surveillance when cameras lurk everywhere to locate Bourne, but also how both the CIA and Bourne use their remotely controlled agents—for Bourne, a journalist as proxy—to play a hide-and-seek role-playing game with each other between the visible and the invisible. The hidden cameras maximize the visual field in which Bourne remains a mobile blind spot, a phasmid-like ghostly shadow: a terrorist by nature. The tension between the system and the terrorist then turns mutual fear into 'dread,' the ubiquitous fear for unpredictable attack immanent in daily life. Normalcy is an emergency.

Each Bourne film comprises such discrete sequences, as if they were levels in a video game that the player completes with increasing difficulty while exploring unknown nonplaces. This double game-narrative of 'leveling-up' and 'navigation' also applies to the entire series. Also, as secret files play the role of a plot-developing archive, all physical actions are driven by the cognitive desire for valuable information. Bourne's body functions here as a sensorimotor system, with the self-backup function embodying a certain undeadness, while his mind is a self-investigating cerebral system that restores damaged memory for identity rebooting. The film series thus appears as a "mind-game" road movie (see Chapter 7) in which a traumatized abject-agent has to follow an undetermined itinerary along contingent spatiotemporal shifts in both fractured memory and disoriented movement. It unfolds a cognitive-corporeal mapping of horizontal global space and vertical subjective time, a struggle of today's pathological subjectivity as abject to orient itself in the threatening world. The terrorist becoming-agent of the abject is then a survival strategy against the global system by reappropriating qualities and skills that are required and trained within the very system; as already noted, this aspect is shared with Daniel Craig's Bond films and harkens back to *Licence to Kill* (John Glen, 1989) as well.

The origin of this antagonism, however, is not merely the corruption of the system. Bourne fails in the initial mission because of his hesitation about killing an African leader in the presence of his children; Bourne takes revenge for the murder of his girlfriend, who was shot instead of him; Bourne apologizes to the daughter of a Russian reformist politician he killed, after discovering the grubby operation and business of his boss who ordered this murder; and Bourne always uses violence in a restrained manner, protecting and never really killing others except for the case just listed. All these suggest Bourne's guilt and responsibility for (possibly) killing (decent) people, his atonement and redemption through paying off this guilt as debt. In *The Bourne Ultimatum*, he finally reaches the CIA training center in New York where, he remembers, he was forced to kill a masked terror suspect as an initiation ritual into a secret team; killing a bare life in the state of exception gained him supralegal sovereignty (see Figure 3.2). The ultimate scene of self-discovery recalls the original sin of killing the Other, whose face was covered to prevent the Levinasian encounter with the "face of the Other" that commands, "You shall not kill," in its absolute vulnerability, which may conversely reveal the potential sanctity of life (see Chapters 4 and 11). At last the post-traumatic restoration of his identity, its ontological and epistemological recovery, ends up with the traumatic revisiting of its initial formation, as in *Skyfall* and *Casino Royale*. But upon finding out the truth of who he was,

Figure 3.2. Jason Bourne became a secret CIA agent through the ritual of killing a masked terror suspect, as seen in *The Bourne Ultimatum*.

Bourne, unlike Bond, decides to abandon this identity, the license to kill, and the system of mechanizing sovereignty and abjection. He is then shot and falls into New York's East River. Real death? We see him swimming away.

It is clear where Bond and Bourne meet and part. Secret agencies as a protective gear of global systems driven by info-capitalist tech-networking inevitably generate symptoms of precarious labor and bare life, and agents as competitive professionals, once excluded, can turn into dangerous hackers or whistleblowers. Bond, particularly in *Skyfall*, undergoes abjection too (evoking *On Her Majesty's Secret Service* [Peter Hunt, 1969], *For Your Eyes Only* [John Glen, 1981], and especially *Licence to Kill*) but fights against such terrorist abject-agents by repeatedly reaffirming the sovereign agency of supralegal power. Conversely, while Bourne's former network agency is more globalized and corrupted at the same time, his traumatic abjection puts him under harsher conditions of bare life in a radically normalized emergency with no room for the hedonistic privileges of the early Bonds. His cognitive-corporeal struggle with a lost memory and threatening space nonetheless unfolds as a convoluted journey for self-discovery in the form of terrorist resistance to the unethical system that trained him. In sum, the continuation of the Bond and Bourne series, in opposing ways, tells us that the sovereign system and the abject agent are inseparable and that their antagonistic hide-and-seek network has no outside. This cinematic logic allegorizes the impossibility of one's ultimate release from the global system, leaving only the fantasy of choice: Bond or Bourne? A blue pill or a red pill?

PART II
CATASTROPHE AND REVELATION

4
Law, Divine Violence, and the Sanctity of Life

Violence as Power: Benjamin, Derrida, and Batman

Part I examined the conflictual entanglements between the sovereign system of abjection and the resistant agency of the abject in view of today's global agenda through French, Korean, and Hollywood films: European, Asian, and American samples of global cinema. Part II extends the critical scope to the foundational level of the system, where we find a 'cinema of catastrophe' from diverse countries. As an initial step toward this foundation, this chapter further develops the Agambenian biopolitics of sovereignty and law in terms of violence. Indeed, the power that constitutes, maintains, overturns, or demolishes the law of a community is violent by nature, whether it causes abjection, change, war, or terror. In this regard, Walter Benjamin's 1921 essay "Critique of Violence" (1978) serves as the guiding text to read carefully and to reinterpret creatively through cinema. Since Jacques Derrida's (1992a) deconstructive reading of it, Benjamin's seminal, obscure, and controversial text has attracted much attention among critical thinkers, if not film scholars (see Moran and Salzani 2015). Building on Benjamin's insights, I delve into the biopolitical and ethical issues that global cinema urges us to tackle beyond aesthetic, media-specific aspects, and which include the question of the sanctity of life raised at the end of Chapter 3.

From his historico-philosophical viewpoint, Benjamin proposes two pairs of concepts regarding violence, or *Gewalt*, which term implies not only physical unauthorized force but also public or legitimate power, domination, and authority, that is, nonphysical or symbolic violence concerning law and justice. The first pair of concepts involves violence as a means of "lawmaking" (founding) and "law-preserving" (conserving). The lawmaking function of violence is to achieve natural, unsanctioned ends as in the case of war, in which a state violently ignores historically acknowledged laws like borders in order to create new laws/borders. In this way, violence founds law and institutes a system of power. Lawmaking is thus power-making. Then, once a new order of law has been established, power confirms and conserves it with the law-preserving function of violence directed toward legal, sanctioned ends. Compulsory conscription, for instance, is a legally forceful imposition of state power on citizens in order to protect the state as well as the law itself. If lawmaking violence goes beyond the legal/illegal boundary, law-preserving violence enforces legal acts and punishes illegal acts.

Second, lawmaking violence is also called "mythical violence" with reference to Greek mythology. For example, when Niobe boasts of her fourteen children to the goddess Leto, who only has two children, Leto kills all of Niobe's children and turns her into stone (a statue), which Benjamin says is not a punishment so much as a manifestation of law (a statute), or the making of a boundary between gods and humans. That is, the law is proclaimed to constitute gods' power over the human hubris that challenged them. But more significant than mythical violence based on power is "divine violence" based on justice. For Benjamin, justice is the unreachable, unknowable end whose justness only God can decide, as often seen in the Old Testament. The angry Jewish God punishes, for example, the company of Korah, who revolted against Moses by causing an earthquake; the ground suddenly splits open, swallows them, and quickly closes. This clean annihilation, a divine judgment, occurs without warning or threat and leaves no mark or trace. Divine violence founds no legal regime for domination. It instead explodes beyond any boundaries (between rulers and subjects, dominant and resistant groups, etc.) in the way of boundlessly destroying law itself, including the law set by mythical violence. It performs divine justice only to purify the world. Benjamin (1978, 297) says: "If mythical violence brings at once guilt and retribution, divine power only expiates; if the former threatens, the latter strikes; if the former is bloody, the latter is lethal without spilling blood."

These two dichotomies of violence—lawmaking/law-preserving and mythical/divine—are, however, unstable. For example, capital punishment is not merely a law-preserving penalty for certain crimes but "the highest violence" over life and death that "manifestly and fearsomely" reaffirms the original foundation of law, in which Benjamin sees "something rotten" (286). What is rotten? Here, we could imaginatively flesh out Benjamin's idea of "violence crowned by fate" as the origin of law. Put differently, the question is about the birth of the king, or the inception of sovereignty. Let's assume that a person commits an unforgivably threatening or condemnable act in a primitive community; the most natural reaction to it would be to kill this person like an animal unworthy of humane treatment, just as animals kill each other instinctively for their survival. But nobody would dare dirty one's hands with blood, because people's underlying ethical sensibility would tell them that killing is horrible, bestial, and inhuman even if naturally needed. Then, if someone bravely stands up and performs the killing, this animalistic act would not only save the community but also cause fear among others that they might also be killed if they do not follow the savior. Violence over life and death would thus bring biopolitical power through the internalization of animality, which paradoxically would bestow some awe-inspiring divinity upon the killer. He would be both below and above humans, descending from humanity to animality and ascending even to divinity. This bestial-divine killer would then become the sovereign ruler by positing the law under which killing is regarded as a crime to punish, but which he could suspend by reaffirming his original lawmaking power in the exceptional case of killing someone as *homo sacer* (see Chapter 3). Capital punishment, though legal, may still evoke this origin of sovereignty as divinity-taken-through-animality, which I propose to see as the "rotten" core of the law. (This divinity concerns the mythical lawmaking violence and not the "divine" law-destroying violence, though I address their overlap.)

By extension, Benjamin argues that the police also use lawmaking as well as law-preserving violence. They "intervene 'for security reasons' in countless cases where no clear legal situation exists" (287), just as the United States has played the role of world police in the name of freedom or the war on terror, and just as numerous American superheroes have done the same on screen. Christopher Nolan's *The Dark Knight* (2008), for example, memorably stages the internal split of Gotham City's public power into two agents: Harvey Dent, the "White Knight" who represents the law-preserving authorities, including elected officials like him, and Bruce Wayne as Batman, the "Dark Knight" who acts as the unofficial vigilante beyond the law. Notable is the White Knight's approval of the Dark Knight. Dent talks about Batman: "Gotham's proud of an ordinary man standing up for what's right" when "all of us . . . stood by and let scum take control of our city." He continues: "When their enemies were at the gates, the Romans would suspend democracy and appoint one man to protect the city. It wasn't considered an honor; it was considered a public service." However, "the last man who they appointed to protect the Republic was named Caesar, and he never gave up his power."[1] This sums up

---

[1] To this last line uttered by his love, Dent replies with his famous adage: "Well, I guess you either

the emergence of sovereignty described earlier: Batman saved Gotham by standing up to kill the enemies and took a tacitly appointed sovereign position without a democratic election. The point is that the animality of killing, however justifiable, underlies this superhero's sovereignty (and 'Bat-Man' literally incarnates animality at that). Caesar became the Roman emperor, a divine sovereign, not because he inherently had divinity but because his animalistic performance of killing *homines sacri* like animals reaffirmed the ancient Roman law allowing supralegal operation; that is, it reaffirmed the lawmaking violence of drawing the boundary between law and its outside. The immanence of the exception to the law in law, of lawmaking violence in law-preserving violence, is not anachronistic but indeed eternal. So now, sovereign agents from James Bond (see Chapter 3) to Batman actively fulfill their public service "in the shadows" at the cost of democracy, as if our modern republic still needs a potential emperor.

Derrida (1992a) rephrases Benjamin in his characteristic deconstructive logic. Lawmaking violence founds "what ought to be conserved, conservable, promised to heritage and tradition"; therefore, "[p]osition [to posit the law through violence] is already iterability, a call for self-conserving repetition. Conservation in its turn refounds so that it can conserve what it claims to found. Thus, there can be no rigorous opposition between positioning and conservation," that is, between lawmaking and law-preserving violence (38). Likewise, deconstruction applies to two kinds of strike that Benjamin, drawing on Georges Sorel, takes as a more significant example of violence. The "political general strike" interrupts the state violently but causes "only an external modification of labor conditions." It actualizes lawmaking violence that can at best change the masters of the workers from one privileged group to another privileged group. Meanwhile, the "proletarian general strike" has the sole task of destroying state power as such. It is law-destroying violence that demands the anarchistic withdrawal of labor, "a wholly transformed work, no longer enforced by the state." The first kind of strike is reformist but still bourgeois; the second is proletarian and revolutionary (Benjamin 1978, 291). Nonetheless, given that destroying the state always ends up making a new state or a new regime of law, Derrida argues that all revolutions, on the left or right, allege the founding of future law. And "[a]s this law to come will

---

die a hero or you live long enough to see yourself become the villain." And he adds that Batman wants someone to take up his mantle, which implies the perpetual need for the supralegal vigilante in the legal community. What matters more than Batman himself is his structurally demanded exceptional role.

in return legitimate, retrospectively, the violence that may offend the scene of justice, its future anterior already justifies it" (1992a, 35). The notion of pure destructive violence is thus no other than the lost origin of its deferred and differentiated actual forms, historical incidents of political violence that only reductively (re)present it while positing another state/law. It is this "*différantielle contamination*" (38) between mythical and divine violence that smells "rotten" to Derrida, as even divine violence cannot but smell bloody. But what truly embarrasses him is not *différance* itself—his keyword underlying all phenomena—so much as its teleological revision that Benjamin proposes, a theological vision that pure divine violence would return through an ultimate revolution like the Last Judgment. Derrida finds this "final solution" to be "too messianico-Marxist or archeo-eschatological" and complicit with crypto-metaphysical thinkers such as Martin Heidegger and Carl Schmitt, who were both involved in Nazism. Here comes the dangerous temptation to regard the Holocaust of the Jews, the Nazi's Final Solution, as a paradoxical manifestation of Judaic divine violence. Did the gas chambers not realize the divine violence of "bloodless" annihilation (62)?

Of course Benjamin, as a Marxist, however mystic, is far from fascism. Some critics criticize Derrida's critique of Benjamin. Robert Sinnerbrink (2006) argues, for example, that Derrida offers a sort of "interpretative violence" by unjustly underplaying Benjamin's anarchistic communist position. For the proletarian general strike does not represent Schmitt's notion of exception to the rule of law but "the 'exception' of any system that can still operate with the political opposition of legal norm and state of emergency" (Hamacher 1993, 134). If Schmitt's state of exception is still defined by, derived from, and dependent on law, Benjamin's radical exception aims at removing the dual framework of the legal/supralegal states itself. In other words, divine violence is not opposed and then reduced to mythical violence on the level of normalcy and emergency; rather, it remains 'undeconstructable' on another level of pure exceptionality: the unconditioned horizon of anarcho-Marxist revolutions.

In this context Batman, whose exceptional status is endorsed by state power, is a sovereign agent of mythical violence and not divine violence. The latter's 'divine' nature is beyond his animality-taking-on-divinity within the law-bound power hierarchy that consists of animality (the abject), humanity (the subject), and divinity (the sovereign), which are respectively positioned below, inside, and above the law. Instead, it is Bane in *The Dark Knight Rises* (2012) who appears like a revolutionary agent of divine violence, at three stages. First, his terrorist bombing of a stadium, streets, and bridges—shot in New York City instead of Chicago, the location of Nolan's earlier Batman films—undoubtedly evokes 9/11, not least because he is a former member of the villainous League of Shadows coming from Central Asia (close to the Middle East). Second, his initial target is the Stock Exchange (on Wall Street), and he provokes a revolt of citizens against the corrupt elite who monopolize politico-economic power. The terrorist then turns into the leader of a leftist revolution subverting global capitalism; the 1 percent top class is tried in the people's court of the 99 percent. The film thus allegorically shifts from 9/11 to the Occupy movement. Third, this revolution does not lead to building a better state but is designed to facilitate Bane's ultimate aim, which is the demolition of the entire city (the global world) by a neutron bomb. Like the Joker in *The Dark Knight*, Bane carries profound disillusionment with humanity and carries out its anarchic annihilating explosion. In sum, Bane is the abject of the global system who also becomes a triple agent: a global terrorist, a communist, and a nihilist.

Things get complicated as, interestingly, Batman also undergoes some sort of abjection. *Batman Begins* (2005) shows that abjection penetrates Bruce's childhood traumas of falling into a well full of fierce bats and of watching a mugger murder his parents. Leading an orphaned, bare life, he wanders around the world until he learns to overcome his fear of bats and violence, which are linked to the world's dread of darkness/apocalypse, in this way incarnating fear itself: first by mastering ninja methods under the League of Shadows and then by becoming Batman after rejecting both the League's cause of destroying Gotham and the League's justification of lethal violence. That is, Bruce as an abject is trained as a terrorist agent but turns into a sovereign agent fighting against the very terrorist agency that trained him; Bane and Bruce thus mirror Silva and Bond in *Skyfall*—though the latter pair belong to the sovereign agency, MI6—when Silva turns into a terrorist against it (see Chapter 3). But more importantly, the sovereign position is practically condoned yet intrinsically questionable in the legal state (again, as in the Bond film), so the Joker in *The Dark Knight* tells Batman: "You're a freak like me. They need you now but they will cast you out like a leper." Gotham indeed discards Batman, blaming him for a killing spree that was in fact carried out by Harvey "Two-Face" Dent as an act of revenge for the death of his love.

Nonetheless, Batman takes responsibility for the murders in order to preserve Dent's positive image as the public White Knight. This self-abjection of Bruce from being the sovereign Dark Knight also overlaps with his retirement as CEO of Wayne Enterprises following his investment in a fusion reactor that is exposed as being weaponizable, in *The Dark Knight Rises*. However, Bruce's financial wrongdoing—which recalls the hazardous practices of Wall Street investors that led to the 2008 financial crisis—is never questioned but rather replaced by Bane's violent occupation of the city. Batman subdues this more visible evil with the sovereign violence he reclaims, just as retired abject heroes in the action genre take up one final mission to dirty their hands with blood. Batman thus turns from a 'bad' man to a 'good' man (for more on capitalist superheroes in the neoliberal age, see Hassler-Forest 2012). Toward the end of the film he hauls the bomb that Bane has constructed from his own fusion reactor far out over the bay, where it safely explodes, at the apparent sacrifice of his life. Though the last shot shows him appearing in Florence, Batman/Bruce is presumed dead in Gotham, honored as its savior and respected for having donated Wayne Manor to be used as an orphanage.[2]

Within the framework of the trilogy, one may feel reluctant to accept Bane as a Marxist messiah for at least three reasons, each related to his triple abject agency. First, Bane's 'divine' violence on the entire world is actually reduced to the anti-Western terror that attempts to counterbalance Western civilization on the plane of 'mythically' violent power struggles. Indeed, the view of Gotham by the League of Shadows echoes Islamic jihadists' view of America: a corrupt, decadent, hypocritical, and irredeemable empire. The anti-imperialist terrorism, then, does not lead to bloodless annihilation but instead provokes an all-the-bloodier reaction of the sovereign empire to preserve itself even by suspending its law. Violence is justified not only for Bane's end of fundamentalist justice but also, too quickly, for Gotham's end of self-defense and its aggressive extension to 'infinite justice against the axis of evil.' The result is the defeat of terrorism, but in the real world, as we have seen, it would most likely trigger the terror-counterterror cycle. Even worse, the relationship between ends and means is nearly reversed in this vicious cycle, as though violence as a means becomes an end itself that justifies the continuation of jihad, the politics of fear, the military industry, and the state of emergency, while justice becomes a mere pretext for achieving this end.

---

[2] This ending does not 'undo' sacrifice, the final topic of Chapter 7, but suggests a step toward it. While Batman is not really sacrificed, his act achieves the full effect of sacrifice: getting social recognition as a heroic sacrifice and individual compensation in the form of the new life that he seems to start with cat burglar Selina Kyle outside Gotham—now no longer as Batman/Catwoman but as a man and a woman.

Second, Bane's Occupy riot does not bring utopian anarchy but only a dystopian regime. Gotham is depicted as destructive, frantic, brutal, and chaotic under the people's proletarian dictatorship. The ideological effect is evident: communism is worse than capitalism; revolution is nothing but catastrophe. Compared to this anticapitalist upheaval, Bruce's mismanagement of money involved in an illegal business is a negligible glitch of capitalism. Bruce/Batman thus returns as a superhero who eradicates the 'Reds' to 'make Gotham great again' and is remembered in the end both as a self-sacrificing savior like Christ *and* as a capitalist philanthropist like his parents. In other words, Wayne Enterprises, founded in the glorious age of industrial capitalism, covers up the risks of financial capitalism in the global age by updating the family legacy of noblesse oblige (fighting terror, donating property). Heroic individualism, here implied along with right-wing Christianity, is a typically American solution to social problems. It protects and justifies the wealth of Wayne Enterprises (America), whose primary sources are the manufacture of arms and stock market speculation. Furthermore, the seamless integration of the sovereign agent and the super-rich CEO into Batman/Bruce allegorically renders acceptable and even admirable the supralegal-neoliberal power of America's politico-economic super-elite, like the Trump family.

Third, although Gotham might deserve a total system reboot to restart from ground zero, as Bane believes, how could we justify this divine justice that inevitably costs a number of innocent people? Do most of them not belong to the very oppressed and exploited 99 percent to be saved? Rather than a sublime deus ex machina, Bane appears as a nihilistic, angry god wielding bloody misanthropic power. His defeat by Batman, a Christ figure, thus seems right and proper. However, such poetic justice reduces their positions to a Manichean dichotomy of good and evil, even though Bane is in theory a divine agent and Batman a sovereign agent, and even though both in reality embody 'hard-ethical' justice, whether it is against the global system or its abject (see Figure 4.1). Moreover, on the side of good in this moralistic battle, Batman/Bruce manifests 'soft-ethical' Christian qualities: love and sacrifice, charity and social altruism. The sovereign vigilante and benevolent capitalist thus personifies the double ethics of the global system in the manner of combining Christian fundamentalism and liberalism, performing powerful justice and social harmony at the same time. Without such a 'soft' facet, Bane's justice is handed down only for the sake of balance (and not harmony) in the world, which can be translated as no different from "the clash of civilizations."

Figure 4.1. Batman and Bane embody 'hard-ethical' justice as violence on behalf of the global system and its abject, respectively, in *The Dark Knight Rises*.

Or at least the film depicts his violence in this manner. That is, it cannot but victimize numerous civilians and make them bleed for his eschatological antihumanism, leaving no room for future potentialities of humanity.

Divine Violence for the Sanctity of Life

These three aspects of Bane's violence may indicate that Derrida is right: pure divine violence for an anarchic revolution cannot but be deconstructed into bloody mythical violence for a power struggle. However, Benjamin (1978, 292) paradoxically argues that, like diplomatic agreements, a rigorous conception of the revolutionary general strike as a pure means of violence can diminish the incidence of actual violence. How can there be 'nonviolent' divine violence that does not shed blood when it is not humanly possible or allowable to cause a bloodless earthquake or holocaust? This question leads us to grapple with the most enigmatic yet crucial point in Benjamin's text, as we will see presently.

Benjamin says that blood symbolizes "mere life" (*das bloße Leben*), and mythical violence is "bloody power over mere life for its own sake." Meanwhile, the lack of bloodshed in divine violence implies that it "'expiates' the guilt of mere life" and purifies "the guilty, not of guilt, however, but of law" (1978, 297). What does "mere life" mean, and why is it guilty? Of course we are tempted to equate it with Agamben's bare life, the guilty *homo sacer* to be killed outside of the law. However, Benjamin calls it pure and simple "natural life" in humans, that is, nature in human beings as such, rather than solely in the condemned abject. "Mere life" thus refers to what Agamben terms *zoē* instead of *nuda vita* (for more on these terms, see Salzani 2015). The "bloody power over mere life" thus concerns not the supralegal banishment of the *homo sacer* but the primordial mythical violence of lawmaking. This violence is exercised at the cost of the mere life that it makes bleed in its own favor, that is, for mighty dominion, "even as it remains precisely within the order of natural life" (Derrida 1992a, 52). As per the aforementioned birth of the king, the initial act of killing as mythical violence is still naturally done to save the community while at the same time instituting law and starting to govern natural beings under the sovereign rule of "guilt and retribution" (Benjamin 1978, 297). Though not guilty, the natural performance of bloody violence thus introduces a sense of guilt to nature/natural life in that it exemplifies who/what is to be punished as guilty from the perspective of the law, which it simultaneously posits and transcends. This is the paradoxical performativity of lawmaking as law-transcending. The state of nature (*zoē*) inevitably, fatefully, turns into the legal state (*bios*), from which *homines sacri* are excluded by a sovereign power that supralegally reaffirms itself. But just as this exception to the law is an exclusion included in the sovereign operation of law, mere life is subject to (the natural order of) lawmaking violence that brings guilt, and consequently the law, as inescapable fate. Life is thus "the marked bearer of guilt" (299), not only liable to do guilty acts but fundamentally guilty about its own bloody mythical "fate" of law that integrates nature.

Divine violence enables not the retribution but the 'expiation' of this guilt. More precisely, the guilty (mere life) are purified "not of guilt but of law," that is, liberated from the legal system of guilt and retribution as a whole. Divine violence is "pure power over all life for the sake of the living," and not for its own sake as per mythical violence (Benjamin 1978, 297). Here, "the living" (*der Lebendige*) is meant to be opposed to mere life, or that which is oppressed by law, and thus should be taken out of the natural-legal life system. The living may be something really *living* in itself but only potentially living in mere life; the potential of life that should be *living* in order for life not to bleed under the power of legal violence. It can therefore be understood as the living potential of "supernatural life" (*übernatürliches Leben*), a life that goes beyond/over (über) the natural life fated in law (Salzani 2015, 111). If mythical violence demands sacrifice, divine violence accepts it in order to save this potential life, or "the soul of the living" (Benjamin 1978, 299). In other words, even if divine violence involves killing, it does so not in the way that power founds law by sacrificing life—that is, by making it bleed—but in the way that justice purifies that very blood by sacrificing law as such and by accepting the unavoidably entailed sacrifice of life so as to expiate its guilt and redeem the living. Justice is not something that is just good, but something that has to be done even at the sacrifice of life insofar as it can revive the living, or the just value of life. This justness could be called the justice of life itself.

Derrida (1992a, 53–54) puts it thus: "What makes for the worth of man, of his *Dasein* and his life, is that he contains the potential, the possibility of justice, the yet-to-come (*avenir*) of justice, the yet-to-come of his being-just, of his having-to-be-just. What is sacred in his life is not his life but the justice of his life." As the living is beyond life, justice is beyond law. Derrida's deconstructionist insight highlights the significant difference between justice and the enforcement of the law, which might otherwise simply be reduced one to the other. Law is the finite, relative product of sociopolitical dynamics grounded in history, whereas the infinite and absolute notion of justice is impossible yet indispensable for the sacredness of life and its utopian futurity/ *avenir*. Justice for Derrida is thus ethical above all, much like his concepts of the pure gift and hospitality (see Chapter 11). In this way, he 'ethicizes' Benjamin, or rather sides with the ethical Benjamin against the political appropriation of him, alerting us to the dubious link between the Benjaminian messianic revolution and Schmittian political fascism.[3]

Here is indeed the core of ethics regarding the sanctity of life. How can we accept that God, who often inflicts annihilating violence, is the same God who ordered "Thou shall not kill"? Referring to Judaism, which does not condemn killing in self-defense, Benjamin (1978, 298) regards this commandment "not as a criterion of judgment" under the law of guilt and retribution "but as a guideline for the actions of persons or communities who have to wrestle with it in solitude and, in exceptional cases, to take on themselves the responsibility of ignoring it." You may kill if you can defend your deed as ethically just and take responsibility for it of your own free will. However, Benjamin also introduces Jewish essayist Kurt Hiller's theorem on which to

---

[3] In comparison, Sinnerbrink radically politicizes Benjamin by emphasizing the leftist anarchism of divine violence over its theological messianism. I explore this position later via Žižek.

base the commandment: "Higher even than the happiness and justice of existence stands existence itself." That is, no righteous cause for killing is more important than life as such. Though Benjamin rejects the sacralization of mere life, he finds this proposition to be truthful if "existence" implies "the irreducible, total condition that is 'man,'" which is more than the simple fact of natural life. By the "total condition that is 'man,'" he means the "not-yet-attained condition of the just man," the yet-to-come of the justice of life, the living as sacred beyond bloody life. Animal as it is, human existence with its potential sanctity of life is less terrible than "the nonexistence of man" (299). Life for itself is not sacred, but sacredness is immanent in it as its potential to preserve. Therefore, you should not kill. However, man's sacredness is not here the sovereign's divinity taken through animalistic power, as mentioned earlier. Rather, sacredness is a certain potential divinity of human life that is yet to come *out of* the very bloody hierarchy rooted in the natural-legal state. Hence there are two kinds of divinity: one within the power system and the other beyond it; one crowns man in the name of the law, while the other dethrones him in the name of justice. The second is easily co-opted by and into the former, as Derrida would say, but we must distinguish between them.

Now, it is evident that divine violence is precisely an exceptional case, in that God himself ignores his commandment in order to redeem the potential divinity of man by destroying the legal state and realizing the potential sanctity of life by sacrificing mere life. The problem occurs when not God but man attempts to be the agent of divine violence. What if killing does not bring this justice of life but reaffirms the domination of law that deprives life of its potential sacredness? How can 'human' divine violence not be alloyed with mythical violence when no clear guideline for its purity seems available? Who can judge that this or that sacrifice of life is objectively oriented to the sacredness of life and not subjectively abused for the interest of bloody power? Benjamin admits that it is impossible "to decide when unalloyed violence has been realized in particular cases . . . because the expiatory power of violence is not visible to men." Violence performs a decision for justice without decidable knowledge or determinant certainty. It is not recognizable in itself but only in its "incomparable effects," which manifest themselves in "a true war" or in other forms that myth, over the course of history, has "bastardized" with law. This bastardization is none other than Benjamin's name for deconstruction, since the vicious cycle of law-destroying and/as lawmaking has "maintained mythical forms of law." Nevertheless, Benjamin believes in the possibility of pure revolutionary violence outside of the law, or "the highest manifestation of unalloyed violence by man" (1978, 300).[4] In sum, human action can still be divine, though human knowledge never is.

Divine Violence without God: Žižek and *The Act of Killing*

Žižek (2008b) explores this dilemma in his typically provocative yet inspiring manner while reinterpreting divine violence. When he says that *homines sacer* are guilty of "leading a mere (natural) life" under the law that is "limited to the living," he indeed mistakes *homo sacer*, mere life, and the living as all the same. This same life "cannot reach beyond life to touch what is in excess of life," whereas divine violence expresses the very excess of life and "strikes at 'bare life' regulated by law." He argues, then, that divine violence "does partially overlap with the bio-political disposal of *Homini sacer*" (198), even though I would contend that they are the abject victims of the biopolitical system of law and power, which is to be destroyed by divine violence. Indeed, Žižek casts no subtle look at the potential sanctity of mere or bare life to be saved. For him, what is potential in life is its own excess as "pure drive," "the undeadness" of one's "desire" that one should follow without compromise like one's "duty." Committing divine violence is thus no different from an ethical act in the Lacanian-Kantian sense of standing by desire as duty (195). It is what man can and should do actually without God. This is why Žižek fearlessly identifies divine violence with existing phenomena in history, avoiding any obscurantist mystification imbued with theological messianism (197). His violent misreading of Benjamin thus leads to the positive humanization of divine violence. Divine justice is to be desired ethically and delivered humanly even if violently.

As Žižek suggests, the dénouement of Lars von Trier's *Dogville* (2003) exemplifies the revelation of such divine yet 'all-too-human' violence. The film tells a fable about Grace, the daughter of a gang leader, who runs away from his dirty work and hides in a small town, Dogville. Villagers kindly harbor her as long as she works for them, but they gradually exploit, abuse, and enslave her until her father appears. He then argues against her dedicated service to the villagers and her gracious understanding of their deeds as done under hard circumstances. In his view, she patronizingly exonerates

---

[4] At the end of his text, Benjamin abruptly states that divine violence may be called "sovereign violence." But I consistently relate sovereignty to mythical violence and not to divine violence.

them out of sympathy, without "judgment," on her condescending assumption that no one can attain her "high ethical standards." Finding her arrogant, he says, "You forgive others with excuses that you would never in the world permit for yourself." In Kantian ethical terms, Grace violates the categorical imperative that an action as permissible must be applied to all people.

Conversely, it is with her final decision on total revenge that she abandons this superior position and achieves universal justice as one of them by exploding her resentment. This "authentic resentment," for Žižek, embodies not the Nietzschean slave morality but a refusal to normalize the crime—like the male villagers' frequent rapes of Grace—and a just punishment (revenge) to move forward to true forgiveness and forgetting. In this sense, "her act of killing is an act of true mercy" (2008b, 189–94). Grace was arrogant when offering mercy as if Christ would have done so, but the true love of Christ, at least its Žižekian version, incorporates cruelty: "Love without cruelty is powerless; cruelty without love is blind." This love-cruelty link exceeds the natural limitations of life and embodies an unconditional drive toward the yet-to-come domain of love (204–5). The gangster father of Grace was initially deemed to be a terrible patriarchal sovereign but turns out to be a divine messenger of humanly possible justice. He helps Grace to perform divine violence that combines the wrath of God with the grace of Christ, the Old and New Testaments doctrines. Interestingly, we see shooting but no blood in Grace's massacre thanks to the theatrical direction of the film. The postcatastrophic last scene shows only the empty stage with nobody alive, and nothing left except a dog named Moses, which Grace did not kill, and the chalk-written word "DOG," which reads backwards as GOD. This dog-god association may symbolize divinity in natural life, its potential sanctity to save and love (I return to *Dogville* in Chapter 10).

The point is that divine violence results from a difficult decision that one must make when no God exists: to kill others or to sacrifice oneself. It is not an almighty God that will intervene directly to solve problems like a deus ex machina or to punish man's excesses as in the Last Judgment. Divine violence is instead the performance of man's will to excess, to a divinely unknown yet desperately desired justice while God remains silently impotent. Put differently, when the big Other, religious or secular (including historical necessity, ideology, etc.) gives an order to kill, it is not divine violence. The agents of a totalitarian massacre are no more than instruments of such a big Other that offers a sort of objective justification for their bloody mythical violence. Žižek puts it in Badiou's terms: while mythical violence belongs to the order of Being, divine violence destroys it as Event. And "it is only for the believer that an event is a miracle"; no objective criteria are available to identify an act of violence as divine (2008, 200). One becomes the subject of divine violence through one's subjective belief in its justness of one's own free will. One must "wrestle with it in solitude," assuming full responsibility for it as Benjamin says. This subjective freedom is dreadful, I claim, because one must be responsible for its unknown result. In turn, one cannot help desiring dread for the unknown because utmost freedom is right there. Divine violence with this human freedom pursues neither sovereign power, transcending yet founding law, nor anarchic self-indulgence in chaos and disorder. It rather performs a Kierkegaardian yet atheist "leap of faith" regarding the potential sanctity of humanity or the divinity that is "in man more than himself" but belongs to no sovereign, no God—or what I might call divinity without divinity.

However, what if leftist or rightist fascists, religious fundamentalists, or rioting youths also had a deep subjective belief in their violence as a free choice for justice? How can we judge which subjectivity is more objectively authentic than others? How is it possible to tell authentic divine violence from 'pseudo-divine violence,' so to speak? To criticize the Nazis is easy because their violence was "a means of the state power" and thus not divine, as Žižek notes (2008b, 199). I add that the Holocaust was not even an unsanctioned burst of lawmaking violence to establish a new state but, despite its massive scale, a well-programmed operation of law-preserving violence to abject an 'impure' race from the already functioning state under its Führer, the sovereign big Other. Therefore, divine violence cannot be evidenced by the simple visual fact of bloodlessness in the gas chambers, despite Derrida's suspicion that this is the case. As Derrida also states, the Holocaust exterminated not only millions of natural lives but, more crucially, "the witness of the other order, of a divine violence whose justice is irreducible to right" (1992a, 60). The Holocaust was indeed a pseudo-divine 'bloody' violence in nature that foreclosed a demand for justice.

True divine violence typically erupts when the abject strike as if from nowhere and demand justice with no cover in the big Other, as, according to Žižek, did many revolutionary peoples, from the Jacobins in France to favela crowds in Brazil. Žižek highlights Robespierre's undefeatable "faith" in a "sublime and holy love for humanity," which constitutes the paradoxical core of cruel divine violence (2008b, 203). By extension, reviewing *The Dark Knight Rises*, Žižek (2012) likens Bane to a modern-day Che Guevara whose violence is also driven, counterintuitively, out of a sense of sacrificial love for humanity, against the structural injustice of the global system. Bane's 'reign of terror' is thus a Badiouan Event for the equal liberation of all humans. It could be what Robert Young (2009) calls "a violent healing," a practice of "an ethics of healing through revolutionary violence," which is found at the heart of the lives of Che and other revolutionary doctors such as Frantz Fanon and Agostino Neto. In this interpretation, the Christ figure is not Batman, as we saw earlier, but Bane.

Nevertheless, even this Marxist-Christian idealization of Bane makes us doubt the nature of his violence. Žižek draws attention to the "People's Republic of Gotham City," which is negatively depicted in the film and yet which should be positively pursued. But to do so would mean that Bane's revolution is inherently lawmaking and state-founding—just like Robespierre's "ambition to establish here on earth the world's first Republic" (Žižek 2008b, 203). Bafflingly, Bane's unconditional love for his partner Talia does not extend to all humanity, as Žižek notes; it instead disrupts emancipatory ideals and colludes in the plot to demolish Gotham (Fisher and White 2012).[5] Bane is above all a traumatized abject whose agency for vengeance as justice is channeled into the megalomaniacal apocalyptic project of Talia's father, the leader of the League of Shadows. The fundamental problem of terrorism is that all its violence opens onto "no future." It lacks "the interest in the perfectibility of the present"—what Derrida identifies with "the inexhaustible demand of justice" (Borradori 2004, 167). Let us rephrase it thus: terrorism pretends to demand justice but tends to exhaust its infinity by obliterating the unknown future of humanity and its potential sanctity. Bane ends up with an anarcho-leftist version of pseudo-divine violence.

A more complicated case is found in *The Act of Killing* (2012), Joshua Oppenheimer's sensational documentary about the perpetrators of the 1965–66 Indonesian genocide, in which a million communists were killed. Leading this massacre, Suharto overthrew the then procommunist government through a military coup and commenced a three-decade dictatorial presidency. The purge thus typifies the bloody use of lawmaking violence to take over power and institute a 'New Order' at the cost of abject scapegoats. What is unique is that Suharto not only pushed his army beyond the law but also recruited gangsters into vigilante corps with a license to kill. These 'Dark

---

[5] Mark Fisher also notes that in reality "neoliberalism has survived the bank crisis," as "the hyper-rich do not fear the poor" and "the peaceable encampments of Occupy have done nothing to induce such fear."

Figure 4.2. Political gangsters called "freemen" nostalgically reenact their past Red Hunt to justify it as patriotic, in *The Act of Killing*.

Knight' mafias were called, appositely, "freemen": sovereign agents free from any legal procedure and responsibility for killing bare lives in the state of exception. Moreover, a few living "freemen" reenact various killings in the film while proudly justifying themselves as patriotic heroes and enjoying their performance with nostalgia (see Figure 4.2). Here we see more than the "banality of evil" that Arendt (2006) saw in the Nazi operatives' thoughtless performance of evil deeds without evil intentions. Arendt found the Nazis "neither perverted nor sadistic" but "terrifyingly normal"; they were not amoral monsters but ordinary bureaucrats who did their daily job mechanically, disengaging from its horrible effects. If this detachment of the Nazis from the Holocaust intimates their lack of faith in Nazism (hence, again, it is pseudo-divine violence at best), the Indonesian killers' ecstatic attachment to their slaughter shows a strong faith in its necessity.[6] They even developed techniques of bloodless murder as if to offer divine violence. Meanwhile, their projection or transference of evil onto the Reds was not rooted in any religious or racial fundamentalism but derived from secular capitalistic nationalism. Their primary motivations were money, power, and fame; they

---

[6] Arendt's view, based only on the war crimes trial of Adolph Eichmann, has been controversial. Some critic finds him to be "a self-avowed, aggressive Nazi ideologue strongly committed to Nazi beliefs, who showed no remorse or guilt for his role in the Final Solution—a radically evil Third Reich operative living inside the deceptively normal shell of a bland bureaucrat" (see White 2018).

were paid for eliminating 'public enemies' and are revered by a right-wing organization that grew out of the death squads and which continues to have a huge influence on national politics today. The film shows their everyday life in their now-globalized country without demonizing them as inhuman psychopaths or 'orientalizing' Indonesia as a primitive hell.

It is in this sense important to look at the protagonists of *The Act of Killing* in a global context. Interestingly, Anwar Congo and his friends were cinephiles of sorts. Before becoming vigilantes, they often sold black market film tickets (serving the extralegal economy) and learned from the cinema that history is always written by the winners (approving supralegal power), just as American films triumphantly depict the killing of Native Americans without guilt. Anwar's squad thus advocates their massacre from a hegemonic viewpoint, reconfirming that a successful coup is unpunishable as it is no longer an illegal revolt but a law-remaking revolution. For Anwar's squad, this is the case with the French, American, Soviet, Chinese, and such other bloody revolutions that led to the foundation of new states or orders. They even adopt the style of their favorite Hollywood genres—westerns, gangster films, and musicals—in order to make a docufiction about their killings, that is, a film within the film. Crucially, Hollywood's stylization of violence reduces it to an enjoyable spectacle, and the global circulation of Hollywood's violent imagery in this case helps the local Indonesians to perform the act of killing like 'acting.' That is, the commodified violence that they consumed in the dark theater served as a mental anodyne of the horror of actual violence. They jumped into the brutal reality of each killing—after a sort of trance-inducing ritual—as if it were an illusion, a simulation, a film in which they should act. In the present, they happily reenact the very past act(ing) of killing. This reenactment reveals their long-repressed desire to be openly acknowledged for their contribution to the nation because the genocide has been a social taboo, hardly told about or taught under the Suharto regime. If they *saw* violence on the screen yesterday, they *show* violence on the screen today. The screen is both a shield against the traumatic Real of bloody violence and a stage of its inscription into the mnemonic Symbolic order.

Their desire for recognition comes true on an absurd television talk show. Anwar's squad boasts of their 'patriotic' homicidal exploits, identifying with action heroes commemorated in American cinema such as Shane and Samson, Al Pacino and John Wayne. The audience gives exuberant cheers to their saga, celebrating them like official White Knights; thus, they are no longer forgotten Dark Knights. They acted like movie stars and have now become national stars. Acting is making believe, believing, and making the belief reality—this performativity underlies their sovereign agency. Most perplexingly, their private story is enjoyed in the public as if their dirty business were not an exceptional crime, horrible yet necessary for the public good, so much as a fun activity that is ordinarily acceptable and pleasurable. They entertain rather than enlighten the audience, sharing their pornographic memories of "wiping out communists" while satisfying the audience's voyeuristic desire amid a moral vacuum. Here works the neoliberal trend of "privatizing the public space," as Žižek (2013c) notes. It is not that private antisocial desires provoke the public in the exhibitionist fashion of transgressing taboos, but that today's postmodern society permits such desires as if there were no solid taboos, no public control of private enjoyment, and no clear boundary between the id and the superego, the Real and the Symbolic. The TV studio thus appears less like a hearing room for Anwar than like his living room, where he, as the host, tells his 'funny games' of murder while guests laugh and applaud. That is, Anwar takes over the position of the big Other from the audience and orders: 'Enjoy!' Around this obscene superego who does not prohibit but who promotes pleasures is formed a fascistic bond between subjects who shamelessly circulate raw desires, including the desire to purge the abject. As we see globally, far-right collective aggression is distributed in just such a mode of daily entertainment, a cultural mode of consumer capitalism. It privatizes the public space while normalizing the act of exception like a comfortably consumable commodity.

Not the local audience of the TV show but global viewers of *The Act of Killing* may feel highly uncomfortable, as if stuck in an ethical deadlock. The killers' retrospection on Indonesia's history and Hollywood's imagery brings no delayed judgment on the traumatic past. It instead justifies the lawmaking violence of all victors recurring in fiction and reality, in the past and the present, in the First and Third Worlds. There is no transcendent justice on the basis of which to judge whose violence is good or evil, not least because agents of violence may have a robust subjective conviction about its cause. In other words, there is no absolute divine violence but only the perpetual, universal mechanism of pseudo-divine violence. It runs on two axes of conviction, faith, or rather fantasy: the fantasy about the self as the savior of one's community and the fantasy about the other as the threat to eradicate, that is, the fantasy of sovereignty and the fantasy of abjection. Cinema is a factory of this double fantasy, full of violent yet unpunishable sovereign agents, from cowboys and gangsters—Anwar's idols—to superheroes and secret agents.

Moreover, various avengers in global cinema tend to enforce subjective justice by privatizing the public sphere of law in a self-created state of exception (see, for instance, Clint Eastwood's *Mystic River* or Park Chan-wook's *Oldboy*). In the real world, this sovereign mechanism is immanent in and between most nations, which are often entangled in each other's bloody violence. No wonder the CIA supported Suharto's communist purge as part of the global Cold War, and the gang-driven vigilantism was a colonial legacy rooted in the Dutch occupation of Indonesia (Anderson 2013). Who could blame whom? The (re)birth of a nation, the United States or Indonesia, almost always reaffirms the mythical origin of power in the name of justice, thereby deconstructing divine justice. We may question pseudo-divine violence ethically, but we may not deny that our nations could not have existed without it. Oppenheimer is right when he says: "We are much closer to perpetrators than we like to think" (McClendon and Oppenheimer 2013).

(Pseudo-)Divine Violence and *Waltz with Bashir*

How can we find our way out of this ethical dead end? Toward the end of *The Act of Killing*, Anwar plays a tortured and strangled communist and doubts whether or not he has sinned. He then retches as if "he himself were strangled and, at the same time, regurgitating, though alas only symbolically, the bodies of his victims" (Nagib 2016, 229). The real terribleness of his own violence hits him belatedly, making him its victim. Of course this dramatic moment does not testify to his authentic atonement or purgation; he was aware of the camera, and a short awakening may not change him forever. Gagging is also an outward sign of rejection, an adverse reaction to what one is not able or willing to accept. Nonetheless, this physiological abjection indicates that the ghost of the past, like the abject, intrudes into the present and pushes Anwar into a state of limbo between his peaceful reality and the excluded Real, between his secured subjectivity and its concealed void. Put in Freudian terms, "acting out" the past in the way of 'countering' traumas turns into "working through" the past in the way of 'encountering' traumas. This unexpected performativity brings back a "flash" of the past in its "now of recognizability," as highlighted in Benjamin's theses on history (1968b), a "fragment" of history to remember and to redeem that has been smothered by "the homogeneous course of universal history" (McAlinden 2013). A "deep memory" of unresolved traumas is reactivated in this process. Anwar, the sovereign agent, now faces a nameless *homo sacer* that he killed, and he perhaps feels the mere life's vulnerability and potential sanctity as his own, embracing, even if subconsciously, its precarious yet precious abjecthood as immanent in everyone. This abject yet potentially sacred humanity has been denied by state power, but its vulnerability to sovereignty is the very basis of human desire for life's sanctity as divinity beyond sovereignty. Even a natural or bare life is a being with this desire for self-transcendence. Anwar's nausea betrays the ethical potential for the living to co-desire the unrealized sanctity of life with the dead.

Let me conclude by briefly noting another documentary about mass murder, and which has a similar but much more shocking ending. Ari Folman's animated autobiography *Waltz with Bashir* (2008) traces the filmmaker's lost memories of his experience as an Israeli soldier in the 1982 Lebanon War. This 'mind-game' odyssey unfolds in a series of talks with his comrades that constitute a collective memory of the war, but which is also punctuated by fragmented symptoms of an unclear yet undead trauma. Among them is the nightmarish visual leitmotif of the film: a repetitive and lethargic scene in which naked soldiers emerge from the sea, don uniforms, and walk like zombies onto the land. This repeated sequence eventually comes to represent how back in 1982 the soldiers headed toward two refugee camps, Sabra and Shatila, in order to back the massacre of innocent Palestinians by Lebanese Christian Phalangists, a massacre that took place in response to the assassination of Phalangist leader Bashir Gemayel, from whose name the film takes its title.

This traumatic Real causes two effects on screen. First is war as spectacle: in animated memories, the past often appears like an aesthetic simulacrum of reality, a sort of virtual reality constructed in cultural forms (MTV, video game, LSD trip, porn). Its stimulating imagery substitutes atrocities and numbs soldiers, like Hollywood cinema in *The Act of Killing*. The screen thus 'screens out' the Real of the war. Second is war as specter: the Real still pierces the screen through spectral images of bare lives, animal or human, which are killed by the soldiers yet haunt them, neither alive nor dead. The sovereign agents of bloody violence cannot completely foreclose or forget the ghostly abject. Thus, the screen obliquely screens what cannot be screened out. This double screen, both protective and projective, embodies Freud's notion of "screen memory" and delivers what Benjamin calls "dialectical images" that evocatively awaken historical truths buried under the phantasmagoric surface of capitalist culture (for more on these concepts concerning

Waltz with Bashir, see Stewart 2010 and Landesman and Bendor 2011). The screen shows the director trying psychotherapy as he gropes to recover from his post-traumatic amnesia. However, in the end his traumatic core is revealed like the last piece of a jigsaw puzzle when animation turns into real footage of the Palestinian refugees crying over their slaughtered families. The Real as disavowed reality, then, tears down the screen of fantasized reality, that is, the screen memory of the sovereign subject. Now in his retrieved memory, Folman faces the Levinasian faces of the *homines sacri* whose unspoken demand to 'not kill' he dismissed (see Figure 4.3). The deep trauma, we see, has been lying in his long-avoided guilt for not having recognized their potential sanctity of life as a universal humanity yet to come.

This self-critical 'remembering as awakening' à la Benjamin leads to the question of whether Israel has become just such a sovereign state for Palestine as Nazi Germany was in its turn for the Jews. What would be possible to stop this eternal return of bloody violence? Perhaps nothing, although we must believe that the potential sanctity of life, the self-transcendent potential of life, is immanent in mere life. This is universal justice beyond the law. And we must desire the freedom of embracing that very potentiality as the divinity within humanity. Indeed, this is our ethical duty in our godless world. In other words, what we might do is to rearticulate Benjamin's anarchism with Derrida's ethics and Žižek's atheism in order to redefine divine violence as redeeming humanity without God. The opposite would be to avoid freedom, dreading to face the unknown in a godless world, and to replace

Figure 4.3. The amnesic protagonist finally faces his traumatic memory of the crying faces massacred in the Lebanon War, in *Waltz with Bashir*.

that dread with a fear of specific social others while reducing freedom to self-making and to the self-preservation of the right to exclude and eliminate these others. This is the right-wing fascist logic of abjection, the fundamentalist hard-ethical justification of pseudo-divine violence committed by the pseudo-divine sovereign power. Again, we must demand violence, if any, to let human divinity live without being crushed by any pseudo-god. When blood is shed locally—in Gaza, Syria, Ukraine, or wherever else—we must struggle globally to build universal solidarity with all bare lives suffering from pseudo-divine violence, as bare life is the base of life. Only from this bottom of life can we leap for the divinity of life. A revolution will end up with a catastrophe if it only attacks economic systems. To avoid this catastrophe, it must also envision this ethical leap *beyond any systems*. Only then could divine violence be freed from the shadow of God and the smell of blood.

5

From the Disaster Genre to the Cinema of Catastrophe

Global Catastrophes, Enforced Cosmopolitanism, and Cinematic Reflections

Today's catastrophes often testify to the inconsistency of globalization. The post–Cold War age saw the integration of different ideologies and identities into the tolerant harmony of rainbow communities, with 'systems of inclusion' promoting liberal democracy, multinational capitalism, and cultural exchanges. However, 'symptoms of exclusion,' like the abject cast out of these systems, exploded most violently on 9/11, and the underprivileged within the systems unexpectedly triggered Brexit and Trumpism. As noted in the Introduction, globalization is thus summed up in three waves, a foundational one followed by two rough ones: the 1990s posthistorical emergence of the single-market multicultural world, the 2000s vicious cycle of terror and war on terror, and the 2010s rise of antiglobalist populism in the wake of the financial meltdown. Inclusive globalism has been debunked for the last two decades by a variety of biopolitical, economic, and environmental catastrophes: terrorist attacks and mass murders, uncontrollable side effects of neoliberalism (economic polarization, casualized labor, illegal migration, refugee crises), and even technological and ecological anomalies (computer hacking, infectious diseases, industrial pollution, climate change). While catastrophes are now global in size and character, they crack and rupture the glamorous system of globalization as its inevitable byproducts. The more globalized the world is, the more globalized its threats are.

Likewise, a local disaster tends to become a global catastrophe that may occur anywhere or impact a large portion of the world. Locality no longer refers to the essentialist particularity of a specific area but takes on some compatibility, contingently embodying global universality. Let's recall Asian catastrophes, for instance. Natural disasters such as the 2008 Sichuan earthquake and Typhoon Haiyan in 2013 affected regions far beyond their epicenters; the 2004 Indian Ocean tsunami resulted in nearly three hundred thousand casualties across about ten countries, followed by a worldwide relief effort. The radiation effects from the 2011 Fukushima Daiichi nuclear disaster (3/11) have been immeasurably spreading over Japan and beyond, via air, seawater, and even agricultural and marine products exported overseas. This industrial catastrophe, the worst nuclear incident since Chernobyl in 1986, aroused global attention anew to the vulnerability of today's civilization depending so much on nuclear power generation. The protests against the importing of US beef into South Korea in 2008, though not a catastrophe, also caused a local eruption of global fear, in this case the fear that degenerative disease in certain herbivores—cattle raised on animal feed to promote rapid growth for capitalistic mass slaughter— (typically referred to as 'mad cow disease') might infect the human food chain. Meanwhile, the artificial disturbance of the planet's ecosystem has been increasingly palpable through global warming and climate anomalies. No local government can handle such global phenomena that affect the entirety of humankind in its interconnected networks. Catastrophe is thus core evidence that we live in a risky global world. It transcends all human boundaries and puts the survival of humanity to the test. It shatters the shelter of our social subjectivity and exposes our immanent bare lives like naked animals, a vulnerable state of nature immanent in culture. The subject is thus abjected, brought down to the abject state of being. What is more, this abjection itself is catastrophic. Even if naturally caused, a catastrophe does not remain a mere horrible event but is experienced like biopolitical abjection.

Traditional politics as the public struggle for legal rights gives way in the global age to a double ethics: the soft-ethical inclusion of ever more others, with human rights taken for granted like ethical default values, and the hard-ethical exclusion of those treated as intolerably harmful or useless, with radical antagonism occurring between the whole society and its abject others deprived of their basic rights (see Chapter 1). This antagonism with no political solution is catastrophic. It only pumps up biopolitical power with hard-ethical violence like the supralegal circuit of terrorism and counterterrorism, abject agency and global biopower, each of which justifies itself in the name of justice against evil. This fundamentalist justice, be it Islamic, Christian, or other, fulfills retaliation at best, only prolonging a postpolitical stalemate: 9/11 was followed by the Iraq War, which was followed by the rise of the Islamic State of Iraq and the Levant, and so on. ISIL has even attracted young Arabs from the West and provoked its autogenic adherents to carry out local attacks (e.g., the mass shooting at the offices of satirical French newspaper *Charlie Hebdo* in 2015), literally globalizing the threat of terror. The global sovereign system has in turn intensified control over (potential) terrorists and wearisome military operations. The vicious circle of violence has indeed been creating a catastrophic downward spiral that is ever more widely coiling around the ever more globalized world, while the state of emergency has been normalized for the past two decades. The American soldiers' daily abuses of the *homines sacri* detained in the Abu Ghraib prison (including torture, rape, and murder) manifested the routinization of human rights violations, the exception to the law becoming the law itself. As Agamben (1998, 168–80) argues, "the camp" is "the nomos" of modern biopolitics; it did not end in Auschwitz but has been updated to Guantanamo Bay. Moreover, suicide bombings are no longer shocking, while global surveillance programs constrict democracy in an increasingly totalitarian but unnoticeable manner, as the US National Security Agency massively scans private emails and online accounts. People are numbed or unhindered by prevalent or immanent catastrophes.

However, alternative biopolitical ethics emerges in the "subpolitical" manner. Sometimes a myriad of subjects or the (potential) abject directly engages in bottom-up activities to cope with "global risks" that are caused or unsolved by top-down malfunctional administration and representative politics, as Ulrich Beck says (2013, 81–108). People participate in a second government, temporary and exceptional, decentered and distributed, to perform democracy that is promised but not realized by the elite ruling class, which is then threatened. The Korean people's US beef protest did not pursue typical political aims like democratization or liberation, but instead demanded the ethical protection of their lives against potential adverse effects of neoliberal state power. The global Multitude in digital agoras actively expresses support or denunciation regarding local events: the independence movement of Tibet from China, antigovernment protests in Myanmar and Hong Kong, the Arab Spring, and the Middle Eastern crises from the Syrian Civil War to the Gaza-Israel conflict. This occurs not because people have personal stakes or expertise in every political situation, but because even local politics touches the global conditions of biopolitico-ethical life and its fundamental rights as shared values. Global citizens then immediately empathize with the local abject who suffer from sovereign power's "pseudo-divine violence," the bleeding bare lives who may still retain "the potential sanctity of life" wherever they are (see Chapter 4). Similarly, many kinds of the "Me Too"/"With You" movements 'go viral,' often entailing the relay of texts or photos showing 'I am XXX (the victim).' Like "a paradise built in hell," "the constellations of solidarity, altruism, and improvisation are within most of us and reappear at these times [of catastrophe]" (Solnit 2010, 12).

I briefly address this 'glocal' solidarity in terms of *cosmopolitanism*. Cultural theorists such as Enrique Dussel (2013), Pheng Cheah and Bruce Robbins (1998), Homi Bhabha, and Arjun Appadurai (Breckenridge et al. 2002) criticize the imperfection of cosmopolitan inclusion, tracing its history from the Roman Empire through the Kantian Enlightenment to modern versions of the "league of nations" and current globalization. They note that classical cosmopolitanism based on universal hospitality disguises the historical hegemony of the European bourgeoisie, who can be capitalist cosmopolites— like the condescendingly tolerant multiculturalists we have discussed. For non-Western critics, Marxist postnationalism as an alternative also fails to overcome the Western colonial paradigm. Through this ideological critique, they propose "cosmopolitics" to pursue "multiple cosmopolitanisms" with an "s" (Robbins 1998, 12–13), advocating pluralism rather than cultural relativism. They support not "universality" rooted in the West's reformative inclusion of the rest but "diversality" enabled by the global subalterns' transformative appropriation of globalization (Mignolo 2002, 179–83). What matters here is not "globalization from above" by supranational institutions such as the United Nations and the EU, which have not always been effective systems of inclusion and intervention. Instead, it is "globalization from below," the subpolitical connection of the worldwide multitude in today's Empire, like the Occupy movement extending from New York to everywhere. This cosmopolitanism has little to do with tolerance or hospitality, political liberalism or cultural modernism, or even the multicultural dialogue that Kwame Anthony Appiah (2006) proposes regarding embracing otherness on the premise of self-fallibility. It rather works as "enforced cosmopolitanism" (Beck 2013, 47–66): we cannot help being cosmopolitan and forming international networks to handle global catastrophes in an everyday connected life. Similarly, Daniele Archibugi (2003) and Seyla Benhabib (2006) envision "cosmopolis" to set up through the democratic reconciliation between the "universality of human rights" and the "partiality of law." It would be a cosmopolitan public sphere in which global systems of inclusion should continually readjust to and negotiate with symptoms of exclusion in order to be ever more flexible and permeable.

Cinema reflects a variety of catastrophes. Regarding those in Asia noted earlier, let me first mention East Asian films, particularly the post-Fukushima films that evoke and update the post-Hiroshima films in Japan. Documentaries such as *Nuclear Nation* (Funahashi Atsushi, 2012) and *Lullaby under the Nuclear Sky* (Kana Tomoko, 2016) address the accident's victims, the citizens who were turned overnight into abject refugees, while they critique the nationalist ideology of development underlying the construction of nuclear power plants. Fictions such as *The Land of Hope* (Sono Sion, 2012), *Peaceful Days* (Uchida Nobuteru, 2012), *Tokyo Family* (Yamada Yoji, 2013), and *Sharing* (Shinozaki Makoto, 2014) blend together the personal and the collective, the direct and indirect traumas of the nuclear incident, while depicting social phenomena: the techno-bureaucratic state control of people, the security industry capitalizing on the disaster, the paranoid fear of death, and the consolation and bonding of the abject. Sono Sion's *Himizu* (2011), analyzed in Chapter 12, impressively portrays the painful outcry of a teenage boy whose patricide and companionship with the homeless stand for the abject's struggle between life and death against the backdrop of the 3/11 earthquake. Meanwhile, Chinese cinema has seen two oppositional tendencies. First, mainstream blockbusters represent catastrophe and redemption in Hollywood style. *Aftershock* (Feng Xiaogang, 2010), for example, is a megahit family drama about a girl abandoned by her parents, who had to choose to save only one of their two children during the 1976 Tangshan earthquake (see Figure 5.1). About thirty years later, the Sichuan earthquake brings about reunion and reconciliation with her mother, that is, the 'suture'

Figure 5.1. A girl is abandoned by her parents, who decide to save their other child during the Tangshan earthquake, in *Aftershock*.

of the abject's postcatastrophic trauma. Second, independent critical films do not compromise with such a happy ending. In *A Touch of Sin* by Jia Zhangke (2013), four unrelated characters exploited by capital explode in vengeful violence like abject terroristic agents (see Chapter 9). Reflecting China's rapid absorption of global capitalism, a relentless rush of greed without political mediation only provokes the catastrophic eruption of accidental terror.

Southeast Asia is ever more visible in world cinema as well. Documentary films often shed light on otherwise unseeable people devastated by natural or social catastrophes. *Storm Children: Book One* (Lav Diaz, 2014) and *Nick and Chai* (Cha Escala and Wena Sanchez, 2014) illustrate the abject lives of Filipino people who have to cope with the aftermath of Typhoon Haiyan. *The Storm Makers* (Guillaume Suon, 2014) traces the misery of young Cambodian women sold off like slaves by Christian recruiters; facing this injustice, one of the trafficked and raped girls even swears to take revenge on her rapist by raising the child born of rape and killing it later. A political struggle beyond such hard-ethical vengeance is found in *Burma VJ: Reporting from a Closed Country* (Anders Østergaard, 2008). In it, under the radar of Myanmar's military junta, guerrilla "Video Jockeys" film the 2007 antidictatorship uprising led by Buddhist monks and smuggle the footage to Thailand, then to Norway, to transmit it finally to the outside world via satellite. They thus build up not personal terrorism but the cosmopolitan solidarity between the local and global multitudes against a catastrophe: the repressive state's violent crackdown on this protest and the sovereign power's brutal abjection of the monks and citizens. As examined in Chapter 4, Joshua Oppenheimer's *The Act of Killing* (2012)—followed by its sequel *The Look of Silence* (2014)— also brings to the fore the universal mechanism of such biopolitical sovereignty and abjection. The former gangsters hired by the Suharto regime for the Indonesian Communist purge reenact their supralegal act of killing and equate it with patriotic genocide, justified in the winners' history and glorified in Hollywood cinema.

Many Middle Eastern documentaries also highlight catastrophes brought about by pseudo-divine violence that claims justice through the fantasy of the other as evil and the fantasy of the self as savior. *Silvered Water, Syria Self-Portrait* (Ossama Mohammed and Wiam Simav Bedirxan, 2014) is filled with brutalized remnants of the Syrian Civil War, evoking the atrocities of the 2003 human rights violations against detainees in the Abu Ghraib prison. *Striplife* (Nicola Grignani et al., 2013) sketches the daily life of the Palestinian abject after the blockade of the Gaza Strip. Furthermore, we might also return to Ari Folman's autobiographical *Waltz with Bashir* (2008), explored in Chapter 4. This animated psychological odyssey through the 1982 Lebanon War reveals the origin of the director's post-traumatic amnesia in the end by showing the real footage of the Palestinian refugees whose massacre he assisted as an Israeli soldier. The traumatic Real erased in his memory then turns out to be the crying or dead faces of *homines sacri* whose potential sanctity of life he dismissed. The (pseudo-divine) sovereign agent belatedly encounters the true divinity immanent even in the abject, that is, in all humanity. This retrospection brings neither a political solution to the Israeli-Palestinian conflict nor a subpolitical solidarity between the multitudes on both sides. Nevertheless, it opens up ethical room for going beyond the soft and hard ethics interlocked in the global system.

Theorizing Disaster, Catastrophe, and the Sublime

Including this alternative ethical stance, fictional films dramatize more diverse responses to various catastrophes centering on individual characters, if not collective societies. I address all such films as the *cinema of catastrophe*, including but not limited to the *disaster genre*. Let me frame these two notions in a discursive context and illuminate how they appear oppositional to each other on the one hand and yet how it is possible to elicit implications of catastrophe from disaster genre films in multiple aspects on the other hand. Disaster etymologically refers to an event affected by a bad (*dis-*) star (*astro*), that is, an ill-starred accident. It typically occurs within a specific time and space and has an identifiable cause and a resolvable effect such as a hurricane, a conflagration, or a bomb blast. Most disaster films begin with the outbreak of a calamity and end with its dissolution, staging their protagonist's "double death" as formulated in Chapter 2: the symbolic death of disastrous abjection leads to the struggle for recovery until the real death or salvation. In Hollywood conventions, disasters are strictly governed by the law of causality, and rescues are heroically led by experts in the goal-oriented, problem-solving, and character-driven manner of classical narrative. This main plot leads to a redemptive finale with poetic justice, often entailing a romantic subplot as in the action genre.

In contrast, catastrophe has certain notable aspects irreducible to disaster. It is more comprehensive, overwhelming, indiscriminate, and unpredictable than disaster—at least conceptually. The Greek origin of the word refers to the downward (*cata-*) overturning (*strophe*) of our footing itself in various cases, from an earthquake or tsunami to a radical sociopolitical upheaval and its extreme ravages. Catastrophe thus turns over/overturns the surface of reality like the eruption of the Real, leaving us with nothing but to hope for a transcendent exit or to pray for an impossible miracle. If the disaster is ultimately manageable, catastrophe provokes the apocalyptic sentiment that only divine intervention could save us, like a deus ex machina. Moreover, catastrophe by definition implies "revelation," in that the unseen/hidden side of our footing is exposed with things turning inside out (Debray 2011, 78). If disaster destructs order temporarily, catastrophe reveals that our system for maintaining order was a disorder in and of itself. Also aesthetically, catastrophe means the poetic dénouement in Greek tragedy in which everything comes to an end, a terminative, helpless state beyond control. These two aspects are contradictorily entangled: catastrophe is already immanent in our reality but has not yet come and will not come as long as it goes unrecognized; upon being recognized, out it bursts. The longer this temporal gap between the catastrophic Real and its recognition, the more difficult it is to evade it when we recognize it. The catastrophic is an epistemic belatedness, the temporality of knowing 'too late to stop it.'

For this reason, it is small wonder that the Cassandra syndrome permeates the cinema of catastrophe. Just as nobody believes Cassandra's prophesies in Greek mythology, a catastrophe is typically pronounced by a character who is initially considered mad or crazy. Furthermore, this kind of "cognitive dissonance" wherein an individual can see the end is symptomatic of today's global tendency for individual, real-life experience to be relied upon less than socially circulating knowledge, not least because reality is already saturated with simulacra and media (Virilio 2009). Even if we feel the effects of global warming, we are not sure of it until scientists confirm it (though they often refute each other). We follow the (pseudo)scientific voice of authority and consult Google, our omniscient digital God, to see if our experience tells truths. This reliance on mediated information and expert discourses does not always decrease the danger of rupture. In some cases, it increases the impossibility of recognizing and escaping unexpected catastrophes that might destroy our reality constructed by the global technocracy. However, this risk in turn reinforces the 'technopolitan' obsession of what Richard Grusin (2004, 8–61) calls "premediation": the media's preemptive simulation of potential catastrophes to reduce their shock effects and to prepare contingency plans. Today's Cassandra is media and science technology.

More crucial from the aesthetic perspective is the ethical dimension of catastrophe.[1] We tend to take an ethical attitude to a past irremediable catastrophe like the Holocaust by endlessly mourning for its abject victims. Art after Auschwitz is obsessed with "the ethical witnessing of unrepresentable catastrophe" and mourning for the dead, as Rancière claims (2004, 129–32). In this sense, the unrepresentability of historical catastrophes has often been both the aesthetic anxiety and ethical kernel of European cinema. Suffice it to remember how Claude Lanzmann's *Shoah* (1985) 'reflects' on the Holocaust without 'representing' it. The Holocaust is deemed comparable to the shocking intervention of the Freudian Thing or the Mosaic Law, which goes beyond human understanding, and toward which one can take only an ethical rather than aesthetic attitude; art should then testify to "the infinite debt of spirit with regard to a law that is as much that of the order of Moses' God as it is the factual law of unconscious" (126–28). Rancière calls this tendency the "ethical turn of aesthetics" (along with the ethical turn of politics), pointing out its key operational concept that he critically examines, the *sublime*. In Kantian aesthetics, the *sublime* is characterized as chaotic, fearful, and boundless outside the agreeable and communicable realm of the *beautiful* (Kant 2000, 131–48). It goes beyond empirical imagination and human capacity in two ways: immeasurable quantity causes the *mathematically sublime*—like too many birds in *The Birds* (Alfred Hitchcock, 1963)—while insurmountable power provokes the *dynamically sublime*—like invincible aliens in *War of the Worlds* (Steven Spielberg, 2005).

However, mainstream commercial cinema represented by Hollywood has never cringed at 'representing' sublime catastrophes as marvelous spectacles in ways that 'beautify' them. Its scopophilic impulse toward catastrophe indeed embodies the cinema's inherent desire to represent the unrepresentable, visualize it within the rectangular field of screen, and transform it stylistically, as if this could make psychological room for, and ultimately overcome any fatalistic suffering from, the traumatically sublime Thing. Steven Spielberg's *Schindler's List* (1993) thus vividly reconstructs German concentration camps from which a German hero redeems hundreds of Jews—for Lanzmann (1994), the film is an inverted American superhero's "kitschy melodrama" that transgresses or trivializes the Holocaust's sublimity.[2] In such

---

[1] The following discussion on the sublime is an expanded revision of the first few pages from my essay on the disaster genre (Jeong 2013c, 72–74).

[2] Notably, Lanzmann's critique of *Schindler's List* recalls Serge Daney's similar well-known critique of *Kapo* (Gillo Pontecorvo, 1960). Daney (2007, 34–35) finds the "pretty tracking shot" of a Jew's electrocution on the fence of a concentration camp in this Academy-nominated film to be "immoral,"

ways—good or bad—Hollywood has incorporated all sorts of catastrophes into the disaster 'genre,' while visual technology has become ever more advanced in its depiction of terror, ruin, destruction, and the like. As many blockbusters depict disastrous events, the sublime on screen is now the most desired cinematic capital; its creation is the core of the film industry. The mathematical sublime of absolutely great things beyond measurability is always fabricated into cultural products, calculable in numbers of comparison and competition (this dinosaur is fifty feet tall, costs $1 million, and so on). Sequels, remakes, and rip-offs follow successful products. The film market lives on commodified disasters. Visual technology never stops intensifying the cinematic effect of special effects to render terror or destruction sensational and even splendid. By extension, dystopian sci-fi films (the *Terminator*, *Jurassic Park*, *Matrix* series, and the like) have anathematized emerging technologies and the human hubris of becoming the creator of machines or lives. However, this technophobia has been depicted ever more graphically through the never-ending advancement of visual technology (see Arthur 2001). Hollywood's 'performative self-contradiction' always capitalizes on public fears of imminent catastrophe by turning them into public pleasures in a cultural mode of "disaster capitalism" (Klein 2008).

On the spectators' side, the cinematic effect of special effects implies the turn of sublimity into something sensible, sensational, splendid, and stimulating. A catastrophic event appears as astonishing yet tamable, devastating yet agreeable, inexperienced yet sharable according to cultural norms. Thus, the fear of being threatened by a sublime event turns into the desire for being only virtually overwhelmed and thus actually entertained by its beautified representation on the screen, from which a safe distance is kept in order to secure *aesthetic disinterestedness* for visual pleasure, as Immanuel Kant states (2000, 131–34). This aesthetic distancing from the sublime reduces the supersensible *noumenon* to the sensible *phenomenon* and replaces unfathomable jouissance with induced pleasure. The formless sublime of catastrophe is often singularized into a small abject other: a monster like Godzilla or a villain like a terrorist. Its elimination is presented as postcatastrophic redemption, bringing psychological comfort to spectators. Well protected, we thus consume the aestheticized sublime by watching devastating events as mere onlookers. The screen not only projects catastrophe but also protects

---

because the spectator has to be "aesthetically seduced" where it is only a "matter of conscience" of being a human. Ethics beyond aesthetics is lucidly presumed here.

us from its danger. We enjoy the aestheticized sublime through all our senses, purchasing and consuming it repeatedly.

Nevertheless, the safety in which we see a fearful thing as attractive enables us not simply to enjoy its sensible aspect but also to experience its power without being really endangered. We, though physically powerless, then find a capacity for resistance, "the courage to measure ourselves against the apparent all-powerfulness of nature," as Kant says. To measure ourselves may mean acknowledging that our aesthetic imagination fails in measuring the sublime but that we have correspondingly immeasurable reason. With noumenal reason, we can subjectively think of nature as more than sensibly imaginable nature, as "the presentation of something supernatural" in its sublime totality. Sublime objects elevate the strength of our soul above imagination toward reason, which ultimately serves as the ground of our "superiority over nature." Thus, genuine Kantian sublimity is not in nature but our minds (144–47). In this case, our free will to resist the sublime outside would be empirically limited but would concern the foundational decision to accept the entire given as unavoidable and assume any responsibility for it. Kantian ethics resides then in this fundamental freedom, that is, the *moral* sublime, as opposed to the *natural* sublime. Psychoanalytically speaking, this moral sublime does not serve the pleasure principle to do whatever our inclinations desire without any constraints, but it somewhat resembles the Freudian "death drive" to do what we do not want to do, "to thwart the 'spontaneous' realization of an impetus" (Žižek 2006, 202). In other words, our free will may be the will to exercise this freedom as the moral law imposed on us so that the given situation is chosen as given by ourselves against our desires. We could then find room for redemption that results from our own sublimity in front of the invincible environment.

In this sense, it is possible to think about the sublime through postcatastrophic redemption instead of the catastrophe itself. Is Schindler's act sublime? Perhaps, as it can imbue us with "respect," it is an aspect of the Kantian moral sublime. Is Lanzmann's attitude sublime? Definitely, according to Jean-François Lyotard (1984, 71–82), who elaborates on "the aesthetic of the sublime," primarily through the avant-garde art that is in the ethical service of witnessing the unrepresentable. For Rancière (2004, 129–32), however, this ethical turn overturns every promise of political emancipation, reducing aesthetics to "the interminable mourning of irremediable catastrophe" from which "only a god could save us." Yesterdays' genocide returns as the never-ending catastrophe of today, as if it were an immemorial trauma. A decisive moment that cuts a time into two is no longer a revolution to come (as in the modernist aesthetics and politics that Rancière hopes to reinstate) but the extreme event that is already past but still present in a "theology of time [. . .] a time destined to carry out an internal necessity, once glorious, now disastrous." The time of today's art is suspended between "a primordial trauma" and "a salvation to come" instead of making a political breakthrough. Here, one could argue for or against Rancière's criticism that Lyotard inverts the Kantian autonomy of the moral law into "an ethical subjection to the law of the Other." Again, theologically, this Otherness is rooted in the Jewish God; Kant (2000, 156) also takes this God's prohibition of the image as the essence of the sublime. However, I claim that Kant's moral sublime may concern a different realm, including our 'resistance' to sublime events. This resistance could take the form of apolitical mourning or emancipatory activity or something else, and this diversity would leave room for diversely thinking about the catastrophic sublime. Then, what can widen this room would be less the image of sublimity visualized in the (post)cinematic age than our diegetic experience of a sublime situation, especially on the side of characters' subjectivity. And not limited to medium specificity, "the (post)cinematic sublime" (Comer and Vayo 2013) would also imply a sublime effect that can intervene in spectators' subjectivity through the cinematic experience, a cinematic effect that leads us beyond the screen toward unthought dimensions of the world and our minds.

The Evolution of the Disaster Genre and the Cinema of Catastrophe

Hollywood disaster films offer a multitude of case study items in this regard.[3] We thus can elicit (ethical) implications of catastrophe from the disaster genre. It is not simply about the visualization of catastrophe but strongly implicates the narrativization of postcatastrophic redemption above all. From the genre's establishment in the 1970s, the classical structure of "situation-action-situation modified"—Deleuze's action-image formula, noted in Chapter 2—underlay such foundational films as *Airport* (George Seaton, 1970), *The Poseidon Adventure* (Ronald Neame, 1972), and

---

[3] The following four paragraphs on the history of Hollywood disaster are taken with revision from my aforementioned essay (Jeong 2013c, 75–76).

The Towering Inferno (John Guillermin, 1974).[4] A disaster usually occurs at an earlier point of the storyline, and the rest of the running time is filled with characters' struggles for rescue, finally followed by the return of the precatastrophic situation, with wounds, victims, or nightmares lingering over it. From the outset of this struggle to its dénouement, the theme of ethical sublimity pervades, especially when involving heroic protagonists' deaths—marking the double death narrative. In *The Poseidon Adventure*, for example, the Nietzschean reverend does not just wait for God's salvation like the chaplain character but leads a group of 'the strong' through the claustrophobic maze of a *Titanic*-evoking wrecked liner. He finally saves people by opening the door to the outside while falling into the fire as he rages against a pitiless God. Through this act declaring the Death of God, he paradoxically incarnates Moses's leadership and Jesus's sacrifice at the same time, a sublime divinity immanent in the impotent human. He embodies the 'moral' sublime through the resistance to the 'natural' sublime in the Kantian terms mentioned previously.

After the 1980s 'campy' genre mutation (*Ghostbusters* [Ivan Reitman, 1984], *Gremlins* [Joe Dante, 1984]), the fin-de-siècle imagination of the 1990s yields various types of cinematic concerns over impending millennial catastrophe. In particular, the catastrophic sublime pervades three types of sci-fi narratives. First, as already mentioned, the standard narrative of postcatastrophic redemption shows how a disaster occurs near the start of the storyline and is overcome at the end (*Jurassic Park* [Steven Spielberg, 1993], *Independence Day* [Roland Emmerich, 1996]). Second, the narrative of precatastrophic prevention depicts how an already identified potential catastrophe is at last stopped from occurring. It consists of suspenseful efforts to prevent an upcoming apocalypse (*Armageddon* [Michael Bay, 1998], *Deep Impact* [Mimi Leder, 1998]). Third, techno-dystopian sci-fi films typically use the motif of time travel to transform postcatastrophic redemption into precatastrophic prevention (*Terminator 2* [James Cameron, 1991], *12*

---

[4] In fact, the disaster film has a long history; the first *Titanic* film traces back to 1913 and the megahit original *King Kong* to 1933. More broadly, diverse catastrophes have enriched cinematic imagination and documentation from the birth of the cinema. But it is in the 1970s that Hollywood set up the specific genre of the disaster film and its consistent industrial, aesthetic identity as a marketing category through technological advancement in the global cultural and commercial arena. Here, a disaster manifests itself as the central event of a film instead of a minor factor or background. It is usually plausible yet ahistorical, involving events like natural calamities, which implies its repetition on a mythical level beyond specific sociopolitical contexts. Disasters are thus represented as part of human civilization, well hosted in the universal form of Hollywood narrative and style (see Keane 2006, 1–43).

Monkeys [Terry Gilliam, 1995]). Mixing the first and second types, the third one starts with a postcatastrophic situation from which the protagonist is sent back to a point in time before the outbreak of the assumed catastrophe to remove or at least identify its cause 'in advance,' thereby changing the future.[5] Here, for instance, against the 'techno' (rather than natural) sublime of Terminators—whose insurmountable power takes on a Kantian dynamical sublimity—the moral sublime manifests itself when the Terminator, fighting on behalf of humans in *Terminator 2*, sacrificially submerges himself in molten metal in order to erase every trace of his cyborg body brought from the dystopian future. At this closing point of the story, a certain divinity exudes out of the machine, as if to embody deus ex machina in a different sense of the term.

The first decade of the new millennium sees the cinematic anxiety about global catastrophe manifest itself in a variety of ways, from (in)direct invocations of 9/11 (*United 93* [Paul Greengrass, 2006], *World Trade Center* [Oliver Stone, 2006]) to imaginations of climate doomsday (*The Day after Tomorrow* [Roland Emmerich, 2004], *2012* [Roland Emmerich, 2009]). A growing number of films update the motif of pre/postcatastrophic preemptive/redemptive struggle with ever more upgraded technology. Notably, post-9/11 action/thriller/sci-fi films in and around the disaster genre present terror as a salient catastrophe and the counterterrorist mission of sovereign agents as the core of the narrative (see Dixon 2004; Comer and Vayo 2013). Their use of time travel for the paradoxical prevention of a past catastrophe becomes increasingly plausible and sophisticated, actively adopting and updating the practice of premediation to the screen. Noteworthy is the origin of this practice: since 9/11, US media have attempted to prevent the immediacy of such a traumatic shock by replaying images of past disasters and anticipating future scenarios of potential ones. As a result, any catastrophe "would always already have been premediated" so that one can be less terrified and better prepared if it really occurs (Grusin 2004, 8–16). I add that

---

[5] Things are more complex in truth. In the *Terminator* series, a hero sent by humans back to the past prevents a terminator sent by machines from killing the future leader of humans. The time travel is done not to defuse the catastrophe of nuclear warfare itself (which is presumed from the beginning and not even represented), but to maintain the postcatastrophic situation (in which the humans' fight against the machine is presumed to continue). In *12 Monkeys*, the hero travels in time not to undo the apocalyptic pandemic that has happened but to gather information about the original virus from which to distill the cure. But it turns out that he is also unwittingly "the source of the catastrophe that he himself is sent into the past to investigate," and that the resolution is "to die and therefore *neutralize* the agency that caused the cataclysmic consequences he was hoping to prevent" (Elsaesser 2021, 131).

digital technology has ever more perfectly simulated such potential terror, oversaturating and trivializing sublime audiovisual stimuli to the extent of leaving nothing unrepresentable and unpredictable.

This obsessive trend of premediation reflects the anxiety about the cognitive dissonance between the unpredictable advent of catastrophes and the aspirations for their proactive control. What matters is that this is Hollywood's way of conducting counterterror operations to protect and reinforce the American-model global sovereign system and its agents. For instance, *Déjà Vu* (Tony Scott, 2006) begins with a terrorist bomb attack in New Orleans that evokes the Oklahoma City bombing, 9/11, and, geographically, Hurricane Katrina. Then, as though these historical disasters should have been averted, a government agent travels back four days into the past, utilizing space-folding technology to forestall the bombing and the murder of a woman with whom he fell in love only through her images captured on the surveillance 'time-warp' screen. Set in the year 2054, the "Precrime" system in *Minority Report* (Steven Spielberg, 2002) carries to an extreme the mission of precatastrophic prevention. If three "Pre-Cogs" (prescient cognitive mediums) report an impending crime visually on their mind-screen, agents rush to the locale, arrest criminals, and rescue their victims at the last minute. Catastrophe is 'represented' through premediation, namely the remediation of the future. In this way, media serve as an interface to and remedy for an event that has not yet occurred so that, in theory, we can proactively parry the blows of future trauma (even though Precrime ultimately fails in the film). In short, the proactive premediation promotes precatastrophic preemption. I further trace the evolution of sci-fi time-travel counterterror films through the 2010s in Chapter 7, focusing on Duncan Jones's *Source Code* (2011).

At this point, however, I emphasize again that the cinema of catastrophe is more than the disaster genre. Without conforming to disaster genre formulas, some catastrophe films show the failure of postcatastrophic redemption, precatastrophic prevention, or their fusion. Not serving the sovereign system fictionally, they shed light on the abject, whose resistance to the sovereign system ends up being catastrophic. Or they draw attention to an inexplicable catastrophe without any hope of salvation, as if it were a divine judgment on the world and humanity. Sometimes these two cases intermingle in realistic or allegorical settings. For example, *Fight Club* (David Fincher, 1999) portrays a community of abject males who desire to feel the Real out of their mundane reality stuck in the consumer society of postmodern simulacra. They liberate themselves through new connections by remasculinizing their bodies while fighting each other. But just as their Fight Club is contained and constrained within a protocol, "they model the future at the same time as they preempt it, and thus potentially short-circuit the very connections they seek to establish" (Elsaesser 2021, 103). In the end, this alternative public space turns out to be confined to the delusional mind of the protagonist, a "risk-insurer" who risks becoming a self-fulfilling prophet in his dissociated identity disorder. That is, while his normal ego has been managing risks in the capitalist system in the daytime, his alter ego has been developing an antimaterialist and anticorporate project at night, a pseudo-divine plan to demolish the world with no constructive vision. His radical but ideational end-of-century sensibility implodes like an apocalypse as finally seen in the 9/11-prefiguring collapse of skyscrapers: the total collapse of buildings in a financial district, and by implication, the neurotic capitalist society. Made a decade later, *Cloverfield* (Matt Reeves, 2008) unmistakably evokes 9/11 by presenting a massive monster's attack on Manhattan from the first-person viewpoint of a New Yorker with a digital camera. The film avoids facing the real trauma by replacing the terrorists of 9/11 with a fictive, alien Thing. Nonetheless, the ending, in which the cameraman is killed—a moment that we feel as though we are being killed—pushes the nihilistic Real of the catastrophe further away from any redemption.

Such extreme apocalyptic imagination peaks in *Melancholia* (2011), which epitomizes the European cinema of catastrophe in Lars von Trier's style once again after *Dogville* (see Chapter 4). *Melancholia* begins with a euphoric wedding party but gradually exposes calculated deals and unresolvable frictions among families and guests. Tired of communication in this community—a miniaturized global network of individual interests and desires—the neurotic heroines rather embrace the impending collision of a mysterious planet called Melancholia with Earth. The closer it comes, the bigger it looks, and it finally engulfs the entire world—the whole screen—to leave spectators with nothing but darkness: an ecstatically melancholic advent of doomsday (see Figure 5.2). We see "a cinema of the after-all"; the end of the world in the film is the end of cinema itself (Szendy 2015, 3). Such a radical apocalypse also concludes the Korean sci-fi film *Save the Green Planet!* (Jang Joon-whan, 2003). Its protagonist, an abject laborer, kidnaps, confines, and tortures the head of a company that he believes is the leader of aliens plotting to destroy Earth. His paranoiac conspiracy theory justifies his ridiculous mission and methods to save the green planet, but in truth, it pumps up his abject agency

Figure 5.2. A mysterious planet collides with Earth to engulf the entire world and the whole screen simultaneously at the end of *Melancholia*.

to subvert the real class hierarchy fictionally. He inflicts vengeful sovereign violence on the evil bourgeois figure (who caused his family traumas) by creating a phantasmatic state of exception in his private prison for private justice. However, this delusional resistance to capitalist power leads to more than a fatalistic failure or terroristic destruction. The supposed alien turns out to be an actual alien, a divine figure who has been testing humanity's promising potential but finally decides to blow up the entire planet.[6] *The Terror Live* (Kim Byung-woo, 2013) takes a similar, less grandiose, but more realistic approach to systemic evil. The son of a construction worker who was killed while fixing a bridge demands an apology for the state-driven industrial accident from the president via a TV news program. When the president declines to apologize, the son ultimately carries out his threat to blow up the bridge. That is, the unheard abject carries out the agency of vindictive terrorism as a desperate attempt to intervene in the public sphere. Evoking some real tragedies caused by state violence in Korea, the film ends with the terrorist's suicide bombing, which demolishes the broadcasting station and the nearby National Assembly Building, where the president is announcing the war on terror. Chapter 6 delves into Bong Joon-ho's *Snowpiercer* (2013) in this direction of today's cinema that stages the extermination of humanity as a not-too-bad scenario.

---

[6] If the alien punishes humankind like an angry God, the abject pursues vengeance out of fidelity to his personal attachments (family), not his class. Both use violence, exposing the catastrophic contradiction between their utopian ideals and dystopian actions. See Peter Y. Paik's (2010, 72–91) close analysis of the film.

In sum, we reach the global cinema of catastrophe wherein catastrophes are not just disasters to shun or subdue but symptoms of the cataclysmic inconsistency of the global system and the political impossibility of utopian change. The multitude turns from exploited consumers into abject agents against Empire, but their resistance to its omnipresent neoliberal biopower ends up being futile or terroristic. Socioeconomic networks are mathematically sublime, as is the global contagion of a local problem such as the domino effect of debt crises, computer viruses, and radioactive contamination, with the uncontrollable power of these problems even taking on the dynamically sublime. While industrial and environmental risks fuse, totalitarian technocracy joins disaster capitalism at the cost of democracy. Postcatastrophic mourning tends to be stuck in the monumentalization of the past and the victimization of the abject.

With all this impasse implied, redemptive efforts are nonetheless made, opening room for rethinking postpolitical ethics in diverse settings and styles. European art films exude the apocalyptic atmosphere of the absurd world (*Songs from the Second Floor* [Roy Andersson, 2002], *Werckmeister Harmonies* [Béla Tarr and Ágnes Hranitzky, 2001], *Time of the Wolf* [Michael Haneke, 2003]). Global action adventures prefigure biopolitical crises in the posthuman age (*Children of Men* [Alfonso Cuarón, 2006], *District 9* [Neill Blomkamp, 2009], *Blade Runner 2049* [Denis Villeneuve, 2017]). While sci-fi horrors cosmically imagine the fate of humankind (*Prometheus* [Ridley Scott, 2012], *Sunshine* [Danny Boyle, 2007], *Us* [Jordan Peele, 2019]), human dramas heal the trauma of the Indian Ocean tsunami (*Hereafter* [Clint Eastwood, 2010], *The Impossible* [J. A. Bayona, 2013]). Some titles designate a year for ecological doomsday (*2012*, *2030* [Nguyễn Võ Nghiêm Minh, 2014]). Abbas Kiarostami searches for his former child actors in their village, which was ruined by an earthquake in Iran (*Life and Nothing More . . .* [1992]), whereas Christopher Nolan searches for humanity's new home across the galaxy as Earth becomes uninhabitable (*Interstellar* [2014]). Furthermore, a catastrophic event has positive potential to reveal hidden truths or open new futures even if nothing appears changed or is guaranteed to change, as we see in later chapters (*Donnie Darko* [Richard Kelly, 2001], *Life of Pi* [Ang Lee, 2012], *Himizu* [Sion Sono, 2011]). Catastrophe thus makes cinematic imagination come into full bloom.

6
Human History in (Post)Apocalyptic Cinema

Apocalypse between Revelation and Repetition

As explored in Chapter 5, the disaster genre tends to conventionalize the sublime dimension of catastrophe while also exposing it and thus can be reframed in the broader cinema of catastrophe. This reframing further opens room for accommodating the most radical sense of catastrophe, the end of the world noticed in some apocalyptic films. It is little wonder that global catastrophes have 'nurtured' the cinematic imagination of apocalypse ever more visibly, either premediating worst-case scenarios about our future or preparing us to embrace them with some perverted fascination or liberating anticipation. The latter, interestingly, evokes the religious etymology of 'apocalypse' as 'un-covering': the ultimate disclosure of something hidden, some higher truth that has been hitherto concealed or ignored in our (sinful) status quo but can shatter it to bring about a more positive (redeemed) order. Implying the revelatory power of catastrophe, apocalypse thus marks not the end of everything but the replacement of the old world with a new one, just as the Book of Revelation foretells divine violence and judgment followed by visionary descriptions of heaven. In other words, apocalypse indicates the tipping point of the need to purify the current world, its turning point to restart from ground zero. What matters is not so much apocalypse as a postapocalyptic tabula rasa on which to write history anew.

However, a postapocalyptic reality would not be paradisiacal, as in the Bible. What if the destruction of the old does not lead to the creation of the new? If our civilization someday causes its own devastation that renders Earth uninhabitable, is it not plausible that a group of super-rich elites will rely on already privatized space travel to abandon the rest of us, as is depicted in *Elysium* and *Interstellar*? What would then happen to the abject people who do not have a ticket to the space station? How would their plight resonate with us now? To tackle these questions, we should address postapocalyptic cinema as a hypothetical platform for revisiting our present and reconceiving its future via dystopian imagination.

I conduct two case studies in this regard, wherein, beyond an individual drama, the entire human history is at stake. First, Bong Joon-ho's *Snowpiercer* (2013) deserves critical attention due to its allegorization of the global system from many angles while narrativizing multiple catastrophes. The initial postapocalyptic situation develops into the abject agents' revolutionary struggle for freedom and equality, which turns out to be just another catastrophe repeatedly necessitated for the sovereign system's self-maintenance. This systemic cycle of catastrophes is eventually broken by another apocalypse that literally leaves nothing but a tabula rasa with some primordial potentialities. Second, what could emerge from such a 'clean slate' can be seen in George Miller's *Mad Max* series. The postapocalyptic wasteland caused by a nuclear war here apparently resets human civilization back to ground zero, but the overall development of a new world through technology and biopower is parallel to the old human history as we know it. We can then assume that this new world might inevitably evolve until it ends with such an apocalypse as has already happened in the film's diegesis. Max's episodic saga continues: a nomadic abject hero, he endlessly avoids settling in the evergrowing world as if to escape his potential trauma of re-encountering the very apocalypse.

These two examples complicate the nature of catastrophe or apocalypse in a sort of virtually infinite regression. What we see is no single decisive event that brings a transcendent epiphany, but a series of cataclysms normalized at a higher level. Moreover, though *Snowpiercer* still invests in the revelatory potential of apocalypse, the apocalypse in the *Mad Max* franchise no longer discloses a new future but encloses us with historical déjà-vu. It is a "naked apocalypse" according to Günther Anders (2019): "the apocalypse that consists of mere downfall, which doesn't represent the opening of a new, positive state of affairs (of the 'kingdom')." Such an "apocalypse without a kingdom"—whose prime example is a total atomic war—challenges the disaster genre's typical narrative arc of fall and rise, abjection and redemption, which still works on a microlevel but is subsumed under the cycle of repetition without change on a macrolevel. In this sense, dystopian sci-fi films are symptomatic of our posthistorical, deadlocked temporality. Postapocalyptic futures connect back to our preapocalyptic present, which is already full of global-scale catastrophes. I illuminated this historical implication reflected in the spy genre in Chapter 3 and further investigate its evolution through the time-travel genre in Chapter 7. The current chapter may serve as a bridge between them via the apocalyptic genre.

Snowpiercer: A Global Allegory of Biopolitical Economy and Ecology

Snowpiercer touches on many of the global issues explored so far, epitomizing the turn of the disaster film to the cinema of catastrophe in South Korea. Korean cinema has been more visible in this regard than any other Asian cinema. In the early 2000s the Korean 'adoption' of the American genre began in terms of narrative, style, and subcategories of disaster (skyscraper fire, terrorist bombing, monster attack, etc.). Spectacular blockbusters were produced in this manner, driven by the industrial ambition to emulate Hollywood. Then the trend developed into the Korean 'adaptation' of the genre beyond its mechanical adoption while reflecting Korea's global connections and local traumas as they were related to sociopolitical abjection, economic polarization, and bio-environmental risks (*Save the Green Planet!*, *Tidal Wave* [Yoon Je-kyoon, 2009], *The Terror Live* [Kim Byung-woo, 2013], *The Flu* [Kim Sung-su, 2013], *Train to Busan* [Yeon Sang-ho, 2016]). It is crucial that the heroes are not professional experts, as in Hollywood, but ordinary people, the working class, and the disadvantaged. They become abject agents who act for the sake of stopping (or bringing about) a catastrophe. They show contingent solidarity with the abject through their symbolic and real deaths, and they reveal Korea's biopolitical system itself as catastrophic. For example, Bong uniquely blends all these features into *The Host* (2006), the first Korean monster film globally circulated. But more audaciously ambitious in both scale and impact is the truly global *Snowpiercer*. Based on the eponymous French graphic novel, this apocalyptic sci-fi film was shot in the Czech Republic with a multinational crew and cast and produced with the biggest budget in Korean film history. A megahit in Korea, it also received critical acclaim as well as commercial attention from all over the world.

The global nature of *Snowpiercer* is not limited to the production/reception side. It is the first major Korean film that tackles outright the fate of humanity facing environmental and sociopolitical crises. The opening prologue states that seventy-nine countries began using an artificial cooling system called CW-7 in 2014 to drastically drop the temperature raised by global warming. The shot of jet aircrafts dispersing CW-7 in the blue sky, however, looks as if they are falling, with a grim sound swelling in the background. Then two intertitles sum up the dystopian consequences of using CW-7: the world froze, and all life became extinct except 'the precious few' who boarded Snowpiercer, a supertrain that endlessly hurtles around the planet so as not to freeze in the new ice age. Set in 2031, the story begins by showing that the postapocalyptic survivors are put into a dystopian caste system. A group of deprived tail-section passengers revolt against this system to break free, spread the wealth around, and take over the engine, the symbol of power. Helped by Namgoong, a security expert who can open the doors to the train's different sections, they pass through kaleidoscopic front cars, including extravagant upper-class areas, while fighting against armed guards, also losing most of their lives all the way up to the engine car. There, the leader of the revolution, Curtis, faces the head of the system, Wilford—the transportation magnate who founded the train's maker, Wilford Industries.

Many viewers see this sci-fi film as a parable of global capitalism projecting its current symptoms onto a dismal future. Globalization is here more complete, no longer transnational but literally stateless. There remains no nation, only the iron ark that annually circumnavigates the single global network loop linking all formerly disconnected (national) railroads. The world is reduced to this private corporate empire, a seemingly ultimate neoliberal society of the 1 percent versus the 99 percent. The elite ruling class takes up most of the space on the train and enjoys all luxuries, whereas a myriad of second-rate citizens suffers from misery under oppression. The have-nots aim to occupy the engine as if to update Occupy Wall Street.

Nevertheless, let me note that the train has less to do with a capitalistic economy than it appears. The tail-section habitants do not strictly represent the Marxist sense of the proletariat as the working class that earns wages by offering labor power. Called the "scum," they are acquiescing stowaways of sorts who do nothing productive, or at least we don't see them working. Instead, they are retained as a pool of potential workers from which to extract a protein gel maker, a sushi restaurant cook, or a violinist for a front-car school, serving the system at assigned places where and when needed. They thus rather embody a type of scavenger-like lumpenproletariat, a classless class exposed to the full force of deprivation, performing duties even out of self-abnegation. And the most crucial place they occupy in the system turns out to be the tiny underfloor engine room where small children, taken away from their parents, are horrendously trapped with no extra space and work as replacement parts for extinct machinery. Because these children must also be periodically replaced (after being exploited to death), the reproduction of the tail car rabble is necessary for the smooth supply of new children. Paradoxically, this biological demographic function of the lumpenproletariat evokes and even realizes the Latin etymology of 'proletariat': *proletarius* denoted those who had no wealth in property, who only served the state by producing offspring, by proliferating (*proles* = offspring). The human waste excluded from the system thus becomes indispensable components of its continuous functioning because of their physical proliferation. It is in the mode of exclusion that they are included in the train. And all this order of social place and human arrangement is controlled under the orders of Wilford, the CEO as sovereign.

What makes *Snowpiercer* a palpable global allegory is therefore its biopolitics underlying the economy. Class economy, though not absent, is biopolitically reshaped, complicated, and encompassed. The "inclusive exclusion" is precisely the condition of bare life, the animal-like subhuman (Agamben 1998, 85). Deprived of political rights, it is to be killed without juridical process, and only through being an outcast is it integrated into the sovereign order, thereby reinforcing its power. Sovereignty is the sovereign's power to proclaim this state of exception to the law. The sovereign can suspend and transcend his legal regime even to save it, especially in emergency crises caused by internal minorities or external enemies, who then are treated as bare lives to eliminate. The biopolitical Latin notion of proletariat may be related to this bare life defined in the Roman law and ruled by divine sovereignty, which underlies the imagery of religious authoritarianism and (non) capitalist fascism in the film.

Not surprisingly, the tail end, where myriad quasi-prisoners are crammed into multideck beds and live in squalor, looks like a concentration camp—the most obvious example of this exceptional state. Anyone who is against the authorities is subjected to an awful summary execution; a man's arm, utterly frozen after being exposed to the icy exterior, is broken into pieces by a hammer. More terrible is the bare life of the child workers. Half-naked and fully shaved, they apathetically repeat some robotic tasks in a virtually zombified state between life and death, truly embodying the ironical Agambenian sense of *homo sacer*: their service for the "sacred engine" is never commemorated as sacred. Compared to the engine compartment, the tail section is in truth less like a Nazi death camp (where inmates are totally mechanized into hopeless passivity since the exceptional state of bare life is already normalized) and more like a normal prison (where inmates could still generate some agency for hopeful activity that could trigger an emergency within the normalcy of incarceration). Indeed, the fighters led by Curtis are sufficiently well organized for a bold riot to subvert the whole regime, a decisive event that amounts to a proletarian revolution. The guards 'kill' them only in this emergency; that is, the normal and the exceptional states are still distinct, unlike their fusion in the camp.

However, it is revealed that Curtis's 'revolution' is merely the sixth in Wilford's program of "revolutions" as repetition (as in *The Matrix* series). It turns out that the train-as-life world, due to its limited space, maintains its homeostasis by regularly reducing the population of the tail car via uprisings. In other words, the regime absorbs the revolutionary force as a structural pretext to activate lethal police violence and to shake off annoying human trash before it overflows. The plot of oversetting the system is already overplotted by the system itself for its necessary resetting. Curtis's mentor, Gilliam, turns out to be Wilford's collaborator; his hidden desire was, shockingly, to have more space in the tail after the envisioned death of many of his fellow riff-raff. And it is Wilford who sent Curtis a series of trigger words hidden in bullets inside protein bars, like fortune cookies, to fire him up for revolution. In terms of class struggle, as the sci-fi trend of apocalyptic catastrophe often shows, the socialist revolution ends up being a simple point of vanishing mediation to the hegemony of the bourgeois master (Paik 2010, 124). Here, an exception is not the breaking of a rule but the rule of the game as such. The emergency is secretly inscribed as part of normalcy via the sophisticated indistinction of the two.

Why is this sophistication preferred to simple killings that could be done anytime? From Wilford's perspective, letting the tail car subalterns have some hope for a better tomorrow might be good to sustain their daily lives with vitality, (re)producing (not commodities but) bodies necessary for the train. They are thus controlled under "cruel optimism" (Berlant 2011): the double bind typical of liberal-capitalist societies in which people are attached to the desire for upward mobility and social equality, though these become unachievable fantasies that impede their flourishing. Wilford modulates the dual frequency of hope and despair and moderates the double track of normalcy and emergency. Besides, the normal, endurable oppression may bring the tailenders some life-simulating tension, whose release is allowed at a tipping point in the form of explosive violence as if their repressed libido climatically blows up. No wonder their bloodiest battle against the guards occurs when the train penetrates a tunnel that has a female name (Yekaterina)—a cinematic cliché about Freudian eroticism, here used for carnage. Of course, the resolution of their deadly drive should lead to the restoration of the system.

This engineering of collective life and death is the core of Wilford's managerial sovereignty. Doing a head count and calculating the desirable scale of a massacre thus become a demographic routine, just as biopolitics began with control over the physical bodies of a population. Watching Namgoong's desperate fight with Franco, the henchman of Wilford's assistant, Minister Mason, Wilford sardonically tells Curtis that they look "ridiculous, pathetic," and that people "devour one another without leadership." A leader is needed to establish order for all lives out of the fatal chaos of animalistic drives; even their explosive release should be for the sake of order. From the Hobbesian viewpoint, this leadership implies power as confiscated from the masses, who make a social contract to overcome the state of nature ('the war of all against all') and keep peace at the cost of some individual liberty under state control. People relinquish their natural power, which is conceded and condensed into political sovereignty, which in turn governs them. Though compared to the biblical monster Leviathan, this sovereignty historically prevented the Church from abusing religious power over law and thus led to the birth of modern secular states.

The problem with Snowpiercer is that the so-called divine Wilford's sovereignty has no basis in social agreement and no boundary between its legal and extralegal exercise because there are only normalcy and emergency as two sides of the same coin without actual law (except for his words as law itself). His guards do not represent public power but evoke the neoliberal trend of privatizing public power, just as his empire is his private enterprise. Its privatized police of sorts protect the high class from the lowest, who are segregated, exploited, and doomed to die somehow for the eternal maintenance of the train. In this regard, Gerry Canavan (2014) reads "necrofuturism" in *Snowpiercer*: anticipation of the dreary future from the perspective of "necrocapitalist colonialism." It means that transnational corporations, even privately mobilizing military forces, continually take over resources and abuse cheap labor from indigenous communities, which are then left devastated. The smooth functioning of today's capitalism depends on the efficient production of death, while this exploitation destroys the conditions for its own expansion (limited resources, labor, their environment, etc.). But we believe that things must remain the same because our society would otherwise be more necropolitically wretched, maybe returning to the anarchic state of nature. Necrofuturism indicates this catch-22 situation: the conditions of the system are unsustainable and futureless, yet there is no alternative to it. Snowpiercer's continual movement at the sacrifice of bare lives is the only possible future for humanity. Likewise, Naomi Klein (2008) critiques "disaster capitalism": the security industry now capitalizes upon disasters by selling surveillance technology, various insurance, and even private rescue corps to those who can afford them. That is, the poorer, the more precarious. Neoliberal free market policies to boost this commodification of safety and its class polarization are pushed through when people are too affected by disasters under the administration of fear. For this "shock doctrine," some catastrophic shocks are intentionally encouraged or even manufactured since the market will eventually benefit from them. Even if Curtis's revolution is carried out as an alternative to the train system, it is induced as an alternative-turning-into-chaos that only justifies the perpetration of a massacre in the interest of the system.

Nonetheless, capitalism as such does not decisively characterize Snowpiercer. Wilford's task is less to benefit a ruling class than to sustain the whole train. Its economy is not about any colonial expansion but about the infinite recycling of finite space and materials, for which revolution as disaster is programmed. While emotionally detached from "ridiculous, pathetic" human nature, Wilford emphasizes his responsibility for continuing 'humanity' in this postcolonial, postcapitalist environment. Not always necropolitics but broadly biopolitics sustains the train as a sort of nature. Wilford may have learned this from experience. For, as Curtis traumatically remembers, the tail end was in the early years a cannibalistic hell because of a lack of food, with people barely living bare lives as they lived on top of each other's bodies, with many older people now being crippled and missing limbs as a result. This self-destructive jungle was worse for the train than real nature, where natural bare lives form the food chain as self-sustaining order, and where each species continues its existence by preying on others. The protein blocks may have been introduced to prevent the tail species' self-devouring, though they were disgustingly made of cockroaches—the metaphoric equation of the scum as worm.

Biopolitical economy thus expands into biopolitical ecology. The entire train should work as a 'closed ecosystem' that keeps in balance scarce resources such as air, water, food, and population in their controlled reproduction. An aquarium section between a greenhouse and a meat freezer, symbolically located near the center of the train, impressively visualizes this ecological equilibrium. It offers sushi, the result of culling some fish, to the resistant group, the target of another culling to happen. The death of one life form feeds another. Among eggs carried to the schoolkids is buried a gun that their pregnant teacher fires at the rebels; signs of life and death mingle. And Wilford peacefully tastes steak, nonchalantly talking about the "thin barrier between life and death." In this respect, the civilization of the train system as opposed to frozen, sterile nature rather emulates another 'state of nature': the lost ideal of fertile nature, a holistic harmony of interconnected species that eat and are eaten along the spontaneous hierarchy of power yet also in a broad circle of energy flow. And for the system's optimization within the worst constraints of space and resources, every class and organism is put in its "preordained position." Each processes given orders while their lives are themselves processed in one way or another for the system's ceaseless operation, its self-sustainability. Nature, including humanity, is perpetuated in this ark, just as Noah's biblical boat was an ecological microcosmos with every kind of animal on board. Its difference from real nature is that the tailenders can proliferate too fast for 'natural selection' to work and can defy the naturalized social order by moving to the front end. So Wilford intervenes to filter some of them off while sending the remainder back to their original place. This modus operandi makes the train a self-sustaining pseudo-nature.

Snowpiercer: Catastrophe as Breakthrough or Dead End

There is, however, a paradox, in that if the engine needs kids from the tail, then their place must change as they are brought to the front. What is more, the young Curtis is supposed to take over the train from the old Wilford, shifting his place, too. This exception to the given positions is essential for the normal functioning of the train. Again, then, the exception is the rule. The first and the last cars thus interlink as if in a feedback loop, with the front fed by the back. The train is like the Ouroboros serpent, its head biting its tail, its linear body forming a circle, just as it runs on the same ring line. The guards shout "Happy New Year!" at the anniversary moment of crossing the Yekaterina Bridge, though nothing is new in the same train circulating the same landscapes. Put differently, the 'cultural' replacement of exceptional elements sustains the normalcy of the system, perfecting its resemblance to 'nature.' The train of the "eternal engine" is equated to nature in its eternal return. Wilford's position is special here. This creator of the train is a godlike figure, worshipped at the church-like school where a video explains the genesis of Snowpiercer. The teacher offers a sermon, "The Revolt of Seven," about a rebellion that ended up with all the rebels' deaths outside, and the schoolchildren chant, "If the engine ever stops, we'd all die!" The school scene makes a musical parody of the religious fundamentalism underlying the politics of fear: be on the road of Wilford the Lord or you shall perish! But paradoxically, his successor would have to be a rebel who can successfully survive brutal battles and knock on the engine car. Revolutions thus function like reviews of job candidates for his position. Curtis, the chosen one, receives the 'fortune cookie' messages like unknown gifts, God's calling, and goes through the test to prove his fortune. The film is then about a divine father's waiting for a qualified son who shall inherit his kingdom. But unlike God, Wilford says, "we are all prisoners," including himself. A mortal being, he is a demigod, not transcendent so much as immanent to the very world that he created and serves as its part.

Curtis stops short of accepting the destiny to be a new pseudo-divine leader, convinced by Wilford's fascist ideology that the leader must do whatever horrible thing is necessary to preserve the community eternally like the genuinely divine engine. Such eternity is also that of the Oedipal cycle: the son becomes a father through the challenge to his father—Curtis's long adventure toward Wilford recalls classic Oedipal journeys (*Apocalypse Now* [Francis Ford Coppola, 1979], *Blade Runner* [Ridley Scott, 1982], etc.). More precisely, Curtis moves from being a good yet weak father (his spiritual mentor Gilliam) to being an evil yet strong father (Wilford), only to find them to be the same big Other, for whom good is nothing but survival and evil is just extinction. However, Curtis rejects becoming a father upon witnessing two kids enslaved for the engine work, or rather, he becomes a father who sacrifices himself to save them, but not a father who sacrifices them to save the engine for all.

This turning point marks his existential decision to overcome his trauma about cannibalism. He was nearly ready to a kill baby, Edgar (whom he later takes as his right arm but eventually sacrifices to capture Mason during a fight). But now he expiates the guilt of being complicit in fascistic bondage among adults who ate the limbs of infants (and the guilt of letting Edgar die) by pulling Timmy, one of the kids, out from the engine compartment at the cost of his arm. For bare life, abandoned by the fascist regime to sustain all humanity, would rather have the potential sanctity of life; without its salvation humanity might be nothing other than machinery that merely works. Curtis's death to protect Timmy from the explosion of the train (and Namgoong's death to protect his daughter Yona) also takes on sanctity by giving life to the next generation. If Wilford is comparable to the authoritative God, the father of discipline and punishment, Curtis turns into a Christ figure, not as God's son but as a new type of father embodying atonement and sacrifice. In sum, he as the abject works as an agent in a double step: first as an agent who acts to regain his subjectivity within the system and then as an agent who deviates from the system and offers himself as a gift to other abject people as an indirect way of paying his debt to the dead abject. The abject becoming a debt-gift in a zigzag contingent connection suggests 'performative agency,' performing the unplanned mission of carrying the potential sanctity of humanity on the edge of the system.

Nevertheless, Curtis's humanistic choice to save the kids and to get off the train (following Namgoong's suggestion) seems naïve, given the unexpected ending that the detonation of the exit door leads to the destruction of the whole train. And it is a polar bear that welcomes into the snowy desert the only two survivors, an Asian girl (Yona) and a Black boy (Timmy)—with the other, White kid slave having died (see Figure 6.1). Life exists out there; however, projecting a magical solidarity or romantic nomadism onto these nonwhite multiracial, even multispecies, orphans might be an unrealistic fantasy. We just face the most primitive state of nature in which the big beast/bear might well prey on the small minors. This is a third ending

Figure 6.1. Only an Asian girl and a Black boy survive the destruction of the train that represents a postapocalyptic human world, in *Snowpiercer*.

that was anticipated in neither Curtis's original plan to make a livable train nor Namgoong's optimistic vision of the thawing livable outside, since both presupposed the continuation of some collective of humanity including themselves. Noteworthy is that the ice age, the initial apocalypse, was unintentionally caused by artificial intervention in global warming, which had already been immanently disastrous. Conversely, global warming had already been characteristic of nature as changed due to the emission of greenhouse gases, threatening yet endurable. It is rather a radical intervention in this nature adapted to long-term polluting human interventions that triggered an ecological breakdown, just as the abrupt cessation of the industrial activity would do (Žižek 2008a, 56). For this reason, the "revolutionary solution" of CW-7 to the climate crisis in the film was more dreadful than the crisis itself. This dilemma foreshadows the dramatic double twist: Curtis's revolution rather brings a massive loss of his class while paving the way for Wilford's system reboot, and Namgoong's solution to this stalemate ends up with the near termination of humanity. We are put in a 'double' double bind: Curtis as an alternative to Wilford fails, and so does Namgoong as an alternative to Curtis. Neither status quo nor change is positive; A is bad, but B is worse; any alternative is sutured back in this hopeless alternative of A or B.

The attempts at postapocalyptic redemption thus bring about the second apocalypse, as if the first one were not enough. In this way *Snowpiercer* exemplifies the cinema of catastrophe beyond the disaster genre. Here, the dazzling spectacle of destruction covers the absence of what should have been there. The extreme imagination of catastrophe betrays the impasse of imagination, the incapacity to imagine a new, better world.[1] Allegorically speaking, it is easier to imagine the end of the world than the end of capitalism, as has often been said. An alternative system is unthinkable even for leftist critics, remaining a negative 'u-topia' or the negative vision of 'no utopia.' And yet Jameson (2004) would elicit "negative dialectics" here. Utopia as negative is a critical response and challenge to the negativity of a nonutopian present, and while the negation of the negative state does not necessarily bring with it a positive synthesis, it could serve as a warning criticism of any imagined alternatives that could cancel each other out, thereby debunking any/every all-encompassing resolution as an ideological illusion. Likewise, we could think that the respective negation of Curtis's and Namgoong's dreams warns

---

[1] This passage on the postpolitical impasse in *Snowpiercer* is developed from my essay on global Korean auteurs (Jeong 2016, 370).

against any easy solution to the complex problems of the train, which resonate with real-world problems. In truth, we could not expect a film to offer a panacea for predicaments that could not be overcome in our reality. Such a happy ending as humans' victory over machines, or the multitude's victory over the dictator, risks being a regressive cliché reviving the good/evil dichotomy (Paik 2010, 129–30).

Not coincidentally, the characters' utopian propositions evoke internegating historical allegories of the train as a nineteenth-century emblem of modern technology. Its spatial movement was a metaphor of historical progress, representing capitalistic expansion, per Wilford's global railway network. Then there was a Marxist turn, with communist revolutions compared to "the locomotives of world history," just as Curtis moved forward to make a better world for the miserable. But when this class struggle is co-opted into the system, Namgoong tries what Benjamin (1968b, 263) suggests is a true revolution: not to stay on the rails of progress for the capitalist or communist utopia, which turned out to be dystopian, but to pull "the emergency break" and exit the train itself. But again, nature as the final utopia is almost dystopian since humanity is nearly extinct. No utopia comes, paradoxically realizing its etymology of 'no place.'

Of course Namgoong had the utopian vision of a thaw, but he did not foresee that the ice was melting to the point of setting off an avalanche that could wipe out the whole train when it was impacted by a small blast, per the butterfly effect. Contrary to the mysterious advent of the ice age following humans' direct intervention in nature, the avalanche is thus caused only by an indirect intervention. That is, it is nature that blows up the world, though signaled by the bombing, as if humans deserved a punishment that they could not directly inflict on themselves. Then who are these humans? The front car residents remaining in the train after the slaughter of the tail car residents draw our attention at this point—the leisure class whose labor is just to enjoy material comfort and physical pleasure. They relax luxuriously in a clinic, a tailor shop, a café, and a beauty parlor. They drink and dance in loud fashion in a nightclub and snort a hallucinogen called Kronole, lying quasi-naked in furs in a sauna-like salon. They do not care about Curtis's group and do not dare fight Namgoong, who takes their Kronole and furs. Do they not summon up the *last man* in Nietzsche's terms, who, fearful of risk and death, only seeks individual ease and security in the modern state, indulging in instant gratification with no greater cause or big Other after the death of God at the end of Western civilization?

Wilford is, as said, not a god but a demigod of sorts, who steers his privatized state as their pleasure dome immanently rather than transcendently. For them, he is like the late capitalist superego of the free market, which does not prohibit but promotes the pursuit of desire and the consumption of pleasure, ordering "Enjoy!" This is the only thing that they can do endlessly in the postapocalyptic cave. Thus we see "a wholly instrumental definition of power coupled with a radically individualistic justification of pleasure" (Paik 2010, 76). The rave party and the Kronole orgy caricaturize their addiction to apathetic ecstasy, locked in a hedonistic cycle of self-indulgent libido. Psychoanalytically, this libidinal impulse is not so much *desire* based on unfulfillable lack as *drive* that is instantly fulfilled and revived while circulating around its object. Addiction is a negative mode of the drive, its self-destructive perpetuation as *death drive*: not jumping into death but continuing to be undead (like Franco the killing machine's repeated revival from seeming death). The half-naked playboys, when tottering toward snatched Kronole like zombies, even look like, and thus become counterparts to, the child workers in the opposite class.

The implication is that for this bourgeoisie, too, the cultural and natural states are indistinct. Their aristocratic elegance and animalistic decadence may be two facets of the same self-modulating enjoyment, just as the perky teacher suddenly turns into a wild shooter. The state of exception not only occurs through the last car's revolution and massacre but is already normalized in the lifestyle of the 'last men' entrapped in the closed circuit of never-dying drives. Likewise, driving Snowpiercer is nothing but circulating its blind drive to perpetuate the pseudo-naturalized system, which does not really move forward but idles in a circle of 'no progress.' And in this 'end of history' loop, different past eras are jumbled in the postmodern way of time being spatialized. We hark back to the Industrial Revolution with child labor, the Nazi camps to which trains carried Jews, and nuclear power evoked by the engine's radiation of light engulfing the kids. If these relate to the history of technological civilization, its destructive effects that lead back to premodern states are intimated in primitive weapons (dagger, axe, torch, etc.) and the religious motifs (Wilford's cope catches the eye too). The train conveys a reservoir of frozen history. Hence the ultimate questions: Is the world worthy of existing when its self-sustainability means nothing more than the eternal return of the same negative? Does humanity deserve to be preserved when life is driven by no more than self-circulatory addictions at the expense of some people utterly deprived of sanctity? The ending shows the last judgment on this posthistorical emptiness. The avalanche occurs like the manifestation of God's anger, a catastrophe as overturning (the train) and as denouement (a deus ex machina miraculously resolving all issues). This divine violence goes beyond both the brutal force of pseudo-divine sovereignty to preserve the law and the counterforce of explosive rebellion to make a new law. Instead, it destroys all law, the entire order of things. Not proposing a future, it just disrupts the present along with our guilty comfort about the status quo (we are the 'last men' in reality).

However, Yona and Timmy survive 'after all.' They are thrown into the absolute outside of the posthistorical world. Back to the other end of history, this outside is prehistorical, with only one bear standing on 'ground zero' (like a dog at the postcatastrophic ending of *Dogville*). Would history as we know it repeat then? Or could an unknown different history start? Or would there be no more history but an epilogue of three bare lives before their slightly delayed death? Whatever may happen, this open ending marks a new start of time whose eternal return should be that of its form and not the same content. Or at least we should believe so because life would otherwise be meaninglessly homogeneous. The tabula rasa onto which the kids step, as if to land on a new planet, is thus extremely precious—precisely because it is not the beginning of the next story/repetition. In this sense, divine violence can be atheistically viewed as rooted in the human will to justice that is divinely unreachable yet necessarily desired. The thaw is not a mystic but a natural phenomenon, which Namgoong captures with his knowledge of snow learned from his Inuit wife, one of the seven who revolted and ventured outside. With no god's order, Namgoong revives the past potential to open a new future, and he uses his hallucinogenic Kronole drug as an explosive to remove the exit door. He is, in short, an addict dreaming of quitting the entire system of addiction. Although nobody else believes conditions to be livable outside the train, true freedom may lie in embracing what is absolutely unknown, or that which we dread. Despite knowing he may die, Namgoong activates this absolute freedom with his subjective, solitary conviction. This is why his performative agency is more adventurous than Curtis's, triggering divine violence unawares. And upon this visionary father's sacrifice, his 'clairvoyant' daughter is given the gift of a new life; Yona—like Jonah, the biblical prophet who survives captivity within a big fish thanks to God—comes out of the train. In *The Host*, a daughter dies in a monster's belly and her father adopts a boy who survives thanks to her care. Now in *Snowpiercer*, a daughter, losing her father, should take care of a boy. A white bear looks at them out there in silence. A truly postapocalyptic time has nothing to begin with but the open unknown.

The *Mad Max* Series: A Postapocalyptic 'Fury Road' of Historical Déjà Vu

Here I move onto the next case studies, but bring back the question left unanswered in the last section. Despite my own conclusion, one could not help wondering what would happen in a sequel to *Snowpiercer* if its ending implied a new beginning of human history. As a way of suggesting a hypothetical answer to this hypothetical question, I draw attention to the *Mad Max* series, a seminal (post)apocalyptic road movie that has tremendously influenced the genre's formation. Since its inception in 1979, followed by two sequels in the 1980s, this Australia-based franchise has retained its legendary status, and after thirty years, the same old director, George Miller, released its impactful update *Mad Max: Fury Road* (2015). In all four installments, what appears left after the end of the world is nothing but an endless road without a home. Each sequel repeats Max the Road Warrior's contingent adventure in spatiotemporal limbo, ending up with him going out alone on the road.

However, under this episodic structure flows a sequential saga of not only Max but also humankind. Evoking the 1970s–1980s oil and nuclear crises, the series initially stages the road as a contested site of declining civilization in the near future, when the lack of energy resources provokes an apocalyptic global war among nations, as narrated in the second film's opening sequence.[2] From then on, the road displays an allegorical landscape of mythic sights, with some clans of survivors emerging on the tabula rasa of history. They struggle for scarce resources like primitive tribes, killing each other to secure water and oil in barren deserts without law. That is, apocalypse leads back to prehistory, as if no future could be imagined, as if history should be rewritten from the beginning, as if the postapocalyptic cinema would thus imagine not any future but an alternative past. Nonetheless, the point is that we see virtually nothing other than a caricature of the same history as we know it. The four *Mad Max* films recycle some phases of humanity's

---

[2] See Doru Pop's (2015) close analysis of the series regarding its historical background, utopia-dystopia dynamics, and aesthetics of recycling.

grand narrative: the lawless state of nature, the transition from nomadism to sedentism, early capitalist imperialism, and absolute monarchy subverted by people's revolution. But then, would this chronology not go on until reaching its apocalypse that rewound time, restarting the very history cycle? What should we see in this closed but potentially endless loop of historical déjà-vu?

It is worth looking at each installment more closely. The original *Mad Max* is set in a preapocalyptic modern society that is already in crisis. The Halls of Justice are destroyed, a policeman peeps at a sex act in the desert like an 'obscene superego,' and crazy bikers go on a rampage and occupy a settlement called Jerusalem. The eponymous hero is a highway patrolman cruising the filthy back roads where criminals forage for gasoline and scraps. But the loss of his buddy and family drives Max mad, and he becomes a vigilante who takes revenge on a motorcycle gang in an off-limits area, that is, in the state of exception to the law. He thus turns into a brutal sovereign killer of bare lives outside the juridical system that he, a former police officer, represented and protected. In other words, social order collapses into an anarchic state, while Agambenian biopolitics replaces institutional politics. The objective justice of law gives way to the subjective justice of vengeance, which will only trigger a vicious cycle of violent retaliation because anybody can claim sovereignty when there is no absolute hegemonic authority. Suffice it to recall such a never-ending cycle of terror and war on terror.

It is no wonder that Max's sovereign vigilantism against self-proclaimed sovereign enemies continues throughout the sequels. As noted earlier, *Mad Max 2: The Road Warrior* (1981) begins with a documentary-style prologue about the global war—supposedly a nuclear holocaust—and a subsequent barbaric state due to the near exhaustion of oil supplies. Through this postapocalyptic return to the prehistorical state of nature, we are introduced to a small community of settlers with an oil refinery under siege by a hoard of biker bandits. Though using remnants of machine civilization, they are virtually primitive-looking nomadic clans fighting for survival in an energy-starved wilderness. Here, scavenging for food and petrol, Max makes a deal with the oil-rich but vulnerable community: to get fuel, he helps the settlers move away from the skinhead bikers hell-bent on destruction and mayhem. But the ending is a bit bitter. Max barely defeats the bandits, only to see not oil but sand leaking from the wrecked tanker he was driving, revealing it to be a decoy. That is, he was caught unaware by the settlers' escape with hidden oil drums. While Max is left for dead, the epilogue says the settlers have later established the "Great Northern Tribe."

The third film, *Mad Max Beyond Thunderdome* (1985), unfolds around one such survivor community named "Bartertown," where Max finds himself after losing his car. No longer nomadic, this big settled market town looks like a mini city-state, signaling the birth of a politico-economic regime for dominion and commerce. It even uses electricity supplied from a methane refinery in the subterranean Underworld. The autocratic Queen of Bartertown, however, wants to take over this underground energy system and makes an offer to Max: he will get back his car and freedom if he accuses the refinery owner of stealing his car and kills the owner legitimately; the town's law allows conflicts to be resolved by a duel to the death in a combat arena called Thunderdome. We then see no other than two gladiators given a sovereign license to kill each other, like *homo sacer* in the Colosseum under the Roman emperor's suspension of the law, which embodies sovereignty at its purest. Put otherwise, the law of Bartertown is self-contradictory yet universal. Thunderdome is in the state of exception to the law against murder, but the exclusion of this state from normal law is included in the sovereign system itself. The law always has its self-transcending potential to be suspended and surpassed by its immanent externality. Again, this sovereignty underlies the vigilantism of Max and many such supralegal (super)heroes too (see Chapter 4).

Interestingly, however, Max refuses to kill the underworld rival, who turns out to have a child's face with Down syndrome. This Levinasian moment of facing the other's face and saving its vulnerable sanctity of life upsets the Queen, who expels Max from her town. He now becomes a sheer *homo sacer*, deprived of any sovereign agency. Here begins a Christian allegory. Near death in the desert, Max is found by a Samaritan girl and hauled to her haven of "The Lost Tribe": a primitive community of marooned children who believe Max to be the legendary Captain Walker they have been awaiting. Max at first denies this role of savior but later helps them, overthrowing Bartertown's ruthless tyrant on their way to find the prophesied "Tomorrow-Morrow Land." While this land of promise turns out to be the nuclear-devastated Sydney (evoking the ending of *Planet of the Apes* [Franklin J. Schaffner, 1968]), it is told that the children have later built a new society, remembering Max left behind in the wasteland.

The latest installment, *Mad Max: Fury Road*, set in a more advanced imperial city-state, further develops the early trilogy's motifs. Its ruler Immortan Joe's immortal power comes from his monopoly on water, oil, and ammunition—three essential biopolitical resources for living, moving, and fighting in the desert. Water falls from Joe's rocky Citadel like a divine gift to people on the ground (evoking Moses's biblical miracle of bringing water out of the rock), but Joe only occasionally permits this, to control people's thirst and submission, echoing the neoliberal trickle-down effect. Joe also commands an army of White skinhead "Warboys" who believe that dying honorably on his behalf would enable their resurrection in (Norse) heroes' heaven Valhalla. They evoke fundamentalist terrorists ready to commit a suicide bombing as a sublime action to glorify their god. The Citadel's biopower system even takes human bodies as energy sources, upgrading Bartertown's methane refinery powered by pig feces. Captives, including Max, are used as "blood bags" for transfusion, imprisoned mothers' breast milk is expressed by force and bartered for other tribes' gas or bullets, and young women uncontaminated by radioactivity are taken as Joe's wives and confined to bear his offspring. If Bartertown blends the Roman Empire with mercantile industrialism, Joe's Citadel eclectically represents patriarchal monarchy, mythic fundamentalism, neoliberal inequality, and industrial bioengineering all together.

The main narrative begins with one of Joe's lieutenants, Imperator Furiosa's, betrayal of Joe, her attempt to flee with his five wives from the Citadel. In pursuit of freedom, she crosses the desert back to the "Green Place," her idyllic childhood homeland. But this nostalgic utopia is revealed to have become a postapocalyptic barren swampland like "Tomorrow-Morrow Land." After a moment of despair, she plans to search for a new shelter across the huge salt flats. However, "hope is a mistake," says Max, who had to join her group for his survival away from Joe. He instead convinces them to return and liberate the watery green Citadel. The only alternative to the oppressive regime would be not the flight toward a lost paradise but the fight to change the regime itself, not the romantic escape into a utopian illusion but the revolutionary struggle for a better system. It should be noted here that Max is no longer a messianic guide to a dream place, a new Christ who is saved by and will in turn save Samaritan neighbors, as in the previous film, but a secular, self-interested man who happens to share the resistant agency of bare lives: in this case, abject wives, Amazonian comrades, and a Warboy awakened to the evil of their patriarch, a Freudian 'primal father.' This contingent female-led solidarity of the abject agents against sovereign power revamps the male hero–centered genre with feminine agency, culminating in the last scene, in which Furiosa—whose prosthetic left arm prefigures 'cyborg feminism'—takes over the leadership of the Citadel in the people's welcome.

Nevertheless, Max is left behind again, or this time, is shown leaving the very utopia he catalyzed. He disappears among the cheering crowd (into the wasteland), just as a typical western hero rides into the sunset horizon of Monument Valley after fulfilling the mission of (re)building a community against villains or indigenous enemies (see Figure 6.2). To reframe Jameson's (1973) concept, the western hero is a sort of "vanishing mediator" who mediates between two opposing states—nature versus culture, freedom versus security, individual versus society—only to vanish upon the transition from one state to the other. If, as Lévi-Strauss (1955) contends, mythologies offer logical models or, say, imaginary solutions to real contradictions, the western should be considered the American mythology par excellence. More dialectically speaking, à la Jameson, the hero vanishes while bringing about a settled, civilized community that contradicts his free spirit of unbound individualism. Notably, this spirit is nevertheless immanent in the community as the American frontier spirit itself. The hero never really vanishes in this sense. That is why the genre sustains itself through repetition, restaging in similar films with similar heroes those same contradictions, which thus remain unresolved and thereby repeatedly remobilize the American ideology.

Without doubt, the *Mad Max* series looks like a motor-driven western, with vehicles replacing horses. But Max's 'recurring' vanishing mediation demands more subtle attention. He does not vanish as the frontier spirit incarnate that should move on along the boundary between nature and culture. His vanishing instead intimates a deep skepticism about any civilized society that might end up with such a catastrophe as he has experienced. Though

Figure 6.2. Just as in the prequels, the road warrior in *Mad Max: Fury Road* leaves the community he has saved, like a vanishing mediator.

seeking peace of mind after the loss of his wife and child, he says he is "the one who *runs* from both the living and the dead, hunted by scavengers, haunted by those I could not protect." Put otherwise, Max has not yet overcome the trauma of failing to save his family while paradoxically avoiding facing their ghosts and resolving his trauma. This self-contradiction continues, as he never settles in a new community of the people that he succeeds in saving, maybe because he is afraid of a much bigger potential trauma he could never prevent, the future self-destruction of the community itself. Does he not repeatedly run from another apocalypse in this sense?

In psychoanalytic terms, Max is still in melancholia without moving on to mourning, without embracing and thereby overcoming the loss of his love object. This trauma, by extension the apocalypse, caused the loss of his social subjectivity and legal identity, too, his abjection from the symbolic order, that is, his symbolic death. Like many abject characters in the cinema of catastrophe, he is in limbo, stuck between two deaths, symbolic and real. A living dead, so to speak, he precisely describes himself as "a man reduced to a single instinct: survive," a man who wants nothing more than mere life. He does not vanish through a self-contradictory, self-sacrificial mediation of a big cause but returns to the road by way of protecting himself from the risk of real death in any potentially catastrophic regime. His recurring vanishing is thus a sort of survival strategy, a nondialectic wish to exist just as an abject rather than regaining subjectivity at the risk of death. Its nomadic instinct is not any unfulfillable *desire* for an unobtainable object but the undead *drive* that only desires its sustainment, instantly fulfilled whenever repeated, satisfying itself by merely circulating the object and not reaching it. The road does not lead to utopia but persists as *atopia*: the place of self-displacement and self-abjection with no origin or destination, no hope or home—I elaborate on these terms in Part IV.

Preapocalyptic Yet Already Catastrophic

In some sense, Max's 'atopian' drift fits for continuing to make deals and connections based on common abjecthood to perform contingent tasks, and this performativity has crucial ethical potential, as we will see later. In the case of Max, however, it is noteworthy that abject agency activated for a temporary mission is prolonged through recurrence and preferred to ultimate resubjectivation. This aspect somewhat resonates with our way of living in this posthistorical, if not postapocalyptic, age. Whether called postmodern or "liquid modern" (Bauman 2000), subjectivity now takes on less fixed identity than modulable agency controlled to freely adapt to new demands, skills, stimuli, and markets in a fast-changing, ever-upgrading world. Corresponding to what Deleuze calls "societies of control"—a free-floating, flexible control (see Chapter 7)—this agency of constant self-modulation underlies the neoliberal lifestyle, in which private security, endless competition, instant pleasure, and social networking are prioritized over public commitment, symbiotic cooperation, sublime duty, and community building. In a nutshell, the law of the jungle or desert, where everyone fights everyone else in the *Mad Max* world, is not too far from the individualistic survivalism permeating our reality. Max's recurrent avoidance of the potential repetition of a past apocalypse is, then, symptomatic of our modus vivendi: living in the so-called perpetual present after the 'end of history,' thereby avoiding confronting the potential end of the world signaled by the global risks that this relentless civilization historically adds up.

There is one further link between Max and us. Given that the nuclear war in the film series was triggered by the international competition for energy as capital, Max's skepticism about any settled community might indicate his concern over its potential development into a nation. Every micronation he encounters is driven by negative biopolitics, and perhaps he cannot surmount his deep disillusionment with any collective form of governance despite his participation in revolutionary fights. At this point, are we not reminded that the past decade—under the third wave of globalization, as noted in the Introduction—has witnessed bizarre extreme variants of such distrust in state power among right-wing freedom fighters, Christian fundamentalists, Trump supporters, climate denialists, anti-intellectuals, conspiracy theorists of the 'deep state,' and recently, self-claimed antifascists like violent opponents of COVID-19 vaccination and regulation? Although it is time for all countries to unite against global crises, those antigovernmental individualists disrupt this collaboration from within their nations. They ignore, overlook, or misrecognize the nature of the crises; chalk them up to politically distorted targets; and absolutize the here-and-now pursuit of free choice and self-indulgence. Facing the pandemic, their 'freedom fundamentalism' without responsibility confuses the rights of life and death and justifies the state of nature in the middle of civilization: the fittest or at least the lucky will survive! Worse still, personal freedom is claimed in public space, increasing public risk, dividing public opinion, causing the enforcement of public power and consequent damage to civil society, and thereby delaying global solidarity for overcoming the crisis. We will have to pay such a disastrous price for avoiding looking into bigger and bigger global risks like climate change. Put otherwise, where we continue to ignore the serious possibility of apocalypse, we already live in a catastrophic world. What we should indeed see in the *Mad Max* series is the potential of this preapocalyptic—yet paradoxically already catastrophic—future. Or we are already in it.

The final title card of *Mad Max: Fury Road* reads: "Where must we go . . . we who wander this wasteland in search of our better selves?" But unfortunately, we cannot help concluding that perhaps no *Mad Max* sequels, if made, could give an answer. The nuclear war in the series triggers the naked apocalypse without a kingdom I mentioned earlier, not starting a new history but restarting the old one. The boy, the girl, and the bear left at the end of *Snowpiercer* could have been a new Adam, a new Eve, and a new serpent in a new Garden of Eden without the old Fall, but their offspring are stuck in the *Mad Max* wasteland, as though they represent fallen abject humanity without redemption. Max is not a new Christ like Neo in the *Matrix* franchise, either. If Neo still incarnates the need to believe in a spiritual dimension transcending the postapocalyptic matrix of programmed reality, Max embodies not such "an inflation of faith" but "a loss of belief." No longer a heroically sacrificial classical savior, Max is close to the precarious and ambivalent "modern self" that Jörn Ahrens (2009, 61–64) finds in modern apocalyptic films, especially *12 Monkeys*—"the impossible self" whose identity crisis is unredeemably marked with "a loss of reason, coherency, and self-confident approach to its artifacts." Let me recall here that like *The Terminator*, as noted in Chapter 5, *12 Monkeys* even sends the protagonist back to a preapocalyptic point for a mission supposed to serve as a postapocalyptic redemption. However, the apocalyptic pandemic itself is not prevented, and the hero falls into the traumatic time loop in which his younger self has always already witnessed his later death without salvation. The next chapter looks into precisely such time travel paradoxes evolving in the cinema of catastrophe and their biopolitical and ethical implications.

7
The Time Loop of Catastrophe in the Mind-Game Film

Mind-Game Time Travel and Retroactive Causality

As explored so far, today's cinema of catastrophe is not a conventionally formulated genre but rather a comprehensively characterized phenomenon that reflects biopolitical, ethical, and aesthetic implications of global catastrophes. It permeates many genre and nongenre films as well as subgenres of the disaster film. Following the previous chapter on postapocalyptic sci-fi, this chapter further investigates the destructive yet revelatory power of catastrophe and its dilemmatic posthistorical repetition through time-travel films. We will see how time travel both promotes and complicates our discussions of the sublime, sacrifice, sovereignty, and abjection. For this study, let me begin by approaching time-travel films as *mind-game films*. By this term, Elsaesser (2021) means a mode or tendency of contemporary cinema to play games with characters who do not know what is going on (*Silence of the Lambs* [Jonathan Demme, 1991], *Se7en* [David Fincher, 1995], *The Truman Show* [Peter Weir, 1998], etc.) or with the audience, from whom crucial information is withheld until the end (*Fight Club* [David Fincher, 1999], *The Sixth Sense* [M. Night Shyamalan, 1999], *Memento* [Christopher Nolan, 2000]). Protagonists usually have an extreme mental condition or a psychic disorder, playing games with other characters' or viewers' perception of reality (*A Beautiful Mind* [Ron Howard, 2001], *Oldboy* [Park Chan-wook, 2003], *Eternal Sunshine of the Spotless Mind* [Michel Gondry, 2004]). Common motifs include the suspension of causality, delusion between reality and imagination, alternative timelines, parallel universes, trauma and emotional disturbances, identity as contingency, and fate as chance. Consequently, mind-game storytelling is as complex as its diverse terminology: "forking-path," "multiple-draft," "modular," "fractal," and "puzzle" narratives.[1] It stimulates philosophical "thought experiments," raising ontological doubts about other minds or worlds and epistemological questions about how we know what we know.

When it comes to catastrophe, such thought experiments are notably activated through the hypothetical imagination of reversing time to disable the chance of catastrophe itself. What has already happened appears as what should/could have been averted and even turns into what has not happened. But this process of 'undoing' a past event involves a step-by-step mind game with causality. The first step is the belated recognition of one's failure in the sense of the 'if-only': if only I had done not 'A' but 'B' to prevent it! This regret begins with Freudian retroaction, the deferred action of looking backward in time to detect causes for later effects. I belatedly understand that 'A' was the real cause of the event, positing 'A' in a causal chain hitherto unknown to my mind. Causality is thus less an objective relation of events than a subjective inference drawn by the observer. That is why historians describe historical events as if they necessarily had to happen from the present perspective, and why a narrative "'configures' what would otherwise be a simple succession of events into a 'meaningful whole'" of causes and effects (Simons 2008, 121–22). Likewise, one can overcome trauma by articulating its fragmented memories in a lucid narrative. This is the symbolic process of facing and accepting the cause of the trauma, thereby leaving the past behind and moving toward the future—like the psychoanalytic turn from melancholia to mourning.

This *retroactive causality* implies our potential to change the past, if not actually at least etymologically and ethically: I do not merely find 'A' in the past but insert 'A' into the past, which thus changes into a new past, and I choose 'A' as the determinant cause of the fateful event. The causality, paradoxically, then loses its fateful force because I embrace the given as chosen of my own free will. My freedom breaks the closed circle of determinism, realizing Nietzschean *amor fati*: love your fate and you will be freed from it! This freedom traces back to Kantian ethics noted in Chapter 5, the moral sublime of our self-determination to accept even an unfavorable and unexpected situation. Instead of trying to avoid it in vain, we can retroactively recognize and choose its cause, which has been hidden in the chain of fatal causality.

---

[1] To map such complex narratives with various cases studies, see, among others, Warren Buckland's edited volumes on puzzle films (2008, 2014). Elsaesser, however, emphasizes multiple dimensions of the mind-game film that are irreducible to narratological puzzles assumed to be solved, as I do.

Even if we decide to avoid a destined situation that we actually want to accept, this may also suggest the exercise of 'freedom against desire' as we enable and choose the possibility of our act changing the causal chain. Likewise, we can change not the actual past but its potential by adding a new possibility and choosing it as the determinant cause of our changed future. In *Minority Report*, despite the Precrime system's prediction that its top agent will kill the murderer of his son, he blocks his explosive inclination to pull the trigger on a man who turns out to be the murderer. By doing so, he breaks the closed circle of determinism and changes "the true value of modal propositions about the past" (Žižek 2006, 202). Kantian freedom is neither entirely determined by preceding causes nor dependent on pure contingency. Although I am determined by various causes, natural or motivated, I have the freedom "to retroactively determine which causes will determine me," including those that I can posit in the past. The courage to accept this responsibility underlies ethics (203). Not opposing determinism, freedom thus takes on retrospective determinism, a self-determined necessity that is recognized, constituted, and assumed after the fact. "The effect is retroactively the cause of its cause" in this *après-coup* (204). Retroaction enables a cognitive time travel to cause an unthought cause of the present effect.

Do time travels in films, then, not physically actualize this virtual time travel in mind, literally going back to the past and engaging in new causes for future effects? That is to say, I see not only 'A,' the cause of my trauma, but also a new possibility of having chosen 'B' that would not have caused the trauma. Not limited to accepting the only option, my free will then turns into 'freedom of choice' among different options. Not loving my fate, I want to cancel it and make a new one. Not moving on to mourning for the dead, I will carry my melancholia until I eradicate its cause and save the dead back in the past. This desire to change the actual past stimulates sci-fi time travel in the cinema of catastrophe. As noted in Chapter 5, the time-travel narrative combines postcatastrophic redemption with precatastrophic prevention by sending the protagonist from a postcatastrophic situation back to a precatastrophic time in order to prevent the assumed disaster. There can even occur multiple time travels with new choices of C, D, E, F, and so on, which multiply a cinematic equivalent of 'virtual history,' pivoting around a fork of the 'if-only' that branches off to multiple 'what-if' situations. The past is repeatedly rewritten with newly posited causes. From the cognitivist viewpoint, the past is indeed a palimpsest overwritten with "nearly true hypothetical points" that may have been elided yet still present within the mind

(Branigan 2002, 109–10)—characters revisit such points in forking-path or multiple-draft films, including time loop films (*Blind Chance* [Krzysztof Kieślowski, 1987], *Groundhog Day* [Harold Ramis, 1993], *Sliding Doors* [Peter Howitt, 1998]). In sum, the cinematic time travel turns the epistemological retroactivation of temporal potential into an ethically sublime act of changing causality with free will. And time travel for a precatastrophic prevention can be the utmost ethical act when costing the time traveler's life. The heroic self-sacrifice for redemption is not a hackneyed theme but, by nature, the culmination of this sublime mind-game action.

Donnie Darko: An Indeterminate Text on Free Will

Admittedly, Hollywood films leave little room for our contemplation of this radical sublime. Time travel often appears as a sci-fi cliché, reducing an ethical act into a superheroic gesture. Suffice it to recall Superman's postcatastrophic redemption, or say, resurrection of his dead girlfriend in *Superman* (Richard Donner, 1978). He flies around the earth in its counterdirection so rapidly that it starts to rotate backwards, and thus time is rewound until before her death. This last-minute rescue achieved through time travel—ridiculously rather than sublimely—only suggests that Superman is divine rather than human. Even the more humanized Spiderman always suddenly appears like a deus ex machina to save endangered people, especially when they fall out of Manhattan's skyscrapers, as if to cinematically compensate for the failed rescue of victims fallen from the Twin Towers on 9/11. Spectators of such superhero-disaster films already know that they will enjoy the thrill of predictable postcatastrophic redemption that is predetermined in the genre system rather than reflecting on the genuine human struggle for freedom or sacrifice. In this context, I draw special attention to Richard Kelly's sci-fi-tinted cult film *Donnie Darko* (2001) as both a unique symptom of and an exception to the Hollywood disaster film. Its unique time travel occurs not along the linear chronology of an actual world (as in the *Terminator* and *Back to the Future* series, etc.) but in a virtual world whose twisted temporality is not determinate. Let me suggest different possible determinations of this indeterminate text.

The standard interpretation is based on the director's fictional *Philosophy of Time Travel*, the book presented in the film as written by Grandma Death and given to Donnie (extracts from it are included on the film's website, DVD extras, and director's cut). In brief, a Tangent Universe (TU) branches off the Primary Universe (PU) when a jet engine crashes into Donnie's bedroom while he sleepwalks outside, led by a giant bunny man, Frank. But as it is inherently unstable, the TU will collapse in twenty-eight days and take the PU with it if not corrected. Closing the TU is the duty of the Living Receiver, a weird teenager, Donnie Darko, who can wield such supernatural powers as telekinesis and mind control. At the end of the given twenty-eight days (during which what we see is the TU and not the presumably suspended PU), let's suppose that Donnie uses his telekinesis to detach a jet engine from an airplane into a "time travel portal" created by God, which appears as a tornado wormhole; this is the way of warping time he learned (see Figure 7.1). Then, at the moment of the engine's fall, he decides to stay home and accept death in the crash to keep the PU going without the intervention of a TU. In short, a disaster occurs at the beginning, Donnie is set as the juncture of two universes, and his time-reversing power enables him to prevent the apocalyptic collision of the two worlds, at the cost of his life. Here, the final destined apocalypse seems assumed to be a one-time event that will end both universes. In this fatalistic chain of time, Donnie ethically exercises his freedom to retroactively insert a choice of life and death in the past, a choice that, however, puts him in a double bind of choosing either dying alone in the original PU (in the case of choosing death) or dying with the whole world

Figure 7.1. Time is reversed at the end of the twenty-eight days given to a postcatastrophic world when a tornado wormhole appears, in *Donnie Darko*.

in the dead end of the TU (in the case of choosing life). That is, he will die in either option, but he can save the world in one of them. The point is that he gives himself this preventive choice only after the original disaster, by way of getting to know about his power to reverse time, and that though this power is superheroic, its exertion is sacrificial. Certainly he looks divine in the opening scene; he wakes up on a hill where he has a godlike view of the world over mountains. But this hill is also evocative of Gethsemane, as he is more like a self-sacrificing Jesus and not a never-dying Superman. Even if his sacrifice is primarily concerned with returning his girlfriend, killed in the TU, to life in the PU—that is, his motivation still recalls Superman—Donnie is morally sublime, whereas Superman is simply visually marvelous.

However, we can take another view of Donnie's power since it is uncertain that he enables the time to reverse by his own free will. On the twenty-eighth day, from the top of the hill, he sees a huge tornado, because of which a jet engine is about to fall off an airplane that carries his mother and sister. Cinematically, the airplane appears like an enigmatic spot in the middle of the natural sublime, unfolding in a Romantic-style extreme long shot, but the next shot shows the engine in close-up, rapidly passing through a supernatural wormhole. These two shots present an epiphanic moment at which the start of temporal reversal is revealed through their spatial juxtaposition, followed by a hyperaccelerated backward montage of events that have happened for the past twenty-eight days. Then, convincingly, the eye-like black hole in the engine, flying within the wormhole, is matched with a skull image residing within an eye, taken from Escher's *vanitas* print that hangs on the wall of Donnie's room. Just beside this print, Donnie, fully awake, is now sitting on the bed, laughing in resignation. The point, presumably, is that the same engine is destined to fall at the end of the world, which then is destined to return to its starting point and not to face a one-time apocalypse. In other words, the TU is trapped in a negative eternal return of the same hellish twenty-eight-day-loop with the same traumata, including the death of Donnie's girlfriend, a vicious cycle that will eternally repeat, unless Donnie takes a decisive action. He thus has no superheroic power but the dutiful freedom to choose death by realizing that the original juncture of the two worlds occurred through his survival of the crash of the engine, and thus that he can only fix the situation by sacrificing himself. His vandalistic rage against the conservative and repressive society of 1980s America then turns into a higher-level ethical act concerning the entire universe. In short, antiheroic Donnie's postapocalyptic adventure ends up becoming a preapocalyptic self-sacrifice to get the world back on the right track and out of the Möbius time-strip that perpetually recycles a periodical catastrophe.

At this point, the film's inadvertent connections to history merit attention. It is not only the jet engine's terroristic attack that evokes 9/11, but also the film's temporal setting; Bush senior's 1988 presidential race resonates with Bush junior's presidency upon the film's release just after 9/11. It would not be odd to see Donnie's retroactive prevention of the apocalypse as embodying America's postcatastrophic "yearning to turn back the clock on tragic events" (Stuart 2001). And if we combine the two former interpretations, Donnie could be viewed as having both the power to change the world and the duty to save the world, just like the United States. Likewise, our "respect" for America, just like Donnie's moral sublimity, would come out if the United States used its superpower for its high duty. But in the years following 9/11, the United States lost international respect due to the vicious cycle of terror and the war on terror, which deprived the postcatastrophic world of redemption. More specifically, this circulation of retaliation was initiated by somebody who stood for America's power but did not take moral responsible for its duty. So allow me to suggest a playful allegory: Who should have sacrificed himself, like Donnie, upon 9/11 to save the world if not George W. Bush? In other words, is Donnie not the virtual verso of actual G. W. Bush? We see in him a sort of parapractical redemption, that is, a postcatastrophic fictive reversal of the US president's failure to learn the nature of his power, as well as an unintended cinematic critique of the president's actions.

One might cast doubt on this reading of Donnie's death as an act of poetic justice, that is, of saving the right world through this sacrifice. In fact, his goal is to overcome the dichotomous moral choice of "love" against "fear," the Christian fundamentalist doctrine promoted by suspicious New Ageist Jim Cunningham and the authorities of Donnie's school. Against this simplistic morality that neglects life's complexity, Donnie denounces Cunningham as an "Antichrist," whose house later turns out to hide "a kiddie porn dungeon." Compared to this false Messiah, Donnie appears to be a true savior who, however, also faces a truly existential choice—life versus death, or, on an epic scale, the death of the world versus the death of his girlfriend—like Jesus in *The Last Temptation of Christ* (Martin Scorsese, 1988), which is briefly noticed in the film. But on the other hand, just as this alternative story of Jesus's individual happiness does not change the actual history of Christianity, so Donnie's death does not necessarily prove to be an effective sacrifice for a better world, because it only closes the TU without impacting the PU, where, for instance, Cunningham's dungeon may remain undiscovered by the police.

Instead of religious morality, then, Peter Mathews (2005) highlights Donnie's doubt of religion and the motifs of the unknowable[2] and draws on Leibniz to argue that although our world is the best of all possible worlds, multiple worlds remain equally possible. Both the PU (where he is dead) and the TU (where he is alive) can thus exist hypothetically, and suspended between them, "Donnie is both dead and alive, trapped inside a cinematic box that cannot be opened" (47). By extension, modern science teaches that every event has an unpredictable ripple effect, a set of contingencies that can change the meaning of an action, just as a red car Donnie passes by in the beginning of the film turns out to be Frank's car, which kills Gretchen in the end, but this causal link emerges only when we recognize it retrospectively. "There are no direct causes, only side-effects: reality is made up of contingencies that project us through our possible lives, and to think otherwise would leave us with the same sense of illusion experience by Spinoza's stone"—the stone that thinks it is flying freely because of its own desire, not aware of its cause (47).

This idea needs more clarification in terms of free will. According to Cunningham's morality, free will awards sovereignty to the individual, who must then use it to create happiness; if you are not happy, it is your fault, and you are guilty. Here, free will is predestined to institutionalized ethical inertia. But regarding Donnie's question about whether one could see into the future through a set path of all time predecided by God, his science teacher notes that if destiny were visibly manifested, the choice to act differently would be available, putting an end to the destiny. This suggests that the TU is to be repeated unless altered by Donnie's suicidal determination. His ethical time traveling is, in this sense, nothing other than "repeating" the past moment of the engine terror "differently," breaking the TU's closed circuit of the same repetitive past. Here works a new concept of repetition: repetition in and of difference. It is proper to the foregoing notion of Kantian freedom as a self-determined necessity, and furthermore, to life as *autopoiesis*: a self-organizing system that does not merely result from past

---

[2] Donnie's view of God is ambiguous. Hypnotized, he obeys Frank's orders without knowing his (or God's) "master plan." He does not reply when asked: "Do you believe in God?" For him, "the search for God is absurd if everyone dies alone," and he dies alone. In a sense, he may be not an atheist but an "agnostic," who believes that there can be no proof of the existence of God but does not deny its possibility (King 2007, 90–91). This uncertainty leads Donnie to science and philosophy.

causes but retroactively posits its own causes. It is not simply determined by contingent conditions but self-reflectively determines this determination itself. Life "posits its presuppositions" in this infinite feedback loop, thereby repeating itself with different outcomes at every moment (Žižek 2006, 205). I further link this idea to Friedrich Nietzsche's *eternal return* in Deleuze's (1983, 175–94) sense. It is not a repetition for sameness but a repetition for difference, an insertion of the possibility of difference back in the past for a different future, whether good or bad. What returns is not a certain content, but the same empty form of difference-in-itself that yields a different content. The affirmation of this generative, positive eternal return is what Nietzsche means by *amor fati*. This "yes" to life begins with our epistemological reconfiguration of sublime fate as the precondition of ethical freedom. Unlike Spinoza's stone, our free will is neither free from fate nor knowledge of it. We rather free ourselves only by consciously (re)embodying fate. One may doubt the positivity of a return that requires Donnie's death. But his *amor fati* is all the more sublime because the positive return of a new life is given to the entire world instead. The world will now live a second time.

Donnie Darko: "Time Is out of Joint" and Postapocalypse

It is therefore possible to take the perspective of the world itself. That is, the TU as such could repeat the PU differently and positively after the decisive moment when "time is out of joint." Hamlet utters this line upon encountering his father's ghost, a shocking supernatural event that alters the way he perceives the world. Only when a radical event occurs, Derrida (1997, 10–24) argues, is time out of joint. In Deleuze's (1994, 119–23) words, time is "unhinged" from its circular, periodic movement and experienced only as a pure, empty form of change, marking the before and after of the crack, becoming no longer cardinal but ordinal: the second, third, fourth. Time then repeats itself as "difference in itself." Put otherwise, time-in-itself is the pure condition of difference, eternally returning not with the same trauma or other thing but with the differential event of "time-being-out-of-joint." Similarly, Frank disjoins Donne's time when appearing like Hamlet's ghost father. This big Other's 'animal' form resonates with the surreal jet engine, a 'mechanical' Thing, in their ontological otherness that interrupts the human world. Back home after the catastrophic night, Donnie faces the uncanny face or dark eye of that Thing, the 'mysterious object at noon' that sucks in our vision as the camera zooms in. Just like Alice's trip down the rabbit hole, this image marks the starting point of Donnie's adventure in the TU.

What happens, then, in the second time of the world? The TU reveals the many negative aspects of Donnie's world: the affluent, leafy, White American suburbia with large houses, spacious lawns, and private expensive schools. The fallen jet engine cracks open this wealthy and peaceful community, while literally tearing apart a big US flag hung on the ceiling of Donnie's room and figuratively delivering Žižek's (2002) ironic greeting framed by 9/11: "Welcome to the desert of the Real!" For the unprecedented attack on American soil revealed the unthought Real of sublime antagonism to what the American people had believed was their well-protected reality. Of course the terroristic engine is purely accidental and not political at all, but it works like a violent *objet a* protruding out of the Lacanian Real, or say, the Deleuzian Virtual, the potential realm immanent in the Actual reality. Notably, Frank is also the name of Frank's father, who is a cursed and dead alumnus of Donnie's parents; Frank junior leads Donnie to engage in arson and vandalism, thereby making him into a sort of terrorist. The Frank family may thus stand for an uncanny and undead exception of the society repeatedly ruled by the Bush family at the national level. This social abject figure is cut off from society but roaming around it like a specter that makes social reality inconsistent and liberates what is repressed in reality. And Donnie, as a sort of postmortem figure (his first encounter with Frank and the following sleep could be seen as his symbolic death), becomes a social abject whose resistance to society, sympathy for the other, and horror about apocalypse all mingle and ultimately open another time-world by his second, real death.

Donnie is thus an abject agent of the Real between these two deaths. He debunks political conservatism, moral impasse, educational repression, and sexual ambivalence, revealing how normal reality is perversely constituted. For example, it turns out that Cunningham's religious morality hides a self-contradictory repression that is resolved through his addiction to child porn, while this sexual crime seems an extreme form of the immanently pervasive sexualization of children—contrast the gaudy but celebrated Sparkle Motion dancers' show to the fat Chinese girl's white angel dance. Likewise, when Michael Dukakis and Bush debate on Panama's drug crimes and American connection, Donnie's family members quarrel about their own drug addiction. Personal or national, the dependence on drugs is everywhere, publicly problematic but privately permissible. The White middle-class Americans at the end of the Reagan age thus appear like the Nietzschean "last men," standing for First World 'passive nihilism.' These postmodern individuals are immersed in ever more refined and artificially aroused daily pleasures like drug, food, and sex. Permissive hedonism allows everything trivial but not an excessive core that can threaten their sound conservative morality.

Conversely, Third World 'active nihilism' is found among fundamentalists who risk self-sacrifice for an alleged universal sublime Cause, just like terrorists attacking the First World (see Chapter 12 on nihilism). Though not from the Third World, Donnie plays the role of a terrorist immanent in his society—not a complete outsider to the First World so much as a subversive insider. The point is not how to judge or justify his violence, but how to read symptoms of the Real in a new time of reality. Donnie inspires us to face terror differently than a disaster, against which society unites its different conflicting members. Far from this suturing function, his terror triggers the revelation of repressed social desires and traumas so that we can better look back on the precatastrophic situation and get it back from a new angle. In short, time-being-out-of-joint is not a state to be fixed but a singular event through which immanent but unrepresented social symptoms of the Real erupt onto reality. Donnie's death may be a sort of narrative compromise to tame the further chaotic eruption of the Real. In the restored PU, Cunningham is alive and Bush will be elected in the history that we know. But what matters much more is the TU itself as a liberated time.

I conclude by drawing attention back to Donnie, as his subjectivity would be the matrix of the ethical sublime against the apocalyptic sublime in the end. In truth, he is not a mature hero, and his terrorism does not open a realistic exit from reality. One could even see the film as having been dreamed by Donnie in the hours immediately preceding the crash of the jet engine. The moving song heard at the moment of Donnie's death, Tears for Fears' "Mad World," includes the expression of "dreams in which I'm dying." In this aspect, *Donnie Darko* resonates with mind-game films whose narrative events occupy some ambiguous hallucinatory dimension or turn out to have been dreamed by a dead or pathological hero under extreme mental conditions, such as *Jacob's Ladder* (Adrian Lyne, 1990), *The Others* (Alejandro Amenábar, 2001), and *Vanilla Sky* (Cameron Crowe, 2001). Donnie cannot fight threatening forces of the world, so he might instead dream of the Virtual as Real, where he can more easily debunk and destruct the world. Like narcolepsy in *My Own Private Idaho* (Gus Van Sant, 1991), a radical daydreaming occupies Donnie's mind in this way. *Donnie Darko* could then be a high teen genre film in which a boy with Peter Pan syndrome takes or avoids the coming-of-age narrative with critical self-consciousness. Conversely, Donnie the Nietzschean last man's idealistic resistance to the world is entrapped in a double bind where neither growing (accepting norms) nor not growing (ignoring them) would be the answer.

The implication is that Donnie is not a predetermined Messiah but an indeterminate mind that continues to determine itself and thus changes predeterminations. Likewise, he is also a postmodern subject who composes himself through the experience and embodiment of floating signs whose meanings are indeterminate and contingent. Grandma Death is waiting for God's letter (death?), and Donnie sends her a letter. Gretchen is a stranger who appears on the day of the engine terror by chance, another *objet a* on the side of love as opposed to Frank's death. Donnie's English teacher says that "cellardoor" is the most beautiful compound word, a word that sounds like a beautiful interface surfacing onto the Real, often in the form of daydream. At the end of this adventure, Donnie, the postmortem subject, dies again. His death, however, is not a return to reality but an opening of just another unknown time, even if it could be cyclical. This is the only ethically sublime way of allowing *atopia*, if not utopia, to be cinematically imagined in the apocalyptic closed circuit (see Chapters 6 and 12): a-topia that is not a topos (place) but the nonplaced movement to a different time itself, the self-displacement of the world without anchorage. We do not know where the world will go after Donnie's death, but we know that the world is not the same any more, in light of one person's absence. This tiny change offers no place; it offers, instead, a postapocalyptic atopian time that we live in and from which we retroactively think over the apocalypse past.

Source Code: Sci-Fi Mind Game and Video Game in Control Society

Let us now move onto the second phase of the chapter, the new millennial evolution of mind-game time travel. *Donnie Darko*'s 9/11 allegory, though tangential, gains more significance in this historical context. Donnie's abject agency to save the world seems to have been concretely but complexly developed into the post-9/11 counterterrorist sovereign agency or terroristic abject agency of subsequent Hollywood films. Chapter 3 explored the spy genre in this regard through the professional secret agents James Bond and Jason Bourne, whose abjection from their state organizations leads to the reaffirmation of, or resistance to, those very sovereign agencies. By extension, a new notable trend is the sci-fi mind-game action thriller that experiments with *Donnie Darko*-style virtual time loops created by the sovereign system conducting war on terror. This trend has been increasingly visualized through the cutting-edge computer-generated imagery (CGI) technology of the 2010s since *Source Code* (Duncan Jones, 2011). I investigate this seminal film and touch on related others, drawing special attention to how they complicate all our debates on sovereignty and abjection, the sublime and sacrifice, and catastrophe as revelation or repetition, just as the *Mad Max* series loops the revelatory apocalypse of *Snowpiercer* in a repetitive world history (see Chapter 6). *Source Code* will then appear as an innovative yet problematic update of *Donnie Darko* (starring Jake Gyllenhaal again), a cinematic symptom of the new normal in which a catastrophic or sacrificial event turns into a 'nonevent' while agency becomes transhuman.

As a mind-game film, *Source Code* plays games with both the protagonist and the audience. It begins with US pilot Colter Stevens waking up on a train for Chicago without knowing why and how, because his last memory was of being on a mission in Afghanistan. More perplexingly, the woman sitting opposite him calls him Sean. This is Christina, a teacher colleague of Sean—whose face Colter sees in the mirror instead of his own. Suddenly the train explodes like a bolt out of the blue and everyone dies. However, Colter again wakes up, this time in a dark cockpit, where someone called Captain Goodwin appears on a screen and orders him to identify the train bomber before another bomb hits Chicago in six hours—as per a warning given by the bomber. This mission to identify the train bomber is conducted inside the "Source Code (SC)," a time-travel device that can repeatedly send Colter back into the last eight minutes of a passenger compatible with him racially and physically, namely Sean, so that he can collect more and more clues regarding the identity of the terrorist. The underlying logic is that postmortem memory lasts for eight minutes, during which Colter, though killed as Sean on the train, can deliver the clues to Goodwin from the cockpit. That said, he has to die and resume his extremely frustrating eight-minute lifespan over and over until he completes the mission. It later turns out that Colter was nearly killed in Afghanistan, losing most of his body, and has since been comatose for two months on life support in the SC chamber beside Goodwin's office. Only his brain and upper torso are alive, hooked up to neural sensors to communicate with Goodwin in the brain-projected cockpit on the one hand

and combined with Sean's body to act for the mission on the train on the other hand.

A turning point occurs when Colter learns about his physical abject state, which is used to test the SC, with no chance of recovery. Angry, he demands to be disconnected from life support once the mission is fulfilled, and Rutledge, the SC designer, agrees. Colter finally identifies the bomber, has him caught by the authorities, and thus prevents the second explosion in Chicago. However, he is betrayed by Rutledge, who orders Goodwin to wipe Colter's memory for future missions—except that Goodwin, out of sympathy, secretly accepts Colter's request for euthanasia and helps him put into action a new plan, namely to go back to the train one final time in order to prevent the first explosion and to save every passenger on the train, this in spite of Rutledge's insistence that such past events cannot be altered. After fulfilling this plan, Colter uses the bomber's phone to send an email to Goodwin and to call his estranged father in order to reconcile with him, under the guise of a fellow soldier (i.e., Sean). Colter then kisses Christina at the moment when eight minutes have passed, and Goodwin takes him off life support. Colter dies in the SC chamber, but he survives in the new alternate timeline in which the train arrives safely at Chicago. Colter, now as Sean, enjoys a romantic walk with Christina around the city center while Goodwin, in this new timeline, receives Colter's email, which says they have changed history thanks to the excellent performance of the SC. The film ends with a chamber scene: Colter is lying there, still comatose, waiting for his first mission, yet to come (see Figure 7.2).

What makes *Source Code* a unique mind-game film is its extreme video-game structure. As typically seen in *Run Lola Run* (Tom Tykwer, 1998)—Lola's twenty-minute rush to save her boyfriend repeats three times until her final success—some video-game features have been adapted for complex films narratives: a serialized repetition of actions, multiple levels of adventure, mastering the rules and accumulating points, immediate punishment and rewards, feedback loops, and deadlines (Buckland 2014b, 187). We saw the *Bourne* series also unfolding the double-game narrative of 'leveling-up' and 'navigation.' in which Bourne's mind and body work like a self-orienting, self-curing system to fulfill a mission (see Chapter 3). *Source Code* further uses a double-layered, self-reflexive 'play station.' It is crucial that Colter's mind is not solely injected into Sean's body but is mediated in the form of his whole figure, confined within the cockpit (unlike the paraplegic hero in James Cameron's *Avatar* [2009], whose mind directly connects to his avatar).

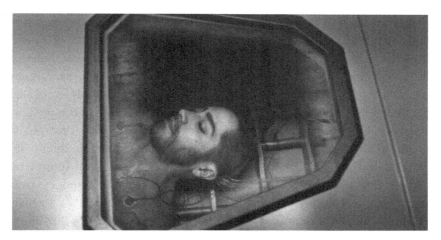

Figure 7.2. The comatose hero of *Source Code* is still alive as a potential sovereign agent even after his sacrificial death during a time travel mission.

This cockpit itself is a virtual space in which Colter as a projected image makes some "rotation adjustments" and "pattern recognition" first to orient himself and identify Goodwin (Hesselberth 2012). In other words, Colter's brain on life support plays a preliminary 'mind-video' game and organizes a virtual psychosomatic system to cope with a new situation and learn from it. This mechanism is extended into the main 'mind-video' game in which Colter sees himself as Sean, his avatar to control in a much more complicated situation. The film then "replicates a role-playing game" by going back and forth between the player in the cockpit (game room) and his performance in the train (game world) (Buckland 2014b, 195). This game world has the structure of leveling-up and navigation, reviving Colter's eight-minute life eight times. Each time he collects pieces of information, explores the train, tests different options, and forms relations with Christina and Goodwin. He thus builds himself up as an efficient cognitive-kinetic mapping system that accumulates data and takes actions in the feedback loop of human and technological interactions, especially learning from his own failures. Apparently nobody could better personify Samuel Beckett's dictum: "Fail again. Fail better."[3]

---

[3] This is often quoted as an entrepreneurial mantra to embrace failure as an essential step for lucrative self-fulfillment. But such positive motivation has nothing to do with Beckett's view of failure expressed in *Worstword Ho!* (1983): the inevitable defeat of every human endeavor and

Source Code also shows a "modular narrative" that presents forking paths (Cameron and Misek 2014). Each train sequence is a module, or rather, the unseen last minutes of Sean's life are the first module that continues to be modulated with differences. David Bordwell (2008), however, argues that although forking-path narratives display alternative worlds or parallel histories, they are not that complex but still conventionally comprehensible. A key convention is "psychological continuity," which the protagonist retains in visiting different futures, growing knowledge and even modifying personality through the accumulated experience of the 'past' futures, as Scrooge does classically (182). That is, different branches of a forking-path narrative do not strictly show incompatible 'parallel' worlds as they are linearly arranged and traversed; therefore, the last branch becomes "the fullest, most satisfying revision" of the past ones (184). *Source Code* is no exception. Moreover, the modulation of the original reality is like refining the selfsame draft instead of writing a totally new one. The mind/video game indeed presumes the gradual development of the mind through the deadline-bound progress of action toward a conventional happy ending. The primary rule of the game is no other than that of classical Hollywood narrative: character-driven, goal-oriented, problem-solving continuity.

Paradoxically, the postclassical newness of *Source Code* comes out of the very continuity that Colter's undamaged, sober mind retains. Though physically comatose, he as the game player has none of the common pathologies among mind-game films, such as amnesia, paranoia, and schizophrenia. But as his inherent brain can adequately function, he is under extreme pressure to maximize its capacity for figuring out a puzzle in an insanely stressful situation set up by a ticking bomb. He suffers not from his mental condition but from this external environment in which his performance, unless correctly done, gets him punished by death again and again in his continuous mind. Traumatic are not only the flames of the explosion that engulf him but also this helpless re-experience of being annihilated, like a repeated torment by an unforgettable, terrible memory. What becomes complex is thus the narrative of double death mentioned earlier; Colter, symbolically dead in a coma, struggles to survive until real death, but this struggle in abjection itself is punctuated with multiple 'deaths' that are both actual (in the train) and virtual (in the SC). That is, within the limbo stage between two deaths, he

---

communication (Schlottman n.d.). Beckett's edging to full failure is co-opted as the progress toward full success in neoliberal capitalism.

dies several times and prepares for revivals in the cockpit—his posthumous limbo in which he is neither really dead nor alive, thus abject by definition. There are abjections within abjection.

Of course, Colter is not biopolitically abjected by his sovereign military system. From his physical abjection, he is instead retrieved to work as an unprecedented sovereign agent who has to tackle an all the more challenging emergency, which no passenger in the train knows about actually. The states of normalcy and exception coexist here on the brink of destruction. This dangerous, precarious condition both requires and enables him to optimize the use of all his abilities and skills trained in the system, including the SC. Although he has no pathology, his agency with this maximal efficiency evokes "productive pathologies" of mind-game film heroes (Elsaesser 2021, 98–104)—just as Bourne's amnesia boosts his activity. The notion of agency implies this ambivalence: it is motivated by a goal in certain restricted circumstances that inhibit its achievement but would dissipate if it is achieved. The agent is then impeded and empowered at the same time by constitutive constraints of action. Deterministic conditions enable the performative activation of free will. Colter's traumatic, claustrophobic train ride is a 'closed circuit' with no end, no exit, but his desperate acts open up unknown choices to make.

Notable is the sociohistorical backdrop of the type of agency that Colter reflects, which broadly resonates with the turn of modern "disciplinary society" to postmodern "control society" (Deleuze 1992). If Foucault's notion of discipline is a long-term process of subjectivation in a set of different, confining, coercive institutions with central systems of plans, rules, surveillance, and punishment, Deleuze contrasts it with his somewhat ironic idea of "control." The society of control does not govern individuals from the top down but promotes self-control with the flexible agency, the capacity for continuous self-modulation through numerous short-term projects as well as endless lifetime education. Individuals are encouraged to be 'free choosers' responsible for their choices, internalizing entrepreneurship and adjusting to decentered environments of information highways, boundless networking, and the free circulation of capital. Control is thus a name for agency optimized for postindustrial cognitive, emotional, and financial capitalism (see Hardt and Negri 2000). Capital exists as immaterial assets overwhelming material ones: intellectual properties, affective services, and financial goods. Its agents are required to acquire knowledge and foreknowledge, relational and communicative skills, and technical adaptability to high-speed data processing. We are in fact all such agents, often distracted by information overload during our daily practices of digital multitasking. Mind-game films, then, appear as disciplinary machines "reformatting the body in view of tasks and affordances the control society requires from its dysfunctional functioning members" (Elsaesser 2021, 291). The new society disciplines us in this new way of controlling—or forcing us to control—new cognitive-kinetic skills.

This late-capitalist society is inseparable from neoliberal globalization. While work becomes flexible in the free market of people, goods, services, and capital without borders, workers become easily hurt, casualized, fired, and dehumanized in an economic 'war of all against all.' In this new Hobbesian state of Nature, the safety net to protect precarious labor from aggressive capitalization disintegrates to the extent that abjection is no longer exceptional but normalized. The abjection, as well as all dangers that Bond and Bourne undergo, allegorizes this working condition. Colter's case is all the more traumatic as he loses not his job but his life, and he needs not just self-healing but self-rebooting with continuous upgrading. Moreover, his temporary work under a pressing deadline leaves no second for leisure. He has to rapidly adjust to unpredictable situations while reinforcing cognitive power, mapping ability, corporeal tenacity, flexible mobility, and other qualities demanded in a globally expanded workspace and competitive market. He is, namely, a casual worker who works like an entrepreneur, "resolving the quandaries generated by vexingly volatile and constantly changing circumstances" in the age that Zygmunt Bauman (2006, 3-4) dubs "liquid times"—the current postpolitical age in which social structures, welfare systems, solidarity, and long-term plans all decompose and melt.

However, it is crucial that the 'liquid' condition of life and work—which are now indistinguishable—is sustained by the 'solid' sovereign system of global capitalism, its security apparatuses for the automated surveillance and supralegal intervention. This system, as well as American cinema reflecting it, adapts "the working population to the social technologies that promise their economic survival, maintain civic cohesion, and assure America's hegemonic position in the world" (Elsaesser 2021, 106). Superhero-like secret agents are "harbingers of the 'new normal'" that applies to us in this context (272). Subjects are thus still ideologically reproduced in this postideological era, but only as self-contradictory agents like 'CEO-workers.' They embody the anarchic notion of control, self-making freedom, and free-floating autonomy, which is virtually controlled by the system that constantly tests their workability or disposability; this ambivalence colors Colter as an apparently sovereign yet potentially abject agent. What matters for the system is not his selfhood based on memory but his action to perpetuate even at the cost of his memory. He at best makes a deal for euthanasia, which the system unilaterally breaches. He is thus less than a mercenary, enslaved forever and deprived of dignity, unable to kill himself yet forced to die endlessly.

Source Code: Time Travel, Performative Agency, and the Sacrifice of Sacrifice

Obviously Colter's agency is defined as nothing but functionality. Time travel (or "time reassignment" in Rutledge's expression) is mobilized to optimize his counterterrorist function. The past is rewritten over and over to "reverse castration in the aftermath of 9/11, for a veteran's severed body and Homeland Security" (Stewart 2014, 172). However, unlike a common belief, *Source Code* does not adequately present a branching multiverse of ontologically distinct worlds parallel to the actual one. The eight-minute train time is a segment of the past that Colter virtually revisits while actual time still passes in the present, in which another bomb is ticking and to which he comes back after every virtual death to talk to Goodwin. The repetition-with-differences of his action does not bring about any actual alternative reality, insofar as the loop of the past remains reassigned by, derived from, and thus subordinated to the present. The only way to create a new reality is to break the linear connection between the past and the present by changing not small details in the self-closed circuit but its constitutive condition itself. That is, 'if only' the train had not been bombed in the first place, the SC would not have been used and reality would have been different. To change this fundamental cause of the present situation, to 'undo' the train bombing, is what Rutledge prohibits—he privileges testing his program to saving passengers—but what Colter finally pursues as an authentic big cause, at the cost of his life. The sovereign agent then turns into a self-abjected agent of a self-imposed mission against the sovereign system. Likewise, phoning his father and growing a romantic attachment to Christina are unexpected outcomes of his performance that go beyond the rules of the game. Evoking and updating Bourne, Colter embodies 'abject agency' to resist his sovereign system, which exploits his abject body and wants to 'abject' the passengers for its self-sustaining mechanism. He does so by abjecting himself from the system while saving the passengers from being abjected by it.

Nevertheless, does Colter really sacrifice himself to save the passengers, including Sean, or does he actually sacrifice Sean in order to date Christina in the alternate timeline? The director approves of the latter (Brevet 2011), but it entails the contradiction that Colter's mind resides in both Sean's body and his vegetative body still alive in the new reality; how could he then work as an SC agent (whose mind plugs into someone's body) without conflicting with his mind inside Sean? Although time travel itself is paradoxical, the film's otherwise entirely realistic diegesis could be consistent on the assumption that the mind-body unity is retained and sustains one's identity even if one's mind takes another's body in a virtual time loop. It would thus be reasonable to consider that Colter's mind died in the train when his life support was switched off, and Sean's mind, which was replaced by Colter's but held in a sort of coma, comes back to his body in the new timeline. It would also make sense that along with Colter's death, the original timeline is closed—we don't see it anymore—because its changed past (no train explosion) cancels the premise of the present (using the SC). In effect, it cannot but be closed somehow once the train is saved because of this linear causality. The new timeline is the only actual reality, and there are no multiple, parallel worlds. Even if Colter had not chosen to die, he would have disappeared with the entire post-terror situation's getting 'undone.' Moreover, though seemingly self-sacrificial, his death is a case of euthanasia for his own 'rest in peace' as well as a kind of 'suicidal terror' against the inhuman sovereign system. It is not a self-sacrificial death.

His sacrifice is made nonetheless, not with the choice of death but with the choice of undoing the bombing. The latter terminates his life as just noted and resurrects the dead passengers including Sean, who may then become Christina's boyfriend on behalf of Colter. The penultimate scene of Colter and Christina reaching the sculpture Cloud Gate in Chicago is telling. Its earlier imagery appears in the flash-forwards that flash across Colter's mind upon his repetitive virtual death, just like "an unconscious scene of desire (almost subliminal in its fragmentation) getting realized by dint of heroic faith and persistence" (Stewart 2014, 81). To put it another way, he may have unconsciously inserted a new 'effect' (enjoying Chicago) in the future and finally chooses the 'cause' (saving the train) that would bring about this effect. Not retroactive but 'proactive' causality works here, just as Christina's ironic words right before the first explosion, "everything is gonna be ok!," promote his performative quest for an alternative future in which 'everything should be ok.' Facing the sculpture, Colter—now Sean, as reflected on its warped surface—recognizes it and asks Christina, "Do you believe in fate?" This sense of déjà vu may imply a residual unconscious link between Colter's and Sean's minds, an uncanny ethical feeling that one is somehow mediated by and indebted to the other. This connection is mutually beneficial: Christina finds Sean (Colter) more than usually active and attractive in the train and falls into a romantic mode in Chicago; Colter finally reconnects with his father by consoling him on his own (impending) death in the name of Sean as if Sean ventriloquized Colter. The time-travel action adventure thus entails a romantic/family subplot of remasculinization and reconciliation. Colter helps Sean to be a charming man, and Sean helps Colter to be a good son.[4]

The ending is open to yet another hermeneutic turn. Garrett Stewart touches on the possibility that the SC might have programmed the flashforwards as "appeasing free-associations of potential escape, anodyne images (u-topic, place-less)" (Stewart 2014, 181) to reward Colter unconsciously for each traumatic death "with an erotic afterlife, the secular correlative of a jihadist's harem in the sky" (177). Although this sounds like a conspiracy theory, it is not unlikely that the system could inject into its agents the illusory hope for escaping from it, a sort of 'cruel optimism' that enslaves them to make any escape impossible. But more crucially, it must be noted that Colter reappears as a potential sovereign agent in the new reality, and in his email to Goodwin he praises the SC and asks her to tell this comatose double of himself, "everything is gonna be ok!" Despite his suicidal resistance to the system, he thus eventually endorses the system and reclaims his recyclable agency in it. Escaping into another reality, he ends up with the same system and job, but now this is 'okay.' The abject agent is replaced by/reset as another sovereign agent, who might work better under the 'okay' sign and even feel 'okay' about the traumatic cycle of virtual death. This self-reaffirmation of sovereign agency, as well as the dream of liberation from the system, indeed sustains the system that has no utopian outside. If each Bourne film ends with Bourne fleeing from the CIA (though he always returns in the sequel), Colter's death as the ultimate nirvana rather brings back his life in the new

---

[4] Let's recall the seminal time-travel film *Back to the Future* (Robert Zemeckis, 1985). A son, sent into the past prior to his birth, plays matchmaker to his future parents by changing a timid boy into a brave man, who will be his father. The son makes his father; the effect is the cause of its cause.

reality with the same old system. That is, he is not really sacrificed. Not only the train bombing but also his self-sacrifice to undo it are undone. Time is rewound and the past is rewritten, but the virtual loop of this process itself is undone. Nothing happened, nobody died, and the entire reality including Colter's sacrifice has disappeared. Not another parallel Colter but the same Colter who was lying in the chamber before the train explosion is still lying there after the train's safe arrival.

What is sacrificed is the value of sacrifice as such. This 'sacrifice' of sacrifice thus poses a new ethical dilemma—albeit one that we can take as an old philosophical aporia to reflect on anew. The appreciation of sacrifice presupposes that a sacrifice 'works' only insofar as it is recognized as an act selflessly done. But this recognition itself repays sacrifice even if symbolically, thus inevitably involving it in an economy of give and take or investment and return. Those who sacrifice themselves are rewarded by the symbolic Other with indebtedness, respect, or honor, often elevated to an ethically superior or privileged position. However, sacrifice essentially implies a "holocaust" of all (*holos*) being burned (*caustos*), a selfless giving without reserve, calculation, or reward (Keenan 2005, 1). It must be "a sacrifice *for nothing*" by transcending all its secular values and severing links to the symbolic order that commemorates it as a sacrifice. That is, it must sacrifice the economic understanding of sacrifice. Like the Derridean notions of gift and hospitality, sacrifice is also "a work that unworks itself in *the very performance of the work*" (3). This sacrifice of sacrifice underlies Jesus's maxim: "Do not let your left hand know what your right hand is doing" and "your Father who sees in secret will reward you" (2). If any big Other exists and repays sacrifice, it is only God. However, this divine reward registers the pure sacrifice back in another secret economy. The sacrifice of sacrifice is thus doubled: the 'terrestrial' economic sacrifice is sacrificed into the 'deconstructive' *an*economic sacrifice, which in turn is sacrificed into the (celestial) economic sacrifice. In sum, I claim, sacrifice 'overdoes' itself; it is inherently 'overdone.'

Colter seems to be a perfect 'secret' agent of pure sacrifice; Sean has no idea what Colter did while borrowing his body, and Goodwin, the only witness to Colter's sacrifice, has no memory of it in the new reality. There is neither social recognition nor divine redemption. Nonetheless, his virtual sacrifice costs him nothing. It instead brings back his actual life, as a potentially more empowered sovereign agent destined to be 'okay.' It is this 'reassigned' life that sacrifices his sacrifice itself, not 'overdoing' but 'undoing' it. In yet another sense it is we, the spectators, who appreciate the ethical sublimity of his sacrifice from an Other's position that is both social—we see him as our hero—and transcendent—we don't belong to his diegesis. The film thus creates the comforting illusion of his sacrifice being remembered and given significance, even though it is skillfully canceled. In this way both the conventions of the tragedy and the happy ending work; his death has a cathartic effect on audiences, who then feel reassured of his survival, which erases the very death just seen. The point is that Colter is not reborn or recreated as a cyborg agent like RoboCop but restarts his life in the changed reality. The traumatic past is not overcome but undone. It serves not as the base of continuous memory but as a sample segment of time to test the potentiality of 'undoable' action. This 'undoability' may signal the future direction of sovereign agency. Agents could perform endless self-sacrifice in secret even without feeling embarrassed by its being undone once they accept it as their normal work. The sovereign system then could not be more hegemonically served by its agents.

The Ideology of 'Undoing' in the Perpetual Present of Action

To recapitulate briefly, the global system of sovereign agency has been ever more monstrous in action thrillers. Bond and Bourne undergo the vicious cycle of terror and war on terror in the normalized state of exception. Their sovereign and abject agency alternate and fuse in the perpetual present of 24/7 labor and precarious life with no utopian future. Colter's traumatic loop intensifies this postpolitical neoliberal temporality while also figuring a way out of it. He pursues not postcatastrophic redemption but precatastrophic prevention by abjecting and sacrificing himself to open up a new future. However, the new world is not new but more monstrous, as it is the same world waiting for (the use of the SC against) unpredictable threats 'minus' the chance and dream of leaving it. Colter starts as a sovereign agent, then resists the sovereign system through abject agency like Bourne, but eventually reclaims sovereign agency to fight potential terrorism, like Bond. A traumatic event is undone but presumed to occur anytime, to redo itself. Colter's self-abjecting sacrifice and its ethical and existential significance are all undone within this system but also could be redone whenever needed. 'Undoing' does not lead to redemption but only to 'redoing,' which nonetheless brings with it the mood of a happy ending.

Recent sci-fi mind-game films go further than *Source Code*. Once a fighter in *Edge of Tomorrow* (Doug Liman, 2014) finds out that time is supernaturally rewound to the starting point of his mission upon his death, he even takes advantage of this loop by killing himself whenever something goes wrong in his mission to stop an alien invasion. Death is no longer a trauma but a simple 'game over' that enables him to immediately 'start over' (as in *Groundhog Day*). It is better to die before the situation gets worse, and undoing it is as easy as deleting what was just written by pressing the backspace key. With no pain or regret, he exhibits ever-upgrading practicality: correcting mistakes, enhancing performance, 'edging' to tomorrow. At the climax of the film, he loses this capacity for resetting time but seizes one final chance to kill the head of the aliens, at the cost of his female colleague. Then, thanks to the transference of the enemy's inherent time-reversing power to him, he awakens in the world of a day ago, in which her sacrifice is undone but retroactively effective, as all the aliens are mysteriously gone. It is not a parallel world but a 'backspaced-then-upgraded' world. Losing nothing, he is even empowered with the time-reset button embedded in his sovereign agency. Likewise, such an unexpected happy ending closes *Oblivion* (Joseph Kosinski, 2013). Though time travel does not occur here, a security repairman on a postapocalyptic Earth discovers that the so-called aliens are not his enemies but the humans fighting against the real aliens, who colonized most of humankind and cloned him into many sovereign agents serving the alien regime. He then joins the resistance group, that is, turns into an abject agent, and sacrifices himself to destroy the alien headquarters. The film ends with a clone of his appearing to his wife in the restored world as if he had not been sacrificed and would resume his marriage.

The undead agency to undo/redo everything could not be more practically efficient but is all the more ideologically dubious. This ambivalence is conspicuous in the Hollywood remake of *Ghost in the Shell* (Rupert Sanders, 2017). Here too, a sovereign agent has an identity crisis. She remembers that she was orphaned by a terrorist attack and transformed into a counterterrorist cyborg, but it turns out that this memory was implanted; she and her cyberterrorist enemy were both anarchic radicals abducted by a cybernetics company as test subjects (like ninety-eight other failed ones), and she had taken her life while in custody before being reborn as the first successful cyborg. However, this self-discovery does not prompt her to resist or leave the sovereign system. She retrieves her former solidarity with the terrorist—now an abject agent—but refuses to merge his mind with hers. She kills the CEO of the company but rejoins her state agency. She reconnects with her original mother but returns to work as an ever-repairable sovereign agent. The film ends with her oft-repeated words: "We cling to memories as if they define us, but what we do defines us. My ghost survived to remind the next of us that humanity is our virtue. I know who I am, and what I'm here to do." In sum, her traumatic past is unearthed only to be sutured into corrected memories, which should not affect her present actions. This mourning process illusively reconciles her past leftist activism with her present sovereign operation while in effect leaving the past behind and embracing the present as the sole base of identity. It reveals the state's involvement in the dirty business of the cyborg industry, yet also legitimizes the state's sovereign agency against terrorism and punishes only the industry's ruthless exploitation of bare lives, although they both work supralegally. The sovereign system is then justified as the guardian of "humanity," in the name of which her posthuman body is reassembled whenever it is damaged as if nothing has happened and no pain is remembered.[5]

The self-reaffirmation of sovereign agency after self-doubt is indeed the core experience of secret agents today. It implies their positive internalization of the system's ever-increasing flexibility and inescapability at the same time. They are trained as subjects with free will to accept sovereign agency, however vulnerable, and to focus only on actions for given missions. They embody neoliberal subjectivity that is both entrepreneurial and precarious, like 'CEO-workers,' perpetually trapped in the present of overworking at the risk of being abjected from the efficiency-driven capitalist market. Sci-fi films further depict the technological recreation and co-option of the abject (agents) as (replaceable) sovereign agents. Time travel or bioengineering brings cloned or reformatted agents at the end, whose memory-based identity is not that of sacrificed protagonists, but whose action-oriented mission is the same. The intended effect that this 'happy' ending seems to achieve poetic justice without sacrificing our heroes is problematic. It indicates a new level of the fictive resolution that Elsaesser (2018a, 26–33) notes. He argues that mind-game films provide "imaginary solutions to real contradictions" (like the myths in Lévi-Strauss) while also exposing the "black boxes" of

---

[5] The paradoxical doubling of liberation and domination implied in her ambivalent abject-sovereign agency is also reflected in her cyborg femininity. Carl Silvio (1999) argues that the original Japanese animation apparently subverts the dominant power structures of "gender and sexual difference" but covertly reinscribes them. The Hollywood remake (starring Scarlett Johansson) overtly presents her nudity, which brings into relief her voluptuous sexuality more than her bare life.

gaming such as time travel that create seemingly valid but ultimately incompatible realities. That is, they suggest dilemmas that have no solutions except formal, ludic ones. Devising such solutions is a productive way of "living with contradiction," but it also implies the impossibility of changing the actual situation (37). However, what is new is that the films discussed so far do not merely offer virtual solutions to the terror-counterterror cycle but instead end up assuming it as the unsolvable contradiction and shifting the focus from breaking the cycle to better preparing for its rerun, by training more adaptable agents who prioritize action over memory or anything else. This shift reflects today's sovereign system and a future model of agency that could be pursued realistically even without time travel or memory implant. In short, these films premediate somewhat feasible solutions and promote the world to pursue them.

Is cinema good for the world, then? Or rather, could we welcome such a future world as that prefigured on screen? Time travel and other mind games are motivated to save the past from trauma or catastrophe, but this salvation appears as if it is the minimal ethical condition for the justification of the present. Essential questions about life, sacrifice, or humanity are put aside while the sovereign system reduces ethics to a simplistic imperative of saving "innocent people" and a Manichean dualism of dividing innocence and evil based on conformity or resistance to the system itself. This moral reductionism allows nothing but action to realize it. Unless sovereign agents kill innocent people, the perpetual present of their action entailing supralegal violence is legitimized. Life is either merely innocent or eternally active. Let's ask: Is this life desirable? Does it have the sanctity of life to save in spite of all?

PART III
COMMUNITY AND NETWORK

8
Narrative Formations of Community and Network

Global Society: Community or Network?

Marshall McLuhan's term *global village*, coined in the 1960s, imprinted the word 'global' on people's minds well before today's full-scale globalization. Looking back on it, however, the implication might be somewhat paradoxical. McLuhan's age was already ultramodern thanks to the unprecedented interconnection of all different parts of the world through electronic media, but the consequent contraction of the globe into a 'village' sounds rather premodern. A village, that is, a small old-fashioned *community* where information is instantly shared from every quarter to every point, is the new form of society brought about by cutting-edge technology. But today, no other notion could better capture our digitally updated global village than *network*. Every day we log in to social networking services (not social community services) to reach out of and transcend our neighborhoods at the speed of light. Or rather, we are involved in a complex 'community of networks' that stretches across cities and nations but also intensifies interconnections in existing social clusters; each SNS is thus a social 'network of communities.'

How then should we understand the partly contrasting, partly confusing usages of community and network? What are meaningful differences between them, and how are they interrelated in our global society? These fundamental questions urge me to theoretically investigate community and network as each implying a different mode of social organization and subjectivity. In this chapter, opening Part III, I take global cinema as a useful stage of this study by focusing on its *network narratives* in comparison with *community-based narratives* and illuminate how this narratology underlies and enriches our biopolitico-ethical approach to global cinema. If Parts I and II have reached the dead end of postpolitical double ethics depending on sovereignty and abjection and ending up with repetitive catastrophes, Part III calls for attention to two universal modes of social formation—since ethics is about relationship after all—and thereby serves as an intermediate platform for thinking further about an alternative ethical direction in Part IV.

The network narrative is one of the buzzwords in recent film narratology about complex storytelling, a framework that also includes puzzle, modular, fractal, hyperlink, database, forking-path, multiple-draft, and mind-game narratives, as examined in Chapter 7. While scholars propose such different terms and taxonomies, there is a consensus that complex narrative films have been increasingly visible since *Pulp Fiction* (Quentin Tarantino, 1994) and conspicuously challenge classical narrative conventions by foregrounding fragmented space/time, temporal loops, different realities, unstable characters, multiple plots, unreliable narrators, and overt coincidences. The "Tarantino Effect" has indeed permeated "alternative plots" (Berg 2006), also pumping up narratological desires to map and theorize the newness of this cinematic trend from aesthetic, cognitivist, cultural, and industrial perspectives. As its multifaceted background, critics have commonly referred to modernity and postmodernism; globalization and network technologies; new media including video game and virtual reality; and even scientific theories of chaos, chance, and quantum physics. A mirror-like feedback or two-way influence has been noted between such external causes and their narratological effects (Everett 2005, 159). Furthermore, the latter is understood not just as a response to the former but as a reflection of a broader epistemological shift in rethinking identity, reality, and time (Cameron 2008, 2).

What is missing, however, is a coherent philosophical framework of such shifts and their explication, which would consider lives and worlds depicted in narrative space and time. Their existential conditions in diegesis allegorize or embody new historical changes of subjectivity and society that we undergo in reality. In this aspect, a framework I propose is to highlight the paradigm shift of social structure at large from community to network and the cinematic transcoding of these entities into community-based and network-oriented narratives. This shift does not merely result from economic, technological globalization but indicates a large-scale transition in the fundamental way in which, I argue, collective life is organized spontaneously and even unconsciously around the core axes of sovereign power and individual desires. I thus build on a range of critical theory to approach aesthetic narratology, drawing primarily on sociological, biopolitical, and psychoanalytic philosophy. The shift from community to network will then turn out to be resonant with the emergence of complex narratives in general and network narratives in particular. Moreover, some network narratives reflecting global phenomena will indicate that this broad shift includes a problematic overlap of community and network in global cinema. I move from this mixed stage to the stage of pure networking, analyzing their implications and related films.

Mapping Network Narratives; Global Community as a Totalized Network

Let me begin with a comprehensive but concise mapping of network narratives, partly building on Bordwell (2006) and Charles Ramírez Berg (2006). Network narratives usually present several protagonists inhabiting distinct yet interlocking storylines. The traditional name "ensemble plot" implies the polyphonic harmony of multiple characters mingling in a single location: it can be as tight as a French chateau in *The Rules of the Game* (Jean Renoir, 1939), a student-share house in *The Spanish Apartment* (Cédric Klapisch, 2002), and a theme park in *The World* (Jia Zhangke, 2004); it can also be as large as a metropolis such as Los Angeles in *Pulp Fiction*, Taipei in *Yi Yi* (Edward Yang, 2000), and London in *Love Actually* (Richard Curtis, 2003). Of course, there is a variety of middle-sized locales like districts or neighborhoods in a big city, as seen in *Hannah and Her Sisters* (Woody Allen, 1986), *Magnolia* (Paul Thomas Anderson, 1999), and *Timecode* (Mike Figgis, 2000). In many cases, time is also restricted, and all events occur within a day or two in *American Graffiti* (George Lukas, 1973), *Do the Right Thing* (Spike Lee, 1989), and *Dazed and Confused* (Richard Linklater, 1993). An ensemble film thus keeps the unity of space and time while often boasting an all-star cast and revealing a social cross-section. It intermingles several voices or worldviews and yet does not necessarily privilege one of them or unify them around a single, shared goal like a planned theft in heist films (*Ocean's Eleven* [Steven Soderbergh, 2001], *The Thieves* [Choi Dong-hoon, 2012]) or postcatastrophic redemption in disaster films (*The Poseidon Adventure* [Ronald Neame, 1972], *Train to Busan* [Yeon Sang-ho, 2016])—these conventional goal-oriented genre films are not polyphonic though they feature an ensemble of multiple stars.

Polyphonic or not, many ensemble films tend to attenuate the proper sense of networking due to their limited spatiotemporal scope. However, the idea of ensemble is shattered in the omnibus-style "parallel plot" that crosses over different times and/or spaces, showing different protagonists. This more distributed form of narrative has in fact long evolved since D. W. Griffith's *Intolerance* (1916) and via modern masterpieces such as *The Godfather Part II* (Francis Ford Coppola, 1974) and *Before the Rain* (Milcho Manchevski, 1994), though the number of subplots rarely exceeds four—hence the "four-plot rule" (Berg 2006, 18). Slightly differently, what Berg calls "the hub and spoke plot" interconnects parallel storylines at certain points that sometimes last only for fleeting seconds or pass unnoticed by characters, as seen in a variety of (art) films that have two to four distinct parts: *The Double Life of Veronique* (Krzysztof Kieślowski, 1991); *Chungking Express* (Wong Kar-wai, 1994); *The Edge of Heaven* (Fatih Akin, 2006); and many titles in Hong Sang-soo's filmography including *The Day a Pig Fell into the Well* (1996), *The Power of Kangwon Province* (1998), and *Virgin Stripped Bare by Her Bachelors* (2000). These films draw attention to chance encounters between characters and simultaneous connections, but paradoxically, such random networking rouses the sense of fate and (often bad) luck and thus stimulates the psychology of 'if only' and the imagination of 'what if.'[1]

Furthermore, there is a case in which characters get hooked up by an occasion, such as a metaphysical mystery in *Terrorizers* (Edward Yang, 1986) or successive ceremonies in *Four Weddings and a Funeral* (Mike Newell, 1994)—whose title tells everything. More palpable in this regard are "converging fates" films that, as Bordwell (2006, 97–102) says, unfold a vast network in which unacquainted characters pursue their own lives with autonomy but occasionally intersect by accident. Robert Altman's trademark style not only merges many characters into events like the lavish wedding in *A Wedding* (1978) or the weekend holiday in *Gosford Park* (2001) but also notably depicts "the sheer contingency of the encounters before bringing nearly all the characters together at the final concert" in *Nashville* (1975) and at the final earthquake in *Short Cuts* (1993). This networking logic evokes "the narrative of simultaneous monadic simultaneity" that Jameson (1995, 114–16) formulates and traces back to modernist novels such as André Gide's *The Counterfeiters* (1925). Here, Jameson argues that coincidences merely emphasize isolated individuals' ephemeral connections, and their "Providence-effect" is little more than a bravura aesthetic gesture. For Allan Cameron (2008, 146), however, this effect also serves as a source of pleasure, "revealing the common temporal medium that unites these disparate

---

[1] The 'if only'/'what if' effects are prevalent in forking-path, multiple-draft, mind-game films, as explored in Chapter 7. However, these films do not necessarily pivot around network narratives but often reinforce the sense and logic of community I discuss later.

characters." Cameron's further point is that the fluid fashion of interweaving multiple stories in this temporal unity disqualifies Altman from making "modular narratives," in which each episode should disconnect the *fabula* (story) on the level of the *syuzhet* (plot). Modular narratives, in Cameron's terms, modulate time by creating or using "anachronic" devices (flashbacks/ flashforwards), "forking paths" (parallel storylines), an "episodic" series (an anthology), or a "split-screen" (spatial juxtaposition) (15). The last two may apply to some network narratives, but I claim the director's intentional modulation of time in these extradiegetic ways is not essential and is even disruptive to my emphasis on 'diegetic' networking. Altman's films exemplify a specific phase of networked if not modular narrativity that deserves full attention itself.

In this sense, I look into the issues of disparity and unity within network narratives, centering on the so-called LA ensemble films, from *Short Cuts* to *Magnolia* and *Crash* (Paul Haggis, 2004). Although an ensemble cast is a selling point, what these films let us feel is "an impossible sense of 'community' or commonality among all Los Angelenos" (Hsu 2006, 134). Los Angeles, well known for its automobile-centered and thus decentered urban sprawl, is indeed "a serpentine network of often jampacked freeways and a crucial node in an international network of commercial, informational, immigrant, and financial flows" (138). This expansive metropolitan network frustrates individuals' attempts to 'cognitively map' its totality à la Jameson—this operation is possible for a community—just as spectators often have difficulty penetrating the subplots, images, or 'short cuts' that are rapidly networked in *Short Cuts*. Consequently, people lose a feeling for the public identity based on trust and respect as well as the private commitment to sustainable community building. Busy adjusting to the chaotic network but often stressed and exhausted, people tend to end up with a "blasé outlook," devaluing external stimuli—this is a protective shell, safeguarding the self from contact with the others, as Georg Simmel (1972, 329–30), a precursor of network sociology, pointed out a century ago.

The problem is that this urban ego also grows into the collective selfhood of certain groups distinguished and detached from other groups. While public space and the public sphere disintegrate, private desires and privatized power prevail without regulations. Forbidden cities are built and gated communities are sealed with high-tech policing methods against racial or ethnic minorities and the homeless, jobless, or moneyless. Postmodern urbanism not only enhances networking but leads to "an inevitable

Haussmannization of Los Angeles," controlling populations and segregating neighborhoods (Dear and Flusty 1997, 158). The network society thus takes back on some qualities of the community such as the territorial, hierarchical boundaries between inside and outside, center and periphery, members and strangers, and friends and enemies. The social barriers among different identity groups are rendered ever more permeable on the one hand and yet, on the other hand, are restructured on an even larger scale. The networked whole becomes bigger and bigger while leaving unnetworked people behind, rendering them invisible. It is noteworthy that *Grand Canyon* (Lawrence Kasdan, 1991), an earlier LA ensemble film, explicitly contrasts the rich White and the poor Black, but *Short Cuts* and *Magnolia* depict people of color only tangentially and stereotypically as offering services or threatening White masculinity. This relegation of the minorities to the sidelines makes "a totalizing image of L.A.'s community" (Hsu 2006, 142). The urban network is, I argue, totalized like a community that closes itself by excluding the unqualified, but without the traditional sense of communal belongingness. In other words, today's global community is a *totalized network* without the pure openness of networking. This double bind is palpable in *Crash*. The metropolis here appears as a vibrant multicultural network, but it turns out to be highly vulnerable to daily racial tensions and deep-rooted biases that explode violently anytime, anywhere among isolated individuals and segregated classes.

By extension, transnational network narratives reveal an immanent plane of global interconnectedness and its traumatic, disastrous effects at the same time. As mentioned in Chapter 1, Paris in Haneke's *Code Unknown* appears as a contingent platform where racial and cultural tensions in French society burst out through chance encounters between a White boy, a black man, a French woman, an East European beggar, an Arab bully, and an old Arab man. Alejandro González Iñárritu's *Babel* (2006) completes his multinarrative Death Trilogy—following *Amores Perros* (2000) and *21 Grams* (2003)—in the largest, global setting: a vacationing American couple is injured by two poor Moroccan boys who simply want to test their father's hunting rifle, which was bought from a tour guide neighbor, who in turn received it as a gift from a Japanese man. While this Japanese man loses connection to his teenage deaf-mute daughter, who was traumatized by her mother's suicide, the US government carries the Americans to a hospital by helicopter and considers the boys' shooting a terrorist act. Pressed by the United States, the Moroccan police chase after the boys, then shoot and take away one of them. In the meantime, the American couple's Mexican nanny in the United

Figure 8.1. In *Babel*, a global network of random connections emerges around a rifle, a moving object that turns from a gift into a weapon.

States takes their two children with her as she travels across the border to attend her son's wedding in Mexico. But on her way back to the United States, she encounters unexpected events on the border and ends up being deported from the United States, where she has worked diligently yet illegally.

Narrative space in these films accommodates a global network of random connections with the so-called six degrees of separation and the butterfly effect. Unrelated characters are tied together by converging fates or a moving object such as the rifle in *Babel*, which turns from a gift into a weapon like Plato's *pharmakon* as both remedy and poison (see Figure 8.1).[2] This ambivalence reflects the dual nature of globalization, which is never fully global, or rather, is full of global schisms, as we have seen. Let's recall the history summarized in the Introduction. The Cold War ended when two ideological blocs merged into one liberal capitalist globe, but the new millennial antagonism occurred between the entire global system and its remnants with new antinomies debunking it in the forms of terroristic, economic, migration, and refugee crises. World politics has given way to the administration of this globe as the World Interior of capital, including policing measures for security and sovereign violence on its threatening outside. Hence the recto

---

[2] One may recall *Winchester '73* (Anthony Mann, 1950), an earlier network film about the eponymous, prized rifle (a gift-weapon), which is lost and pursued by different characters until its owner reclaims it.

and verso of globalization: a single market of social networks, multicultural harmony, and transnational neoliberalism forms a planetary system of inclusion, yet it generates symptoms of exclusion like inassimilable others and catastrophic risks as inevitable byproducts to control or remove. Nonwhite or immigrant characters in the films just discussed are thus accepted and often needed but are also suspected, humiliated, or even deported by mainstream society in the name of the law. This exclusion, in turn, triggers their violent backlash or terroristic return that breaks the law. No doubt this loop can be extended to the vicious cycle of terror and war on terror that perpetuates extralegal violence. Here is a crucial turning point. As mentioned previously, our global society is not just an open, diverse, malleable, and permeable network, but even reinforces the way a community demarcates its boundaries, members, and rights, always ready to take actions beyond its own law in order to protect itself against any security threat.

Theorizing Community and Global Network Narratives

At this point I examine the notion of community theoretically, from biopolitical and psychoanalytic perspectives; I later take this approach to the notion of network as well. As Jean-Luc Nancy (2008) and Roberto Esposito (2010) suggest, the essentialist view of community assumes an inherent human desire to fuse different others into a unified identity that shares political ideals while building up biopolitical immunity. The others are then incorporated into the Same or cast out of it if they are harmful, threatening, or too different. This Same makes the totality of the community, the totality that often takes on an exclusive purity and tends to become totalitarian, as proved in modern projects of nation-building and utopian revolution, based on ideologies from nationalism to fascism, whether right wing or left wing; communism, literally rooted in the sense of community, was fascist in its historical regimes. Here, biopolitics concerns not only the Foucauldian biopower that regulates populations and disciplines their bodies under ideological state apparatuses, but as we discussed, Agambenian sovereignty that creates the boundary between such subjects in the state or law and mere bodies cast out of it. This casting out, social abjection, is thus the biopolitical deprivation of social subjectivity. When a community wields its sovereign power to declare a "state of exception" to the rule of law, a subject ineligible to be in the community may be reduced to the abject like those deported migrants, degraded to *homo sacer*, the animal-like "bare life" expelled from both human law and divine law with no rights or sanctity of life. Only on this biopolitical ground of sovereignty can institutional politics be formed.

The implication is that the desire for community is structured along with power. Let me further develop this idea, now psychoanalytically, through Jacques Lacan's (1999) formula of *sexuation*: not biological sexuality but the unconscious differentiation of the masculine and the feminine logic of desire (see Figure 8.2). Its masculine logic is that all are submitted to the phallic function, with one exception. That is, all men follow the law of symbolic castration that, in the name of the father, states the prohibition against incest and the foundation of desire. The desire of the son-as-subject is then destined to fill in the lack of the primordial object (mother) with its replacements (other women) but never reaches satisfaction in the Symbolic Order of reality. One exception to this phallic law is, so to speak, the Freudian 'primal father,' who is supposed to have the phallus and enjoy all women, the mythical father who transcends the law of castration, prohibition, and repression that he imposes upon the others, his sons, in order to sustain the social order as the control system of desire. The name of the father is thus the signifier of the phallus (Φ) that all others lack and desire in vain, the signifier of primary repression for them and of supreme enjoyment for him. The phallic father thus embodies both the superego and the id, the Symbolic and the Real, the law and beyond. Of course, this Father is not an actual father who is another

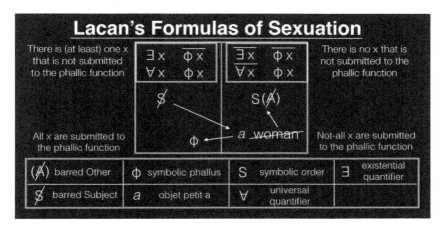

Figure 8.2. Lacan's masculine (left) and feminine (right) formulas of sexuation resonate with the organizing principles of community and network, respectively.

mere human. But this inconsistency is reified through the phallus into an exceptional Other who accesses jouissance beyond limited pleasure. Not a biological entity, the phallus is thus a fantasized signifier of fullness or an empty signifier into which the full satisfaction of desire is projected and toward which the subjects of desire are oriented. It turns the inconsistent Other into a sublime object of desire, just as God is projected to fill the gaps in our imperfect knowledge as if it is the invisible hand pulling the strings of reality that seems to us often unpredictable and inexplicable.

Psychoanalysis and biopolitics interlock with each other in this context. Their structure of subjectivation is homological, centering on the analogy between the sovereign's divine power and the father's unrestrained desire in terms of supralegal exceptionality.[3] The Father-as-Sovereign, like God, takes the center of his community under his law (which he can transcend), thus setting its ideal goal or utopian destination for which a collective but unfulfillable desire is internalized in subjects. This process works as the ideological mechanism of shared subjectivation in the same structure of power and desire. The subject is a particular example of the universal set organized by the phallus-as-sovereignty, while this set is closed because the very exception to it transcendently delimits it and all its particulars. The center of structuration is outside the structure; the democratic multitudes are subject to that big Other and are the subjects of that big Other. A unified community then emerges, nurturing the sense of belongingness, membership, or nationality among the subjects and forming the boundary between inside and outside, 'us' and 'them,' our friends and enemies—the latter is the potential object of collective abjection. In this way, a biopolitical topology of the sovereign, the subject, and the abject is hierarchically established.

This biopolitical community, historically patriarchal, typically appears in a variety of films about a dominant father figure who controls a family, a city, an army, or a religious group. To take just a few contemporary examples, *Pan's Labyrinth* (Guillermo del Toro, 2006) stages a post–Civil War fascist Spanish army that hunts Red guerrillas to abject in order to make a "new clean Spain." The leader of this military community incarnates sovereign power and desire as the near-divine center of misogynic patriarchy and far-right nationalism. In *Timbuktu* (Abderrahmane Sissako, 2014), such a community is run by Jihadist fundamentalists who legally ban music, smoking,

---

[3] More precisely, Lacan's psychoanalysis has an affinity with Carl Schmitt's political theology that underlies Agamben's biopolitics (Reinhard 2013).

and immodest clothing in an old town in Mali, while they remain exceptional to the very laws, like an obscene superego who enjoys. *Ju Dou* (Zhang Yimou, 1990) depicts rural China, where a superego figure embodies the feudal Confucian patriarchy that invincibly continues the Oedipal father-son lineage. In *The Master* (Paul Thomas Anderson, 2012), a charismatic patriarch appears as the transcendent center of a semireligious autonomous community that pursues a utopian alternative to postwar American society. Despite their different cultural backgrounds, these films commonly indicate the "all vs. exception" logic of masculine sexuation.[4]

The global network-narrative films at issue do not exhibit such an authentically unified, self-closed community ruled by a negative father figure. Nevertheless, it is true that their characters experience various modes of abjection (humiliation, deportation, etc.) as a traumatic event and then struggle to regain their sociopolitical subjectivity and re-enter their sovereign community as a totalized network, though often in vain. Reflecting global conditions of life, this structure of abjection and redemption itself is reasonably classical, resonant with Deleuze's action-image formula (Situation-Action-Situation modified) as seen in Chapter 2. A fatal occasion destroys everyday reality, causing protagonists' abjection and redemptive action, and the original state is finally restored with some changes. As Bordwell (2006, 98–103) points out, each storyline in a network narrative also takes this classical form, centering on a cluster of intimate, long-lasting relations arranged in sketchy vignettes and goal-achievement pathways. It has all that is needed for mainstream storytelling: causality, motivic harmony, temporal sequence and duration, character wants and needs, and the like. Coincidences are not purely contingent but serve to build "small worlds" of common goals, obstacles, appointments, and deadlines. In sum, the innovative network structure still resorts to classical norms, working within what I call the community-based narrative logic.

What demands further attention is the ideological dimension of this logic in network narratives. Hsuan Hsu (2006) sharply criticizes LA ensemble films for their apolitical moralistic attempts at redemption. In *Crash*, the racial scars of abject individuals end up being sutured by the liberal gesture of forgiveness and reconciliation; White masculinity, which is threatened by

---

[4] At the same time, these films also reveal that the crisis of this masculine logic is mostly triggered by female characters, even if it does not always bring about their liberation. This crisis suggests the point of the shift from community to network, which I elaborate on later.

carjacking and a black man driving a nice car, is re-established through a White man's heroic agency to save a passive, victimized black woman. This "melodramatic vision" reduces the institutional, historical complexity of racism to interpersonal relationships and the matter of mutual respect or formal equality. As a paradoxical consequence, it tends to be racially blind, to "exorcise this racism by exorcizing race itself" and create "a false totality" of the multiracial ensemble in "a universal neoliberal form of inclusion" (146–49). This vague sense that "we are all in this together" is also brought about through the shared experience of an earthquake and a rain of frogs at the end of *Short Cuts* and *Magnolia*, respectively. Such divine disasters falling over the network city evoke "a nostalgia for a lost community" (143) and the holistic desire for redemption, rather than emancipation from a materialistic, intolerant regime. Hsu's point is clear: we should re-politicize racism and find viable public responses to it from sociostructural viewpoints instead of pursuing "facile solutions," melodramatic or religious (149).

It should be noted that in our terms, such moral solutions resonate with the soft-ethical construction of inclusion/tolerance/pity, whose counterpart is the hard-ethical exclusion/violence/hate. These two contrasting facets of global ethics, respectively based on the all-embracing attitude of networking and the community operation of self-closed sovereignty, interlock to make the 'totalized network' of the global community. As I have argued, however, political struggles for freedom and equality have historically led to the soft-ethical system of inclusion while entailing hard-ethical effects, so this double ethics is not antipolitical so much as postpolitical. It underlies the double bind of the totalized network's status as neither an authentic community nor a pure network, the dilemma that leaves little room for proper political solutions. No wonder it is easier to imagine the end of the world than the end of capitalism, as suggested in the cinema of catastrophe (see Chapter 6).

The catastrophic finales of *Short Cuts* and *Magnolia* could then be viewed not as a nostalgic evocation of a paradisiacal community but as an allegorical exposure of the sublime catastrophes immanent in cognitively unmappable yet totalized networks. The sense of being together caused by such catastrophes would not be that we are finally in a community, but that we are all nothing but bare lives, vulnerable to abjection. Only with the basis of this abjecthood as the most fundamental commonality of our being could we experience unexpected new connections between individuals stripped of established identities, even if no utopian political community is possible. People in the films at least have some potential to make solidarity without unity through this commonality without community by sharing their suffering from all causes of individual-level abjection (loneliness, depression, alcoholism, adultery, disease, sexual frustration, loss of dignity). Not disavowing "the need for more larger-scale public solutions" as Hsu (2006, 137) claims, this intimacy between the abject might open up an ethical, if not political, alternative to the double ethics of the global system, a precarious yet precious potential that should not wholly be downplayed from the political angle—this is the theme of Part IV. Cinema as an art form, with all political limitations, sheds light on existential singularities and their new potentialities above all.

Pure Network Narratives with Free-Floating Agents

In the direction of further exploring this cinematic nature, I now move on to another set of network narrative films, which are not reputed as network films but show a more radical type of networking that deserves to be highlighted. These are 'pure' network films, in which abject figures turn into the agents of free-floating networking instead of pursuing reintegration into their original community. In truth, the latter case also implies the crucial point about abjection: after losing subjectivity, one may try to regain it. We have seen many films in which the abject do not remain passively victimized but activate agency, the temporary and transitional mode of subjectivity as being-in-action. Even when aiming at resubjectivation, the core of agency is thus the potential for becoming-other, not a fixed identity. It is performative, creating its content at the moment of performing it instead of representing a predetermined entity. We have seen many abject agents, the abject reloaded with this agency, and now see abject figures, such as the White savior in *Crash* and the Mexican nanny in *Babel*, turn into action-leading agents as well. Only in doing so do they also realize the previously unknown possibility of forming solidarity with the (abject) others beyond their former subjectivity.

The case I introduce here suggests that the abject can be further liberated from any fixed subjectivity and community, thereby increasing the sense of agency and networking to various degrees. They become agents performing a task that may even be just to wander around a networked space with no other goal. Jacques Tati's *Playtime* (1967) is a seminal example. Tati, playing the protagonist himself, takes a one-day roundabout tour of Paris, on which he initially tries to meet with a business contact but gets lost in an urban maze of glass and steel buildings. Though abjected in some sense, he then weaves through innovative rooms, offices, apartments, a chaotic restaurant, and busy streets like a modern flâneur, a carefree, strolling agent, intermittently encountering an American tourist and her group along with other quirky people. The film stages nothing but this 'playtime' of networking, which entails many actions as sensorial reactions to the artificial environment of ultramodern architecture and simulacra. The teleological trajectory typical of conventional road films dissipates into a sort of spatialized temporality, a series of events that could repeat with random differences in a potential loop.

Updating *Playtime* in the global age, *Holy Motors* (2012) by Leos Carax follows a day in the life of a mysterious man named Oscar. He is driven around Paris by a loyal driver; stops by different places; dresses up in unique costumes; and plays a variety of bizarre, semiscripted roles in the manner of abjecting himself and becoming others: an old beggar, a sex performer, a father, a musician, a Chinese gangster, a dying man, and an ordinary man whose wife and child are chimpanzees. These roles are "appointments" he carries out as a nearly surreal agent, sometimes on behalf of others but often for no reason. As his name suggests, Oscar is in effect a kind of actor, who misses the days when he was aware of cameras. All those performances are thus fulfilled as part of his actual profession, and his stage is now the real world, where he even shoots someone and encounters other performing agents like him, including his ex-lover, whose sudden suicide makes him cry. At the end of the day we see his car entering the Holy Motors garage, where other identical cars are parked after having carried other performers around the city in the same way; the cars even talk to each other, sharing their fear of being outmoded and unwanted—the fear of abjection (see Figure 8.3). No longer a civil community at all, Paris then turns out to be a network platform of nomadic semi-abject agents whose mission is to circulate between eternal or ephemeral appointments, as if to disperse and dissolve any memory or trauma in the present of performance without (knowing) a big cause, an ultimate goal, or a sustainable plan. It is a universe of imperfect intimacy or bare relation of witness between different parts of the whole, or it is a chaos whose cognitive mapping is impossible. What matters is solely the continuity of "networking as process rather than map or figure," a process of navigational, performative movement liberated from any universal social model that enforces and rigidifies habitual modes of living (Munster 2013, 12).

This liberating agency is not preformed but rather performed only in the process of networking, and is potentially reperformed through temporary

Figure 8.3. The network narrative of *Holy Motors* unfolds around a mysterious man, or rather his car, which is one of many identical cars moving around Paris.

modulation and flexible adaptation to changing circumstances. It enables the malleable 'reassemblage' of subjectivity facing unpredictable events, crises, wounds, and the like. Networking in *Holy Motors* further blurs the boundaries (or networks) between life and performance, real action and virtual acting, the world and the stage, and humans and cars. More experimental in this regard is Richard Linklater's animated docufiction *Waking Life* (2001), which conveys several parallels to his other network narrative film *Slacker* (1991). The protagonist, from the beginning, feels that his life is ethereal, lacking transitions between daily events. This experience progresses toward an existential crisis, a sort of psychological abjection. Then he travels through a series of chance encounters with various people and conducts philosophical discussions on free will, metaphysics, situationism, André Bazin's film theory, and so on. This surreal network flourishes with ideas and observations in a world that may be reality, dreams, or lucid dreams, leading him to realize that he is living out a perpetual dream. He eventually awakens to the meaning of life: that life may be an instant illusion that the individual believes to be real while negating God's invitation to become one with the infinite universe. In the end, he suddenly levitates and disappears into the endless blue sky. Although this final 'leap of faith' seemingly marks a teleological 'yes' to God's invitation, the point of the narrative lies in the journey of pure networking driven by the agent in search of the truth. Crucial is not transcendent truth but its pursuit itself on the illusory ground of life. One may take this perspective in earlier truth-seeking, (anti-)religious network narratives such as *The Milky Way* (Luis Buñuel, 1969) and *Taste of Cherry* (Abbas Kiarostami, 1997).

I briefly note Iñárritu's *Birdman* (2014) in this regard. In the opposite direction to the global-scale *Babel*, *Birdman* stages everything within and around a building in New York City. The film centers on a faded Hollywood actor best known for playing the superhero "Birdman," a half-abject figure undergoing a midlife crisis in both his career and life. But while trying to regain recognition as a real artist, he serves as a mobile agent who introduces and interconnects his team and family at different spots in his theater. Their side stories apparently form a traditional 'ensemble plot' rather than a free-floating network narrative. However, it is notable that the camera autonomously shifts from one person to another whom the hero encounters, without cutting and often without his presence. The entire film indeed looks like a single-shot long take, which renders palpable the camera's own agency, unlike the cross-cutting made under the director's full control. This 'camera with or without a man' is the real agent of networking on the ground, turning claustrophobic space into a community of micronetworks, whereas the man gains redemption, surreally disappearing into the sky like a bird at the end—evoking *Waking Life*.

One might recall that such a camera-agent embodies the movement of networking in Buñuel's *The Phantom of Liberty* (1974). Though it does not have a single-shot look, we sometimes even feel the camera's hesitation about whom to follow between different characters whose paths cross. This surrealist film is a remarkable precursor of the "daisy chain plot" (Berg 2006, 24–26) in which one character's story leads to the next without a central character like the 'Birdman.' An extreme case is *Mysterious Object at Noon* (2000), an experimental documentary film by Apichatpong Weerasethakul. Its networking principle is the 'exquisite corpse' party game: a surrealist technique of assembling a series of words or images collectively. Each player adds to a composition in sequence, usually by seeing only the end of what the previous player contributed, by writing in turn on a sheet of paper and passing it to the next writer for a further contribution. In an attempt to create a unique cinematic version of the exquisite corpse, the film crew travels across Thailand, interviewing random people and asking each person to add their own words to an unscripted story about a boy and his teacher, which is re-enacted. The director himself appears and recruits a hodgepodge of people to continue the story in a completely unpredictable direction creatively. Embodying performativity par excellence, the film is the process of filmmaking itself. It tests and realizes the purest form of networking without structure or a community that is preplanned and organized, only enjoying the artistic creativity of chance, contingency, and connectivity among real lives.

Theorizing Network and the Shift from Community to Network

Now it is time to reformulate network in comparison to community theoretically. I begin with the other half of Lacan's sexuation, that is, the feminine formula—though it may sound unrelated to the films just discussed (see Figure 8.2 again). It is that there is no exception to the phallic function, but not all are submitted to it. Like men, women are under castration and thus lack and desire the phallus, but there is no transcendent center, namely no primal 'mother' enjoying all men. This absence of exception suggests that no boundary makes a closed set of women under the law, that each woman is radically singular and not a member or example of generalized essential femininity. In this Lacanian sense, unlike Man, Woman as universal with a capital W does not exist. This does not mean that the Symbolic is foreclosed, but that the feminine 'not-all' is a phenomenon of discordance with the phallus when it comes to the Real. What underlies this phenomenon is not any positive feminine content of some women or some part of a woman beyond the male gaze, desire, or representations, but a pure formal cut that inherently occurs between the woman for the other (in the man's full fantasy) and the woman in herself (as empty substance). This fissure itself defines the subject as such, the Subject as immanently barred ($). The sexual difference is that a woman knows this fundamental void of content as well as how to veil the abyss, whereas a man believes illusively in some substance in himself, some phallic potential that he wants to realize by reducing her to a partial object-cause of desire (*objet petit a*) in his fantasy, projected onto her veil without knowing that there is nothing behind it. The woman then partially enjoys the phallus that the 'stupid' man believes to be his own, while still preserving her 'nothingness' out of his possessive desire (Žižek 1995).

This paradoxical freedom opens up room for a woman to not fully belong to a biopolitical community in which masculine sovereignty sets the boundaries between inside and outside, self and other, friend and enemy, subject and abject. More precisely, the woman is freed from the phallic function without leaving the phallic order, in the proper sense of being the abject that is neither fully included nor wholly excluded. Like hair just cut off, the abject is by definition no longer part of the subject but not yet a mere thing, and it thus lingers in the limbo state between subject and object, between the law of subjectivation and its outside. In this aspect, I emphasize, abjection implies not only deprivation but also liberation from subjectivity, from a particular way of subjectivation under a certain mode of sovereignty. 'Abjecthood' could then be considered the most universal and foundational mode of being, the degree zero of life unconditioned by any biopolitical subjectivation. Here is the positive power of the pure abject. She takes on an "unassimilable foreignness" to the self/other dichotomy (like the *objet a* that is detached from the subject) and floats like an "internal stranger" whose enjoyment may lie in the transgression of subjectivity. She even embodies what any subject might keep as the "unrecognizable yet intimate secret," that is, some latent drives toward an asubjective state of free, equal relations. Neither friend nor enemy, this 'Third' is none other than the *neighbor* in ethics (Reinhard 2013, 30–46) with whom to make the relationship of "beside yet alike, separation and identity" (Lacan 1997, 51). We could then imagine a move from the vertical hierarchy of the sovereign-subject-abject to the horizontal equality between the abject who meet each other as neighbors; a move from the closed totality of 'all vs. exception' bound in their metaphoric semblance to an infinite series of particular abject-neighbors in the 'not-all' of metonymic knotting; and a move from a utopian community unified for a transcendent ideal to an 'atopian' connection grounded on no fixed place of identity but only on the commonality of immanent abjecthood without community—I further develop this atopian notion of the abject-neighbor in Chapter 11.

This is the point where I propose to address 'neighboring' as networking. If community forms the totality of all and an absolute exception that fuels the universal desire to make it utopian, the network has the infinity of drives to (dis)connections in the way of dismantling the community, yet thereby leaving no exceptional outside. Community is a closed set of subjects who may be abjected from it, but network is an open Whole of endless links along which the subject-abject shift continually occurs. In Deleuze and Guattari's (1987) terms, community operates as a "tree-like," vertical system of hierarchical units that takes a historical trajectory toward its own perfection, whereas network creates a "rhizomatic," horizontal movement of molecular forces that endlessly continues in nondialectic, nonlinear directions with no utopian terminus. Community works in the 'in/out' mode, network in the 'on/off' mode. People in a network have no binding belongingness to it but simply make connections and disconnections. Network thus only has permeable boundaries, if any, and proliferates as an open whole in democratic, fragmentary, amorphous, and schizophrenic ways. In a traditional community, Foucauldian "discipline" is key to subjectivation, as noted in Chapter 7; the disciplinary society confines bodies in an isolated space and for a long-term period, while disciplining them into its skilled members under surveillance and punishment. However, discipline turns into a Deleuzian "control" in the control society that does not actually control each individual from the top down but instead promotes flexible agency and continuous modulation, thereby making everyone internalize entrepreneurship and adjust to consequently decentered environments, whose ever-changing boundaries do not allow any stable outside (Deleuze 1995). This new, anarchic notion of control, I argue, underlies the network that enables self-making freedom and free-floating autonomy with no boundary, no exception, and therefore no externality, either.

Actor-network theorist Bruno Latour (2009) distinguishes two ways of understanding space. On the one hand, space is seen as a vast ground inside which objects and subjects can reside. If these entities are removed, an empty space remains and reappears. But on the other hand, many connections between these entities generate their space(s) as they trudge along, so if they are taken out, nothing is left, especially space. The choice is thus not between nature and society but between two different spatial distributions: one in which there is an infinite outside where every organism is cramped, unable to deploy its life forms, and another in which there are only tiny insides, "networks and spheres," but where life forms are fully deployed through their relations. For me, the first case concerns the way a community occupies a part of space, forms its boundaries, and confines its members inside. In the second case, nothing precedes and exists outside incessant relations; there is no space as *res extensa*, the cartesian realm of matter separated from the act of networking, which itself creates space performatively. Everything is performed and thus produced in this 'immanent plane of networking,' to rephrase Deleuze's "plane of immanence"—not an actual material ground but the virtual in itself. In an empiricist context, William James's concept of concatenation applies well to pure connectivity. Networked experience as concatenated is assembled and sensed through "ambulatory, peripatetic, and transitory movements" of relations. At the same time, recursion and its redundancies lend a flavor to both "the banality and euphoria of networked encounters" (Munster 2013, 7–11). Here appears a "relational database" (77), relations operating like data that are combined, cut, or crossed endlessly. This network even includes nonhuman connections, opening up "a relational field of both techno- *and* biodiversity" in which neither humans nor things are privileged (7), just as both performers and cars are networked in *Holy Motors*.

In aesthetic and media studies, George Landow's (1994) notion of hypertext no doubt shows a literary form of network based on new information technology: nonlinear, intertextual, nomadic, rhizomatic, and schizophrenic. Such poststructuralist and postmodernist concepts indeed dismantle the totalizing "master narratives" as well as hierarchical frameworks of representation and interpretation. But it should also be noted that earlier modernism—James Joyce's *Ulysses* (1920), for instance—experimented with avant-garde techniques such as stream-of-consciousness and surrealism to articulate new connections between classes, religions, sexualities, and histories while aesthetically reflecting a sense of societal fragmentation against totalization (Beal and Lavin 2011, 6–10). In this sense, according to Jan Simons (2008, 114–23) it is debatable that database/modular narratives conform to the modernist/structuralist paradigm of "spatializing/de-chronolizing time." Structuralist narratology revealed a universal structure of mostly classical narratives like myths and folktales—in my terms, the community-based narrative logic—whereas modernist narratives dissolved this logic into a new, network-oriented one. If structuralism illuminated communal systems of narrative, poststructuralism deconstructed them, and this deconstruction aesthetically evolved from modernism to postmodernism. The question is, again, the shift from community to network. In the community-reflecting narrative, time is also structured like a community: linear, accumulative, and teleological, with a utopian, redemptive closure projecting an atemporal transcendent point of pursuit. This totality is disrupted or pulverized by the networked narrative time that flows in the perpetual present without origin or orientation. Yes, time is spatialized in database/modular narratives, but as I have noted, these are not necessarily network narratives, and a loop of recursive networking does not spatialize time. Networking, in any case, embraces "the contingent, the possible, and the probable" that Simons says is opened up by time.

In conclusion, network narratives by nature perpetuate the present of networking in a space that only emerges at the very time of networking. Global cinema experiments with this unique spatiotemporality to different extents. *Birdman* centers on the hero's organic temporal structure of the glorious past, the abject present, and the redemptive future while also opening it up to a fragmentary community of micronetworks beyond his cognition and control. *Holy Motors* hints at the traumatic past of the performing mobile agent but dissolves this past into the potential loop of networked performances by both humans and machines in the eternal present. *Waking Life* replaces the question of the past and the present with that of dream and reality, mingling them in a virtual plane of truth-seeking networks, often without the presence of the walking dreamer. *Mysterious Object at Noon* radically goes without the past, or only with the past as a collection of temporal fragments that relay a story through many authors, in a continuous yet contingent, linear yet disoriented way. The crucial point is that these network narratives that spectators appreciate and diegetic networks that characters experience are inseparable, mirroring each other in the almost classical concordance between form and content. And we, as well as they, may live networked lives instead of keeping community-based spatiotemporal identities and continuity.

Nevertheless, I briefly re-emphasize that the global community contradictorily appears as a 'totalized network' that has both utopian interfaces for connectivity and dystopian symptoms such as mechanized sovereignty/abjection, lost causes, addictive indulgence, and extremist violence. That is why relatively moderate network narrative films such as *Crash*, *Code Unknown*, and *Babel* deserve critical attention. In particular, the unpredictable eruption of violent tension or action in these films proves the global paradox that ever more connections increase the potential for ever more catastrophes. Terrorism is the most uncontrollable danger immanent in uncontrollable networks, whether it devastates a single American high school as in Gus Van Sant's *Elephant* (2003) or randomly explodes here and there in vast China as in Jia Zhangke's *A Touch of Sin* (2013). Stephen Gaghan's *Syriana* (2005) most ambitiously highlights how our global network is totalized by owners of power and wealth like neoliberal corporations, sovereign agencies, political elite, and mercenary lawyers, while they are also vulnerable to abjection from their organizations and terrorist attacks from the abject of the global system as such. This dilemma underlies our increasingly networked, yet all the more precarious, life, which we discuss further in the next chapter.

9
Nation, Transnationality, and Global Community as Totalized Network

Community and Network in the National, Transnational, and Global Frames

If Chapter 8 illuminated the general mechanisms of community and network, now let me investigate their historical resonances with national and transnational forces. As formulated in the Introduction, the national frame of world cinema implies nation-based "territorialization," while the transnational frame suggests its "deterritorialization." These Deleuzian notions, along with the "tree vs. rhizome" metaphors, characterize community and network in a nutshell. Community-building involves establishing boundaries, designating members, and denominating norms around common features and values. It claims, governs, and sustains its land, people, and law in centralized, hierarchical, organic systems. The nation is the most comprehensive perpetual unit of this territorialization, constructing a collective identity as cohesive and consistent. Conversely, network traverses the national territory, transgresses its stable identity, and trades differences within or across the nation. Never fixed, the network emerges in the performative mode of networking; the act of connection forms a temporary, contingent, relational space whose territory disappears when disconnected. It deterritorializes national borders, citizens, and sovereignty into a dynamic web of chance encounters, floating agencies, and various exchanges.

Here I attempt to map various regional films comparatively for biopolitico-ethical critiques in terms of nation-building, transnational experience, and globalization's effects on community and network. Each film reflects one of these aspects strongly but is also approachable from all of the national, transnational, and global frames. This complexity matters because I highlight a selection of ten films from the Global South—including three pan-Arab, three pan-Indian, and four pan-Chinese films—that have been mainly received under the rubric of non-Western world cinema and yet can be reviewed in the context of global cinema issues no less significantly than films from the Global North can.

Malian auteur Abderrahmane Sissako's *Timbuktu* (2014), for instance, draws our attention to the multiple contradictions in an African Muslim pseudo-state: between pacifist and jihadist Islamic sects, between divine and human laws, and between a fundamentalist community built around the transcendent center of God and a global network of secular desires and cultures. Abbas Kiarostami guides us to Iran, another Islamic region, where a further secularized mode of networking unfolds abject figures' existential search for the sanctity of life or divinity immanent in human senses and connections. *Taste of Cherry* (1997) and *Life and Nothing More . . .* (1992), among others, can be seen as Middle Eastern network films in this regard. Moving further East, *Roja* (Mani Ratnam, 1992) and *Rang De Basanti* (Rakeysh Omprakash Mehra, 2006), two representative Indian nationalist films, conduct modern nation-rebuilding projects on screen. They unify ethnic and cultural differences in India through romanticized patriotism against public enemies but also solidify the Hindu middle-class hegemony while diluting revolutionary potential in a postpolitical manner. A global Bollywood production, *Slumdog Millionaire* (Danny Boyle, 2008) disrupts this hegemony by mediating an utter abject boy's contingent adventures across India via a television quiz show, which both catalyzes a mind-game network narrative and remediates the nation as an imagined community. By extension, pan-Chinese cinema offers a rich platform for exploring the community-network entanglement. Transnationally coproduced, Ang Lee's global hit *Crouching Tiger, Hidden Dragon* (2000) appears as a Chinese wuxia and Western film at the same time, negotiating the nostalgic sense of an honorable martial arts community with liberational, nomadic, and transgressive networking forces. But community disintegrates drastically into network in the postmodern city-state of Hong Kong. Four urban youths in Wong Kar Wai's *Chungking Express* (1994) interconnect—as they often do in his films—contingently and ephemerally, adrift yet stuck in a 'glocal' circuit of mobility full of crowded yet lonely places. Jia Zhangke unsentimentally reveals the dark sides of such networked life caused by mainland China's relentless globalization. If the theme park in *The World* (2004) is a miniaturized global village of nearly imprisoned poor workers, the entirety of China captured in *A Touch of Sin* (2013) looks like a mini global network in which people, deprived of dignity under a brutal capitalist power system, turn into abject agents of terroristic violence that bursts out with no exit to any organized politics or alternative public sphere.

In short, community and network appear in every film, while the films in each region are arranged with the overall focus shift from community to network. Though the degree of national community-based narrativity varies among these films, all of them engage transnational networking in some way, involving either various forms of cross-border experience (*Timbuktu, Roja, Rand De Basanti, Chungking Express*), or the inner-state deconstruction of national integrity (*Taste of Cherry, Life and Nothing More . . ., Slumdog Millionaire, Crouching Tiger, Hidden Dragon, A Touch of Sin*), or both (the Indian films in particular). The networking aspect of these films is especially pronounced in their contexts of transnational production and reception. As emphasized in Chapter 8, however, the crucial point is that the global community takes on a totalized network in the end. If Kiarostami experiments with pure network narratives, Jia suggests that what permeates our global network is not the liberating potential of pure networking so much as the constant risk of drifting precariously and exploding violently individually. The transnational deterritorialization of the national community is then reterritorialized into the globalized matrix of biopower and desire, which leaves no outside but a closed circuit of the abject floating without community. We will see what questions should be asked at the end of this networking with global network films.

Islamic World: *Timbuktu, Taste of Cherry, Life and Nothing More . . .*

Timbuktu is worth examining first because it spotlights a prototypical biopolitical community in relation to networked globalism and violent fundamentalism—that is, the soft- and hard-ethical aspects of globalization. Set in Timbuktu—an old Islamic center in Mali and a sub-Saharan hub of trading networks—the film is indeed based on the 2012 occupation of the city by Ansar Dine, an Islamic militant organization. The radical group of oppressive outsiders appear in the film with a jihadist black flag, take over Timbuktu by force, and impose an extremist interpretation of Sharia law on the open-minded Muslim denizens of the city. In Benjamin's terms discussed in Chapter 4, the jihadists destroy the existing regime by wielding the law-making power of violence and then govern their new city-state with the law-preserving violence of administering strict rules. Their community policing is nothing but ruthless biopolitical law enforcement, the primordial politics of fear that normalizes a constant lethal threat. They pass sentences of lashes for singing, smoking, playing football, and being in mixed-sex settings outside of one's family; they even stone an unmarried couple for adultery. Not to mention the absurd patriarchal sexism: a middle-aged woman who sells fish in the market is made to wear gloves, and a young woman is forcibly married though her family declines a jihadist's proposal.

While this totalitarian biopower constructs a fundamentalist religious community, the film acknowledges its inner contradictions. Some music, sports, fashion, and love affairs are banned, but jurisdiction often executes arbitrary arbitration rather than fair justice. The jihadists are unsure how to handle a song in praise of Allah and a football game with an imaginary ball. They even fail to live up to their own rules, arguing for Zidane or Messi as their favorite football star and enjoying smoking, which is an open secret among themselves. While this inconsistency apparently exposes their hypocrisy, it structurally implies their extralegal status as well. They are sovereign agents exceptional to normal laws and entitled to exclusive pleasures, evoking the primal father of the primitive community (see Chapter 8). The inconsistency thus indicates "a parallax gap between the public letter and its obscene superego supplement" (Žižek 2006, 10). The superego is by nature obscene as the embodiment of enjoyment beyond the reach of the subject; the permissive order of "Enjoy!" by the postmodern superego is the explicit externalization of this inherent obscenity. The law is split in itself in this sense.

At the same time, those supposedly antiglobalization militants are already placed within the same global flows (Holtmeier 2019, 72–80). Let's note that Sissako is an African epitome of the global auteur, trained abroad and coproducing all his films across continents (Gabara 2016). In a proto-network narrative form, the ensemble cast of *Timbuktu* speaks Arabic, French, English, and African languages, which are constantly translated between the townspeople and the jihadists. The latter even make a propaganda video to upload on the internet while, interestingly, admitting their lack of conviction in their faith (see Figure 9.1). The ideal of their divine war, the transcendent center of their community, is hollowed or rather filled with personal interests and cultural issues in daily life. Fundamentalism dissolves from within. No wonder today's terrorist organizations like the Islamic State (IS) use social media to recruit "the new rock stars of global cyber jihad," promising opportunities to enjoy adventure, find camaraderie, make history,

Figure 9.1. The jihadists in *Timbuktu* make a propaganda video to upload on the internet, but they secretly admit their lack of faith.

and impress the opposite sex (Taylor 2020). Reportedly, seductive benefits for new recruits include the offer of cars, houses, or women, as if the so-called reward of seventy-two virgins waiting for Muslim martyrs in heaven were given in this world before dying (though the misinterpreted word 'virgin' in the Quran means 'raisin' actually).

Such material and carnal motivations might explode into the IS members' "full-scale grotesque orgies, including robberies, gang rapes, torture and murder of infidels," as Žižek (2014) says. He argues that these violent libidinal outbursts prove their perverted resentment and envy of the permissive hedonistic First World. They are in effect "pseudo-fundamentalists [. . .] deeply bothered, intrigued and fascinated by the sinful life of nonbelievers." Why? Because they lack true conviction in their own belief, cause, and superiority. In other words, the IS members lack a feature of authentic fundamentalism as indifferent to and unthreatened by the nonbelievers' lifestyle. "The problem is not cultural difference (their effort to preserve their identity), but the opposite fact that they already like us, that, secretly, they have already internalized our standards and measure themselves by them." Though they behave like a local superego, they are globalized Oedipal subjects in this sense, driven by anger and desire for the obscene superego of the global system. Everyone, even terrorists, belongs to this globally networked system. *Timbuktu* shows nomads in the desert using mobile phones and naming a cow "GPS." The traditional, sacred, nationalistic sense of community gives way to the modern, secular, transnational flux of networking.

If pseudo-fundamentalism indicates a deeper parallax gap that emerges between the jihadists' local and global statuses, their sovereignty may employ a 'pseudo-divine violence' that does not save the potential sanctity of life but exerts domineering power over life in the name of (subjective) justice (see Chapter 4). The militants in the film justify their actions by cherry-picking only some points of Sharia when arguing with the local imam, who preaches genuine divinity in his peaceful temple. Indeed, two versions of Islam appear—that of the jihadists and that of the imam—which represent human law and divine law, respectively. The former exploits the latter, taking on pseudo-divine law and taking advantage of God as the pretext for sanctifying sovereign power to impose obedience and make any dissident a *homo sacer*. Noteworthy is the townspeople's futile but moving resistance to the law as pseudo-divine violence: the female fishmonger refuses to wear gloves, young people play forbidden music and soccer without a ball, and a Vodoun priestess blocks the jihadists' progress through an alley "in a global political alliance that evokes Mali's francophone colonial past" (Gabara 2016, 56). The most dramatic event unfolds around herdsman Kidane and fisherman Amadou. Amadou kills Kidane's cow, which damaged his net, so Kidane shoots Amadou dead, but accidently. Arresting Kidane, the jihadists offer to spare his life if Amadou's family forgives him and receives the compensation of forty cattle from him. Though Kidane's family gathers the cattle, Amadou's family declines this settlement. Kidane is sentenced to death and executed when running to his wife in the prison yard. The jihadists chase the motorcyclist who brought her to Kidane, and his daughter is shown running in the desert at the end.

However, Kidane's tragedy does not result from the direct enforcement of law as in other cases but from the seemingly objective mediation of law between two families in dispute via two traditional Sharia punishments: *diya* (financial compensation) and *qisas* (equal retaliation). This double measure evokes the origin of law tracing back to the Code of Hammurabi. Its 'eye-for-an-eye' principle sounds barbaric but was deemed just because it restricted compensation to the value of the loss; vengeance would otherwise tend to become unrestrained in the manner of harming the other's two eyes for one lost eye and then triggering an ever-growing vicious cycle of retaliation. Law was invented to intervene in such direct reprisal from the third-person perspective of judgmental authority. It prevents private vengeance; performs the public redemption of the victim; and thus replaces subjective justice with objective justice, which has taken increasingly indirect, civilized forms ranging from corporal punishment to fines and incarceration. But at this point, let's recall that according to René Girard (1979), there was a primary means for avoiding the escalation of violence even before the birth of law: ritual sacrifice. To sacrifice a victim to a deity was to purify the guilt and destructive potential of the community, quell the desire for revenge indirectly via divine power, and thus resolve bloody conflicts and unify the community. (Human) law took over the social role of this sacrificial ritual, which was a sort of divine law.

In *Timbuktu*, the shaman-like Vodoun priestess, a witch doctor, sacrifices an animal to divert violence from humans. Kidane might have felt humiliated and vengeful because Amadou had violated his vision of divine law—that nature (water, cattle) is sacred and shareable—which contradicts human law based on possession and calculation. His final acceptance of death may imply his submission to 'Inshallah' rather than Sharia. The film exposes multiple layers of law and/as violence this way. The point is that far from a modern judicial system, the jihadists' Sharia is not only applied arbitrarily and brutally but easily metes out capital punishment to achieve literal retributive equality. This law-preserving violence reaffirms the lawmaking violence of killing humans like animals, the foundational "rotten" core of law, "the origin of sovereignty as divinity-taken-through-animality" as explored in Chapter 4. This paradox resonates with the link between sacrifice and law. Law inherits divine power over sacrifice but risks distorting divine violence into pseudo-divine violence from subjective human standpoints. No matter how just their Sharia may be, the jihadists thus embody supralegal sovereignty, ready to kill *homo sacer*, who may be "killed and yet not sacrificed, outside both human and divine law" (Agamben 1998, 73). The general economy of theological abjection working in sacrificial rituals is then reductively reactivated as the scapegoat mechanism of biopolitical abjection in the name of law. Not to mention the fact that this mechanism defines all sorts of fascist communities that unite against an arbitrary abject who is blamed for all the chaos.

Is there any way out of such a repressive biopolitical local community or its self-contradictory (dis)integration into a permissive postpolitical global network? I propose a review of Kiarostami's Iranian road movies as Middle Eastern network films that invite an alternative mode of networking in Islamic culture and reinterpret the fundamental topics of life/death and humanity/divinity framed by the fundamentalists in *Timbuktu*. Kiarostami's road films typically take a repetitive, cyclical narrative in the form of journey or quest, made in minimalistic neorealist style with marked uses of long take, long shot, weak montage, nonprofessional actors, and natural locations. No doubt Kiarostami exemplifies the Bazinian "cinema as discovery" (D. Andrew 2010b, 52) or "cinema of uncertainty" (Mulvey 2006) that opens room for revelatory reality and interpretive freedom. This aesthetic realm also hosts poetic modernism in such docufictions as *Close-Up* (1990) and *Shirin* (2008), which blur the boundary between life and art or reality and cinema by reflecting on the filmmaker, the filmed subjects, and the spectator at the level of equally shared sensory experience. Building on Rancière's aesthetics, Nico Baumbach (2016) appreciates this "shareable cinema" as politically emancipatory in form, though not content, and defends Kiarostami against the common accusation of his "sanitized politics."[1] My point is that without losing these aesthetic implications, his films also open room for our further discussion of networking and its ethical, if not political, potential in content as well as form.

Let's focus on *Taste of Cherry*. It follows Badii, a seemingly wealthy, middled-aged Tehranian man, driving his truck around the city in search of someone who is willing to bury him in a pre-dug mountain grave after he kills himself with sleeping pills. He offers a lot of money to people he meets, including a Kurdish soldier and an Afghan seminarian, but nobody wants to assist his suicide. Eventually an old Turkish taxidermist in need of money for a sick son agrees to do so and yet also tries to save Badii's life, while talking about his own failed suicide attempt. In the past he had nearly hanged himself in a tree one night, but he happened to taste the delicious mulberries growing there; he then saw a magnificent sunrise, shared mulberries with passing children, and brought home and ate mulberries with his wife, happily. This narrated beauty of life does not seem to affect Badii, but he later asks the old man to make sure he is indeed dead before burying him. That night, Badii is seen lying looking up to the sky from his grave. But the film ends abruptly with a blackout followed by a short montage of handheld video footage depicting the making of the film, leaving his fate unknown. We see the film crew in bright daylight, including the actor playing Badii and

---

[1] It is noteworthy that another Iranian New Wave auteur, Mohsen Makhmalbaf, who appears as himself in *Close-Up*, represents a cinema of action unlike Kiarostami's. Makhmalbaf is known for his political dramas critical of the Islamic regime and ideology, as seen in *The Cyclist* (1989), *Kandahar* (2001), and *The President* (2014).

Kiarostami himself, smiling while working, along with a group of soldiers enjoying a break at the location.

Taste of Cherry shows nothing more than a nomadic man engaging in a tiring odyssey, only to end his life through a temporary network of chance encounters, without community-building. Badii's solitary depression, whose origin is never specified, intimates his total disconnection from any cohesive form of community that would have sustained his raison d'être and social identity, whether his family, people, nation, or religion. There is no transcendent center of communal life in which he keeps faith and for which his suicide can serve as a self-sacrifice. He is an abject in this sense, already symbolically dead; a living corpse who drives his car like a claustrophobic mobile coffin until his real death. The double death narrative in the cinema of catastrophe works perfectly in this film, which narrates an individual catastrophe. What is distinct is that Badii pursues postcatastrophic redemption not by struggling to restore his lost life but by taking a journey into the void, a godless pilgrimage to ultimate death that will terminate his hellish undeadness. His horizontal movement in a barren no-man's land is destined for his vertical fall into the grave as a symbolic rise to rest in peace—a kind of spiritual rise above nature, given his Antigone-evoking wish to be buried and thus protected from being preyed on by wild animals. This pursuit of human dignity implies his still-lurking desire to save his life at least from being bare life. By extension, the long and winding road to his grave might paradoxically indicate his unconscious delay of death, during which he might find a meaning in life and rekindle his will to live, that is, the possibility of redirecting postcatastrophic redemption back to life.

Of course this redemption never comes easily, as Badii remains apathetic toward everything and everyone he encounters. When people refuse to help him commit suicide because they are busy with work or performing a given duty, it may seem to him that they stick to life for clichéd reasons. His three car passengers are not that different. The Kurdish soldier accompanies him to his grave but runs away from assisting with the killing, though he serves a state-level killing machine. The Afghan seminarian preaches that suicide is a sin prohibited by God just like any other killing. The Turkish taxidermist tells the story of how he found life's value in everyday sensorial happiness. Overall, each of these interlocutors represents a certain social position with an existential contradiction: the soldier, trained for institutionalized killing, precludes the potential of death to be a gift; the seminarian applies a dogmatic religious judgment when practical flexibility is needed; and the taxidermist delivers the seemingly hackneyed wisdom that life can be either suffering or pleasure depending on one's mindset. None of them offers Badii a sufficiently convincing solution to what the existentialist Albert Camus (1991, 3) declares to be the "one truly serious philosophical problem," that is, "suicide," the question of whether and how life, absurd and meaningless in essence, is still worth living.

There are a few subtle yet more important points to make. Those three companions reflect Iran's ethnic diversity, which underlies Badii's transnational networking within his national community. However, the soldier's and the seminarian's values are still rooted in moral communities that determine their behavior and language. Conversely, the taxidermist speaks in his own voice about his own experience of the existential crisis that he overcame not in the name of law or God or any communal superego, but through his primordial awakening to the joyful sense of being-in-the-world as such.[2] The sacredness of life, if any, is not transcendent but immanent to anyone connected with this living world. It is not predetermined by a community but shareable with connected others like unknown children and maybe a stranger on the verge of suicide too, on the borderless egalitarian plane of people's contingent networking. The final camcorder footage of filmmaking radicalizes this networking mode. This epilogue, rather than diegetically extending to Badii's memory, dream, utopian afterlife, or renewed life, appears as a small piece of shareable cinema that mingles fiction and reality, diegesis and extradiegesis, interspersing the film crew and the onlookers while depicting a slice of life that they all share at that moment of temporarily activated networking. That lively, lighthearted moment of being happy together suddenly shatters the dry, gloomy, and serious mood of Badii's existential journey as if to confirm that, despite any lonely nihilist's pessimism, life goes on in the sensorial world of endless networking.

Here we cannot help recalling that another English title for *Life and Nothing More . . .* is *And Life Goes On*. An autobiographical docufiction, this road movie depicts Kiarostami's journey with his son back to the village featured in his earlier film *Where Is the Friend's House?* (1987). The village was devastated by an earthquake in 1990; Kiarostami hopes to find the children he filmed there five years prior. Against the bleak landscape of ruins, *Life and Nothing More . . .* epitomizes a genuine yet unconventional cinema

---

[2] See Alberto Elena's (2005, 122–43) rich film analysis and survey of other reviews, especially about Kiarostami's controversial approach to death/suicide in postrevolutionary, post-Islamic Iran.

of catastrophe, in which not the protagonist so much as an entire community grope for postcatastrophic redemption. Every bit of raw reality, from a cracked picture on the wall to a deep fault plane, evidences the 'dynamically sublime' earthquake, but the abject villagers who lost everything still live their uncertain life to the fullest, reconciled yet resilient to their terrible fate and silent God. Likewise, the film remains ambiguous about the child actors' lives until the end, while continuing a decentered narrative of the director's casual encounters with survivors; one may recall Jacques Tati's roving director-protagonist in *Playtime* (Saeed-Vafa and Rosenbaum 2003, 23). In this respect, we see a pure narrative film. Those survivors are not transnational, but their locality is already networked to the global media system indicated by the mentions of TV centers and World Cup matches, while their marginality leaves room for pure networking unbound by the system's reterritorializing totality. The director's car, again, appears like a mobile agent of this endless networking, carrying him over and over to an elsewhere that is not given beforehand. As Nancy (2001) says, we see nothing other than "the acute and tenuous point of a forward movement that precedes itself indefinitely" (68) and "only this sliding along by means of which it leads itself from one image to another," with no spectacle, voyeurism, or sentimentality (78).

It is no surprise that the film begins with the car passing a toll gate and ends with the car crossing a hill, already and always in the middle of movement without origin or end. It shows only the continuation of 'and,' as the title says: (catastrophe occurs) "and life goes on." The director's words to his son, "we'll see later," promise no utopian destination but just 'atopian' motion without topos/place (see Part IV). This mode of networking does not build any cohesive community or bring divine redemption; instead it motivates unexpected connections based on the commonality of (potential) abjecthood. Particularly memorable is the last shot, an extreme long shot set in a cosmic long take: the director passes a man carrying heavy luggage and drives up a hill until the overheated engine stops. The man with the tank helps restart the engine and walks uphill once the car leaves. But after barely climbing the hill, the director stops his car and picks up the man; they move on together. The zigzagging, hilly road then appears as the figurative stage of 'gift-giving' that goes back and forth between these two strangers who offer their hands to each other, adjust to each other's pace, and accompany each other in the end. The nearly abject, solitary strangers form a temporary relationship of precarious yet precious solidarity without unity. We cannot but endure their toil virtually together for its whole duration without a cut, but this cinematic experience lets us sense an ethical, if not political, potentiality of abject agency emerging slowly and gradually beyond the double ethics of pity and hate in the global system.

India's Nationalist Cinema and Beyond:
Roja, Rang de Basanti, Slumdog Millionaire

Since Part IV delves into the alternative ethics discussed earlier, let me now move on to Indian cinema for a case study of nation-(re)building in the proper sense of the term and its complications in our global age. Apt as a starting point is Mani Ratnam's 'terrorism' trilogy from the 1990s—*Roja*, *Bombay*, and *Dil Se*—which expands the locus of desire from the small community-as-nation typical of early Bombay films to the outside, the borders where phantasmatic encounters with the other are staged along with the interstices between civil society and the state, Hindus and Muslims, and terrorists and 'benign' citizens. Alluding to actual political events, these films shed light on "the danger zones of national self-awareness, those nebulous regions hitherto unrepresented but now rendered seductive and compelling" (Chakravarthy 2000, 231–32). This audacious move is palpable in full scale in *Roja*, a romantic thriller about a simple village girl named Roja in Tamil Nadu. Though she unexpectedly marries her sister's unwanted arranged partner Rishi, who is an urban cryptologist and state intelligence agent, the couple fall in love quickly and deeply. But soon after they move to the beautiful yet troubled region of Kashmir, where Rishi is sent for work, he is kidnapped by Islamic militants pursuing the separation of Kashmir from India; their leader, Liaqat, wants to free his associate from judicial custody in exchange for Rishi. To rescue Rishi, Roja desperately begs for help from the creaking government machinery, which finally decides to do the prisoner exchange. However, Rishi refuses to be used as a pawn to release a notorious terrorist and convinces Liaqat that his war is immoral. The film ends with Rishi escaping the terrorist group to join Roja at the exchange spot on his own, while Liaqat escapes the Indian army after letting Rishi go.

Roja has become an influential nationalist Indian film, not despite but thanks to its integration of transnationality. It exemplifies Tamil cinema, dubbed in Hindi and set mainly in Kashmir, thus simultaneously representing South, Central, and North India. Roja evokes a rural premodern India with her subalternity turning into an idyllic backdrop, Rishi embodies an urban modern India as a middle-class yuppie seemingly unbound by the caste system, and Liaqat represents an antagonistic other of India who threatens the nation-state's unity by vying for independent sovereignty. If Roja and Rishi combine touristic and patriotic India, Liaqat incarnates its terroristic heterogeneity. Roja's love and Rishi's loyalty transcend Liaqat's separatism; the narrative flows toward the ultimate reunification of both the couple and the nation. Far from re-enacting the nation's foundational liberation from British colonialism, this new India emerges by both accommodating and subduing a recent rise in independence movements within India's borders. It is a postcolonial nation wherein a formulaic and utopian interplay of major and minor ethnicities occurs through the heroic middle-class Hinduism that takes on a new universality of nationalism: not anti-Western but anti-Muslim. Hinduist multiculturalism serves as the secular mainstream ideology of tolerance, integrating cultural and regional differences into one holistic, inclusive nation, while Islamic terrorism is excluded as the fundamentalist ideology of intolerable violence. Roja and Rishi's India is therefore a national community reimagined with "a new globalized national imaginary purveyed through a visual language of exotic abandon, as well as the terror of the unassimilable stranger" (Chakravarthy 2000, 235). Here, the soft and hard ethics of the global regime underlie the (self-)orientalist film style in a similar double way: voyeuristically exhibiting touristic spectacles of landscapes, musicals, and stars on the one hand and fetishizing the distanced stranger obsessively—even fascistically (Bharucha 1994)—on the other. This abject stranger sacrificed for the fictive resolution of conflicts through a globally updated nationalist hegemony is obviously the farthest from Kiarostami's networked strangers.

Reimagining the national community of India is further refined and complicated in a new millennial Bollywood phenomenon, *Rang de Basanti* (Paint it saffron). It dramatizes the title's symbolic meaning of sacrifice and courage in a mise-en-abyme narrative of nation-(re)building via filmmaking. Sue, a British director, comes to India to make a docudrama about folk heroes of Indian nationalism under British rule. With her Indian friend's help, she casts a group of graduates from Delhi University who haunt their old campus for aimless pleasure. Though they are apolitical, jaded urban youths, they gradually become interested in the film's production and inspired by the historical freedom fighter scenes they re-enact. This political awakening leads to their own activist engagement in the world. When one of them, a pilot in the Indian Air Force, dies in a MiG-21 jet crash as a result of avoiding crashing into a populous city, the government ascribes the accident to pilot error, though it turns out that the greedy defense minister had faulty MiG parts imported from Russian dealers in exchange for a personal favor. Devastated by this shameful treatment given to their friend and their nation as well, the group decide to fight for justice against the corrupt state power. They organize a peaceful protest, but police brutality triggers their further, more radical reactions. They assassinate the minister to avenge the pilot's tragic death and briefly take over the national radio station to publicly clarify that their intention is not terroristic but patriotic. After they are all killed by the police, the epilogue shows the butterfly effect of their deaths: a wave of demonstrations demanding state reform across India.

While updating *Roja*'s postcolonial India, *Rang de Basanti* does so via colonial India. Sue's film within the film, set in the 1930s, intercepts the main story set in the 2000s at decisive moments, as if crosscut in parallel montage. The climax of the film blurs the past and the present, reiterating nationalism as not yet dead and reawakening people's passion for action to change the system and rebuild the nation. The world history of colonialism indeed teaches that nationalism, despite its fascistic potential, can work as the abject nation-people's pivotal and inevitable agency of resistance to the actual fascistic sovereign empire. The fighters for Indian independence personify this abject agency, with their sublime spirit already freed from the British regime of biopolitical oppression and even the fear of torture and death in prison. Sue's film romanticizes their transcendent martyrdom for a big cause in nostalgic sepia tones, while motivating the actors to inherit its abiding communal values. These actors, often shot in MTV style, stand for pop culture, urban youth, individual freedom, and liberal hedonism in a postcolonial, postpolitical India, but the history lesson of anticolonialism enlightens this carefree, cynical generation to lead an anticorruption movement. It even takes on an Oedipal struggle as one of them kills his father, who was involved in the corrupt MiG deals; here we see a patricidal resistance to a power system colluding with dirty money. Young Indian sons want to replace a bad patriarchal state with a good one, a more transparent democratic modern state to be remarried by 'Mother India.' Nationalism is naturalized in this family tie between the community and the land.

Notable is the ideological way of representing the historical abject agency. Sue restages the marginalized saga of a guerrilla group led by the Punjabi revolutionary Bhagat Singh and re-evaluates their militantism as more apt for political change than Gandhian pacifism, which British producers, when

Figure 9.2. *Rang de Basanti* re-enacts the past of Indian freedom fighters, whose slogan *Inquilab Zindabad* means "Long Live the Revolution."

rejecting her project, say they prefer to see on screen (see Figure 9.2). The film justifies violent resistance to power by reaffirming both the past and present freedom fighters as patriots instead of terrorists. To rebuild the nation, *Roja* conducts war on terror, but *Rang de Basanti* reappropriates terrorism and turns it into patriotic abject agency. However, if Gandhi's nonviolence has been co-opted into the orientalist imagery of a peace-loving, other-worldly India, Bhagat Singh's radical violence is co-opted by the middle-class hegemony that fictively sutures social divisions into a nationalist India. The guerrilla leader's original Marxist support of social revolution is diluted and repackaged for regime change within the existing political system. The film thus delivers "a confused and simplistic reformist message aimed at its target audience, young middle-class Indians [. . .] entrusted with 'saving' the nation from corruption" (Srivastava 2009, 713). In Benjamin's terms (see Chapter 4), the abject guerrillas' law-breaking divine violence is reduced to the urban elite's lawmaking mythical violence. Indian cinema has indeed served to converge divided castes into the bourgeois version of "the national-popular" when this notion, in Antonio Gramsci's original sense, centers on the working class or the rural poor, as Italian neorealism shows (Srivastava 2009, 705–6). By extension, trendy nationalist films upgrade Bollywood family entertainment to youth-oriented, commercial, hip culture, staging the filial bonds between cultures, religions, and generations. The gang in *Rang de Basanti* teams up with a political member who opposes their Western culture. Sue, the granddaughter of a British colonel who executed Bhagat Singh's group, purges her country's historical guilt through her filmic tribute to the past Indian 'terrorists' and the present patriots—she even falls in love with one of her actors. This postcolonial position shift and unity between the United Kingdom and India occur at the multicultural crossroads of nationalism and transnationalism, as well as of community and network.

No doubt such a political film loses radical potential while stylizing it with a mainstream multiculturalist sensibility and thereby moves toward the foreseeable turning point at which politics, in the wake of bringing about a more inclusive free society, would paradoxically dissolve into postpolitical soft ethics (see Chapter 1). It is in this context that we can move on to *Slumdog Millionaire*, a British director's Indian film—doesn't Danny Boyle play Sue's diegetic role extradiegetically? Loosely based on a best-selling novel, this global Bollywood hit stages eighteen-year-old Jamal Malik's performance on the Indian version of the TV quiz show *Who Wants to Be a Millionaire?* He is only one question away from winning the grand prize, while the entire nation watches. But the police arrest him on suspicion of cheating before the final round of the show, assuming that a street kid like him from the slums of Mumbai could not know so much. Jamal desperately proves his innocence by telling his survival stories as the keys to his performance: he grew up with his brother as an orphan, went through adventures on the road across India, encountered vicious gangs, and fell in love with a girl, later losing her. Depicted in flashbacks, these episodes reveal that he happened to learn the answers to various difficult quizzes at unforgettable moments in his short but turbulent life experience. After convincing the police, Jamal returns to the show and answers the last question correctly, but this time just by chance. As his girlfriend watches and joins him in a happy ending, it turns out that his motivation for the show was not simply the money but the love he wanted to regain.

The film draws the typical narrative arc of abjection and redemption as Jamal, a slumdog, undergoes and overcomes his status as a catastrophic bare life cast out of society. This 'down-and-up' story is literally condensed into his first anecdote: at the age of five, he manages to obtain a Bollywood star's autograph after falling into and rising from a cesspit full of excreta, the material abject par excellence. The rest of the film is nothing other than the symbolic expansion of this vertical movement. Though thrown into the bottom of the world, the abject scrapes by with small jobs and becomes a kind of agent who fulfills the mission of solving quizzes, until he reaches the highest spot on the show, thereby recovering social subjectivity. Interestingly, another vertical movement occurs in Jamal's mind, entailing the horizontal movement of his body. As the quiz game does not progress in a linear leveling-up video game structure (later quizzes are not necessarily trickier than earlier ones), the film's setting contingently shifts from one place to another, where Jamal's memories evoked by the quizzes were formed. We are prompted to explore different strata of his past 'geologically' and related areas of India 'geographically' accordingly. That is, his present mind goes up and down vertically alongside his past memory—whose Deleuzian model looks like an inverted cone storing sheets of the past—while his abject body drifts here and there horizontally like a spatial agent navigating the nation in the video game mode of space navigation. The quiz game thus catalyzes the fusion of a sort of mind game and a navigation game into a cerebral-corporeal game. It unfolds across time and space, memory and matter, materializing a pop-culture version of the Proustian remembrance of the past against the backdrop of diverse landscapes open to often dark realities. The screen works like a Deleuzian brain and a Bazinian window at the same time.

More importantly, this layered game narrative traverses a contingent network of people and places that interconnect through chance encounters, nomadic moves, and serendipities. *Slumdog Millionaire* adopts the structure of a road movie, guiding us to Mumbai's massive ghetto and historical station as well as travel hotspots including the Taj Mahal, where Jamal pretends to be a tour guide. Like a precarious migrant worker, Jamal does everything ad hoc to survive in a capitalist, tourist, urbanized, and polarized network society under global cultural flows and market forces. Notable is India's new service economy, with implicated issues of labor, transforming the caste-based opportunity system and enhancing urban prospects for mobility (Parthasarathy 2009). Moreover, the gambling-like quiz show, driven by the escalating equation of information and money, reflects cognitive-financial capitalism in a globalized entertainment format. The media industry, in a sense, redistributes wealth to quiz participants, including the underclass, but this social function enabled by commercials resorts to media consumers, thus celebrating not only the winner but the whole market system in the end. And it is this system that totalizes a vast network. When numerous Indians cheer and enjoy Jamal hitting the jackpot, their national community is reimagined via TV as a dreamland where a slumdog can become a millionaire. Updating

Roja and *Rang de Basanti*, this fairytale of *Slumdog Millionaire* resolves real contradictions with a fantastic postpolitical suggestion that it can happen to anyone, just as everyone dances happily in the musical ending scene. Though the film has been acclaimed by global multicultural audiences, this postpolitical aesthetic inevitably reduces or exaggerates the Real of India while 'selling' its superficial experience. As often critiqued, the film displays a still-orientalized India with postcard images of landmarks and 'poverty porn' while consuming social issues—the Bombay riots, street kids abused as beggars and prostitutes, crime organization networks, and so on—as the sensational backdrop of a heroic individual's success story. It appeals to Western culture and development models, but with "hollow idioms of social justice" (Sengupta 2010). This controversy sums up the complexity of the community-network transition in the Global South.

Pan-Chinese Global Cinema: *Crouching Tiger, Hidden Dragon, Chungking Express, A Touch of Sin*

To further our discussion, let's go farther east and examine the community-network transition in a larger region through pan-Chinese cinema. This term includes the cinemas of mainland China, Hong Kong, and Taiwan, which are more culturally interrelated than nationally distinct. Among many films in this context is the uniquely hybrid *Crouching Tiger, Hidden Dragon*, a Hollywood-made, Chinese-language global hit directed by Taiwanese American Ang Lee and coproduced by many companies across the globe, involving a transnational crew and pan-Chinese, all-star cast. My point is that (global) networking is not limited to production but is reflected on screen even in this martial arts film set in a nineteenth-century Chinese (local) community. It begins with renowned swordsman Li Mu Bai leaving Mount Wudang, the base of his sect, to end his blood-stained career. He asks Yu Shu Lien, a female warrior in Beijing, to give his legendary Green Destiny sword to their benefactor. However, the governor's daughter, Jen, steals it to become a supreme martial heroine right before her arranged marriage. Lo, a desert bandit who fell in love with Jen in the past, comes back and asks her to leave with him. But Jen refuses him, runs away from her husband, and enjoys her victorious fights with a local gang. She then engages in duels with Yu and Li respectively, never giving up the sword even when defeated. However, Jen tries to save Li (in vain) when he is poisoned by Jade Fox, her former teacher, who slept with Li's master to learn Wudang skills but killed him because he refused to take a female pupil. Li kills Fox but dies in Yu's arms, confessing his love for Yu. Jen finally goes to meet Lo.

To get back to my point, this film is about a multilayered dialectic interplay of apprenticeship, antagonism, negotiation, and transition between two generations, representing the community and network principles. The old generation, Li and Yu, stands for China's traditional community and fights for its values as *wuxia* (martial heroes), which literally means 'martial vigilantes.' The wuxia genre indeed shows Chinese 'dark knights' who wield supralegal violence to redress wrongs, exact retribution for past misdeeds, and thereby sustain law and order. Li, one such sovereign agent, is also a patriarchal master who inherited the Wudang sect; he tries to retrieve the lost sword, wants to have the talented Jen as his successor, and avenges his master's death on Fox. Vigilantism is intimated in Yu's management of a private security company, too. Moreover, Li and Yu repress their mutual love due to their loyalty to his dead friend, who was engaged to her. Their personal desires are always restrained for the sake of communal security and moral duty, for fidelity and honor. Conversely, Jen and Lo embody the new generation's untamable desire for freedom and equality. Their fervent passions, ignited in the western desert, are far from the unrequited loves of Li and Yu; they are unbound by the class/status gaps and social codes/customs set in the conservative hierarchical community. If Beijing refers to this secular community of law, and Mount Wudang is its sacred sovereign outside, the desert appears outside both spaces. Jen's free love with Lo, her accidental networking with this romantic nomad, thus deterritorializes her community toward a new horizon of life. But it also matters that back in Beijing, Jen pursues independence more than love. Learning martial arts from Fox, Jen not only surpasses Fox in combat skills but overcomes Fox's vengeful feminism stuck in the yoke of patriarchy. We see a coming-of-age story about a next-generation feminist warrior.

The generational gap is visually conspicuous when they fight, such as in the famous bamboo forest scene. When Li and Yu try to pull Jen down to the ground, Jen's gravity-defying body soars lightly in flight.[3] These opposite vertical movements create a symbolic choreography of balance and peril, tradition and transgression, past and future. One is centripetal, toward the

---

[3] Digital special effects in wuxia/action films often display this stark verticality as the referential axis of narrative conflicts. Jen's upward mobility embodies aspiration, vitality, defiance against burdens, inertia, and subordination (Whissel 2006, 29–30).

community; the other is centrifugal, away from it. However, their long duels with dialogue catalyze their mutual understanding and appreciation as well. Jen's effort to prevent Li's death reveals her realization of his legacy and respect for his life, only after which she is liberated from her obsession with the sword, the phallic object of desire for sovereign power. The ambiguous ending that shows her jumping into flight among the clouds may thus signal less her suicide than her genuine freedom emerging from self-growth and not stolen power. It represents her openness to an unknown second life (with or without Lo), liberated from the community world without destructive rebellion. Likewise, Li and Yu do not behave like a strict superego but like exemplary seniors, who also see what they lack through Jen and Lo. The seniors facilitate the juniors' reunion and express their own long-suppressed feelings for each other in the end, as if they have found their true selves in love rather than in the righteous causes that have driven their heroic lives. Li's retirement, which he planned due to his inability to find desired enlightenment through martial arts or zen, is at first disrupted by Jen but then completed via her in the way he is freed from his burdened fate, which she eventually honors.

As the title suggests, *Crouching Tiger, Hidden Dragon* thus dramatizes two generations' delicate negotiation and remediated reconciliation in the waning years of the Qing dynasty and its community values. The film is an ode to "Good old China" in wuxia fiction, "a dream that all the Chinese people in the world have, an impression. Gone with the wind" as Ang Lee says (S. H. Lu 2005, 225). It is a nostalgically reimagined Chinese community, honoring the old generation's dignity, authenticity, and cultural identity. At the same time, this homage to wuxia is fused with other genre elements (romance, melodrama, journey, coming-of-age). The film even looks like a Chinese western in the scenes that unfold in an exotic desert similar to Monument Valley in the United States. It opens an uncharted territory of networking with transgressional outsiders, circulating nomadic, feminist, individualist desires that challenge the community model of relationship and lifestyle. This cultural hybridity made an appeal to the transnational network of film reception and contributed to the Hollywood action film trend of co-opting martial arts style in an orientalist manner without its real locality. In this sense, Sheldon Lu claims, Ang Lee's imaginary China is "a dehistoricized, disembedded entity in the global commercial film market [. . .] a shallow fantasy world, a wishful thinking, a stage for global entertainment" (231). The transition from the old to the new generations, from community to network, does not make the former's culture obsolete. It is recycled in the new media logic of "remediation" (Bolter and Grusin 1999), yet also reduced to surface images in the postmodern logic of multiculturalism.

Without falling into the orientalist trap, Wong Kar-wai's contemporary Hong Kong shifts us to the next phase, in which the community-network transition is completed and the question is no longer the liberation from any community but the lack thereof. Among others, *Chungking Express* is not only a network narrative film but a film about life in network society. Its double-pronged structure follows two heartsick policemen in sequence, who mull over their romantic relationships with a lost lover as well as a new woman; the first cop's story switches to the second one's when they cross paths at a food stand. Cop 223, jilted by his girlfriend May on April 1, keeps buying cans of her favorite pineapple with the expiration date of May 1; he will buy them continually until that date, trying to see if his love will return or expire forever. Meanwhile, he encounters a mysterious underworld woman who is exhausted by her failed drug smuggling activities and feels attached, only to spend an eventless night with her. Cop 663 breaks up with his flight attendant girlfriend and spends time talking to objects in his home. Meanwhile, the food stand server, Faye, falls for him and frequently enters his apartment with the keys left by his ex-girlfriend to clean it, unknown by him. Upon realizing Faye's secret service, he proposes a date and waits at a restaurant called California, only to learn that she has left for the real California, leaving him a boarding pass drawn on a napkin dated a year later. One day Faye returns as a flight attendant to the snack shop, which he now owns, and writes him a new boarding pass before leaving again.

Set in the early 1990s, *Chungking Express* exhibits Hong Kong at the peak of its spatiotemporal postmodernity, before its 1997 retrocession to China. The city appears doubly compressed into a splendid global hub of capitalist flows and a dense local hive of multiethnic populations. Prevalent in both are "non-places" (Augé 2009): spaces of transience where people remain anonymous and stay only temporarily, in passing; these spaces are not "places" where people live, share social references with others, and build their stable cohesive identity. Evidently the notions of place and nonplace resonate with community and network. Most of the film narrative unfolds in nonplaces, including an airport, a hotel, a bar, a restaurant, a convenience store, a street market, and the shopping mall in Chungking Mansions—an urban jungle where the black market of drugs flourishes through transnational networking. Even the cops' homes lose their proper sense of place, filled only with pets or fetishes to soothe their melancholia and remaining mostly vacant or doubly occupied by an ethereal figure (Faye). In these nonplaces, time passes, or say, evaporates like the air, with no anchor, as visualized in step-printing shots of speedy, blurred, disjoined motions. The characters set up deadlines like expiration/reservation dates, send birthday messages, delay reading ex-lovers' letters, and wait for new lovers endlessly, in the way of creating a private temporality to hold fleeting relations against this free-floating time. They attempt in vain to shelter eternal memories from ephemeral temporality. Eventually the two cops in 'romantic abjection' overcome their melancholic attachment to the lost object of desire by mourning for the dead past and embracing an unknown future in solitude. This post-breakup transition to a more solid self may be all the more crucial since there is no community that sustains them in the world of networking.

Indeed, Hong Kong looks like nothing but a pure network space where even the cops appear less as sovereign agents of the city-state and more as lonely walkers among the crowd, that is, metropolitan flâneurs. In this regard, Tsung-Yi Huang (2001) aptly points out that Cop 233 wanders and approaches the drug dealer like a "hunter," whose proximity to the "prey" ends up with failed reciprocity (135). Cop 663's failed recognition of changes wrought by Faye in his apartment relates to what city walkers experience as "reverse hallucination"; he is unable to see the obvious in what Ackbar Abbas dubs a "space of disappearance" that is constantly rebuilt to the extent of being subtly unrecognizable (141). Similarly, the drug dealer is a *flâneuse*, a female walker whose failed mapping of fragmentary urban space leads to the failure of her job. Her femme fatale look, with a blond wig and sunglasses, rather turns her into a "disoriented dupe" with an impaired gaze in an unfamiliar global city (131). All these cases are symptomatic of modern urban walkers' difficulty in resisting, tracing, and navigating a sprawling, ever-changing, chaotic network society. They are maladjusted flâneurs who are unable to establish an intimate relationship, numbed to new external stimuli and lost in unmappable rhizomatic settings. This social environment provokes and frustrates their desires at the same time, fascinating them yet also trapping their lives in a local area compressed with global allure.

Of course there is Faye, the only character who does not fail to meet her desire, reshape her life, and realize a global dream unbound by locality. Unlike Cop 233's conventional flirting approach to the blond-wigged woman, Faye intrudes upon Cop 663's intimate space to improve it invisibly like a positive 'parasite,' an agent of symbiotic change near (*para-*) its host (*site*). This is her dreamy way of living together even without expecting a direct immediate reciprocity, just as she constantly plays her favorite classic pop song, "California Dreamin'" (and sings the Cranberries song "Dreams" in Cantonese extradiegetically), as if to stay in these dreams happily alone. It is unclear why she leaves the cop, delaying a date until a year later; she might have preferred her enjoyable solitude to an actual relationship, lost her long passion due to his too-late response, found a new dream to be a flight attendant while sharing his past, or wanted to replace/revive his lost love with another flight attendant. For whatever reason, she frees herself from the Hong Kong that confines the others toward a vast network of global (airline) connections. But California may not have been a dreamy utopia for her, as it never appears in the film. It rather exists as a restaurant name, a multicultural simulacrum in postmodern reality filmed in impressionistic splashes of motion, color, and mirror images that reflect the double structure, identity, and occupancy of the film, the city, and its people. In sum, two men long for the past and two women drift into the future, while chance encounters link all of them in a bipartite narrative, with each man and woman shot alternately in each part. The film epitomizes 1990s youth culture (visualizing Murakami Haruki's literary postmodernism) in an exhilarating romantic fashion, especially in Faye's story. This dizzily charming style, however, betrays the uncertainty and impermanence of network-driven precarious love and floating life. With no community, sustainable relationships give way to a regressive yet manageable solitude that both opens to constant connections and defends itself against painful disconnections. How 'cool' is this lifestyle?

Let's move on to the final stage of our trajectory. If Wong Kar-wai's Hong Kong takes on a relatively 'pure network' of the middle class, Jia Zhangke's mainland China typifies the global community as a 'totalized network' of the underclass. To briefly bring back *The World*, mentioned in Chapter 1, the eponymous theme park is nothing but a mini simulacrum of the global village as a splendid prison of migrant workers. It manifests China's transition from its communist past to a capitalist future, which will entail the global symptoms of polarization and abjection. While the park publicly stages kitsch multicultural attractions and ahistorical monuments (including the still-standing Twin Towers), the narrative flows around the workers' dingy semiprivate nonplaces (the backstage, the bathroom, the bar, etc.). Here, we see not only microlevel human dramas from romance to suicide but macrolevel networking among those circulated and exploited by capital, including Russian dancers. These underpaid laborers cannot afford to escape the park World, but even their escape would lead to another prison, as one of them ends up being stuck in a Chinatown in Paris, a simulacrum of China. The implication is not just that they are excluded from the capitalist benefits of China's globalization, that "no money to travel outside China means no upward mobility either" (T. Lu 2008, 172). More crucially, the real world outside the simulated world is ever more simulated. The park World is to the real world what Disneyland is to America, if we recall Jean Baudrillard (1981, 12), for whom Disneyland "exists in order to hide that it is the 'real' country, all of 'real' America that is Disneyland (a bit like prisons are there to hide that it is the social in its entirety, in its banal omnipresence, that is carceral)." The simulacrum is thus a disguise of reality itself, as full of simulacra with no original outside.[4]

Likewise, the global village is a totalized network with no exit. Some workers leave for Mongolia, but this peripheral alternative land hosting migrants from both China and Russia may be on the verge of globalization, following its two former communist neighbors. Some workers funnel their hopes for escape into cell phones, but their virtual communication has all the features of new media networking—rapid turnovers of connection/disconnection, attachment/detachment, attraction/distraction, and seduction/protection—which both facilitate and limit social relations as amorphous, unstable, pragmatic, and ephemeral. Their text messages are even inflated into wide-screen shots of flash animation, which turn the gray theme park into a colorful dream space, but the fantastic flight from reality leads nowhere even within the animation. One worker says in an immobile airplane simulacrum, "If I stay only here, I would become a ghost." Indeed, the dead couple still speak in the last scene as though they have become ghosts confined in their dirty, shadowed underground dormitory, the postmortem abject entrapped forever in the closed circuit of World.

Jia's network narrative space expands from the Beijing theme park to all of China in *A Touch of Sin*. If *The World* is technically an ensemble film, *A Touch of Sin* showcases a global network narrative per se by loosely connecting four

---

[4] I have discussed elsewhere *The World* as "a modest critique of the 'society of the spectacle' that Guy Debord radically debunks, and fundamentally, an ironic critique of what Heidegger calls the 'world picture,' not a picture of the world but 'the world conceived and grasped as picture,' i.e. as habitual image" (Jeong 2013b, 130). By extension, the film could be seen as a critique of the world of simulation or a simulacra network.

vignettes of four outcasts set in vastly dispersed regions that are nonetheless totalized under the sway of neoliberal capitalism. The film is based on recent newsworthy events that evidence how the postpolitical combination of the communist state and the capitalist market permeates and impacts every corner of daily life in today's postsocialist China. Its authoritarian neoliberalism has brought about the world's fastest-growing economy and upgraded China to a global superpower, yet it has also triggered increasingly complicated systemic injustice and class division. Four main characters in the film are poor, rural, migrant, or nomadic underclass people, who all undergo some sort of social abjection and then turn into abject agents of violence: vengeful, impulsive, feminist, or suicidal. It is the abject's inevitably reactive violence against the structural violence of the system enacted on them. In Žižek's (2008b, 2) terms, it is "subjective violence" performed by identifiable agents whose normal subjectivity is threatened by the "objective violence" inherent in the normal state of things. The four episodes chronicle four variations of this double violence while also drawing from traditional culture, including animal symbolism, the Chinese opera, and wuxia stories, but in the manner of updating Ang Lee's 'good old China' to Jia Zhangke's 'dark new China.'

The first segment centers on Dahai, a miner in a northern village where the community-run coal mine has been sold off cheaply (through the village chief's influence) to Dahai's former classmate and current boss, a pompous nouveau riche who behaves like a head of state while exploiting poor workers. Dahai raises the question of inequality overtaking the village as a consequence of this exploitation, but his voice is dismissed and met with physical violence by his boss as well as the village chief and the Communist Party. The state-capital complicity in the neoliberal privatization of the public sector is not an abstract concept here. It palpably causes the exponential class disparity between the old friends and treats the oppressed loser like an animal, just as Dahai, when beaten, is shown with a whipped horse. This humiliating abjection drives him to become an angry agent of explosive vengeance, a modern wuxia who brutally kills those corrupt authorities with his rifle, draped in the tiger-patterned cloth that symbolizes his sovereign turn from the horse-like bare life (see Figure 9.3). Shifting to southwest China, the second story follows Zhou San, a lone killer, whose home village bespeaks the stagnation of rural areas, left behind in China's rapid urbanization. The countryside, once a Maoist sanctuary of communist enlightenment, now stands for "the despised antithesis of modernity," emaciating the youth and emasculating

Figure 9.3. In *A Touch of Sin*, a humiliated miner becomes a modern wuxia, who explodes vengeful violence against China's neoliberal capitalism.

the men in particular (Wang 2015, 163). Zhou escapes this "boring," lifeless wasteland to be a roaming robber, traveling around aimlessly on his motorcycle and impulsively killing whoever gets in the way. Like a gangster hero, he wields his phallic firearms and makes his own fireworks as if to remasculinize himself, even just to "feel alive." His Chicago Bulls hat catches the eye as an animal symbol of power and valor like the Ox of the Chinese zodiac, though it is shadowed by tethered cattle that impede his path, evoking his past rural, abject life.

In the third section, Xiaoyu, a sauna receptionist in central China, is forced to 'sell' her body by corrupt local officials, who even whip her face with a wad of cash upon her refusal and shout with anger, "I have money!" Not merely a means of transaction, money manifests itself as "a law onto itself" (Wang 2015, 163) that takes on sovereign power, suspending social norms and degrading women to the status of sexual commodities, that is, bare lives in the sex industry. Similarly, a gaudy van displays the "snake lady" surrounded by crawling snakes and touted as a divine fortuneteller. Aligned with such abject women, however, Xiaoyu turns into an agent of feminist punishment for patriarchal capitalism. She kills one of the dirty, greedy officials in wuxia style, evoking the unruly folktale heroine of *Green Snake*

(Tsui Hark, 1993) seen in the sauna and the female knight-errant in *A Touch of Zen* (King Hu, 1971).[5] By contrast, the fourth chapter sheds light on abject agency's self-destruction, partly adapting the sensational news of the horridly exploited Foxconn workers' suicides. Xiaohui is a rural teenager who works but keeps changing jobs in a coastal city, enchanted by the China Dream of consumerist fantasy and upward mobility and yet entrapped in the prison of "cruel optimism" (Berlant 2011) that only brings him social alienation and unfulfilled desires. After being rejected by his love, a nightclub hostess—who services her client sexually in front of him—and abandoned by his family, Xiaohui jumps off his dormitory to end his abject life. Like the confined migrant workers in *The World*, Xiaohui's social ascent, future, and manhood are thwarted, as he has no money, hope, and love. He even has no clear sovereign enemy to resist, stuck in a Deleuzian control society where governmentality widely diffuses responsibility over networked individuals. His online ID 'Little Bird' ('bird' means 'penis' in Chinese slang) only allows him to take a symbolic flight from the net of social biopower when it signifies an act of self-castration cunningly pushed by the invisible hand of structural violence.

In sum, *A Touch of Sin* connects four tableaux of abject agency that are symptomatic of the dehumanizing side effects caused by China's relentless biopolitical, neoliberal turn. The outcasts channel their rage into deadly violence, exploding their depression and degradation. But even when fighting for dignity, they take at best private vengeance for subjective justice outside the law by resorting to pseudo-sovereign, even terroristic uses of violence. With no community to rebuild, they cannot play the role of classical wuxia, either. As the director calls them "damaged knights-errant" (Wang 2015, 165), they are terrorist-wuxia, so to speak, the Dark Knight turning into Bane (see Chapter 4). Their bloody rampage partakes of convulsive pseudo-divine violence and not truly liberational divine violence, temporarily disrupting personal relations in solitude without any social solidarity. The film's omnibus structure implies this limitation of individual resistance to the system. The network narrative form reflects its diegetic content: abject agents of spasmodic violence emerge contingently and fragmentarily on the edges of the global system as a totalized network of chance encounters and shared fates

---

[5] The bamboo forest scene in *A Touch of Zen* is remade in *Crouching Tiger, Hidden Dragon*, and its English title is revised in *A Touch of Sin*. These different uses of the same wuxia classic indicate the distance between Ang Lee and Jia Zhangke. See Wang (2015, 167–68) regarding the Green Snake legend and those Hong Kong films.

without a public political unity. At the end of the film, Xiaoyu reappears in Dahai's village and seeks a job in the mine, now run by his boss's wife. This random connection between two segments indicates the possible repetition of Xiaoyu's bloody story at another corner of the same network without an outside. She encounters a street opera, in which the judge asks, tellingly, "Do you understand your sin?" This line certainly questions the ethical justifiability of her homicidal justice, but the Chinese word for sin (*zui*) implies Buddhist responsibility for "one's karmic past, or a larger social or cosmological order," even if one may have done nothing illegal (Fan 2016, 338). The question then penetrates both the deadpan viewers of the opera and film viewers facing them directly in the final, front shot. It asks if people are not too desensitized to objective violence and systemic abjection. It challenges us to ask ourselves what can and should be done in this political impasse.

The best answer to this question that we could find in global cinema is not to reorganize politics in the strict sense of the term. It may be either already impossible or only possible in the inevitable way of leading to postpolitics and its double ethics, as we discussed from the beginning. It is therefore time to search for an alternative ethical, if not political, direction, in the next and last part of this book.

PART IV
GIFT AND ATOPIA

10
Alternative Ethics through the Paradox of the Gift

Positive Modes of Abject Agency: Artistic Creativity and Ethical Gift-Giving

Our discussions of global cinema have been critical attempts to address globalization's effects on subjectivity and society. What is global in this postpolitical age is the biopolitical system of neoliberal sovereignty and abjection, the uncontrollable prevalence of various catastrophes, and the paradigmatic dissolution of the totalizing community into the anarchic network. The global community here turns out to be a totalized network whose double ethical operations—soft inclusion and hard exclusion—contradictorily interlock, rendering the ideal of globalism inconsistent. Though activating active agency in films, the abject often end up being stuck in the loop of retaliatory violence, revolution as repetition, or self-undoing sacrifice, from which no escape seems possible except for embracing (suicidal) death or apocalypse. How then could we sustain our belief in the sanctity of life if we still want to, that is, if we do not want to succumb to nihilistic pessimism about humanity and its future? With this question in mind, I grope for some positive modes of abject agency that might not open new political horizons on a collective scale but might inspire us with meaningful potentialities to develop on the existential level of personal relations, the foundational level of ethics. Part IV thus sheds light on alternative ethics irreducible to politics, a third way beyond the stalemate of postpolitical double ethics.

We could begin by finding the positive turn of abject agency as potentially immanent in the ambivalent notion of abjection itself. Undergoing abjection implies the traumatic loss or degradation of stable identity and status and, conversely, the transformative liberation from the established structure of fixed subjectivity. The abject as neither subject nor object threatens or thwarts the Symbolic order in this sense, arousing both the terror and fascination of those securely stuck in the status quo of reality. This ambivalent transgression is most noticeable in creative works; Kristeva (1982) illuminates abject figures' "perversion" of the law—not obeying/denying but disrupting/corrupting it—in her reading of modern literature, as noted in Chapter 1. By extension, the abject symptomatizes the subversive eruption of the Real onto the surface of reality in Lacanian psychoanalysis while, in the opposite direction, it may signal the submergence of reality into the Real or, say, the deindividuation of the subject into its unregulated molecular state in Deleuze and Guattari's (1986) schizoanalysis (though abjection is not a concept they use). In the latter, Kafka's monstrous human-vermin in *The Metamorphosis* (1915) may represent not a degenerative symptom of the patriarchal big Other so much as a "desiring machine" of "becoming-animal" that deterritorializes the Oedipal structure of desire and the social system of subjectivation. A similar case is the "horse-man" in Artaud's play *To Have Done with the Judgment of God* (1947), from which Deleuze borrows and develops the notion of the *body without organs*: the undifferentiated potential of a body whose constituent parts are not yet organically structured. It resonates with Deleuze's other concepts like the plane of immanence, the virtual state of things as immanent (not transcendent) to the actual. Everything is generated from this ontological ground of "becoming" before "being," intensities before identities, and pulsation before thought. Abjection, I note, can free the subject from its solidified organization toward this unthinkable fluidity of the body that manifests the infinite potential of "becoming-other," assembling organs anew and thus producing a changed being (Deleuze and Guattari 1977, 1987).

Art is full of abject bodies that are detached, decapitated, dismantled, or dehumanized. Interestingly, even when delivering religious or mythical messages, classical paintings' graphic depictions of horrible violence evoke some perverted fascination with atrocities that may have captivated the artists themselves. Recall Bosch's numerous naked bodies chaotically brutalized in hell; Caravaggio's bloody beheadings implying self-castrations; or Goya's monstrous cannibalism, animal invasion, and meat. In the modern paintings of Francis Bacon, as Deleuze (2003) demonstrates, bodies are deformed as if disassembled or dissipated into bodies without organs. Their "faces" as the spatially privileged human centers turn into the "heads," mere body parts as zones of indiscernibility between human and animal. This implies that the proper sense of "becoming-animal" is not the imitation of an animal but the abjection of any organism. No wonder animals often appear as nothing but meat, the slaughtered body, with their virtual death cries lingering in our ears, like the actual scream of the transgender abject Elvira, who identifies herself with slaughtered cows in Rainer Werner Fassbinder's *In a Year of 13 Moons* (1978). Though expressing pain in this case, such pure affects penetrate all beings, free-floating across indeterminate bodies, along with rhythms, waves, sensations, or vibrations. Contemporary "abject art" (see Chapter 1) also experiments with this centrifugal emancipation from organic bodies as prisons of life, even when seemingly aiming at the provocation of disgust and disruption.

From this avant-garde aesthetics of abjection, we can move on to the case in which the potential liberation of the abject from the rigidified system of subjectivation is realized through the abject agency of artistic creativity, if not the radical dissolution of the actual body. Not only art's contents but many artists themselves are the abject, like the famous Van Gogh. His illness (of the inner ear) and madness (the act of cutting his ear) made him isolated from society yet also generated extreme creativity beyond normativity. Likewise, many abject characters with bodily disabilities or social restrictions discover and develop their inexperienced artistic and creative potential on the big screen. Ada in *The Piano* (Jane Campion, 1993) becomes mute in the manner of self-abjection, but this traumatic regression from communication in the Symbolic leads her back to the Semiotic chora (see Chapter 1), the prelinguistic realm of sonic, rhythmic, tactile signification, which she sublimates into playing music. Her piano performance and the love affair it catalyzes provoke her possessive husband's vengeful act of abjection—cutting off her finger—but ultimately liberate her from both autistic self-confinement and brutal patriarchy. In *The Diving Bell and the Butterfly* (Julian Schnabel, 2007), the editor of fashion magazine *Elle* suffers a massive stroke, causing locked-in syndrome, an individual catastrophe resulting in total paralysis except for one eye. However, this vegetative state of abjection enables him to maximize the potential use of his left eye—a sort of organ without body—as a writing machine. He makes words and sentences by blinking, like clicking, on a letter from the alphabet constantly recited by his therapy team. This incredible toil of writing culminates in the publication of his memoir before his death (see Jeong 2013b, 207–8). Similarly, *Hana-bi* (Kitano Takeshi, 1997) shows a detective who cannot walk or work after a terrible incident but devotes his vegetative time to art, sublimating violence in his life to beauty. As the title means 'fireworks' ('fire' and/as 'flower'), he paints imaginative figures fusing human and nature, flowers and animals, femininity and masculinity. These oppositional states of being are 'reassembled' into artistic symbols of transient life's transformative body until this creative agency is exhausted, ending with his aesthetic suicide.

One may then ask: Does this artistic agency of an abject individual for self-redemption also have the potential to affect the relationship with the other positively? Let me bring back two German films from Chapter 1. In *Goodbye Lenin!*, we can now say that Alex's simulation of the collapsed East Germany manifests his creative agency, coming out of his guilty feeling for traumatizing his loyal communist mother, who fell into an abject vegetative state upon witnessing his anti-GDR protest. He is an ethically motivated creative agent who tries to save his mother while internalizing and redeeming socialist ideals abjected from the reunified capitalist Germany. More importantly, this double redemption is fulfilled because the son and the mother pretend not to know the truth so that their ritual give and take of care continues as if in a gift exchange, but without revealing this act as a gift. Though opposite to this nostalgic comedy about the GDR, *The Lives of Others* also implies a paradoxical gift exchange. In East Berlin in 1984, Stasi officer Wiesler spies on a playwright and his lover but becomes absorbed in their lives, increasingly sympathetic and disillusioned with his totalitarian regime. When the corrupt authorities threaten the couple's love, he makes false reports to protect the couple's freedom and is later abjected from the state. He thus turns from a secret sovereign agent of surveillance into a creative abject agent of writing who supports the other abject agent of political dissidence. The playwright learns of this secret agent's help only after the fall of the Berlin Wall and writes a novel dedicated to him. Much later, Wiesler happens to notice and buy the book, saying "it's for me" when asked about "gift-wrapping it." In sum, the two creative abject agents give and take secret gifts of empathy, solidarity, indebtedness, and gratitude, but this exchange is possible only insofar as it is unrecognized; when it is recognized belatedly, it is already impossible to repay the gift directly.

This paradox of the gift contingently but profoundly connects the abject while thwarting its development into a stable bond or a sense of community. Here emerges a singular relationship of performative gift-giving: vulnerable, unnoticeable, delayed, relayed, yet life-changing, and even self-sacrificing. It is ethical, if not political, implying the alternative potential of ethics I mentioned earlier. Throughout Part IV I investigate a series of films that pave the way for the ethics of the gift, starting in this chapter with three films visibly centered on the motif of the gift. They look like three film fables about gift exchange with interrelated but different focuses: Lars von Trier's *Dogville* reveals the ground zero of being-as-gift through divine violence, Clint Eastwood's *Gran Torino* (2008) leads to the birth of a multicultural nation and law through sacrificial gift-giving, and Ang Lee's *Life of Pi* further experiences the paradox of the gift through the ontological other of the human. However, before delving into these themes, it may be helpful to take a preliminary theoretical step. What follows is a brief overview of crucial discourses on the gift that underlie my film analysis.

Among others, Marcel Mauss's (1967) foundational study of archaic societies situates gift culture in a broad anthropological framework. He elucidates the system of "total prestations" in which groups exchange not only goods but women, children, courtesies, entertainments, dances, and feasts. Far from individualistic capitalism, this primitive gift economy is a collective culture like the Native American "potlatch": an opulent festival at which a tribal head gives away possessions or purely destroys accumulated wealth to display it, eclipse a rival chief, or enhance prestige (4). An exchange occurs here as if gift-giving is free, voluntary, benevolent, and pacific, to cover the "reciprocity of exchange" associated with "the logic of revenge" detrimental to the social bond. The potlatch is thus "the 'pre-economy of the economy,' its zero-level, that is, exchange as the reciprocal relation of two non-productive expenditures" (Žižek 2009, 24–25). In Polynesia, the magical notion of *hau*, the spirit of things that "wants to return to the place of its birth," works as "the motivating force behind the obligatory circulation of wealth, tribute, and gifts" (Mauss 1967, 10). It underlies an exchange system with three obligations—to give, receive, and repay gifts received—to perpetually interchange things between people, clans, ranks, sexes, and generations (12). In short, at the core of all gift cultures is some moral surplus in the exchange economy. Even if there is an equal exchange, its operation as gift-giving is good, and "this 'goodness' of the given equivalence is in excess over the equivalence itself" (Derrida 1992b, 67). If a "white man keeper" pursues individual savings via commodity exchange based on market transactions, which can remove goods from circulation when driven by pure egoism, "an Indian giver" exchanges gifts based on reciprocity as freedom and obligation as generosity, which keeps circulating goods (Hyde 2007, 3–12). A gift-giving community is sustained thanks to its luxurious nature, its "inexhaustible eros, which is not lost when given away" (24). Gift-giving is thus not capitalist but slightly socialist. It takes on "a non-Marxist socialism, a liberal anti-capitalism or anti-mercantilism" (66).

Derrida (1992b) deconstructs Mauss by radicalizing the paradoxical excessiveness of the gift over the exchange. For him, two axes of economy, law (partition) and home (property), condition the symmetrical exchange of the gift as debt and countergift as repayment in circulation, thus operating the circular time of return. The economic reciprocity and temporality are suspended by the pure sense of the gift as totally given away without return, in theory. But such a pure gift is impossible because even just the recognition of a gift already inscribes it into the exchange order of credit and restitution; even saying 'thank you' inevitably reinstitutes the economic structure in which a gift turns into a gift-debt to repay. The gift-debt is thus indeterminately ambivalent like Plato's *pharmakon*, remedy-poison (Derrida 2017, 103–10); tellingly, the German word *Gift* means 'poison.' In today's neoliberal system, debt is ever more poisonously normalized in economic life. Indebtedness is ethically internalized as guilt in the aforementioned German films, but now ethical indebtedness is externalized as economically measurable. "Debt has become our universal condition, and the 'servicing' of debt—that is to say, the extraction of payments for debt has become a major resource for capital accumulation in the world today" (Shaviro 2011). As Deleuze (1995, 181) says, "a man is no longer a man confined but a man in debt" in this "control society." By contrast, Derrida (1992b) argues, "the gift as gift ought not appear as gift: either to the done or to the donor [. . .] the simple phenomenon of the gift annuls it as gift, transforming the apparition into a phantom and the operation into a simulacrum" (14). Any phenomenological gift is a simulacrum of the noumenal gift, the unthinkable gift that exists in absolute forgetting of circular time, or the *aneconomic* gift outside any exchange. This gift is thus a transcendental illusion of being given and not a present(ed) gift, just as Heidegger's notion of Being is not being as something, being-present or present-being. It is not that "Being is," but that "there is [given] Being (es *gibt Sein*)" before beings exist. If Mauss explains that "the gift exists" in circulation beyond capitalist exchange, Derrida claims that "there is gift" outside this pre-economic circulation as such (20–25).

Derrida's gift is deconstructive precisely because its exteriority makes it impossible to be realized as such in any gift economy while, nonetheless, the very transcendent sense of pure giving is immanent in the exchange of actual gifts, preceding, underlying, conditioning, and setting economy in motion. "It is this exteriority that engages in the circle and makes it turn" (1992b, 30). The impossible gift renders an account of the possibility of its simulacrum and the desire for it, just as "absolute hospitality" is impossible yet immanent in "conditional hospitality" (Derrida and Dufourmantelle 2000). How could we sense and address this paradoxical gift in our phenomenal world if it remains unthinkable beyond our sensorial experience? The films I examine open access points to this noumenal realm by staging the abject as a lost gift whose value is recognizable only after it becomes impossible to return. This abject as a gift then retroactively re-emerges in our minds to evoke the gift of Being and enable the gift exchange. It is thus re-embodied through retroactive causality. And just as such retroaction opens room for the ethical sublime (see Chapter 7), we will see how it guides us to a new ethics of the gift.

Dogville: Being as a Gift beyond Gift Economy and Biopolitical Ethics

Chapter 4 touches on the *Dogville* heroine Grace, who ultimately turns from a Christian angel enslaved in the evil, eponymous village into an angry God whose last judgment is to punish and demolish it. That is, the abject becomes an apocalyptic agent of divine violence. Now, let's take a closer look at the trajectory of her life that leads to this radical change and delve into its complex implications, moving from the biopolitics of violence to an ethics of the gift. Indeed, the crucial keyword in *Dogville* is the "gift" repeatedly discussed by Tom, an aspiring writer and moral leader of the village. As he has been searching for an "illustration" of a gift to preach the value of "receiving," he thanks gracious God for bringing the gift named Grace. This gift is given free of charge like a sacred object, but it also takes on exchange value when shared by people. Those who decided to accept Grace get some smug pride in return for the good deed, and she looks for something to do in return as well. Therefore, the gift initiates the exchange system in which the obligations of giving-taking-returning are regularized with apparent spontaneity stemming from generosity. It is an economy that seems free and fair yet is pretentious, coercive, computational, and selfish. Of course the superiority of the giver is not vice, as it underlies the potlatch and facilitates the donation culture that supplements capitalism with alms and charity. However, people's hints of tricks prevalent in Dogville imply that a rigid hypocritical gift culture and an invisible wall of self-interest—'law' and 'home' in Derrida's economy—are dividing the empty, open stage set as Dogville in the film. Tom, who introduces only people's shortcomings to Grace by comparing them to ugly dolls, knows well that his seemingly 'lovely' village is deeply "rotten from the inside out," as says the cynical Chunk.

Grace awakens the villagers to the authentic virtue of gift-giving, the voluntary creation of surplus value, by doing "something that you would like done but that you don't think is necessary." She gives what they desire, if not need, a surplus satisfaction beyond the symmetrical exchange. Though by way of her return, her gift-giving with the sincerity of '+α' not only beautifies the gooseberry bush but also restores love to Tom and a smile to Chuck, thus making Dogville "a wonderful place to live in." What is genuinely given is the very excess over equivalence that lubricates the gift exchange. People's gifts poured on her after two weeks of her stay in the village beautifully illustrate that the potlatch-like gift economy is growing out of asymmetrical reciprocity. However, from the time when Grace not only complements Jack's lonely life with her company but replaces his blind eyes, her labor turns from surplus to necessary, her sincerity is converted into quantifiable reward, and her gifts are subject to the code of measured exchange. The more Grace is integrated into Dogville, the more residents' benevolent gift-giving crystallizes into an organized pattern of social transactions, a seemingly hospitable but increasingly hostile practice of exchanges (Nobus 2007, 34). As a wanted criminal, Grace is further put in a legal exchange system in which reporting her will get one paid compensation. Dogville then operates a sort of supralegal exchange system in a state of exception. People compensate themselves for the risk of hiding her by depriving her of any choice but to submit to their needs and desires under collective sovereignty.

This biopolitical economy takes the typical capitalist step of intensifying labor and cutting wages. The gift economy that forms a personal, qualitative relationship between transactional subjects is entirely replaced by the commodity economy that allows only an objective, quantitative relationship between transaction objects. Here, Grace is not only objectified as a labor commodity under surveillance and punishment but also degenerates into a physical commodity, men's sexual plaything, under the threat of reporting her. Tom's betrayal is shocking; apart from his twisted desire for love and sex, his plot to eliminate her as a threat to his fame and authority after she notices his duplicity manifests the sovereign mechanism of making an abject *homo sacer*. The cowardly opportunism of this hypocritical intellectual, who teaches a "lesson" until his death, brings about the arbitrary abjection of a gift from God. If "Grace personifies the gift's inexhaustible power" to shake and reshape the economic and ethical codes of the closed community, Tom mistakenly interprets this power "as a further illustration of what is already known. The result is that [. . .] Dogville becomes ever more dogmatic in the affirmation (and acceptance) of its perfidious core" (Nobus 2007, 35).

Worse still, male villagers excuse themselves for sexually abusing Grace, telling her secretly that "it's nothing to be ashamed of" since everyone does the same. This dirty ruse to obtain indulgences by transferring individual guilt to the collective is central to the fascism of desire that mingles the private and the public and justifies unjust desires as universal and natural. Under this upside-down order, there is a kind of master-slave dialectic, too. When good men turn into rapists who share their beautiful object of desire one by one, Grace, a sexual slave, also behaves like a master who allows them to have her, forgiving "their own nature" that they obey like slavish "dogs." Likewise, the women who blame Grace's indolence are her masters and slaves, who cannot live without her labor once her gratuitous service becomes indispensable for their increased comfort. These villagers exploit her not because they are inherently sadistic or greedy but because capitalist relations subordinate them to the exchange system of desire and labor, relentlessly and irreversibly.

This master-slave ambivalence resonates with the narrator's conclusion: it is uncertain whether Grace left Dogville or vice versa. The film questions the capitalist community and the legitimacy of its sheer destruction at the same time; the director debunks Grace's 'pride and prejudice' while making us doubtful about her father's judgment. Coincidentally, the anonymous 'others'—Black, homeless, old—in the end-credit photo montage set to David Bowie's song "Young Americans" evokes *The Others* (Alejandro Amenábar, 2001), whose heroine is also named Grace and is played by Nicole Kidman. Grace, who put down her rifle aimed at the others after realizing her own ghostly otherness in *The Others*, now shoots all the others who have othered her in *Dogville* as if to protest America's exploitation and exclusion of social minorities, its acceptance-as-abjection of strangers, migrants, or refugees, especially in the post-9/11 age, which Dogville allegorizes in the setting of 1930s post–Great Depression America. It is also noteworthy that puritan asceticism and its hypocritical underside, represented by Tom, aligns with the roots of American capitalist morality and desire.

However, the film's anti-American stance could not avoid seeming simplistic and facing its own ambivalence. Yes, the abject Grace performs the cathartic agency of divine violence for justice, but there is only a thin line between divine and pseudo-divine violence, as discussed in Chapter 4. In effect, Grace's extremely vengeful solution to the systemic violence of injustice is not too far from radical terrorism, which is liable to launch a vicious cycle of retaliation without a genuinely divine outside that guarantees objective justice. No wonder that for Rancière (2004, 110–16), *Dogville* reflects the post-9/11 double ethics: the soft-ethical democratic consensus of tolerance and the hard-ethical infinite justice in the fight against the axis of evil. This evil appears primarily moral, detached from sociopolitical and economic structures of dominion, and so does its annihilation. Evil and justice thus fall into "a state of indistinction" like terror and war on terror, destructive nihilism and neoconservative militarism, mirroring each other endlessly without political resolution (114). We cannot help but wonder then: Does Grace represent America's evil or justice? Does she attack or defend America?

Undoubtedly Grace is just such a multifaceted figure, more than ambivalent. She allegorizes God's grace, strong will, the American dream, romantic or erotic fascination, and the asylum-seeking refugee. Sinnerbrink (2007) critically updates Rancière in this regard, claiming that the evil of Dogville is not purely moral but concerns precisely the hegemonic structure of power and the libidinal economy of desire that sustain injustice and inequality in modern society. The systemic violence of exploitation is "at the heart of liberal democracy"; the film implies that this deadlock could also be resolved only through violence. Sinnerbrink views this violence as the "rotten core" of law, drawing on Benjamin and Agamben: lawmaking violence (see Chapter 4). He says that "the possibility of a pure violence clearly slides back here into *retributive* violence once Grace abandons her compact with the community, and takes up her 'proper' place in the symbolic and social order—an order predicated on the kind of symbolic violence and naked exercise of power that her grace and forgiveness had attempted, in vain, to overcome" (Sinnerbrink 2007). In other words, even Grace's violence is not "pure" divine violence but "retributive" pseudo-divine violence, which is immanent to Dogville or any community in the mode of supralegal sovereignty. The film is thus seen as a fable of not only postpolitical ethics or post-9/11 America but also "the emergence of law" and "violence in law and in sacrifice" (Brighenti 2006, 107). In truth, this conclusion is not far from Rancière's point that Dogville and Grace are indistinctly positioned on the ethical horizon of today. We are then left stuck between the possibility and the impossibility of revolutionary, liberational divine violence.

However, we should note that *Dogville* does not show proper 'lawmaking' violence (unlike *Gran Torino*, which I review soon) but rather a normalized state of exception and its catastrophic termination to reveal its empty ground, its foundational nothingness before any law. On this ground zero, we can break away from the debate about the nature of Grace's violence and rethink her being as a gift ontologically outside any systems of exchange and exploitation, power and desire, politics and economy, and judgment and violence. Put otherwise, "to question the hypocritical and 'rotten' systems of solidarity on which the community is based is not with a view to developing better forms of solidarity, but with a view to constantly reorganize the community around the central figures of impossibility and loss, and the essential lack of reciprocity they entail" (Nobus 2007, 36). The transition of Grace's agency from maternal forgiveness to paternal punishment, from Jesus to Moses, does not simply explode the wrath of God at the evil of humanity but interrogates the universal exchange system and inspires us to think outside of it. This system represented by America is based on Christian gift-giving (for-giving) but has distorted it unforgivably, as Tom, the hypocritical puritan who imitates Christ by preaching 'love thy neighbor,' corrupts the neighbor's love. But as Derrida sees, the pure gift without return cannot even be recognized since its recognition always already mobilizes an exchange relationship, an exchange of appreciation and obligation at the least. The unrecognizable gift nonetheless works as the foundational sense of surplus giving, like Grace's '+α,' based on which actual gifts are circulated. But unlike her good deeds that were exploited, the genuine surplus gift is never confined to the exchange system. It is the transcendental kernel of the very system that it enables, yet to which it does not belong. It is the ontological basis of human life while remaining outside human thought.

Dogville exposes this basis exterior to phenomenal experience in the form of a blank floor where even chalk-marked boundaries of homes and shops, partitioned like parking spots, have disappeared after the massacre. The outside of the community, to which people and properties were ordered, turns out to be literally its ground. This tabula rasa is immanently given yet never perceived like the pure gift that enables gift-giving, like Being (*Sein*) that generates beings. In another Heidegger term (1971, 51), it evokes a "clearing" in a forest, a "lighting" (*Lichtung*) amid beings. More than just a space where things are cleared away, the clearing is an opening through which things emerge out of hiddenness or become visible, brought into the light. "This open center is therefore not surrounded by what is; rather, the lighting center itself encircles all that is, like the Nothing which we scarcely know." Thanks to this clearing, beings are "unconcealed," or, let's say, given like gifts. In this sense, existence (*Dasein*) is a given being, a being as a gift. We cannot thus

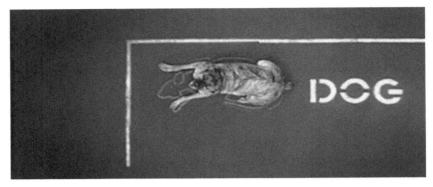

Figure 10.1. After Grace's love for the villagers turns into divine violence, a dog named Moses is given the gift of life on the empty stage, in *Dogville*.

ask who exists for whom at what price. Just as Grace is a gift from heaven and the survival of only one dog from the massacre is "a miracle," being is given miraculously. On the empty stage, the only remaining sign, "DOG," turns into the very dog named after the prophet who received the gift of God's first law, Moses (see Figure 10.1). Only this animal outside the human system is given life and leaps into the sky, unchained and saved, instead of the dog-like humans who have damaged the gift of being. Shot from God's point of view, that animal being-gift barks directly at the audience as if to ask what kind of system we live in and how we exist.

In sum, *Dogville* ends with the denouement of a revelatory catastrophe that renders unconcealed the immanent outside of the human system from which every presence is given as a gift/present. Grace gives away everything and then destroys everything to reveal this clearing of gift-giving. In Rancière's view, the film's theatrical stage evokes Brecht stylistically but lacks Brechtian revolution, stuck in today's depoliticized, ethical deadlock. However, von Trier's minimalist aesthetics experiments with the potential to clear away everything but the essence of existence, like Giacometti's sculpture, and lets us sense Being given under the system of beings and gifts.

Gran Torino: A Global Aporia of the Gift and the Birth of a (Multicultural) Nation

If *Dogville* is a fable of the gift and America seen from without, *Gran Torino* is its domestic American counterpart, rooted in an authentic insider's experience. While von Trier obsessively produces controversial critiques of America in his American trilogy—including *Manderlay* (2005) and *The House That Jack Built* (2019)—and *Dancer in the Dark* (2000) without ever traveling to America, Eastwood prolifically offers multiple entry points to the history and culture of his national community lived from within; suffice it to list some of his millennial films, such as *Mystic River* (2003), *Million Dollar Baby* (2004), *Letters from Iwo Jima* (2006), *Flags of Our Fathers* (2006), *Changeling* (2008), *Invictus* (2009), and *American Sniper* (2014). Among these, *Gran Torino* appears as a rich text comparable to *Dogville* in addressing the postpolitical double ethics—relatively more about multiculturalism and terrorism respectively—and yet takes a different direction of gift-giving. When *Dogville* uncovers the primordial 'givenness' of being through the apocalyptical eruption of law-destroying violence, *Gran Torino* evokes the pure gift through the inevitable sacrifice of supralegal agency and the consequent institution of the law. Grace, created by von Trier, shifts from the New Testament back to the Old Testament, whereas Walt Kowalski, played by Eastwood, moves from justice to love.

Walt is a bigoted and cantankerous old white man in Detroit. Though he is Polish American, he derides a young Catholic priest's formulaic sermon on death at his wife's funeral, not least because he is a Korean War veteran haunted by the dark memory of killing and living with death. Suffering from unresolved trauma, Walt has become an unhappy, grumpy, action-oriented macho man with a loaded gun at the ready. This manhood combines with a professional identity rooted in a bygone white, working-class America. He is a retired Ford factory worker who treasures a 1972 Ford Torino, emblematic of the glory days of American automobile manufacturing. This prized, grandiose 'muscle car' also symbolizes his once-heroic but now alienated masculinity, though it is still seductive to covetous young street gangs. His generational outmodedness further isolates him from his careless sons, who sell and drive Japanese cars, and his spoiled grandchildren, whose liberal, materialistic behavior annoys him. His family is comparable to the Hmong family who move in next door. The generation gap within this large Southeast Asia family is less conflictual than complex. The first-generation immigrants are Vietnam War victims turned refugees who keep their Confucianist tradition and ethnic culture without speaking English, and the second-generation settlers have their own issues: "The girls go to college, the boys go to jail." Sue, a witty, educated teenage girl, is Americanized enough to date a white boy (though he is too weak to protect her), but her effeminate and unconfident brother Thao is bullied and coerced into joining his cousin's Hmong gang, which is in rivalry with other Asian, Black, and Latino gangs in their neighborhood.

Gran Torino centers around an unlikely relationship between Walt and Thao in this 'glocal' setting of transracial space and transitional time. After their initial hostile encounter—Thao tries but fails to steal Walt's Gran Torino under pressure from his cousin—Walt is reluctantly but gradually drawn into Thao's hospitable family, building a mutual bond. Thao helps with Walt's home repair job, and Walt teaches Thao to be a man. Meanwhile, the Hmong gang's threat to Thao's family also intensifies to the point of raping Sue. Enraged, Walt then enacts an ultimate vengeance, but by self-sacrifice: he attracts the neighbors' attention and provokes the gang to shoot him by suddenly pulling his hand out of his jacket as if he were drawing a gun that he does not have. The police arrest the gang for the witnessed murder, and Thao later receives the Gran Torino, according to Walt's will. In short, the film unfolds a quasi father-son relationship beyond blood ties. On the one hand, this relationship is about a white American father's designation of his successor, a rightful heir of his values accrued in a system that is rendered old-fashioned in the age of globalization but redeemable through intercultural intimacy. The arrangement is thus color-blind yet still based on the male-centric, homosocial "logic of inheritance." But on the other hand, the relationship is about a fatherless nonwhite immigrant's development into a surrogate son of a white American man. It is thus "a coming-of-age story," a young boy's internalization of manhood and successful masculinization (Davis 2010, 167–68).

This father-son connection resonates with life-death circulation as well. The film starts with symptoms of Walt's abject status: he is a widowed, retired, lonely old man, waiting out the rest of his life while coughing up blood. However, this symbolically dead hero is reanimated to save his partly abject neighbors from the enemies of his community. He thus becomes an abject agent who tries to fulfill a self-imposed sovereign mission for the public good, like many vigilante (super)heroes. But importantly, he does so by entering the gang-infested lawless state of nature, that is, by symbolically returning to the traumatic battlefield in Korea where he had to kill people. There is always one final dirty job for such an abject agent, who must revisit the past to be redeemed from it; it's an old, bloody business from which one has retired, but which one must do for the last time to quit it forever, as in Eastwood's own *Unforgiven* (1992). *Gran Torino* revives this western film structure yet also revises it by sublimating revenge into sacrifice. Walt restages his original sin (killing) in reverse (being killed) and dies in a Christ-like posture, with his arms outstretched. He thereby restores law and order without triggering further retaliation, redeems himself from his trauma and abjection, and is remembered as a local hero who can rest in eternal peace. This salvation comes out of his determination to embrace actual death, which closes the double death narrative of the abject agent. At the same time, it initiates Thao's new life. The film introduces Thao's family celebrating a birth and ends with his rebirth as a true heir of Walt's legacy, signaling the birth of a multicultural nation.

This double circle of father-son and life-death in the abjection-redemption narrative structure is completed so naturally that *Gran Torino* looks like a just moral drama or just a fine drama as publicly received. Nevertheless, I argue, this old-school film has multiple layers under the surface of its humanistic multiculturalism and morality. First, let's revisit multiculturalism as the core soft-ethical ideology (see Chapter 1). It can be further critiqued in the historical context of national identity-building that Žižek (1997) explains. In the modern era, particular identifications with the ethnic (family, neighborhood) undergo "transubstantiation" into the universal identification with the nation-state. However, this nationalization of ethnicity does not work in America, where one can be "a good American" by keeping one's particular ethnic identity without renouncing it—Italians, Blacks, Koreans, are "all Americans." The postmodern era further sees the ethnicization of the national: "The American state is more and more experienced as a simple formal framework for the coexistence of the multiplicity of ethnic, religious or life-style communities" (41–42). This umbrella framework is no different from the global system of inclusion in which the capitalist multiculturalist tolerates and enjoys mediated forms of other cultures while filtering their toxic otherness. His liberal respect for the Other thus betrays a "racism with a distance" taken from his universal privileged position (44). It is not the old, direct, and raw racism but a new, indirect, and reflective racism that, though seemingly antiracist, "legitimizes apartheid to prevent racial tensions" (Žižek 1993). This pacificist law of 'social distancing' is based on tacit fantasies about the threatening Real of the Other, who is believed to possess excessive enjoyment allegedly stolen from us (Jews have too much money; Blacks have too much fun; gays have too much sex). But obviously such racist fantasies are precisely the content of the old racism. The new racism only represses its immanently explicit version to avoid being bothered by the conflictual confrontation with the Other.

How then can we characterize Walt in *Gran Torino*? On the one hand, he stands for a (pre)modern conservative individualism that blends American vigilantism with Republican nationalism. For him, his Midwest town is still the Old West in the state of nature in which one should be able to protect oneself and one's community without law. The national flag over the porch represents sovereign power, reminiscent of his survival in a war zone. A growing number of racial others then alert and threaten him, intensifying the old racist bigotry that he does not shy away from uttering, often aggressively with slang and slurs, just as gangs do. On the other hand, Walt is a postmodern liberal multiculturalist who does not bother others insofar as they do not bother him. His first words toward the gang crossing the line are just "get off my lawn," and his later friendship with the Hmong family is mediated through their lavish food and exotic culture, which he gets to relish. Interestingly, his crude racism does not literally underlie his racial jokes, which are enjoyed as playful, if controversial, lubricant for communication; his favorite barber brandishes a shotgun in jest at Thao, who lacks "macho and racist etiquette" (Jalao 2010, 2). The old racism is thus distilled into the empty form of ritualized etiquette to confirm and consolidate the shared social code and sense of community. Like a tasteful dose of obscene humor, racial jokes without toxic racism serve as innocuous multicultural gestures that might help reduce social distancing between races.[1] Above all, Walt's showdown with the gang ends the retributive law of the jungle by introducing the institutionalized law of civil society, replacing lawmaking pseudo-sovereign violence with law-preserving public power. It is taken as an inevitable step toward a more positively multicultural (rather than multiculturalist) America.

Of course we should not forget the abject rabble as the inevitable byproduct of any multicultural society. Though appearing like an axis of evil, the Hmong gang is structurally stuck in a situation with nothing but two dilemmatic choices: "Either accept the gender and racial hierarchies and protocols for success as laid out in Walt's racist universe, and for which He sacrificed himself; or remain among the wretched of the earth, forever doomed to the inner

---

[1] Žižek often advocates telling racist jokes as nonracist icebreakers. For him, covering up racism with politically correct words does not eradicate it, whereas laughing at each other's differences unites others. My point is that this 'gently racist' verbal ritual, assumed to be safe, is not radically different from the cultural simulation of others without otherness, though it can be less hypocritical and more comfortable at least among people who share the same degree of racial sensitivity than is the multiculturalist language.

cities of America" (Jalao 2010, 3). Hollywood imposes a law-abiding, middle-class life for Hmong people from the multiculturalist standpoint while eliding America's bellicose treatment of Southeast Asia driven by supralegal violence and domestic racial violence, discursive or physical, exposing the verso of multiculturalism. However, it would be inappropriate to blame *Gran Torino* for not shedding enough light on the convoluted international history beyond the film's diegesis. Nor would it be productive enough to take the Žižekian class determinism and leftist alternative to the still racist and capitalist multiculturalist ideology. We could instead see through the multidimensional relationship between economy and culture and ask if there isn't any 'cultural economy' free from capitalist relations, an 'ethnic ethics' of communal life irreducible to market multiculturalism—put otherwise, a sort of 'eth(n)ic ecology' beyond the economy. Here comes the gift.

The multicultural bond in *Gran Torino* begins and grows through the gift exchange. Walt throws out the gang who forced Thao to steal his car and sends Thao back home, but this initially self-protective action is regarded as an invaluable life-saving gift by Thao's family. As a gesture of appreciation, they serve him endless food, invite him to their house, and offer Thao as an assistant who has "dishonored the family" and thus "has to work off his debt." They behave as if to say: 'Whatever cultural differences there may be, we must repay our indebtedness with this food, service, and labor, so please accept it!' Restrained civility and excessive consumption overlap here, as "it is polite to behave impolitely" (Žižek 2009, 26). This paradox is precisely that of potlach, which escalates the reciprocal exchange of gifts beyond the capitalist balance of give and take. Walt is initiated into this gift culture, and as he gradually learns its lesson from his Asian neighbor, his multiculturalist distancing turns into tribal intimacy. Meanwhile, in return, Walt initiates Thao into manhood, offering tools for home repair, teaching him how to talk to men and women, and helping him get a job. Except for the mere $25 that Walt pays Thao for carrying up his freezer, no money intervenes in their later uncalculated relationship.

However, this virtuous cycle of soft-ethical gift-giving is threatened by a vicious cycle of hard-ethical violence, a counter-potlach of aggravating reprisals. The gang bullies Thao, Walt drives the gang away, the gang burns Thao's cheeks, Walt beats up a gang member, and the gang fires at Thao's house and rapes Sue. Walt takes measures at every step, dirtying his own hands, like Dirty Harry redux. But as if Eastwood is revising his own iconic 1970s hero character, Walt finally decides to terminate the bloody eternal return by terminating himself (saying, "I've got blood on my hands / I finish things") since he is at the exact juncture of the two cycles—as Donnie Darko's self-sacrifice disconnects two universes (see Chapter 7). The result is the intervention of the law: the police take legal vengeance on the gang, and the lawyer administers Thao's legal ownership of Walt's postmortem gift. These third-party authorities execute objective justice, that is, the law's initial function of prohibiting subjective pseudo-sovereign retaliation (see Chapter 9).

The film then looks like a doubly twisted western. First, a retired gunman in a lawless society is guided back to a primitive community, where he rediscovers the meaning of life as a gift. Then he dies to save the community by necessitating the law and thus instating a law-governed multicultural nation, where unregulated gift-giving dissipates into the Symbolic order of crime and punishment, inheritance and documentation. The gift is accordingly put in a double bind. On the one hand, the precapitalist gift culture helps realize the American myth of the melting pot, but it is vulnerable to violent threats triggered by abject immigrants and racial tensions. On the other hand, for the gift culture to continue, its ethical ideal cannot but get lost under juridical, bureaucratic codes that reduce the gift to part of the legalized economy. This process inevitably compromises the precarious yet precious gift-giving between the abject while saving them legitimately regardless of their race. *Gran Torino* thus performs a paradoxical self-reflection of America as a premodern-to-postmodern nation. Eastwood's contemporary filmography, as noted earlier, indeed abounds with various versions of the 'birth-of-a-nation' allegory in the struggle for a positive multicultural society.

This positivity suggests that the gift culture in the film deserves attention from Mauss's anthropological standpoint as a potential antidote to capitalist multiculturalism. But there is one more turn to make in Derrida's ontological direction. Let's recall the lyrical last scene, in which Thao drives the Gran Torino, accompanying Walt's dog (see Figure 10.2). The car is a metonymy for Walt, who is given as dead and thus is not actually given. But then Walt is the invisible condition of this automobile gift, evoking Heidegger's Being, the ontological ground immanently external to all beings. Walt gave birth to Thao as his true son and America as a multicultural nation. He gave this son/nation time for a new era in which he does not exist and cannot be paid back anymore. His whole being is thus remembered as a paradoxical gift that was not recognized as a gift when he was alive and cannot be returned when it is recognized as a gift. What was genuinely given away was his being and

Figure 10.2. In *Gran Torino*, the old white American hero sacrifices himself and leaves his treasured car and dog to his Asian immigrant neighbor.

not his material properties or life lessons exchanged with Thao. Like Grace in *Dogville*, Walt himself, even before any gift exchange and even unknown to himself, was a gift whose pure meaning is only retroactively redeemed through its metonymic trace. Therefore the car is a simulacrum of the pure gift that only Walt's death can evoke as impossible to grasp among actual gifts. But since the pure gift is the inner dynamic of gift-giving that mobilizes gift exchanges, the car could be given to someone else in a new circle of gift-giving that Thao could open in Walt's spirit; gift-giving potentially draws not a closed loop but a zigzag spiral, as we will see in Chapter 11. *Gran Torino* leads us to this ethics of the gift beyond its circular/twisted narrative and multiculturalist pitfalls.

Life of Pi: The Ontological Other as a Precarious Yet Precious Gift

Let me move on to my final cinematic illustration of the gift. *Life of Pi* further inspires us to think about the unthinkable gift through an animal simulacrum via multicultural experience. The film ecologically widens the scope of gifts to all beings, not limited to sociocultural others of the subject but including ontological others of the human. Typically, animals on-screen are personified into conventional characters as in animation—good or bad, and so on—or represent overwhelming ferocity that erupts from behind the aesthetic harmony of nature, as in the disaster genre. The lion prince in *The Lion King* (Roger Allers and Rob Minkoff, 1994), who flees home after being framed for patricide but returns later to punish his uncle, the tricky usurper of the kingdom, is nothing other than a Disney-style combination of Oedipus and Hamlet. Biotechnologically created dinosaurs in *Jurassic Park* suddenly turn from marvelous spectacles in a theme park into uncontrollable monsters running amok. Animals do not remain as animals themselves but are somehow subjectivated or objectified from human standpoints.[2] *Life of Pi*, though based on a best-selling novel and adapted by a mainstream director, draws our attention to the margin of this anthropocentrism. It unfolds an "incredible" story about the multistep development of a human-animal relationship.

In a mise-en-abyme structure, the film begins with a middle-aged Pi telling a writer his story in Canada. We are then introduced via flashbacks to his teenage years in India and his family, which runs a zoo, where he encounters a Bengal tiger nicknamed Richard Parker. Pi feels this animal's "soul" while looking into its eyes, but his father forces him to realize that he sees nothing more than his own emotions reflected back at him, human projections. The face is not the window of its inner soul but the mirror of the beholder. Indeed, the tiger mercilessly devours a goat thrown to it as prey (like a scapegoat) as if tearing apart Pi's naïve sensibility. Up to this point, we have not gone beyond the familiar dichotomy that animals are either domestic or dangerous, helpful or harmful; the prevailing binary of 'friend or enemy,' 'pet or pest.' It is also evident that 'caring' for a wild animal to make it a pet begins with 'caging' it to keep a safe distance from it. The distanced human care for the animal Other is not essentially different from the multiculturalist's hospitality given to the cultural Other on the condition that the line between them should not be crossed.

The story changes as Pi's family sells the zoo due to economic hardship and boards a Japanese freighter with a few remaining animals to move to Canada. Out of the blue, a terrible storm sinks the ship, leaving Pi alone in a lifeboat with Richard Parker—after this tiger kills a hyena, which killed a zebra and an orangutan. Pi needs to find a way to survive (with) this fearsome beast, adrift in the vast Pacific Ocean without knowing for how long. As the Canadian

---

[2] Starting briefly with these two examples, I have elsewhere explored a series of films about animals that challenge this anthropocentric framing of "the Animal as/for the Human" (Jeong 2013a).

dream of the Indian migrant family is wrecked, the modern temporality of linear navigation is stranded in the mythical temporality of primitive drift. In this aspect, *Life of Pi* is a disaster film about a personal catastrophe. It takes a normal subject, degrading him into an abject deprived of everything that sustained his civilized life, even just human superiority to the animal. Pi is now nothing but a bare life just like the tiger, thrown into the state of nature wherein one must kill to survive, the state of exception wherein no murder is a punishable crime. However, Pi misses out on a golden opportunity to kill the animal enemy when, drowning, it looks up at him desperately but miserably. He puts down the ax and saves the poor being upon facing the face of an unexpectedly fragile and vulnerable life, as though this face of the other whispered the words of the divine commandment, "You shall not kill," calling in all the gods he has worshiped—Hindu, Christian, and Islamic— I elaborate on this Levinasian face of the other in Chapter 11. What these different religions commonly imply, or rather, what is crucial regardless of beliefs, is that although there is no objective ground for life's sacredness being deemed as given only to humans to not to be killed, we must believe in the sanctity of life as potential and thus worth saving; humanity would otherwise be no different from animality (see Chapter 4). Conversely, Pi keeps the tiger as a way of investing faith in the potential sanctity of this animal other's life as well, maybe because, in our terms, it is another living being that shares abjecthood on the ground of which they are equal and equally worth saving.[3]

From this point on, the human abject activates agency to live together with the animal abject. Pi's survival strategy exemplifies Lévi-Straussian bricolage, combining whatever is in the boat to create something new and drawing maximal effects from minimal resources. This creative, if not artistic, abject agency catalyzes his relationship with the tiger. He learns to care for the tiger without a cage, just as the Little Prince 'tames' a fox in Saint-Exupéry's novella. This taming is not a one-sided appropriation but affords mutual benefits. When he offers food to the tiger, he feels some energy to sustain himself, some vitality that he could otherwise not have maintained. The tiger thus turns into his indispensable counterpart and company for co-existence. Pi's 227-day journal of drifting is like a human's love letter to an animal, the very ontological other without whom his mere existence would

---

[3] In *Gran Torino*, Walt confesses to Thao his unforgettable guilt about killing, which Pi would have suffered if he had killed the tiger: "You want to know how it feels to kill a man? It feels goddamned lousy. And it feels even worse when you get a medal for bravery right after you mowed down some scared kid when he tries to give up. A dumb, scared, little gook, just about your age."

not have been possible. Their relationship develops palpably as their physical distance decreases and their tactile interaction increases. When the tiger falls ill, Pi hugs and strokes the giant predator's wounded body in the posture of the Pietà. Animal suffering is experienced as the suffering of an intimate other, embraced with compassion. The animal is a companion, a "companion species," as Donna Haraway (2008) dubs it. When humans leave their position as masters and enter the middle of nature, what should be possible may not be killing but caring without caging. Pi's adventurous symbiosis of being in common with the animal appears to be a genuine mode of accepting and embracing its otherness beyond human-centered hospitality and tolerance.

However, the film's highlight lies in the scene where the very one-of-a-kind animal friend vanishes; the lifelong lover instantly becomes a stranger. Richard Parker disappears into the Mexican coastal jungle without looking back at Pi, ignoring his simple and earnest expectations for a minimal farewell gesture (see Figure 10.3). But the point is not the uncomfortable truth that the interspecies utopian bond is nothing more than the human's unrequited love and that the animal is the other wholly different from the human, no matter how much they may seemingly foster companionship. The holistic vision of nature, including the idea of companion species, turns out to be inconsistent, mistaken, and thus 'holed,' but the irresistible sense of loss caused by this hole instead leaves room for reflecting on the irretrievable

Figure 10.3. The tiger in *Life of Pi* disappears into the jungle without looking back at his human companion, Pi, leaving him saddened forever.

animal other as a pure gift. The gift is not merely a metaphor in the film. Pi, who thanks Lord Vishnu for "coming in the form of a fish" he catches, gives the tiger the divine gift and feels rewarded for himself. The gratuitous gift introduces a lively give and take and circulates some exchange value in a kind of gift economy, albeit a primitive one. Recalling this past, the middle-aged Pi sheds tears at the fact that he did not even take a moment "to say goodbye" to the tiger. More precisely, in my view, he is saddened not because he lost the animal friend but because their mutual gift-giving was left incomplete without his last chance to say "goodbye" as a 'thank you' for the will to live, the tiger's invaluable gift given to him, and without the tiger's final symbolic gesture of recognizing his farewell as a way of rewarding him. Therefore, what was lost is the possibility of believing that the animal could also acknowledge the virtuous cycle of gift exchange with the human. In other words, Pi still clings to the anthropocentric gift economy to the extent that even when letting go of one's lover, one wants to feel comfortable by sharing a final thank-you note in the symbolic form of symmetrical exchange.

However, the irreversible loss of Richard Parker is indicative of the pure gift, as in the cases of Grace and Walt. What frustrates Pi's last human desire is not untamable animality but the ungraspable otherness of the gift. The tiger was given to him without being requested and disappeared without being repaid, which implies the tiger was purely given away. What Pi received in the symmetrical relationship with the tiger was the sensorially reduced form of the pure gift, no matter how positive and uncalculated it may have been. When the tiger can no longer be rewarded with a specific gift like food, it is clear to us, if not to Pi, that the tiger belonged to and yet remained outside the symbiotic give and take it enabled, like the impossible gift that renders the gift exchange possible. The potential of being such a contingent yet epiphanic gift, precarious yet precious, must also have been immanent in Pi's existence, which the tiger must not have recognized as a gift. No wonder this potentiality beyond recognition and rational measurement is implied in the name Pi (3.14159 . . .), the irrational number whose infinity resonates with divinity. But although Pi himself humanizes this infinity in the form of gods he worships, its fundamental exteriority to humanity is not translatable into practical faith or any harmonious multicultural combination of diverse religions. The catastrophe that Pi undergoes is revelatory, like other cases explored, to let us sense the infinite horizon of Being across which the abject others intersect as potentialities of the gift, even when they are physically apart. Pi could grieve over this fate less and love it more.

In truth, *Life of Pi* takes a doubly ambivalent position in this regard. First, it ends while leaving another version of the story as if to enrich interpretative freedom. But the second short version, which Pi tells to the Japanese freighter insurers who do not believe the tiger story, is nothing but a source for another Disney animation: what happened in the boat was a bloody survival game between Pi, his mother, a sailor, and a cook, who killed each other, and so Pi transformed them into the orangutan, the zebra, and the hyena in his animal fable to forget the traumatic event. This 'human' drama implies that Pi survived as a cannibal, eating the cook whom he killed without any experience of gift-giving. Also, crucially, the first version cannot be an escapist fantasy, as it has the profoundly traumatic event of losing the tiger, which indeed opens the door to the pure gift. We thus see no value in replacing the tiger as the ontological other/gift with a humanized animal character.

Second, the film appears like a visual feast of cutting-edge 3D digital images that reproduce even the whiskers of the ultimately uncapturable tiger more realistically than reality. The 3D pop-up screen effect—the illusion of figures protruding toward the audience as in *Avatar*—is updated in the opposite direction when the sea and the sky look infinite, like outer space, as though the screen recedes backward endlessly. The film aspires to realize 'total cinema' with this scopophilic desire to obsessively paint and package even the sublime of infinity in hyperreal aesthetic frames.[4] In fact, there is no real tiger that threatens Pi. We see just an endlessly modulable single image into which the ontological other is 'sutured' at our blind spot, which is covered by computer simulation. Digital technology has already disrupted and expanded the nature and scope of cinematic images, replacing the indexicality of the celluloid with the iconicity of animation. Nevertheless, *Life of Pi* leaves an unrepresentable black hole in the middle of nature, copied by this overwhelming technology. The dark entrance of the jungle into which the tiger has walked looks like a visual symptom of an invisible 'clearing' in the forest, where beings as precarious gifts reside. The camera does not follow the tiger. So the film leaves a blank space like a gift on the fully saturated screen.

---

[4] See William Brown (2020) regarding the computer-generated "sublime entanglement." Similarly, Rachel Wagner (2016) analyzes the film's CGI as a means of visually affirming multireligious themes.

11
The Abject as Neighbor beyond Cultural Mediation

Ethical Philosophy on Abraham and Isaac

Jean-Pierre and Luc Dardenne once did an interview in which the biblical story of Abraham and Isaac came up. No myth could be more straightforward yet profound: God commands Abraham to offer his son Isaac as a sacrifice, and Abraham complies. But after he binds Isaac to an altar, a messenger from God stops him and says, "Now I know you fear God." Abraham then sees a ram and sacrifices it instead (Figure 11.1). When the interviewer noted that this story was related to the Dardennes' film *The Son* (2002), the brothers said: "Yes, because Abraham doesn't have to kill Isaac, and that's the foundation of humanity" (G. Andrew 2006). The father figure in the film eventually renounces his revenge plan to kill the murderer of his son, the young apprentice he has accepted like a surrogate son and taught carpentry. A moral lesson of forgiveness? But it is never easy to tell why humanity should be founded on the mandate "not to kill" when God's order was for Abraham to kill even his son. We encounter this question in *The Child* (2005) and *The Kid with a Bike* (2011) as well, as if it is the Dardennes' leitmotif. Indeed, we can trace it back to their first international success, *The Promise* (1996), with more interesting twists of the religious source.

Notably, unlike those films with only white characters, *The Promise* presents African illegal workers in Belgium against the backdrop of globalization in Europe. It is the very backdrop of postpolitical double ethics in our study: the soft-ethical inclusion of cultural differences in (neo)liberal network systems and their hard-ethical underside of sovereign exclusion, migration and refugee crises, and fundamentalist (counter)terror. As seen in Chapter 1, here lurks the European subject's double stance on the migrant Other from the Global South. It is either a precarious Other to protect in the name of European Enlightenment values or a dangerous Other to prevent from threatening the traditional European cultural identity. Likewise,

Figure 11.1. The biblical story of Abraham and Isaac has been depicted in many paintings, including Rembrandt's *The Sacrifice of Isaac* (1635).

human rights are ethically taken for granted on both sides: Europe must save the basic and absolute right of the Other through humanitarian efforts or keep its own self-defensive right not to be harassed but even to 'kill' the terrorizing Other. The soft ethics of tolerance and hospitality is inseparable from the hard ethics of security and violence.

Interestingly, the Abraham-Isaac story is directly mentioned in another notable film reflecting the double face of today's Europe: Fatih Akin's *The Edge of Heaven* (2007). German and Turkish characters here include not only native and immigrant European citizens but also a sort of citizens-turning-into-refugees outside the law, structurally unanchored and nomadically floating. These abject people are none other than global noncitizens bereft of legal rights and sociopolitical identity, treated with either soft-ethical pity and compassion or hard-ethical hatred and discrimination. No doubt *The Promise* and *The Edge of Heaven* serve as two rich texts that allow us to look at non-Western migrants in Western Europe as the abject in the background of cultural conflicts between global (Christian) Europe and its (Islamic) periphery. But more crucially, the abject in both films inspires us to reinterpret the biblical story so as to make a breakthrough in today's ethical double bind. An alternative ethical path is then opened beyond a global multiculturalist Europe and an antiglobal nationalist Europe. To follow this path, let me first briefly introduce the context of ethical philosophy in which the Binding of Isaac has been seriously debated, then delve into *The Promise* and *The Edge of Heaven*.

It is no wonder that the Dardennes mention Søren Kierkegaard and Levinas when talking about their ethical themes.[1] However, the term 'ethics' needs careful attention. In his book *Fear and Trembling* (2006), Kierkegaard criticizes the Kantian ethical paradigm of his times in which one's actions should be based on universal maxims one can will. Each individual should be able to take a set of universal moral laws of one's own free will as coming from within. Conversely, the individual is believed to have the autonomy to extend and represent the universal by internalizing it. However, Abraham abandons the moral code of parental love universally shared in his community to follow God's secret command, something that he does not tell anybody. Kierkegaard defines religious faith, in opposition to ethics, as assuming this highest responsibility for the Other, whose divine law is unknown and unknowable. Its incomprehensible irrationality causes the 'madness' of the leap into faith, a madness that one may reach, like Abraham, only through 'fear and trembling' before the sublime Other. The absolute alterity of this Other demands not autonomous freedom but heteronomous dedication in the individual's singular solitude beyond any communicability. In short, Kierkegaard criticizes the Kantian oneness between the individual and universal law. The (Kierkegaardian) individual transcends the law toward a singular encounter with 'otherness' outside any community.

In the same line of thinking, Levinas (1979) redefines the opposition 'ethics vs. faith' as 'politics vs. ethics.' Kierkegaard's idea of faith corresponds

---

[1] See Joseph Mai (2010, esp. 94–96) regarding Kierkegaard and Sarah Cooper (2007) for a Levinasian (aesthetic) reading of the Dardennes.

to Levinas's notion of ethics, which is less religiously characterized but still transcendent. For Levinas, "the face of the other" is an interface with its invisible otherness, the infinite Other. The face is thus not like an idol that is materially visualized and culturally worshiped but rather like an icon that is transparently open to a beyond, leading to the void. The face-to-face relationship does not build a sense of communal totality but deconstructs it toward infinity. It is a "relation without relation," an asymmetrical, unexchangeable, unequal relation irreducible to the subject-object dyad, which is only initiated by the calling from the Other. One can only respond to this calling, displaying 'response-ability' and thus taking responsibility. Here, the message of the other's face, the appearance of the face itself as speech, is "You shall not kill!"—one of Moses's ten commandments received from God, which Levinas theorizes ethically. Only through the acceptance of this ethical imperative can one have a place for living, room for human subjectivity as given and allowed by infinite otherness. The ethics of the Other thus precedes the ontology of being; the relationship between the two preconditions the existence of one. The intervention of a new, third one in this dyad would open room for politics because it introduces the issue of justice and equality among three, that is, the multiple in society, beyond mercy and grace between two. Levinas prioritizes ethics over politics, emphasizing the significance of infinity in the dual relationship, which should not be flattened among social relations in collective totality.

We may ask, then: How can God, the infinite Other, command Abraham to kill his son? Whatever divine plot may be hidden, this order to kill is given to Abraham by the same Jewish God who gives Moses and all men the order not to kill. This self-contradiction may not just indicate God's caprice, given that the ritual of child sacrifice was historically normal in the period of Abraham, who lived several generations earlier than Moses. Killing to make an offering to God was part of Abrahamic culture. Moreover, Benjamin's idea of "divine violence" originates from the Jewish God's frequent performance of punishment, killing people as a way of expunging human trash to start over from ground zero (see Chapter 4). This 'rebooting' of the world occurred periodically until God had the Mosaic Law established to define murder as a crime. Of course, Abraham's faith in God could still be authentic, as he is to kill not the very Other that he faces, God, but someone outside this dual relationship. But at least in the Bible, we do not see Abraham's 'fear and trembling.' His agony and suffering in following the inhuman order exist only in Kierkegaard's poetic imagination. Abraham almost mechanically takes actions to fulfill his mission, with no hesitation, like the Terminator. He has no question about why God gives him such a cruel order and what the big Other desires; —he does not ask '*Che vuoi?*' ('What do you want?').

In this sense, Abraham's act may represent the then-standard culture of collective servitude to God, who takes the transcendent center of the worshipers' community. This big Other's order may have been obeyed like a Kantian categorical imperative, an unconditional moral obligation binding in all circumstances beyond any individual interest. Although the Kantian universal is universal humanity and not divinity, Kant claims that the single individual expresses his telos in the universal. This ethical claim sounds like an update of the religious faith in the way of annulling singularity to form oneness with universal divinity. Interestingly, the Quran tells that Ibrahim (Abraham), in anxiety, reveals the divine order of filicide to his very son Ismael (Isaac), who instead encourages his father to follow God and kill him. More father-like than his father, Ismael determines even to make a self-sacrifice through a sort of democratic discussion with his father. Ismael thus evokes some tragic nobility that such Greek heroes as Oedipus, Agamemnon, and Sisyphus embody when taking responsibility for their divinely imposed fate in the lucid consciousness of its 'absurd' meaninglessness, thereby paradoxically opening room for sublime humanity. The paradox is that once you accept the given order as retroactively chosen of your free will, you are no longer the servant of your fate but the master of your life. Hence Nietzschean *amor fati*: love your fate, and you will break its grasp and free yourself (see Chapter 7).

The Promise: Walking Side by Side with the Abject Neighbor

Now let me go back to *The Promise*. Here, Igor is a teenage boy, but he can be seen as an Abraham figure who is under the power of his godlike father Roger, a smuggler and capitalist exploiter of undocumented immigrants to Belgium (see Small [2016] for another reading of the Abraham story in the film). One day, when one of his undocumented West African workers, Amidou, is fatally injured while hiding from the authorities, Roger tries to cover up this accident, letting him die and then burying him with Igor's reluctant help. Then the film reaches a turning point. Roger prohibits Igor from helping Amidou's wife, Assita, and plans to sell her to a brothel, but Igor saves her and leaves home with her. Igor does everything, no matter how helpless he is, to take care of Assita and her baby because he promised Amidou to do so right before his death. If Abraham's blind obedience to God conformed to the universal norm of his religious community, unlike Kierkegaard's claim, Igor's resistance to Roger rather embodies a truly Kierkegaardian singularity outside the universal order of sovereign economic power represented by his father. Igor performs this radical transgression not in fear and trembling but in fury, fighting against the global system of labor exploitation and human trafficking that permeates today's Europe.

This singularity, however, does not go 'above' the universal plane of globalization but 'below' it because Igor steps down from the privileged father-son dyad and stands by the alien Third. It is noteworthy that the dual relation between Abraham and God leaves no place for Isaac. Isaac does not count as a dialogue partner at all and thus is not a Third who can open the closed circuit of one-to-one ethics toward sociopolitical relations in which justice and equality matter. Deprived of human subjectivity by divine and patriarchal sovereignty, Isaac is nothing but an abject, a 'bare life' only to be killed like an animal, as Agamben would say: literally bare as seen in many classical paintings of his binding. Conversely, Igor undergoes self-abjection from his father's sovereign realm after facing the face of the abject in our age. Such immigrant laborers as Amidou's family from Burkina Faso, a former francophone colony, are near-neocolonial others of the global system, economically included in and legally excluded from it. This 'internal exclusion' precisely defines the status of bare life: being "included in the juridical order solely in the form of exclusion (that is, in its capacity to be killed)" (Agamben 1998, 8). Igor, then, decides 'not to kill' the abject immigrant family. This order is self-given, embraced from within and not enforced by God's categorical imperative, maybe because abjecthood is the common bottom of all beings. At this bottom one would have to believe in the potential sacredness of human life, the potential to be realized above mere animality without God's predetermination of its value. This is maybe why the commandment "not to kill" is the foundation of humanity. Igor makes the promise while looking at the face of the dying worker whose sanctity of life is yet to come (*à venir*) through his wife's survival and is thus potentially infinite. A Levinasian Other, if any, appears as an abject life killed by the irresponsible sovereign father, and the son atones for this original sin by not killing another related abject.

Igor's becoming-abject is thus not a subservient sacrifice but a subversive challenge to the symbolic order of his big Other. True otherness does not lie in any divine superego's kingdom but in the abject who are cast out of it. Igor goes down to the same level as Assita, who is not transcendent to his reach but is immanent in the egalitarian ground of abjecthood. His move implies more than unselfish love for the marginal and miserable in society. Such a humanitarian gesture still treats the abject as the victim for which our dispensation of sympathy and charity, generosity and hospitality is often offered conditionally, with regulations and calculations from the patronizing position of the subject just as the liberal 'multiculturalist' condescendingly celebrates other cultures commodifiable in the logic of multinational capitalism. In other words, Igor does not practice the soft ethics of tolerance and charity. To become abject is to renounce that hierarchical subjectivity and embrace common 'abjecthood' on the open plane where the inequality of the father-son ethics is restructured for equality and justice through the intervention of a Third. In this way, a minimal social relationship is formed between the three, with sovereignty put into question. It makes a breakthrough in Levinas's dilemma between ethics and politics and in Europe's deadlock between soft and hard ethics.

Another crucial concept to rethink here is the gift. As Jean-Luc Marion (2011, 84–90) argues, the original lesson of Abraham's story is that Isaac was born as God's gift to Abraham—who was already about one hundred years old, thus sexually impotent without a doubt—and is regiven to him when he passes God's test of his faith. This test teaches him that the 'givenness' of Isaac could be taken back anytime and thus must be appreciated. In short, a being as such is a gift. In *The Promise*, however, it is Igor (the Abraham figure) who is a gift given to Assita (the Isaac figure), not in the way of giving something out of pity but in the way of becoming an abject just as she is. Of course Igor's being itself is a gift here too—and the greatest gift possible at that, as he sacrifices his whole life to help Assita. The point is that this existential gift is recognized as a gift by neither the giver nor the givee. It goes beyond the actual mode of the gift as exchange, the capitalistic calculation of give and take, and thus performs Derrida's pure sense of the gift (see Chapter 10). Igor-as-gift is indeed driven by pure indebtedness to Assita's husband, the dead abject whom Igor cannot directly repay. Put otherwise, a pure ethical debt, impossible to pay back, causes a pure ethical gift impossible to return outside their secular economy.[2] This becoming-abject as gift breaks the tautological circuit

---

[2] The debt is indeed an underlying motif. In the opening scene, Igor operates a gas pump, which indicates "amount to be paid" and "debit." It means the rate, a financial debt, but foreshadows his

of God regiving what he gave. It opens room for solidarity between the abject as strangers outside the closed totality of gift-giving in the patriarchal lineage from God/father to the father/son and outside the global system of capitalist economy and its soft ethics.

In some sense, Igor's self-abjection evokes Lacan's (1997, 311–25) formulation of the ethical act as "not giving way on one's desire," the desire to go beyond the symbolic order. Antigone is Lacan's ethical heroine (270–90). Her pursuit of the banned funeral of her dead brother embodies her attempt to take ultimate responsibility and her infinite mourning for the abject cast out of the state law. This act for the abject and against sovereign power makes her another abject between symbolic and real deaths, neither socially alive nor physically dead. Her desire is thus a rather Lacanian death drive, some 'undead' urge persisting over the boundary between life and death. However, Igor is not such a terrorist militant dedicated to a transcendent divine law in absolute solitude. He is an 'abject agent' who helps Assita regain social subjectivity in temporary solidarity with her. And his abject agency is liberated from his fixed identity of being Roger's son and connected with 'any-abject-whoever' in its unanchored drift. It is thus not firm and permanent but only provisional and vulnerable. Agency performs a contingently given task only until it is completed in the transitory mode of identity and through its transformative modulation between subjectivity and objectivity.

More importantly, agency is never guaranteed. Agency is not preplanned but generated when it performs itself, precisely embodying the concept of (linguistic) 'performativity.' Just as *promise* is a 'performative' verb—that is, the utterance of the word itself performs its meaning—so Igor's promise to Amidou is made only at the moment he says "I promise." But the content of this promise—to take care of Assita and her baby—is only to be realized in the future, an uncertain future that even God does not know. This paradoxical temporality of performativity has nothing to do with Abraham. Although he does not know the reason for God's command to kill Isaac, his act to perform this horrible command is rooted in his firm belief in unknown divine providence, in the certainty that God knows and does everything. Inshallah (if Allah wills it) is just such a magical chant of dispelling doubt and displacing it to God, who will do his job well. The paradoxical implication is that we humans do not have to care about what we do as servants of God

---

ethical debt. And Assita, unaware of Amidou's death, thinks that he has disappeared due to gambling debts (Small 2016, 18).

and are thus exempted from responsibility for our actions, taking comfort in a sort of slave morality. In contrast, Igor acts as the master of his existential choice to abject himself, to take responsibility for the unknowable result of his free will. This absolute freedom and responsibility may be the real source of fear and trembling, the fear for the unseen horizon of future possibility that Kierkegaard calls dread. Again, genuinely Kierkegaardian is Igor, who goes through this dread even without Kierkegaard's God.

It is no surprise that the film leads to an open ending. After wandering homelessly, Assita is planning to join her cousin, who she believes is in Italy, and wait for Amidou, who she believes is working somewhere else as Igor said (lied). These beliefs, although groundless, still sustain her version of the European immigrant dream. But on the way to the train station where she is leaving for Italy, Igor finally tells her the hidden truth that he and his father let her husband die. Silence reigns between them for a while. Then Assita slowly turns around and hopelessly walks back even though she has no home to return to. Igor walks along with her in the endless-looking underpass (see Figure 11.2). This aimless walk, however, is not tragic. It instead endures the suspension of subjectivity to regain, the vacuum of sociopolitical support, the deracination of a place to reside, that is, a topos to occupy. They head to no utopia but to 'atopia': a place abjected from its identity and telos, a

Figure 11.2. The Belgian boy in *The Promise* walks with his abject neighbor from Africa in the endless-looking underpass at the film's end.

place taking no place in the Symbolic order of the world, the global system of Europe (see Chapter 12).

The crucial point is that Igor confesses his guilt while looking at Assita's back and not her face. That is, he tells the truth when he does not face her face, when she is faceless, maybe because he 'loses' face by facing his guilt. This guilt exceeds his self-control and binds him to the faceless other who can be neither redeemed nor removed. The traumatic Real of the buried past penetrates and connects both subjectivity and otherness. The core of the 'neighbor,' Žižek (2013b, 140–41) says, is not his/her familiar face but this terrifying Thing, which makes one ashamed or guilty. In effect, Igor's act of making the promise to the face of dying Amidou may just have come out as a socially pertinent gesture: —Who would say "I won't promise" in that situation? However, the promise becomes binding to the extent that he cannot help choosing the abject over the father, that is, the faceless Third over the face of God. And this Third, who came from the Third World, does not represent cultural differences to tolerate and assimilate, or hate and eliminate, but the sameness of human abjecthood to embrace and overcome at the same time. It is noteworthy that Igor is not bothered that Assita's ethnic culture looks exotic and often irrational. This 'indifference' to differences that exist, which comprise reality as such, may enable a new global ethics of sameness, as Badiou (2012, 27) suggests. The cultural barrier is not something one must cross to reach the true other behind it. Without being mediated by such collective identity as culture, one could immediately connect with the other in the common struggle with the human condition. Igor's walk side by side with Assita on the same ground of abjecthood is thus the best image of a new ethical relationship: not the face-to-face interpellation but the side-by-side accompaniment. It shares the whole weight of existential abjection in 'atopian' movement, without optimism or pessimism, terror or suicide, passion or compassion.

Psychoanalytically, this atopian ethics could be examined in light of Lacan's formula of sexuation (see Chapter 8). On the masculine side, all men are under the law of symbolic castration, but one figure transcends it to fulfill desire. This obscene superego, like the Freudian primal father, puts all his sons on the Oedipal trajectory. He is analogous to the biopolitical sovereign who can go beyond his law, abjecting the normal subject into bare life. Similarly, Igor's father imposes the prohibition (of helping Assita) and brutal punishment on Igor for violating the prohibition in the name of paternal love. The injury to Igor's foot—which evokes the meaning of Oedipus ('swollen feet')—intimates his Oedipalization in the father-son lineage. By extension, the father represents the universal regime of global capitalism, including its illegal underside of taking benefits from exploiting the immigrant abject. Igor's atopian flight from this regime, then, takes on the logic of femininity: that there is no exceptional woman to the phallic function, but not all feminine sexuality belongs to it. This 'not-all,' in Igor, resonates with the very abject that cannot belong to the totality of the father's regime. Moreover, it is infinitely not-all, as Igor's guilt for the death of Amidou cannot be expiated by him anymore and is thus redirected to Assita. The Levinasian ethics of dual relation is then opened up to the potential replacement of one end of the two by a Third, who could also be replaced by another Third, and so on (in theory). This openness of not-all draws a zigzag path of 'becoming-abject as a gift' through deferred actions and belated revelations of indebtedness.

The Edge of Heaven: Relaying Gift-Giving in Zigzag as Atopian Ethics

To further develop the idea of the zigzag gift-giving between the abject, I now move on to *The Edge of Heaven*. The story goes back and forth between Germany and Turkey, following six main characters from three families, that is, three parent-child pairs: Ali (father) and Nejat (son) are Turkish German, Yeter (mother) and Ayten (daughter) are Turkish, and Susanne (mother) and Lotte (daughter) are German. To be brief, the complex plot unfolds as follows. A professor of German literature, Nejat seems disapproving about his widower father Ali's choice of prostitute Yeter for a live-in girlfriend. But Nejat grows fond of Yeter as he discovers that she sends money home to Turkey for the higher education of her daughter, Ayten. Yeter's accidental death caused by Ali makes Nejat distance himself from his father. Nejat travels to Istanbul to meet and take care of Ayten on behalf of her mother. However, political activist Ayten has fled from the Turkish police and is already in Germany. Homeless and moneyless, Ayten is assisted and befriended by university student Lotte, who even invites rebellious Ayten to stay in her home. They fall in love, but Ayten's stay is not particularly pleasing to Lotte's conservative mother, Susanne. Later, Ayten is arrested, and her asylum plea is denied; she is deported and imprisoned in Turkey. Lotte travels to Turkey, where she happens to rent a room from Nejat and struggles to free Ayten, but she is killed by a kid who fires a gun unintentionally. After Lotte's death, Susanne goes to Turkey, meets Nejat by chance, and decides to take on her daughter's mission of freeing Ayten. Touched by Susanne, Ayten exercises her right of repentance and wins her freedom. She stays with Susanne at Nejat's house, while Nejat journeys to reconcile with his father, who has come to Turkey.

Let us start with one notable scene in the middle of the film. It shows a quarrel between Ayten and Susanne, who is reluctant to welcome the stranger. Susanne asks what Ayten is fighting for, and their conversation goes like this:

AYTEN: We are fighting for 100% human rights, and 100% freedom of speech, and 100% social education. In Turkey, just people with money can get an education.
SUSANNE: Maybe things will get better once you get into the European Union.
AYTEN: Ah, I don't trust the European Union. [. . .] Who is leading the European Union? It's England, France, Germany, and Italy, and Spain. These countries are all colonial countries. It's globalization and we are fighting against it.
SUSANNE: Maybe you're a person who just likes to fight.
AYTEN: You think I am crazy? If a country kills the people, the folk, just because they think different, or look different, or because they protest to have a bulb, and energy, and schools, you have to fight back.
SUSANNE: Maybe, everything will get better once you get into [the] European Union.
AYTEN: Fuck the European Union!
SUSANNE: I don't want you to talk like that in my house. You can talk like that in your house. OK?

It is clear that Susanne stands for and even idealizes the EU as a soft-ethical global utopia, whereas Ayten pinpoints its politically divisive structure controlled by a few dominant colonial powers. However, what matters is not the opposition between the soft ethics and politics but the problems with each. Germany refuses Ayten's asylum plea and deports her as an illegal alien, judging that there is no legitimate fear of political persecution in her case. In Turkey, however, she is imprisoned as a political dissident. Here is a paradox: the inclusion of a refugee in the soft-ethical system requires her legalized qualification, which is precisely what this outsider calls for to be there. The tolerance of this system only works softly for the qualified insiders of the boundary between tolerable and intolerable in the name of the law.

"Once you are a member, you are free and equal." However, the legalization of the very membership inevitably causes inequality, producing the abject, who are judged without careful consideration of a country's political reality outside the system. The institutionalization of ethical values such as tolerance and hospitality is thus nothing else but the administration of regulations through biopolitical apparatuses, which govern the EU's soft-ethical rainbow community.[3]

Another paradox is that Ayten's political struggle is not really opposed to, but rather virtually oriented to, the ideal of soft ethics, that is, 100 percent freedom and radical equality. Indeed, is politics today not destined to achieve the very soft-ethical goal of making the current imperfect global system more perfect? The ethical turn of politics, which Rancière has criticized, seems inevitable, as I noted in the Introduction. The pursuit of politics will ultimately bring its own dissolution (at least in theory if not in reality). This dilemma is related to two delicate, contradictory points in the film. First, when Ayten's international allies in Germany almost abandon her due to her inability to pay them for support, their political group appears rather like a sort of soft-ethical community whose hospitality to a new member is conditional, depending on her financial power. Second, when Ayten's comrade inmates in Turkey spit on her after her decision to exercise her right of repentance and be released from prison, their political group turns out to be rigidly isolated in a sort of hard-ethical dogmatism with no room for embracing existential concerns. Ayten 'betrays' them because Lotte was absurdly shot with a pistol that Ayten asked Lotte to secure for future activism—that is, she was sacrificed to fulfill her lover's political mission—and Susanne, saddened but moved by this tragedy, also travels to Turkey to fulfill her daughter's ethical mission to save her foreign lover. Ayten's and Susanne's guilt over Lotte's death and their final reconciliation thus resonate with the ethics of indebtedness and gift-giving mentioned earlier. That ethics enables contingent solidarity between the abject (including the self-abjected subject) and their redemption between life and death on the concrete existential level of individual relations, not on the abstract ideal level of collective destiny.

By extension, a scene toward the end of the film evokes the ethical core of my discussion of *The Promise*. Susanne notices a procession of people in the

---

[3] Elsaesser (2011) reviews the film by precisely drawing on Rancière's view of "the ethical turn," and Dudley Andrew (2016) appreciates "an ethic of viewing" that the film inspires as a binational epitome of world cinema. Starting from here, what I attempt is to take another, alternative ethical turn.

street from the apartment of Nejat (who also came to Turkey to repay an ethical debt to Yeter by offering Ayten a gift of educational support). Nejat tells Susanne that people are participating in a Bayram festival commemorating Ibrahim's sacrifice of his son Ishmael, which she finds equivalent to the Abraham-Isaac story (see Figure 11.3). Nejat reminisces about being terrified by the story as a child and asking his father if he would sacrifice him to obey God. As Susanne wonders about his father's answer, Nejat says: "He said that he would even make God his enemy in order to protect me." No doubt the same story of sacrifice in the Quran and the Bible builds a cultural bridge between the two people, between Germany and Turkey, between Judeo-Christian and Islamic religions. They are indeed not enemies but brothers. "We are the world, we are the children" of the same God, to borrow Michael Jackson's 1985 Live Aid theme song. The scene seemingly teaches that one can understand and accept the other by overcoming a cultural barrier and finding a common denominator that connects them to a universal community of humanity. It epitomizes the soft-ethical vision of a harmonious multicultural world more ideally than Susanne's former remark about the EU.

However, the real point about this scene is the position that Nejat's father Ali takes with regard to the Abraham story: if he were Abraham, he would tell Nejat about God's inhuman command and conduct a war against God. This radical resistance is different from delaying or ignoring the execution of the

Figure 11.3. *The Edge of Heaven* shows a Bayram festival in Turkey commemorating the Islamic version of the Abraham-Isaac story.

command, which is the case of failure in the divine test of faith and would thus result in the killing of the son by God himself as punishment. Here lies Abraham's double bind: if he obeys God, Isaac is supposed to be killed, but even if he does not, Isaac will still be killed. Both options are alternatives set within the divine paradigm of faith as obedience. In contrast, Ali rejects this paradigm itself. If Abraham represents the universality of religious culture, unlike Kierkegaard's view, as we saw, it is Ali who is a singular Kierkegaardian individual outside his religious community: an 'all-too-human' solitary warrior who expresses not 'fear and trembling' but furious antagonism toward divine sovereignty. In this sense, Ali and young Nejat correspond to Igor and Assita in *The Promise*. Ali breaks his upward connection with God and stands by his son whom God makes an abject. He abjects himself from the privileged divine relationship by facing this bare life, whose potential sanctity of life is to be believed as open and undecidable, to be saved and not killed. A Levinasian 'relation without relation' would be made between two abject beings whose otherness is equally bare yet infinitely sacred. In sum, the true other for Ali is not the superego-like God that he is supposed to internalize as his telos but his son as the abject abandoned by the very big Other. Ali steps on the same ground as this abject by abjecting himself. He performs not soft-ethical humanitarianism for social minorities to include in the community but identification with the abject without pity and openness to the Third outside the theological Levinasian dyad. As Žižek (2013b: 146–48) criticizes Levinas, we could further claim that the primordial ethical obligation is toward this abject Third in shadow beyond the face-to-face relationship. It is to fight against the face of God and fight for the faceless Third. This fight is for justice beyond the universal law of faith in God or any sovereign big Other.

The idea of the gift also applies here. In Ali's case, the gift of a being is not his son given from God but Ali the father himself, given to his abject son to protect him. That is perhaps why Nejat never forgets Ali's words. His becoming-abject as gift destroys the self-closed circuit of giver-givee (God-Abraham) and creates the unprecedented solidarity of the abject against this sovereign power structure of gift-giving. Moreover, just as the father is not regiven to the son but given as a gift for the first time outside this structure, so their solidarity could be seen as that between the strangers, or the 'neighbors' if we want, beyond the universal humanism of paternal love. This 'abject-gift' thus challenges the big Other's universal law. Consequently, God is no longer the highest center of multicultural harmony but is pulled down to the same egalitarian ground as the abject and repositioned as nothing but an enemy.

Ethics is then opened to a minimal level of the social relationship between the three, including a sort of political antagonism. By extension, Ali's antagonistic self-abjection evokes Lacanian desire or Antigone's death drive but does not explode for any suicidal terroristic mission. Like Igor, Ali becomes an abject agent for the self-imposed mission to save and sustain life, although the outcome of this agency is never guaranteed. Without chanting Inshallah, Ali decides to be the master of his fate, to be responsible for the unknown future chosen of his free will.

The ending of the film remains open. In fact, Ali first appears as a lonely old patriarch, who 'hires' Yeter as a sex partner only to kill her accidentally out of rage. We do not see the Ali who would challenge God for his son. The scene described previously suggests that Nejat, having been shamed and feeling guilty for Ali's crime, finally re-embraces his father as a potential gift. However, the ending shows Nejat just waiting for Ali on a beach, on the edge of Europe, or 'heaven,' while their reunion remains uncertain. Far from being predictable or determinable, the relationship between the abject implied here is only precarious and temporary. Their contingently generated tasks of meeting or helping are not accomplished directly and immediately but put in delay and differentiation. Conversely, however, this sort of Derridean *différance* enables the relay of contingent relations among the abject agents. Listening to Nejat's story, Susanne virtually, if briefly, takes the place of his father (or his lost mother). Indeed, she seems touched by Ali's parental love, which is shared as the motivation for her to become an abject-gift to Ayten. Far detached from her heavenly EU, she finds, supports, and accepts Ayten like a surrogate daughter who takes the place of the dead Lotte. Interestingly, Nejat has no chance to meet Ayten but offers a room to Susanne, who offers it to Ayten, as if they are in an open circuit of indirect gift-giving. The dual relationship between father and son, mother and daughter, is thus not symmetrically stable but dynamically shifting, with one of the two replaced by a Third, who can also be replaced by another Third, and so forth. The asymmetry inherent in the pure sense of the debt/gift (as opposed to symmetrical exchange) lies not only between individuals but also between generations on a zigzag path of belated revelations of indebtedness and deferred acts of gift-giving: A is a gift to B, who can give herself back not to A but to A's friend/daughter C, who can give herself back not to B but to B's friend/daughter D, and so on.

This nontotalizing abject agency of gift-giving does atopian networking in the mode of 'not-all.' There is no utopia, a nostalgically or futuristically idealized place, but only atopia, or rather, the atopian movement of losing/leaving one's place or being abjected from one place to another. What I call 'atopian ethics' only contingently emerges on the edge of the global system through its abjects' connection and disconnection, transition and modulation, supplement and replacement (see more in Chapter 12). It is based on their commonality without community, identity without pity, solidarity without unity. The face-to-face dyad, whether it brings soft-ethical grace or hard-ethical desire, is then opened to the potential intervention and embrace of the Third, while one's abject agency is set in motion by one's indebtedness or responsibility for the other. This performative agency puts the circulation of gifts/debts in perpetual *différance* without optimism or pessimism. Irreducible solely to the Kantian imperative or Kierkegaardian singularity, atopian ethics calls for attention to abject agents' existential consciousness about the absurdity in the big Other's morality and the freedom of self-abjection for solidarity as *amor fati*. What is universal here is potential abjecthood, and what is singular is existential agency. This ethics opens the Levinasian dyad to a potential triad, but it is not subsumed to political collectivity and assimilated to a global community. Instead, it keeps its atopian dynamics of the precarious yet precious gift-giving relation without relation while challenging or abjecting the big Other that governs biopolitical subjectivity. We should thus embrace the adventure of taking atopian subjectivity to stand by the abject. What would happen, then? Let us not say Inshallah because we have nothing but the will to love our unknown fate.

12
Atopian Networking and Positive Nihilism

Negative, Passive, and Active Nihilism in the Global Frame

Our journey into global cinema began with the framing of today's postpolitical double ethics: the soft-ethical inclusion of differences in multicultural, neoliberal systems and their hard-ethical symptoms of fundamentalist exclusion and terror. Mapping a global range of films in this frame, we have critically delved into the biopolitical abjection of subjectivity, the sociostructural shift of community to network, and the political deadlock of utopian change as allegorized in various forms of catastrophe and some nihilistic characters. Yet as also highlighted, an ethical alternative irreducible to collective politics emerges when abject figures become contingent agents of existential gift giving. This creates 'atopian' networking beyond the problematic soft/hard ethics of pity/hate or tolerance/violence. This last chapter, though short due to limited space, will further illuminate atopian ethics while positively reformulating nihilism via two films resonant with two former chapters and, finally, close the book with the appreciation of cinema as an ethical art.

Let me start with a quick overview of nihilism as a pertinent conceptual lens through which to review today's subjectivity and society on the existential level. Nihilism is, in effect, not a single philosophical trend but an ideological frame of reference that conditions life values in various modes, as profoundly critiqued by Nietzsche (2009).[1] It is worth rephrasing and updating his multistep analysis in our terms and context. First, "negative nihilism" is derived from the Judeo-Christian mentality. After the fall of Adam ("the First Man") from heaven, the actual world is deemed a negative version

---

[1] See Simon Critchley (2013, 4–6) for a brief summary of Nietzsche's viewpoint and Bulent Diken (2009) for a book-length study of nihilism.

of the lost paradise, which can be rejoined only in the hereafter, through the faithful atonement for one's (original) sin in a doomed, resigned life. Heavenly salvation comes as postmortem compensation for this self-sacrificial asceticism, which denies any earthly meaning of life and is subjugated to the divine master. Hence the "slave morality" that Nietzsche trenchantly reveals as underlying and generating pessimism, cynicism, and ressentiment, as well as the model Christian values for the weak or powerless (humility, charity, pity, etc.). In Lacanian language, the devotional pursuit of God is analogous to the subject's illusory 'desire' for oneness with the Other: the transcendent center exceptional to the law of castration who is supposed to enjoy jouissance, the total fulfillment of desire. All subjects are repetitively frustrated under this law, but their fatalistic failure of desire instead makes them subject to the Other's order. Similarly, as we saw in Chapter 8, the Symbolic order of biopolitical community is sustained through the dynamics between the big Other's utopian ideals and the normal subjects' internalization of them. This power structure organizes sovereignty and subjectivity while also producing social abjection and pseudo-divine violence as well as pathological symptoms from nationalist neurosis to fascist paranoia.

Negative nihilism gives way to "passive nihilism" after "the death of God" that Nietzsche sees through the disintegration of Christianity and the rise of secularism. With no sacred Other anymore, one is then publicly disoriented while privately seeking apathetic comfort in security and individual pleasures among secular others, people or things. This nineteenth-century "Last Man," as allegorized in some of the dystopian films we examined, is updated to the postmodern consumerist, whose big Other, if not dead, only fosters enjoyment in this postpolitical age after the "End of History." One finds no great passion for life beyond 'small but secured happiness,' hedonistic self-indulgence in personal gratifications that are easily accessible in the late-capitalist global market, the World Interior of capital. Passive nihilists in our times thus lose big causes but gain small object-causes of desire, or rather, drives that can be instantly satisfied while repeatedly circulating around their object. They are mostly the First World global citizens immersed in ever more artificially aroused "stupid daily pleasures" in Žižek's view (2008b, 29). By extension, their permissive hedonism resonates with the multiculturalist consumption of 'decaffeinated' cultures without their sheer or toxic otherness. Human rights are then normalized not only to tolerate others but to keep distance from them, including the sovereign right to defend territorial security and deprive any threatening others of their human rights.

As a form of backlash, the abject cast out of the multicultural global system often return to it, becoming radical extremists or religious fundamentalists who can even sacrifice themselves for alleged universal Causes, incarnating "active nihilism." This implies the "will to power" for negating the Symbolic order, the spiteful passion for the Real to activate even at the cost of their lives in the name of their endangered God. We know, however, that actively nihilistic terrorists provoke the global system's war on terror and the subsequent vicious cycle of retributive violence, each side claiming its sovereignty to destroy the other in the state of exception. This nihilistic synthesis between McWorld and jihad turns politics into the moral dichotomy of good and evil, the dilemmatic choice of either/or, while fetishizing their lifestyles based on religious orthodoxy and sanctified security, respectively. The point is that both sides fight each other in such a way that their causes get lost for the sake of fighting itself, to the extent that fact and right are indistinguishable. They both lose the political edge of democracy and aggravate biopolitical conflict without ultimate resolution, as if in a clash of civilizations. The passive and active nihilisms therefore reflect the recto and verso of the world in the global frame, the double ethical turn of politics into soft globalism and its hard antinomies.

We can sum up the three phases of nihilism psychoanalytically (see Jeong 2016, 373–74). If negative nihilism is based on the logic of desire whose object is utopian but thus unobtainable, passive nihilism centers around the drive that can trigger the consumerist addiction to capitalist simulacra for the object of desire. Noteworthy is another mode of drive: the death drive that transgresses this circuit of pleasure toward jouissance, which is achieved only by negation—the free will to death that rejects any symbolic semblants of the Other (Lacan 1997, 205–17). Active nihilism embodies the death drive to destroy the Symbolic; it runs the risk of self-sacrifice, but as seen in suicidal terrorists, it can also take on negative nihilism, desiring supralegal sovereignty while killing others and negating everything. In truth, Nietzsche's sense of active nihilism is rather positive. It realizes the will to power to overcome the passive nihilist's decadent individualism by destroying the status quo and further creating new values. Positively active nihilists are thus strong-willed individuals who bravely forge ahead to bring new meaning to the world, like political activists dedicated to their public causes. In other words, Nietzsche reaches antinihilism or a sort of metanihilism that annihilates all these nihilisms by overcoming their reactive forces and affirming life anew.

Children of Men: Atopian Networking in Global Dystopian Cinema

Alfonso Cuarón's dystopian film *Children of Men* (2006) is apposite to illuminating multifaceted nihilism in global cinema. It is set in the United Kingdom of 2027, when humans can no longer give birth to children for an unknown reason. Facing the imminent extinction of humanity, the literally last men on the planet live like the Last Men without any hope for the future, just stuck in their bubble filled with trivial pleasures and artistic simulacra (Bell's whiskey, Strawberry Cough, Pink Floyd, *Guernica*, *David*, etc.). Theo, a former activist turned cynical lowly bureaucrat, even says: "World went shit. [. . .] It was too late before the infertility thing happened, for fuck's sake." That is, some catastrophe was immanent in the preapocalyptic world, but it was recognized too late to prevent. What then would be the already potentially catastrophic world if not the current postpolitical global system that, without any change, must have changed Theo's frustrated activism into passive nihilism and yet has always been at risk, as indicated in the opening scene of a sudden terrorist bombing? Tellingly, the United Kingdom, the one remaining civilized nation in this dystopian world, appears as a sovereign police state to handle the mass influx of illegal immigrants, using draconian security policies and xenophobic border controls. Refugee camps, though sketched, do not fail to evoke Abu Ghraib and Guantanamo. Indeed, the film transposes the actual conflicts in Iraq, Palestine, Bosnia, Somalia, and Ireland to a fictional England while depicting military campaigns, generational inequalities, and ecological deterioration as well (Boyle 2009).

The main story begins with Theo being kidnapped by the Fishes, a militant immigrant-rights group led by his ex-wife Julian, from whom he was estranged after their son's death due to a flu pandemic. Julian offers Theo money to get transit papers for, unbelievably, a pregnant refugee named Kee and helps transport her to a sanctuary at sea for the sake of future humanity. Theo, though reluctant at first, accepts this dangerous mission and escorts Kee to the coast while escaping both the Fishes, whose new leader kills Julian to use Kee's baby as a political tool for a refugee revolution, and the British military, which not only fights against this activist terrorist group but forces fertility tests on women. To put it in our terms, Julian stands for the positive potential of active nihilism, whereas the post-Julian Fishes are on the side of its negative version mirrored by their enemy, the state army. Theo turns from a passive nihilist back into a positively active nihilist for a final big cause demanding fatal sacrifice, just like Walt in *Gran Torino* (see Chapter 10). No wonder this change involves the transformation of his initial capitalist deal with Julian into an ethical act of gift-giving among the abject. The only pregnant woman on Earth, a miraculous gift to humankind, is a Black abject, whose naked body (bare life) is seen among animals. She flees from the biopolitical battlefield thanks to a White man, who became an abject agent of gift-giving after self-abjection from his comfort zone; Theo's name tellingly means 'gift of God.'

Indeed, the film stages the religious allegory of the Nativity with multi-layered revisions. Kee delivers a new Christ in a barn like the Virgin Mary, while Theo takes Joseph's place, but they are a secular alternative family formed out of the global abject. Certainly not God but an anonymous wacko is the real father of Kee's baby, now a 'female' Jesus named after Theo's lost son Dylan, who is thus redeemed circuitously to Theo, a surrogate father. Kee, a Third World Black woman, symbolizes not only the Madonna but the wretched of the earth, emancipated as a new Eve or Mother Earth, evoking the African origin of humankind. Also notable are their "amigos," who help them on their journey one by one or together. A midwife, an aged hippie, a gypsy woman, and a Georgian couple host, guide, assist, and feed them in unexpected ways by relaying collective gift-giving without return as a motley crew of sacrificial abject agency. In short, humanity is reborn and regiven through the contingent but continuous processes of adoption, fusion, resurrection, connection, and devotion across origins, borders, races, sexes, and generations.[2]

As suggested in some characters' discussion of faith and chance, it is crucial that their abject agency is driven by taking responsibility for contingent events, believing in the events' potential meaning, though it is yet to be realized through performative praxis. This performance enables precarious yet precious solidarity between abject agents as positively active nihilists who go beyond the law to create an indeterminate yet radically other future at the cost of their lives. Shot by the Fishes, Theo finally dies after reaching the coast, while Dylan sees the dark dystopian sky in a drifting boat. Then,

---

[2] In fact, too many allegorical references appear too briefly or repeat somewhat fetishized stock images, like Kee's racially otherized body (Chaudhary 2009, 90–91). Even in this way, however, Cuarón signals his political position and cultural background. Byzantine icons of Christ and busts of Lenin scanned in the Georgians' apartment typically suggest "an image of Jesus the Left can live with" (Boyle 2009).

Figure 12.1. The only newborn baby in a dystopian world of infertility is carried in a drifting boat to the ship of the Human Project, in *Children of Men*.

as planned, the *Tomorrow*, the ship of the Human Project—a secretive scientific group formed to cure infertility—appears to save Dylan (meaning 'son of the sea'), the germ of a new community (Figure 12.1). Nonetheless, it is uncertain if *Tomorrow* is a deus ex machina promising a utopian future in a happy-ending mood. It would be better to say that those active nihilists' zigzag relationship of gift-giving opens, by its contingent movement, just another possibility of postcatastrophic redemption without utopian promises. Here, as an alternative to utopia, one might think of Michel Foucault's (1967) *heterotopias*: cultural, institutional, discursive spaces or "counter-sites" that are somehow "other," disturbing or transforming, often mirroring yet upsetting, the outside, representing or inverting all the other sites. Interestingly, he takes the boat or ship as a heterotopia par excellence: "a floating piece of space, a place without a place, that exists by itself, that is closed in on itself and at the same time is given over to the infinity of the sea." It is a mobile heterotopia, connecting ports, brothels, or colonies and mobilizing both economy and imagination.

If the heterotopian notion of the ship concerns its site-specific nature and civilizational vitality in modern history, I instead draw attention to the potentially *atopian* navigation of the ship: drifting without anchor or orientation, yet attracting drifters aboard and catalyzing their new relationships on the edge of the world. 'Atopia,' literally meaning 'placelessness' (*a-topos*), describes the ineffable and unique, if not ideal, quality of things or emotions that are seldom experienced.[3] But let's develop this notion more topologically through its deconstruction of any topological definition as follows. If utopias are unreal sites and heterotopias are real sites, atopia cannot take the plural form because it does not exist as a spatial entity but only appears and disappears through the gap between established sites and ideal/other sites. This gap sparks the driving force of leaving the former for the latter, and atopia emerges and submerges in the mode of the very movement. Even without a destination, the possibility of escaping or negating the here and now itself sets off this movement. In other words, atopia barely refers to a place in motion that tentatively surfaces when the terra firma of reality is erased into terra incognita without coordinates, a place 'under erasure' that is constantly displaced without territorial boundaries or topological markers. Occupying no place in the system, it is sensed only as the trace of perpetual flight, leaving itself at the moment of taking a place. Thus, atopia functions as both the performative condition that makes it possible to move to a utopia or heterotopia and the intrinsic aporia that makes it impossible to settle there. We could even say that it exists only in its dynamic adjective form, 'atopian.'

A sort of abjected space, atopia resonates with the abject mode of subjectivity and the fundamental precarity of life as such. The abject who lose their places in the system of identity or are displaced from it, and who even abject themselves to join abject others, are atopian. Even if they embark on a journey to a future utopia or struggle to recover their past subjectivity, this transposition in the present is atopian. But far from romantic nomadism, atopian life is restless and rootless, without job or home, without safety net or stable belongingness, and without a utopian ideal or a community built on it. Nonetheless, the abject can make an alternative form of relationship based on the commonality of 'abjecthood,' the immanent state of any subjectivity. They encounter each other as faceless neighbors, whose potential sanctity of life is relayed and redeemed through a contingent networking of zigzag gift-giving without return but with successive turns. This networking of atopian solidarity is neither inside nor outside of the global system. It develops into

---

[3] The Greek word *átopos* was attributed to Socrates as unclassifiable, outstanding, of high originality. Though not widely used, the term gains significance in Roland Barthes's late works, including *A Lover's Discourse: Fragments* (2010), in which it depicts the object of love as irreducible to certain characteristics. Roland Barthes's (2012) idea of atopos resonates with his other concept, "idiorrhythmy," an alternative mode of "living together" by recognizing and respecting each other's individual rhythms.

neither a utopian community nor an anarchy network, taking on neither totality nor infinity. The abject neighbors connect with the inside of the system while deviating from its law; they keep an open relationship while dedicating themselves to their mission of performing 'love thy neighbor' in their atopian way. The motley crew of abject agents who arrive at the ship *Tomorrow* in *Children of Men* exemplify this sense of atopian networking.

Notably, many thinkers have envisioned alternative forms of human relationships unbound by the universal logic of community, the cohesive principle of totality with totalitarian risk. Bataille (1986), for instance, elucidates the lovers' "inner experience" of erotic ecstasy beyond social bonding and state power. Maurice Blanchot (1988) imagines an "unavowable community" that does not bind its members to a pledge of loyalty and can thus render its destiny open. Drawing on this idea, Nancy (2008) proposes the deconstructive notion of "inoperative community" that does not work as a community in totality but "unworks" its essentialism. Everyone here exists as a singular finitude exposed to other singular finitudes, and the distance or passage between them hosts "being-in-common": a collective existence through which one can perceive one's separate singularity with plurality and experience the newness of presence without building a community for a destined future. Agamben (1993) pursues an insurmountable disjunction between state organization and nonstate singularity and claims that the latter is not an individual identity needed for the bond of belonging but the proper "being-thus" that does not form a *societas*, a union for a common purpose. Humans as being-thus rather co-belong to what should be a "coming community" without any representable condition of belonging. All these communities commonly suggest an unbound being-together of singularities, evoking the Heideggerian clearing as an ontological community of potential begins as such (Chapter 10). In this inspiring philosophical lineage, however, the social dimension of community is radically dissolved into the ontological ground of phenomenological relations, the fundamental experience of whatever singularities are immanent in the world at every moment. I instead reorient this community discourse back to the lifeworld of existential relationships, eliciting its networking potential from the abject's zigzag connection that sets in motion such alternative communities. 'Atopian networking' better serves our study of global cinema for this reason, especially when it comes to dystopian films that pose the question to all of humanity: Where should we go?

Himizu: Existential *Amor Fati* in Positive Nihilism

My final film to move atopian ethics forward is Sono Sion's *Himizu*.[4] This post-3/11 Japanese film unfolds the postcatastrophic redemption story of two fourteen-year-olds whose lives are devasted by the 2011 Tohoku earthquake and the Fukushima nuclear disaster. Sumida, the protagonist, wants nothing but a regular life running his parent's rental boat business, but his harsh environment drags him into the mud. His promiscuous mother has affairs with various men and leaves home entirely; his alcoholic father only comes around looking for money after getting into debt through gambling. Shazawa, a classmate of Sumida, harbors a severe crush on him, but her situation is no better than his. Her mother, after losing her husband, says that she would be better off without Shazawa and kills herself on the gallows built for her daughter she hates insanely. Fleeing from this hellish home, Shazawa tries to befriend Sumida and sticks around without being deterred, though he berates and even assaults her. One day the yakuza visits Sumida's home and beats him to retrieve money lent to his father, who later comes to wish bitterly that Sumida were dead so that he could get his hands on the insurance money. The already abandoned and abused Sumida then nears a tipping point and kills his father. But soon after this abrupt patricide Sumida is tormented with guilt, which drives him to restart his life as a punisher of social evils such as wanton murder, only to end up in failure and a suicide attempt.

Up to this point, *Himizu* looks like an extreme apocalyptic depiction of Japan in crisis. Addicted to gambling and cheating, the parents sacrifice their children for selfish pleasures, even brutalize them sadistically, and desert them while leaving behind only insurmountable debt and a sense of abandonment. They behave like an obscene superego abusing pseudo-divine power. Noteworthy is a TV panelist seen at some point who argues that Japan's pursuit of self-interest without a monotheistic God or rational control resulted in the atomic ruins of Hiroshima and Fukushima, as if the unregulated development of civilization led back to the state of nature. What is implied is the disintegration of the decent big Other, the proper Symbolic order at all levels of Japanese society from the family to the nation. Sumida is doubly put in a double bind here. On the one hand, his burdensome inheritance of

---

[4] This and the next sections incorporate some parts of my forthcoming essay "Shedding Light on Abject Lives: On Global Cinema as Ethical Art," in *What Film Is Good For: On the Ethics of Spectatorship* (ed. Julian Hanich and Martin Rossouw; University of California Press).

his father's debt leaves no option but patricide, but this extralegal liberation from the father rather binds him to traumatic guilt, just as the sons of the Freudian primal father are haunted by the postmortem father after killing him. On the other hand, Sumida attempts to atone for this sin by assuming the role of a pseudo-divine vigilante who metes out subjective justice, but this self-claimed sovereign agency is thwarted by the still minimally working law, as the police block him from directly punishing a criminal. He becomes no more than an impotent sociopath, so to speak. The film thus seemingly presents a typical double death narrative wherein he is stuck between the symbolic death of abjection and a likely real death without redemption.

At the end of the film, however, Sumida stops short of suicide and walks with Shazawa, who was heartbroken by his disappearance but relieved by his emergence from the lake where he seemingly drowned himself. He heads over to the police to turn himself in. Shazawa walks beside him. Though abjected by her parents, too, she has always taken care of him, dreaming of living with him. They begin to run, crying and shouting over and over, "Don't give up, Sumida!" (Figure 12.2). *Himizu* ends while we accompany them in the endless-looking ruins of Japan. This ending makes the film a cathartic coming-of-age drama in which a teenager's simple dream of normalization, of becoming a "respectful adult," undergoes the unbearably abnormal process of abjection to overcome, a dream that someday should come true through becoming a father without (being) a pseudo-god. By extension, the film

Figure 12.2. The abject teenage boy in *Himizu* stops short of suicide and begins to run with his girlfriend, crying and shouting, "Don't give up!"

envisions postcatastrophic nation rebuilding, the dream of making Japan a respectful society. This is suggested by a group of people who have lost their homes due to the earthquake and live in makeshift tents near Sumida for some time. They temporarily make an alternative family of the abject, sharing misery and pain while relying on each other. They have fun with Sumida and cheer him up until they depart. An old man even repays Sumida's debt to the yakuza after making money illegally—dirtying his hands one final time self-sacrificially like Walt in *Gran Torino* (see Chapter 10)—as he, the last generation of the crumbling old Japan, hopes to clear away the burden of the past and pave the way for the Japan of the new generation. They thus work like abject agents, forming contingent solidarity and performing gift-giving without return in the aftermath of the catastrophe that makes them atopian.[5]

This atopian gift-giving of the homeless evokes that of the motley crew in *Children of Men*, but if Cuarón's adult hero is the action-driven sacrificial leader of the very crew, Sono's adolescent hero suffers a lot from the inner, nearly impossible struggle to find any meaning or mission that can sustain life in himself despite those caring people around him. Indeed, Sumida's abjection concerns not only the deprivation of social subjectivity but the deeply existential question of life value: Camus's ultimate philosophical question of suicide, of whether absurd life is worth living, as noted regarding *Taste of Cherry* (see Chapter 9). For Camus, our daily life is not that different from Sisyphus's meaningless repetition of rolling a boulder uphill that always rolls down from the top: the eternal punishment by Zeus for his trickery. This cursed fate could be escaped by either completely submitting to the god or committing suicide, but both solutions imply giving up human freedom per se. Camus's Sisyphus instead becomes a tragic hero who embraces his absurd fate in full consciousness and takes responsibility for it of his own free will as a way of resisting the divine order, debunking its own absurdity, and thus breaking its fatal force. As Oedipus ironically commits patricide and incest while fleeing from the horrible oracle, Sumida's patricidal escape from his fate enslaves him to its patriarchal order, leading to a suicidal impasse. His final turn from this impasse is thus another illustration of *amor fati* as

---

[5] Noticeably, various Japanese films stage atopian movement that reaches the sea/death, the nation's endpoint or the end of the world, as seen in *Hana-bi* (Kitano Takeshi, 1997), *Pulse* (Kurosawa Kiyoshi, 2001), and *Still Life* (Koreeda Hirokazu, 2008). Though moderate in style, Koreeda often sheds light on the abject, including children, who struggle to survive for themselves, reconnect with their disintegrated families, or form alternative, adopted families on the periphery of the law and normal order: *Nobody Knows* (2004), *Like Father, Like Son* (2013), *After the Storm* (2016), *Shoplifters* (2018), and the like.

illuminated in Chapter 11, based on the paradoxical sense of freedom: not freedom against fate but freedom for it, the free choice to accept it as affirmed from within, to say 'all is well,' including suffering like a Nietzschean 'yes-sayer,' and thereby to become the genuine master of one's life as freed from the contradictory big Other toward an unknown land of potentialities. Sumida is running to the police not so much to surrender to the crumbling yet enforced law but to embrace responsibility as freedom in this sense. As Camus (1991, 123) imagines a "happy Sisyphus" walking down to the tumbled rock, we should imagine a happy Sumida embarking on his atopian journey to a new life.

Let's generalize this existentialist core in our discussion of nihilism. Life is contingently thrown into the world without any a priori meaning or purpose, but it can be valued as more than mere or bare life, more than being destined by nihilistic dogmas. This 'more than itself' is life's self-transcending potential immanent in the affirmation of its meaningless or traumatic condition, whose fatal grip on life would only then be loosened. Sumida retroactively inserts in his life the possibility of choosing between escaping and embracing the absurd nothingness of life. To borrow from Žižek (2013a, 765–68), it is similar to the choice between "coffee without milk" and "coffee without cream." Though they are the same coffee objectively, what is missing determines the true nature of each type of coffee subjectively. Negativity determines subjectivity. Likewise, the orientation toward the negativity of life determines its potentiality, its self-transcendent power. By embracing his nothingness, Sumida turns it into the ground zero of new subjectivity to perform. The most fundamental freedom is thus not to go beyond inhibitions and do whatever one desires; rather, it is to activate the potential to be more than oneself by inserting the choice between two negativities and choosing one, to say yes to one's not-really-free life, even one's abject life. Crucially, one often goes down to this existential zero ground through abjection. Sumida's symbolic suicide on top of his total (self-)abjection from society—visualized in his multicolor face painting that ends up looking like nothing but a muddy mess—touches the real bottom of life. There, he does not simply give up something precious to him but has nothing to lose in a loss. Conversely, such severe abjection enables one to break free of the spell of any overpowering social domination. It nurtures agency for one's psychic annihilation and rebirth ex nihilo.

At this point I am tempted to juxtapose the two similar endings of *Himizu* and *The Promise* (see Chapter 11). They are left open in the middle of the action, so we cannot imagine what will happen to those miserable characters. They just walk together on the road with no promise for a better future other than still enduring their fate. What they share is nothing but the experience of being marginalized and degraded to the bottom of human life at the edge of a malignant global system and a crumbling postcatastrophic society. However, this shared 'precarity' makes their contingent relationship all the more 'precious,' as they have nothing more to lose but their being as such to give each other like a gift. They have no political power to change the world but some ethical agency to take care of humanity crushed in the same world. They embody, as it were, an ethics of 'walking side by side,' an alternative ethics in global cinema regardless of whether it hails from the West or the East. I here see some *positive nihilism*, to reshape Nietzschean antinihilism and refine atopian ethics in the global frame. Positive nihilism affirms not death but the eternal return of life as nothingness and nothing but potential at the same time. The abject are often left alone with the task of having to go on with life in a world with no big Other, where suicide seems like the easier solution. They are thus abject agents of *amor fati*, 'positive nihilists' who can open a nonutopian yet nonsuicidal networking of giving themselves in their love of fate. By embracing the void of being with this potential only, they step away from the dominant regime of power and desire. They do not stand 'for' each other as do the big Other and the subject in the community, but they stand 'by' each other as neighbors in atopian networking. This solidarity without unity signals today's new ethics on the margin of the global regime, beyond the dominant and emergent (de)globalizing ethical modalities.

In sum, abject agents of atopian ethics are neither negative nihilists who renounce freedom nor passive nihilists who consume secured pleasures without big causes. They are not active nihilists who pursue transcendent values through self-sacrifice but positive nihilists who embody the void of being and nothing else, and yet by doing so, they liberate themselves from the illusion of subjectivity generated in the global system. Though promising no utopian finale, their atopian movement makes room for contingent yet transformative relations wherein one does not just talk to the other face to face but walks with the other side by side indefinitely. This precarious yet precious solidarity of gift-giving among abject neighbors epitomizes atopian ethics. It emerges between community and network and moves beyond both. Community has the tree-shaped centripetal structure of imagined totality, oriented to future utopia at the risk of being dystopian and driven by linear, dialectical historicity. It operates various dichotomies like subject/abject, master/slave, desire/lack, and discipline/emancipation, while the dissensus between such antagonistic forces mobilizes political change. Its subjects internalize neurotic and melancholic negative nihilism or explode with sovereign or sacrificial active nihilism. By contrast, network has the rhizomatic centrifugal structure of deterritorial, nonlinear, and schizophrenic connection, proliferating in the perpetual present. It blurs the distinctions between subject and abject, utopia and dystopia, or control and freedom, with one rapidly turning into the other. Its (neo)liberal consensus and libidinal economy generate the postpolitical culture of compulsion and addiction with the (death) drive of passive nihilism. However, atopia takes only a zigzag form of movement open to linear delay and nonlinear deviation. It is driven by abject agents' ethical indebtedness/guilt and freedom/responsibility, their performative gift-giving and existential becoming-gift beyond the exchange economy and social normativity. Its contingency and precarity cannot guarantee a utopian future, but this nihilism still positively affirms all that is inevitably given and symbiotically relays all that is potentially precious (see Table 12.1).

Cinema as an Ethical Art

Let me conclude by illuminating the fundamental relationship between cinema 'and' ethics via global cinema's atopian ethics. As Elsaesser (2016, 21–26) suggests, the ontological and aesthetic questions that have penetrated film studies in its photographic and digital periods ("What is cinema?" and "Where is cinema?") should be followed by an ethical question in a postclassical, postmedia, posthuman era: "What is/was cinema good for?" Let's then ask: What is cinema good for in our postpolitical age? In a nutshell, it is good for highlighting what both politics and postpolitics miss or even dismiss. Politics is always based on collectivity, involving people's organization, maintenance, and change of their communities. It makes, preserves, and reforms the law that represents the generality of rules, norms, and universal imperatives. As a political ideal, even Kant's cosmopolitanism (without a world government) was also envisioned as creating an orderly cosmic world regulated by principles and laws. It can be seen as a "Habermasian program" of world citizenship based on "conditional hospitality," holding the right to invite the others governed by the economy of sovereignty and jurisdiction (Habermas and Derrida 2003, 163–68). Doesn't this vision sound like the

Table 12.1. Three Types of Social Relations Staged in Global Cinema

	Community	Network	Atopia
Structure	Tree (centripetal)	Rhizome (centrifugal)	Zigzag (rootless)
Modality	Utopia vs. dystopia (imagined totality)	Utopia-dystopia (deterritorial connection)	No utopia/dystopia (open contingency)
Temporality	Linear dialectics (future)	Nonlinear schizophrenia (present)	Linear delay, nonlinear deviation (retroaction)
Subjectivity	Subject vs. abject (identity)	Subject-abject (agency)	Abject agent (performativity)
Motivation	Desire (master/slave)	Drive (user-player)	Gift (host/parasite)
Pathology	Neurosis, melancholy (discipline/ emancipation)	Compulsion, addiction (control-freedom)	Indebtedness, guilt (freedom-responsibility)
Nihilism	Negative/active (sacrifice)	Passive (pleasure)	Positive (accompaniment)
Economy	Political (dissensus)	Libidinal (consensus)	Ethical (symbiosis)

postpolitical soft ethics with all the problems we have discussed? We could pursue this cosmopolitanism only by continually having it face and redraw its limits, especially "in the face of a stranger" (163). In other words, however utopian the world may be, it would inevitably need the sovereign law to govern itself as a peaceful whole while producing and encountering someone outside it. Yet in close-ups from most films, what we see is not a political project or multitude but this individual's singular life.

In global cinema, such individuals appear as living symptoms of the global system. Often becoming or accompanying an abject neighbor, they embody what this system's law cannot represent: particular justice, unique situation, liminal experience, incalculable exchange, and unconditional responsibility without which there cannot be ethics per se. But their ethics is not Antigone's terroristic, self-destructive desire to go extremely against the law. Instead, they wander like walking atopia, settling in no place, seemingly ideal yet keeping open the impossible promise of utopia. This ongoing 'edging' to an 'unpromised' land on the edge of the world performs existential *amor fati* to embrace their abject being as such and as a gift. Here is the artistic potential of cinema. It can reflect harsh realities and social contradictions but not bring about political solutions or radical changes. Instead, it can shed light on abject lives generated unavoidably in any system, even if utopian, and let them speak in distinct ethical ways that are irreducible to collective identity formations or the Rancièrian political redistribution of the sensible. That is, cinema, if not a political practice, can be an ethical art that questions the political order but always in concrete situations, that draws attention to politically unresolvable ethical dilemmas, and that gropes for new ethical directions away from established politics and ethics.[6]

In fact, many socially conscious films are criticized for lacking a collective political vision, reducing structural problems to personal issues, or dramatizing fictive solutions led by individual heroes. While this criticism has been valid, alternative films have depicted a revolutionary class with no central character since Eisenstein's *Strike* (1925). Vertov radicalized this approach in the documentary genre, which has since been much better suited for directly presenting political reality. Likewise, political modernism in the 1960s–1970s emerged through discontent with narrative cinema's "institutional mode of representation": illusionistic, reactionary, capitalist, patriarchal, and phallocentric (Burch 1990, 1–5). The ideological critique of cinema was then driven by the political desire for Brechtian or more experimental alternative modes, as seen in film practice (from the French New Wave to Third Cinema) and theory (Noël Burch, Laura Mulvey, Jean-Louis Comolli, among others). This cinematic politics takes on ethics in Serge Daney's (2007, 17–38) famous critique of *Kapo*. For him, the film's tracking shot toward a Nazi camp inmate's electrocution on a barbed-wire fence beautifies death so dramatically in the way of representing the unrepresentable so cheesily (see Chapter 5). In fact, Daney's lengthy essay is an updated elaboration of Jacques Rivette's (1961) short review of *Kapo*, titled "On Abjection." However, the word 'abjection' never appears in the text and only vaguely indicates Rivette's contempt for the very tracking shot as a sort of 'death porn.' I mean to say, it has nothing to do with Kristeva's abjection.

Global cinema, in my framework, pursues no such antirepresentational ethical aesthetics but instead antihegemonic ethics within the represented diegesis. It does not confine us in the modernist impasse of elitist experimentalism but confronts us with abject others in ways we would otherwise not encounter in today's real world. The ethics of global cinema is the ethics of the

---

[6] Not coincidentally, "contemporary political cinema" in Matthew Holtmeier's book (2019) turns out to be ethical rather than political, as he himself claims and admits.

abject in this world. The abject are reductively typified as global news items in reality. Still, on screen we palpably experience their singular existence and our potential abjection at the same time, thereby virtually walking side by side with them. This contingent solidarity, if not politicized, is crucial as the ground of potential social relations. Indeed, almost all narrative films center on protagonists and have limitations in staging a whole class or a social structure. But by the same token, films unfold narratives of individuals who symptomatically embody systemic inconsistencies and thus urge us to critique them existentially while raising unthought questions or possibilities that could not be answered or performed in any hegemonic collective logic. This artistic potential makes cinema ethical, and further, philosophical. Whether or not cinema itself does philosophy, often asked in film-philosophy circles, might be the wrong question here. It is already philosophical, inspiring our thoughts on what is unthinkable in reality.

References

Agamben, Giorgio. 1993. *The Coming Community*. Translated by Michael Hardt. Minneapolis: University of Minnesota Press.
Agamben, Giorgio. 1998. *Homo Sacer: Sovereign Power and Bare Life*. Translated by Daniel Heller-Roazen. Stanford, CA: Stanford University Press.
Ahrens, Jörn. 2009. "How to Save the Unsaved World? Transforming the Self in *The Matrix*, *The Terminator*, and *12 Monkeys*." In *Media and the Apocalypse*, edited by Kylo-Patrick R. Hart and Annette M. Holba, 53–65. New York: Peter Lang.
Anders, Günther. 2019. "Apocalypse without Kingdom." *E-Flux*, no. 97 (February). https://www.e-flux.com/journal/97/251199/apocalypse-without-kingdom/.
Anderson, Benedict. 1991. *Imagined Communities: Reflections on the Origin and Spread of Nationalism*. London: Verso.
Anderson, Benedict. 2013. "Impunity and Reenactment: Reflections on the 1965 Massacre in Indonesia and Its Legacy." *Asia-Pacific Journal: Japan Focus* 11 (15–4). https://apjjf.org/2013/11/15/Benedict-Anderson/3929/article.html.
Andrew, Dudley. 2006. "An Atlas of World Cinema." In *Remapping World Cinema: Identity, Culture and Politics in Film*, edited by Stephanie Dennison and Song Hwee Lim, 19–29. London: Wallflower Press.
Andrew, Dudley. 2010a. "Time Zones and Jetlag: The Flows and Phases of World Cinema." In *World Cinemas, Transnational Perspectives*, edited by Nat Durovicová and Kathl Newman, 59–89. New York: Routledge.
Andrew, Dudley. 2010b. *What Cinema Is! Bazin's Quest and Its Charge*. Chichester, West Sussex, UK: Wiley-Blackwell.
Andrew, Dudley. 2016. "Fatih Akin's Moral Geometry." In *The Global Auteur: The Politics of Authorship in 21st Century Cinema*, edited by Seung-hoon Jeong and Jeremi Szaniawski, 179–98. New York: Bloomsbury.
Andrew, Geoff. 2006. "Luc and Jean-Pierre Dardenne." *Guardian*, February 11, 2006, sec. Film. https://www.theguardian.com/film/2006/feb/11/features.
Appadurai, Arjun. 1996. *Modernity at Large: Cultural Dimensions of Globalization*. Minneapolis: University of Minnesota Press.
Appiah, Anthony Kwame. 2006. *Cosmopolitanism: Ethics in a World of Strangers*. New York: W. W. Norton.
Archibugi, Daniele, ed. 2003. *Debating Cosmopolitics*. London: Verso.
Arendt, Hannah. 1973. *The Origins of Totalitarianism*. New York: Harcourt, Brace, Jovanovich.
Arendt, Hannah. 2006. *Eichmann in Jerusalem: A Report on the Banality of Evil*. London: Penguin Classics.
Arthur, Paul. 2001. "The Four Last Things: History, Technology, Hollywood, Apocalypse." In *The End of Cinema As We Know It: American Film in the Nineties*, edited by Jon Lewis, 342–55. New York: New York University Press.

Arya, Rina. 2014. *Abjection and Representation: An Exploration of Abjection in the Visual Arts, Film and Literature*. Basingstoke, UK: Palgrave Macmillan.

Augé, Marc. 2009. *Non-Places: An Introduction to Supermodernity*. Translated by John Howe. London: Verso.

Badiou, Alain. 2015. "The Red Flag and the Tricolore." Verso Books. https://www.versobooks.com/blogs/1833-the-red-flag-and-the-tricolore-by-alain-badiou.

Badiou, Alain. 2012. *Ethics: An Essay on the Understanding of Evil*. London: Verso.

Badley, Linda, R. Barton Palmer, and Steven Jay Schneider, eds. 2006. *Traditions in World Cinema*. New Brunswick, NJ: Rutgers University Press.

Balibar, Étienne. 2002. *Politics and the Other Scene*. Translated by Christine Jones, James Swenson, and Chris Turner. London: Verso.

Balibar, Étienne. 2005. "Difference, Otherness, Exclusion." *Parallax* 11 (1): 19–34.

Barber, Benjamin. 1996. *Jihad vs. McWorld: Terrorism's Challenge to Democracy*. New York: Ballantine Books.

Barthes, Roland. 2010. *A Lover's Discourse: Fragments*. Translated by Richard Howard. New York.

Barthes, Roland. 2012. *How to Live Together: Novelistic Simulations of Some Everyday Spaces*. New York: Columbia University Press.

Bataille, Georges. 1986. *Erotism: Death & Sensuality*. Translated by Mary Dalwood. San Francisco: City Lights Books.

Bataille, Georges. 2002. "Abjection and Miserable Forms." In *More & Less: No. 2*, edited by Sylvere Lotringer, translated by Yvonne Shafir, 8–13. Los Angeles: Semiotext(e).

Baudrillard, Jean. 1981. *Simulacra and Simulation*. Translated by Sheila Faria Glaser. Ann Arbor: University of Michigan Press.

Baudrillard, Jean. 2015. *Jean Baudrillard: From Hyperreality to Disappearance; Uncollected Interviews, 1986 to 2007*. Edited by Richard G. Smith and David B. Clarke. Edinburgh: Edinburgh University Press.

Bauman, Zygmunt. 2000. *Liquid Modernity*. Cambridge, UK: Polity.

Bauman, Zygmunt. 2006. *Liquid Times: Living in an Age of Uncertainty*. 1st ed. Cambridge, UK: Polity.

Baumbach, Nico. 2016. "Shareable Cinema: The Politics of Abbas Kiarostami." In *The Global Auteur: The Politics of Authorship in 21st Century Cinema*, edited by Seung-hoon Jeong and Jeremi Szaniawski, 271–85. New York: Bloomsbury.

Beal, Wesley, and Stacy Lavin. 2011. "Theorizing Connectivity: Modernism and the Network Narrative." *Digital Humanities Quarterly* 5 (2). https://www.digitalhumanities.org/dhq/vol/5/2/000097/000097.html.

Beck, Ulrich. 2013. *World at Risk*. Hoboken, NJ: Wiley.

Benhabib, Seyla. 2006. *Another Cosmopolitanism*. Edited by Robert Post. New York: Oxford University Press.

Benjamin, Walter. 1968a. "On Some Motifs in Baudelaire." In *Illuminations: Essays and Reflections*, edited by Hannah Arendt, translated by Harry Zohn, 155–200. New York: Schocken Books.

Benjamin, Walter. 1968b. "Theses on the Philosophy of History." In *Illuminations: Essays and Reflections*, edited by Hannah Arendt, translated by Harry Zohn, 253–64. New York: Schocken Books.

Benjamin, Walter. 1978. "Critique of Violence." In *Reflections: Essays, Aphorisms, Autobiographical Writing*, edited by Peter Demetz, translated by Edmund Jephcott, 277–300. New York: Schocken Books.

Benjamin, Walter. 1996. "Critique of Violence." *Walter Benjamin: Selected Writings, Volume 1: 1913–1926*, edited by Marcus Bullock and Michael W. Jennings, 236–52. Cambridge, MA: Belknap Press.

Bennet, Tony, and Janet Woollacott. 2003. "The Moments of Bond." In *The James Bond Phenomenon: A Critical Reader*, edited by Christoph Lindner, 13–33. Manchester, UK: Manchester University Press.

Berg, Charles Ramírez. 2006. "A Taxonomy of Alternative Plots in Recent Films: Classifying the 'Tarantino Effect.'" *Film Criticism* 31 (1–2): 5–61.

Bergfelder, Tim. 2005. "National, Transnational or Supranational Cinema? Rethinking European Film Studies." *Media, Culture & Society* 27 (3): 315–31.

Berlant, Lauren. 2011. *Cruel Optimism*. Durham, NC: Duke University Press.

Bernstein, Michael André. 1992. *Bitter Carnival: Ressentiment and the Abject Hero*. Princeton, NJ: Princeton University Press.

Betz, Mark. 2009. *Beyond the Subtitle: Remapping European Art Cinema*. Minneapolis: University of Minnesota Press.

Bharucha, Rustom. 1994. "On the Border of Fascism: Manufacture of Consent in 'Roja.'" *Economic and Political Weekly* 29 (23): 1389–95.

Blanchot, Maurice. 1988. *The Unavowable Community*. Translated by Pierre Joris. Barrytown, NY: Station Hill.

Bloom, Peter. 2006. "Beur Cinema and the Politics of Location." In *Transnational Cinema: The Film Reader*, edited by Elizabeth Ezra and Terry Rowden, 131–42. London: Routledge.

Bolter, Jay David, and Richard Grusin. 1999. *Remediation: Understanding New Media*. Cambridge, MA: MIT Press.

Bordwell, David. 2006. *The Way Hollywood Tells It: Story and Style in Modern Movies*. Berkeley: University of California Press.

Bordwell, David. 2008. *Poetics of Cinema*. New York: Routledge.

Borradori, Giovanna. 2004. *Philosophy in a Time of Terror: Dialogues with Jurgen Habermas and Jacques Derrida*. Chicago: University of Chicago Press.

Boyle, Kirk. 2009. "*Children of Men* and *I Am Legend*: The Disaster-Capitalism Complex Hits Hollywood." *Jump Cut*, no. 51. http://www.ejumpcut.org/archive/jc51.2009/ChildrenMenLegend/text.html.

Branigan, Edward. 2002. "Nearly True: Forking Plots, Forking Interpretations; A Response to David Bordwell's 'Film Futures.'" *SubStance* 31 (1): 105–14.

Breckenridge, Carol Appadurai, Sheldon Pollock, Homi Bhabha, and Dipesh Chakrabarty, eds. 2002. *Cosmopolitanism*. Durham, NC: Duke University Press.

Brevet, Brad. 2011. "Spoiler Talk: Is the Ending of 'Source Code' Open to Interpretation?" April 3. https://www.comingsoon.net/movies/news/551446-spoiler-talk-is-the-ending-of-source-code-open-to-interpretation.

Brighenti, Andrea. 2006. "Dogville, or, the Dirty Birth of Law." *Thesis Eleven* 87 (1): 96–111. https://doi.org/10.1177/0725513606068778.

Brown, William. 2018. *Non-Cinema: Global Digital Film-Making and the Multitude*. New York: Bloomsbury.

Brown, William. 2020. "Knowing Not What to Believe: Digital Space and Entanglement in Life of Pi, Gravity, and Interstellar." In *Screen Space Reconfigured*, edited by Susanne Ø. Sæther and Synne T. Bull, 55–76. Amsterdam: Amsterdam University Press. https://doi.org/10.2307/j.ctv12pnt9c.6.

Buckland, Warren, ed. 2008. *Puzzle Films: Complex Storytelling in Contemporary Cinema*. Chichester, UK: Wiley-Blackwell.

Buckland, Warren, ed. 2014a. *Hollywood Puzzle Films*. London: Routledge.

Buckland, Warren. 2014b. "Source Code's Video Game Logic." In *Hollywood Puzzle Films*, edited by Warren Buckland, 185-97. London: Routledge.

Burch, Noël. 1990. *Life to Those Shadows*. Edited by Ben Brewster. Berkeley: University of California Press.

Butler, Judith. 1995a. "Contingent Foundations: Feminism and the Question of 'Postmodernism.'" In *Feminist Contentions: A Philosophical Exchange*, edited by Seyla Benhabib, 35-58. New York: Routledge.

Butler, Judith. 1995b. "For a Careful Reading." In *Feminist Contentions: A Philosophical Exchange*, edited by Seyla Benhabib, 127-44. New York: Routledge.

Butler, Judith. 2006. *Gender Trouble: Feminism and the Subversion of Identity*. New York: Routledge.

Cameron, Allan. 2008. *Modular Narratives in Contemporary Cinema*. London: Palgrave Macmillan.

Cameron, Allan, and Richard Misek. 2014. "Modular Spacetime in the 'Intelligent' Blockbuster." In *Hollywood Puzzle Films*, edited by Warren Buckland, 109-24. London: Routledge.

Camus, Albert. 1991. *The Myth of Sisyphus: And Other Essays*. Translated by Justin O'Brien. New York: Vintage Books.

Canavan, Gerry. 2014. "'If the Engine Ever Stops, We'd All Die': Snowpiercer and Necrofuturism." *Paradoxa*, no. 26: 1-26.

Cazdyn, Eric M., and Imre Szeman. 2012. *After Globalization*. Hoboken, NJ: Wiley-Blackwell.

Chakravarthy, Sumita S. 2000. "Fragmenting the Nation." In *Cinema and Nation*, edited by Mette Hjort and Scott MacKenzie, 222-37. London: Routledge.

Chanter, Tina. 2008. *The Picture of Abjection: Film, Fetish, and the Nature of Difference*. Bloomington: Indiana University Press.

Chapman, James. 2005. "Bond and Britishness." In *Ian Fleming and James Bond: The Cultural Politics of 007*, edited by Edward P. Comentale, Stephen Watt, and Skip Willman, 129-43. Bloomington: Indiana University Press.

Chapman, James. 2008. *Licence to Thrill: A Cultural History of the James Bond Films*. London: I. B. Tauris.

Chaudhary, Zahid R. 2009. "Humanity Adrift: Race, Materiality, and Allegory in Alfonso Cuarón's Children of Men." *Camera Obscura* 24 (72): 73-109.

Chaudhuri, Shohini. 2005. *Contemporary World Cinema: Europe, the Middle East, East Asia and South Asia*. Edinburgh: Edinburgh University Press.

Chaudhuri, Shohini. 2014. *Cinema of the Dark Side: Atrocity and the Ethics of Film Spectatorship*. Edinburgh: Edinburgh University Press.

Cheah, Pheng, and Bruce Robbins. 1998. *Cosmopolitics: Thinking and Feeling beyond the Nation*. Minneapolis: University of Minnesota Press.

Choi, JungBong. 2010. "Of the East Asian Cultural Sphere: Theorizing Cultural Regionalization." *China Review* 10 (2): 109-36.

Choi, JungBong. 2012. "Of Transnational-Korean Cinematrix." *Transnational Cinemas* 3 (1): 3-18.

Civitarese, Giuseppe. 2015. *Losing Your Head: Abjection, Aesthetic Conflict, and Psychoanalytic Criticism*. Lanham, MD: Rowman & Littlefield.

Clover, Carol J. 1993. *Men, Women, and Chain Saws: Gender in the Modern Horror Film*. Princeton, NJ: Princeton University Press.
Comer, Todd A., and Lloyd Isaac Vayo, eds. 2013. *Terror and the Cinematic Sublime: Essays on Violence and the Unpresentable in Post-9/11 Films*. Jefferson, NC: McFarland.
Cook, Roger F. 2007. "Good Bye, Lenin! Free-Market Nostalgia for Socialist Consumerism." *Seminar: A Journal of Germanic Studies* 43 (2): 206–19.
Cooper, Sarah. 2007. "Mortal Ethics: Reading Levinas with the Dardenne Brothers." *Film-Philosophy* 11 (2): 56–87.
Costanzo, William V. 2014. *World Cinema through Global Genres*. Chichester, UK: Wiley-Blackwell.
Covino, Deborah Caslav. 2004. *Amending the Abject Body: Aesthetic Makeovers in Medicine and Culture*. New York: State University New York Press.
Creed, Barbara. 1993. *The Monstrous-Feminine: Film, Feminism, Psychoanalysis*. London: Routledge.
Critchley, Simon. 2013. *Infinitely Demanding: Ethics of Commitment, Politics of Resistance*. London: Verso.
Daney, Serge. 2007. *Postcards from the Cinema*. Translated by Paul Douglas Grant. Oxford: Berg.
Davis, Adrienne D. 2010. "Gran Torino and Star Trek." *New Political Science* 32 (1): 163–68.
Dear, Michael, and Steven Flusty. 1997. "The Iron Lotus: Los Angeles and Postmodern Urbanism." *Annals of the American Academy of Political and Social Science* 551: 151–63.
Debray, Regis. 2011. *Du Bon Usage des Catastrophes*. Gallimard ed. Paris: Gallimard.
Deleuze, Gilles. 1983. *Nietzsche and Philosophy*. New York: Columbia University Press.
Deleuze, Gilles. 1986. *Cinema 1: The Movement-Image*. Translated by Hugh Tomlinson and Barbara Habberjam. Minneapolis: University of Minnesota Press.
Deleuze, Gilles. 1992. "Postscript on the Societies of Control." *October*, no. 59 (Winter): 3–7.
Deleuze, Gilles. 1994. *Difference and Repetition*. Translated by Paul Patton. New York: Columbia University Press.
Deleuze, Gilles. 1995. "Postscript on Control Societies." In *Negotiations*, 177–82. New York: Columbia University Press.
Deleuze, Gilles. 2003. *Francis Bacon: The Logic of Sensation*. Translated by Daniel W. Smith. Minneapolis: University of Minnesota Press.
Deleuze, Gilles, and Félix Guattari. 1977. *Anti-Oedipus: Capitalism and Schizophrenia*. New York: Viking Press.
Deleuze, Gilles, and Félix Guattari. 1986. *Kafka: Toward a Minor Literature*. Minneapolis: University of Minnesota Press.
Deleuze, Gilles, and Félix Guattari. 1987. *A Thousand Plateaus: Capitalism and Schizophrenia*. Translated by Brian Massumi. Minneapolis: University of Minnesota Press.
Dennison, Stephanie, and Song Hwee Lim, eds. 2006. *Remapping World Cinema: Identity, Culture, and Politics in Film*. London: Wallflower Press.
Derrida, Jacques. 1992a. "Force of Law: The 'Mystical Foundation of Authority.'" In *Deconstruction and the Possibility of Justice*, edited by Drucilla Cornell, Michel Rosenfeld, and David Gray Carlson, 3–67. New York: Routledge.
Derrida, Jacques. 1992b. *Given Time: I, Counterfeit Money*. Chicago: University of Chicago Press.
Derrida, Jacques. 1997. *Politics of Friendship*. Translated by George Collins. New York: Verso.

Derrida, Jacques. 2017. *Dissemination*. Translated by Barbara Johnson. Chicago: University of Chicago Press.
Derrida, Jacques, and Anne Dufourmantelle. 2000. *Of Hospitality*. Translated by Rachel Bowlsby. Stanford, CA: Stanford University Press.
Didi-Huberman, Georges. 1998. *Phasmes: Essais Sur l'apparition*. Paris: Editions de Minuit.
Diken, Bulent. 2009. *Nihilism*. New York: Routledge.
Dixon, Wheeler Winston. 2004. *Film and Television after 9/11*. Carbondale: Southern Illinois University Press.
Douglas, Mary. 2002. *Purity and Danger: An Analysis of Concepts of Pollution and Taboo*. London: Routledge.
Durovicová, Natasa, and Kathleen Newman, eds. 2010. *World Cinemas, Transnational Perspectives*. New York: Routledge.
Duschinsky, Robbie. 2013. "Abjection and Self-Identity: Towards a Revised Account of Purity and Impurity." *Sociological Review* 61 (4): 709–27. https://doi.org/10.1111/1467-954X.12081.
Dussel, Enrique D. 2013. *Ethics of Liberation in the Age of Globalization and Exclusion*. Edited by Alejandro A Vallega. Durham, NC: Duke University Press.
Dussel, Enrique, and Eduardo Ibarra-Colado. 2006. "Globalization, Organization and the Ethics of Liberation." *Organization* 13 (4): 489–508.
Eco, Robert Angus. 1966. "The Narrative Structure in Fleming." In *The Bond Affair*, edited by Oreste Del Buono and Umberto Eco, translated by Robert Angus Downie, 35–75. London: Macdonald & Co.
Elena, Alberto. 2005. *The Cinema of Abbas Kiarostami*. Translated by Belinda Coombes. London: Saqi in association with Iran Heritage Foundation.
Elsaesser, Thomas. 2001. "The Blockbuster: Everything Connects, but Not Everything Goes." In *The End of Cinema As We Know It: American Film in the Nineties*, edited by Jon Lewis, 11–22. New York: New York University Press.
Elsaesser, Thomas. 2005. *European Cinema: Face-to-Face with Hollywood*. Amsterdam: Amsterdam University Press.
Elsaesser, Thomas. 2011. "Politics, Multiculturalism and the Ethical Turn: The Cinema of Fatih Akin." In *Just Images: Ethics and the Cinematic*, edited by Boaz Hagin, Sandra Meiri, Raz Yosef, and Anat Zanger, 1–18. Newcastle: Cambridge Scholars Publishers.
Elsaesser, Thomas. 2012. *The Persistence of Hollywood*. New York: Routledge.
Elsaesser, Thomas. 2016. *Film History as Media Archaeology: Tracking Digital Cinema*. Amsterdam: Amsterdam University Press.
Elsaesser, Thomas. 2018a. "Contingency, Causality, Complexity: Distributed Agency in the Mind-Game Film." *New Review of Film and Television Studies* 16 (1): 1–39.
Elsaesser, Thomas. 2018b. *European Cinema and Continental Philosophy: Film as Thought Experiment*. London: Bloomsbury.
Elsaesser, Thomas. 2021. *The Mind-Game Film: Distributed Agency, Time Travel and Productive Pathology*. Edited by Warren Buckland, Dana Polan, and Seung-hoon Jeong. London: Routledge.
Esposito, Roberto. 2010. *Communitas: The Origin and Destiny of Community*. Palo Alto, CA: Stanford University Press.
Everett, Wendy. 2005. "Fractal Films and the Architecture of Complexity." *Studies in European Cinema* 2 (3): 159–71.
Ezra, Elizabeth, and Terry Rowden, eds. 2006. *Transnational Cinema: The Film Reader*. London: Routledge.

Fan, Victor. 2016. "Revisiting Jia Zhangke: Individuality, Subjectivity, and Autonomy in Contemporary Chinese Independent Cinema." In *The Global Auteur: The Politics of Authorship in 21st Century Cinema*, edited by Seung-hoon Jeong and Jeremi Szaniawski, 323–42. New York: Bloomsbury.

Fisher, Mark, and Rob White. 2012. "The Politics of 'The Dark Knight Rises': A Discussion." *Film Quarterly* (blog). September 2012. https://filmquarterly.org/2012/09/04/the-politics-of-the-dark-knight-rises-a-discussion/.

Fletcher, John, and Andrew Benjamin, eds. 1990. *Abjection, Melancholia, and Love: The Work of Julia Kristeva*. London: Routledge.

Foster, Hal, Benjamin Buchloh, Rosalind Krauss, Yve-Alain Bois, Denis Hollier, and Helen Molesworth. 1994. "The Politics of the Signifier II: A Conversation on the 'Informe' and the Abject." *October* 67: 3–21.

Foucault, Michel. 1967. "Of Other Spaces: Heterotopias." Foucault.Info. 1967. http://foucault.info/documents/heteroTopia/foucault.heteroTopia.en.html.

Foucault, Michel. 1995. *Discipline & Punish: The Birth of the Prison*. Translated by Alan Sheridan. New York: Vintage Books.

Fukuyama, Francis. 2006. *The End of History and the Last Man*. New York: Free Press.

Gabara, Rachel. 2016. "Abderrahmane Sissako: On the Politics of African Auteurs." In *The Global Auteur: The Politics of Authorship in 21st Century Cinema*, edited by Seung-hoon Jeong and Jeremi Szaniawski, 45–60. New York: Bloomsbury.

Galt, Rosalind. 2006. *The New European Cinema: Redrawing the Map*. New York: Columbia University Press.

Galt, Rosalind, and Karl Schoonover, eds. 2010. *Global Art Cinema: New Theories and Histories*. New York: Oxford University Press.

Giddens, Anthony. 2001. *Runaway World: How Globalization Is Reshaping Our Lives*. London: Routledge.

Girard, René. 1979. *Violence and the Sacred*. Baltimore, MD: Johns Hopkins University Press.

Goodnow, Katherine J. 2010. *Kristeva in Focus: From Theory to Film Analysis*. New York: Berghahn Books.

Gorfinkel, Elena, and Tami Williams, eds. 2018. *Global Cinema Networks*. New Brunswick, NJ: Rutgers University Press.

Grusin, Richard. 2004. "Premediation." *Criticism* 46 (1): 17–39.

Guneratne, Anthony R., and Wimal Dissanayake. 2003. *Rethinking Third Cinema*. New York: Routledge.

Habermas, Jürgen, and Jacques Derrida. 2003. *Philosophy in a Time of Terror: Dialogues with Jürgen Habermas and Jacques Derrida*. Edited by Giovan Borradori. Chicago: University of Chicago Press.

Hamacher, Werner. 1993. "Afformative, Strike: Benjamin's Critique of Violence." In *Walter Benjamin's Philosophy: Destruction and Experience*, edited by Andrew Benjamin and Peter Osborne, 110–38. London: Routledge.

Haraway, Donna J. 2008. *When Species Meet*. Minneapolis: University of Minnesota Press.

Hardt, Michael, and Antonio Negri. 2000. *Empire*. Cambridge, MA: Harvard University Press.

Harvey, David. 2006. *Spaces of Global Capitalism: A Theory of Uneven Geographical Development*. London: Verso.

Hasian Jr., Marouf. 2014. "Skyfall, James Bond's Resurrection, and 21st-Century Anglo-American Imperial Nostalgia." *Communication Quarterly* 62 (5): 569–88.

Hassler-Forest, Dan. 2012. *Capitalist Superheroes: Caped Crusaders in the Neoliberal Age*. Winchester, UK: Zero Books.

Hayward, Susan. 2000. "Framing National Cinema." In *Cinema and Nation*, edited by Mette Hjort and Scott MacKenzie, 88–102. London: Routledge.

Heidegger, Martin. 1971. "The Origin of the Work of Art." In *Poetry, Language, Thought*, translated by Albert Hofstadter, 15–86. New York: Harper & Row.

Hesselberth, Pepita. 2012. "From Subject-Effect to Presence-Effect: A Deictic Approach to the Cinematic." *NECSUS* (Autumn 2012). https://necsus-ejms.org/from-subject-effect-to-presence-effect-a-deictic-approach-to-the-cinematic/.

Higbee, Will. 2014. *Post-Beur Cinema: North African Émigré and Maghrebi-French Filmmaking in France since 2000*. Edinburgh: Edinburgh University Press.

Higbee, Will, and Song Hwee Lim. 2010. "Concepts of Transnational Cinema: Towards a Critical Transnationalism in Film Studies." *Transnational Cinemas* 1 (1): 7–21.

Higson, Andrew. 1989. "The Concept of National Cinema." *Screen* 30 (4): 36–46.

Higson, Andrew. 2000. "The Limiting Imagination of National Cinema." In *Cinema and Nation*, edited by Mette Hjort and Scott MacKenzie, 63–74. London: Routledge.

Hill, John, Pamela Church Gibson, Richard Dyer, E. Ann Kaplan, and Paul Willemen, eds. 2000. *World Cinema: Critical Approaches*. Oxford: Oxford University Press.

Hjort, Mette. 2005. *Small Nation, Global Cinema: The New Danish Cinema*. Minneapolis: University of Minnesota Press.

Hjort, Mette. 2010. "On the Plurality of Cinematic Transnationalism." In *World Cinemas, Transnational Perspectives*, edited by Nat Durovicová and Kathl Newman, 12–33. New York: Routledge.

Hjort, Mette, and Scott Mackenzie, eds. 2000. *Cinema and Nation*. London: Routledge.

Holtmeier, Matthew. 2019. *Contemporary Political Cinema*. Edinburgh: Edinburgh University Press.

Houser, Craig, Leslie C. Jones, Simon Taylor, and Jack Ben-Levi. 1993. *Abject Art: Repulsion and Desire in American Art*. New York: Whitney Museum of Art.

Hsu, Hsuan L. 2006. "Racial Privacy, the L.A. Ensemble Film, and Paul Haggis's Crash." *Film Criticism* 31 (1–2): 132–56.

Huang, Tsung-Yi. 2001. "Chungking Express: Walking with a Map of Desire in the Mirage of the Global City." *Quarterly Review of Film and Video* 18 (2): 129–42. https://doi.org/10.1080/10509200109361519.

Huntington, Samuel P. 2011. *The Clash of Civilizations and the Remaking of World Order*. New York: Simon & Schuster.

Hyde, Lewis. 2007. *The Gift: Creativity and the Artist in the Modern World*. New York: Vintage.

Jalao, Ly Chong. 2010. "Looking Gran Torino in the Eye: A Review." *Journal of Southeast Asian American Education & Advancement* 5 (1). https://docs.lib.purdue.edu/jsaaea/vol5/iss1/15/.

Jameson, Fredric. 1973. "The Vanishing Mediator: Narrative Structure in Max Weber." *New German Critique*, no. 1: 52–89. https://doi.org/10.2307/487630.

Jameson, Fredric. 1995. *The Geopolitical Aesthetic: Cinema and Space in the World System*. Bloomington: Indiana University Press.

Jameson, Fredric. 2004. "The Politics of Utopia." *New Left Review*, no. 25 (February): 35–54.

Jay, Martin. 2012. *Cultural Semantics: Keywords of Our Time*. Amherst: University of Massachusetts Press.

Jeong, Seung-hoon. 2013a. "A Global Cinematic Zone of Animal and Technology." *Angelaki* 18 (1): 139–57.

Jeong, Seung-hoon. 2013b. *Cinematic Interfaces: Film Theory after New Media*. New York: Routledge.

Jeong, Seung-hoon. 2013c. "The Apocalyptic Sublime: Hollywood Disaster Films and Donnie Darko." In *Terror and the Cinematic Sublime: Essays on Violence and the Unpresentable in Post-9/11 Films*, edited by Todd A. Comer and Lloyd Isaac Vayo, 72–87. Jefferson, NC: McFarland.

Jeong, Seung-hoon. 2014. "DMZ: Atopia in Global Korean Cinema." In *DMZ: Stories of Today and Tomorrow*, edited by Jeong-bok Kim, 125–54. Seoul: Space for Contemporary Art.

Jeong, Seung-hoon. 2016. "A Generational Spectrum of Global Korean Auteurs: Political Matrix and Ethical Potential." In *The Global Auteur: The Politics of Authorship in 21st Century Cinema*, edited by Seung-hoon Jeong and Jeremi Szaniawski, 361–78. New York: Bloomsbury.

Jeong, Seung-hoon. 2021. "World Cinema in a Global Frame." *Studies in World Cinema* 1 (1): 29–38.

Jeong, Seung-hoon, and Jeremi Szaniawski, eds. 2016. *The Global Auteur: The Politics of Authorship in 21st Century Cinema*. New York: Bloomsbury.

Johnson, Audrey D. 2010. "Male Masochism in Casino Royale." In *Revisioning 007: James Bond and Casino Royale*, edited by Christoph Lindner, 115–27. London: Wallflower Press.

Kant, Immanuel. 2000. *Critique of the Power of Judgment*. Edited by Paul Guyer. Translated by Pau Guyer and Eric Matthews. Cambridge: Cambridge University Press.

Kapur, Jyotsna, and Keith B. Wagner, eds. 2013. *Neoliberalism and Global Cinema: Capital, Culture, and Marxist Critique*. New York: Routledge.

Keane, Stephen. 2006. *Disaster Movies: The Cinema of Catastrophe*. 2nd ed. London: Wallflower Press.

Keenan, Dennis King. 2005. *The Question of Sacrifice*. Bloomington: Indiana University Press.

Kierkegaard, Søren. 2006. *Fear and Trembling*. Edited by C. Stephen Evans and Sylvia Walsh. Cambridge: Cambridge University Press.

Kim, Soyoung. 2013. "The State of Fantasy in Emergency." *Cultural Studies* 27 (2): 257–70.

King, Geoff. 2007. *Donnie Darko*. London: Wallflower Press.

Klein, Naomi. 2008. *The Shock Doctrine: The Rise of Disaster Capitalism*. New York: Picador.

Krauss, Rosalind. 1996. "Informe without Conclusion." *October* 78: 89–105.

Kristeva, Julia. 1982. *Powers of Horror: An Essay on Abjection*. Translated by Leon S. Roudiez. New York: Columbia University Press.

Kristeva, Julia. 1994. *Strangers to Ourselves*. Translated by Leon Roudiez. New York: Columbia University Press.

Kundnani, Arun. 2014. *The Muslims Are Coming! Islamophobia, Extremism, and the Domestic War on Terror*. London: Verso.

Lacan, Jacques. 1997. *The Ethics of Psychoanalysis: The Seminar of Jacques Lacan (Book VII)*. Edited by Jacques Alain-Miller. Translated by Dennis Porter. New York: W. W. Norton.

Lacan, Jacques. 1999. *On Feminine Sexuality, the Limits of Love and Knowledge: The Seminar of Jacques Lacan (Book XX)*. Edited by Jacques-Alain Miller. Translated by Bruce Fink. New York: W. W. Norton.

Landesman, Ohad, and Roy Bendor. 2011. "Animated Recollection and Spectatorial Experience in Waltz with Bashir." *Animation* 6 (3): 353–70.

Landow, George P. 1994. *Hyper/Text/Theory*. Baltimore, MD: Johns Hopkins University Press.

Lanzmann, Claude. 1994. "Why Spielberg Has Distorted the Truth." *Guardian Weekly*, April 3: 14.

Latour, Bruno. 2009. "Spheres and Networks. Two Ways to Reinterpret Globalization." *Harvard Design Magazine*, no. 30 (Spring–Summer): 138–44.
Levinas, Emmanuel. 1979. *Totality and Infinity: An Essay on Exteriority*. Translated by Alphonso Lingis. Boston: M. Nijhoff.
Lévi-Strauss, Claude. 1955. "The Structural Study of Myth." *Journal of American Folklore* 68 (270): 428–44.
Lotringer, Sylvere. 2002. *More & Less: No. 2*. Los Angeles: Semiotext(e).
Lu, Sheldon H. 2005. "Crouching Tiger, Hidden Dragon, Bouncing Angels: Hollywood, Taiwan, Hong Kong, and Transnational Cinema." In *Chinese-Language Film: Historiography, Poetics, Politics*, edited by Sheldon H Lu and Emilie Yueh-yu Yeh, 220–33. Honolulu: University of Hawaii Press.
Lu, Tonglin. 2008. "Fantasy and Reality of a Virtual China in Jia Zhangke's Film The World." *Journal of Chinese Cinemas* 2 (3): 163–79.
Lykidis, Alex. 2020. *Art Cinema and Neoliberalism*. London: Palgrave Macmillan.
Lyotard, Jean-François. 1984. *The Postmodern Condition: A Report on Knowledge*. Translated by Geoffrey Bennington and Brian Massumi. Minneapolis: University of Minnesota Press.
Magistrale, Tony. 2005. *Abject Terrors: Surveying the Modern and Postmodern Horror Film*. New York: Peter Lang Inc., International Academic Publishers.
Mai, Joseph. 2010. *Jean-Pierre and Luc Dardenne*. Champaign: University of Illinois Press.
Marion, Jean-Luc. 2011. *The Reason of the Gift*. Translated by Stephen E. Lewis. Charlottesville: University of Virginia Press.
Martin-Jones, David. 2011. *Deleuze and World Cinemas*. London: Continuum.
Martin-Jones, David. 2018. *Cinema against Doublethink: Ethical Encounters with the Lost Pasts of World History*. New York: Routledge.
Mathews, Peter. 2005. "Spinoza's Stone: The Logic of Donnie Darko." *Post Script* 25 (1): 38–48.
Mauss, Marcel. 1967. *The Gift: Forms and Functions of Exchange in Archaic Societies*. New York: Norton.
Mbembe, Achille. 2003. "Necropolitics." *Public Culture* 15 (1): 11–40.
McAlinden, Carrie. 2013. "True Surrealism: Walter Benjamin and The Act of Killing." BFI. December 2013. http://www.bfi.org.uk/news-opinion/sight-sound-magazine/features/true-surrealism-walter-benjamin-act-killing.
McClendon, Blair, and Joshua Oppenheimer. 2013. "Joshua Oppenheimer and The Act of Killing." *Los Angeles Review of Books*. August 14, 2013. https://lareviewofbooks.org/article/joshua-oppenheimer-and-the-act-of-killing/.
Mignolo, Walter D. 2002. "The Many Faces of Cosmo-Polis: Border Thinking and Critical Cosmopolitanism." In *Cosmopolitanism*, edited by Carol Appadurai Breckenridge, Sheldon Pollock, Homi Bhabha, and Dipesh Chakrabarty, 157–88. Durham, NC: Duke University Press.
Mignolo, Walter D. 2011. *The Darker Side of Western Modernity: Global Futures, Decolonial Options*. Durham, NC: Duke University Press.
Moran, Brendan, and Carlo Salzani, eds. 2015. *Towards the Critique of Violence: Walter Benjamin and Giorgio Agamben*. London: Bloomsbury.
Mulvey, Laura. 2006. "Abbas Kiarostami." In *Death 24x a Second: Stillness and the Moving Image*, 123–43. London: Reaktion Books.
Munster, Anna. 2013. *An Aesthesia of Networks: Conjunctive Experience in Art and Technology*. Cambridge, MA: MIT Press.

Murray, Jonathan. 2016. "'I've Been Inspecting You, Mister Bond': Crisis, Catharsis, and Calculation in Daniel Craig's Twenty-First-Century 007." *Cineaste* 41 (2): 4–11.
Murray, Stuart. 2009. *Images of Dignity: Barry Barclay and Fourth Cinema*. Honolulu: University of Hawaii Press.
Naficy, Hamid. 2001. *An Accented Cinema: Exilic and Diasporic Filmmaking*. Princeton, NJ: Princeton University Press.
Nagel, Mechthild. 2002. *Masking the Abject: A Genealogy of Play*. Lanham, MD: Lexington Books.
Nagib, Lúcia. 2011. *World Cinema and the Ethics of Realism*. New York: Continuum.
Nagib, Lúcia. 2016. "Regurgitated Bodies: Presenting and Representing Trauma in 'The Act of Killing.'" In *The Routledge Companion to Cinema and Politics*, edited by Yannis Tzioumakis and Claire Molloy, 218–30. London: Routledge.
Nagib, Lúcia, Christopher Perriam, and Rajinder Kumar Dudrah, eds. 2012. *Theorizing World Cinema*. London: I. B. Tauris.
Nancy, Jean-Luc. 2001. *L'évidence Du Film: Abbas Kiarostami = The Evidence of Film: Abbas Kiarostami*. Translated by Christine Irizarry and Verena Andermatt Conley. Bruxelles: Yves Gevaert.
Nancy, Jean-Luc. 2008. *The Inoperative Community*. Minneapolis: University of Minnesota Press.
Nietzsche, Friedrich. 2009. *On the Genealogy of Morals*. Translated by Douglas Smith. Oxford: Oxford University Press.
Nobus, Dany. 2007. "The Politics of Gift-Giving and the Provocation of Lars Von Trier's Dogville." *Film-Philosophy* 11 (3): 23–37.
Nochimson, Martha P. 2010. *World on Film: An Introduction*. Chichester, UK: Wiley-Blackwell.
Nowell-Smith, Geoffrey, ed. 1997. *The Oxford History of World Cinema*. Oxford: Oxford University Press.
Nowell-Smith, Geoffrey. 2008. *Making Waves New Cinemas of the 1960s*. New York: Continuum.
Omry, Keren. 2010. "Bond, Benjamin, Balls: Technologised Masculinity in Casnino Royale." In *Revisioning 007: James Bond and Casino Royale*, edited by Christoph Lindner, 159–72. London: Wallflower Press.
Paik, Peter Y. 2010. *From Utopia to Apocalypse: Science Fiction and the Politics of Catastrophe*. Minneapolis: University of Minnesota Press.
Parekh, Bhikhu. 2002. *Rethinking Multiculturalism: Cultural Diversity and Political Theory*. Cambridge, MA: Harvard University Press.
Parthasarathy, D. 2009. "Of Slumdogs, Doxosophers, and the (In)Dignity of Labour(Ers)." *Social Science Research Network*, September 30. https://doi.org/10.2139/ssrn.2096954.
Pheasant-Kelly, Frances. 2013. *Abject Spaces in American Cinema: Institutional Settings, Identity and Psychoanalysis in Film*. London: I. B. Tauris.
Pieterse, Jan Nederveen. 2017. *Multipolar Globalization: Emerging Economies and Development*. London: Routledge.
Pop, Doru. 2015. "Mad Max: Spare-Parts Heroes, Recycled Narratives, Reused Visualities and Recuperated Histories." *Caietele Echinox* 29: 185–206.
Pratt, Mary Louise. 2010. *Imperial Eyes: Travel Writing and Transculturation*. London: Routledge.
Rancière, Jacques. 2004. "The Ethical Turn of Aesthetics and Politics." In *Aesthetics and Its Discontents*, 109–32. Cambridge, UK: Polity Press.

Reader, Keith. 2006. *The Abject Object: Avatars of the Phallus in Contemporary French Theory, Literature and Film*. Amsterdam: Rodopi.
Reinhard, Kenneth. 2013. "Toward a Political Theology of the Neighbor." In *The Neighbor: Three Inquiries in Political Theology*, by Slavoj Žižek, Eric L. Santner, and Kenneth Reinhard, 11–75. Chicago: University of Chicago Press.
Rivette, Jacques. 1961. "On Abjection." *Cahier Du Cinéma*, no. 120 (June): 54–55.
Rivi, Luisa. 2016. *European Cinema after 1989: Cultural Identity and Transnational Production*. New York: Palgrave Macmillan.
Robbins, Bruce. 1998. "Actually Existing Cosmopolitanism." In *Cosmopolitics: Thinking and Feeling beyond the Nation*, edited by Pheng Cheah and Bruce Robbins, 1–19. Minneapolis: University of Minnesota Press.
Rosen, Philip. 1984. "History, Textuality, Nation: Kracauer, Burch and Some Problems in the Study of National Cinemas." *Iris* 2 (2): 60–83.
Saeed-Vafa, Mehrnaz, and Jonathan Rosenbaum. 2003. *Abbas Kiarostami*. Urbana: University of Illinois Press.
Salzani, Carlo. 2015. "From Benjamin's Bloßes Leben to Agamben's Nuda Vita: A Genealogy." In *Towards the Critique of Violence: Walter Benjamin and Giorgio Agamben*, edited by Brendan Moran and Carlo Salzani, 109–23. London: Bloomsbury.
Schlottman, Andrea. n.d. "Samuel Beckett: Fail Better and 'Worstword Ho!'" *Books on the Wall* (blog). n.d. https://booksonthewall.com/blog/samuel-beckett-quote-fail-better/.
Sengupta, Mitu. 2010. "A Million Dollar Exit from the Anarchic Slum-World: Slumdog Millionaire's Hollow Idioms of Social Justice." *Third World Quarterly* 31 (4): 599–616.
Shaviro, Steven. 2011. "The 'Bitter Necessity' of Debt: Neoliberal Finance and the Society of Control." *Concentric* 37 (March): 73–82.
Shimakawa, Karen. 2002. *National Abjection: The Asian American Body Onstage*. Durham. NC: Duke University Press.
Shohat, Ella, and Robert Stam. 1994. *Unthinking Eurocentrism: Multiculturalism and the Media*. London: Routledge.
Shohat, Ella, and Robert Stam, eds. 2003. *Multiculturalism, Postcoloniality, and Transnational Media*. New Brunswick, NJ: Rutgers University Press.
Shohat, Ella, and Robert Stam. 2014. *Unthinking Eurocentrism: Multiculturalism and the Media*. London: Routledge.
Silvio, Carl. 1999. "Refiguring the Radical Cyborg in Mamoru Oshii's Ghost in the Shell." *Science Fiction Studies* 26 (1): 54–75.
Simmel, Georg. 1972. *On Individuality and Social Forms*. Chicago: University of Chicago Press.
Simons, Jan. 2008. "Complex Narratives." *New Review of Film and Television Studies* 6 (2): 111–26.
Sinha, Amresh, and Terence McSweeney, eds. 2012. *Millennial Cinema: Memory in Global Film*. London: Wallflower Press.
Sinnerbrink, Robert. 2006. "Deconstructive Justice and the 'Critique of Violence': On Derrida and Benjamin." *Social Semiotics* 16 (3): 485–97.
Sinnerbrink, Robert. 2007. "Grace and Violence: Questioning Politics and Desire in Lars von Trier's Dogville." *Scan* 4 (2). http://scan.net.au/scan/journal/display.php?journal_id=94.
Sloterdijk, Peter. 2013. *In the World Interior of Capital: Towards a Philosophical Theory of Globalization*. Cambridge, UK: Polity.
Small, Andrew. 2016. "Fetish, Sacrifice and Tragic Freedom in the Dardenne Brothers' La Promesse." *Journal of Religion & Film* 20 (2): 1–23.

Smith, James. 2016. "'How Safe Do You Feel?': James Bond, Skyfall, and the Politics of the Secret Agent in an Age of Ubiquitous Threat." *College Literature* 43 (1): 145–72.
Solnit, Rebecca. 2010. *A Paradise Built in Hell: The Extraordinary Communities That Arise in Disaster*. Reprint ed. New York: Penguin Books.
Srivastava, Neelam. 2009. "Bollywood as National(Ist) Cinema: Violence, Patriotism and the National-Popular in Rang De Basanti." *Third Text* 23 (6): 703–16.
Stafford, Roy. 2014. *The Global Film Book*. London: Routledge.
Stahl, Roger. 2009. *Militainment, Inc.: War, Media, and Popular Culture*. New York: Routledge.
Stam, Robert, and Ella Shohat. 2012. *Race in Translation: Culture Wars around the Postcolonial Atlantic*. New York: New York University Press.
Stewart, Garrett. 2010. "Screen Memory in Waltz with Bashir." *Film Quarterly* 63 (3): 58–62.
Stewart, Garrett. 2014. "Fourth Dimensions, Seventh Senses: The Work of Mind-Gaming in the Age of Electronic Reproduction." In *Hollywood Puzzle Films*, edited by Warren Buckland, 165–84. London: Routledge.
Stuart, Jan. 2001. "Inside the Brooding Mind of 'Donnie Darko.'" *Los Angeles Times*, October 26, 2001. http://donniedarko.tripod.com/article/la10262001.html.
Szendy, Peter. 2015. *Apocalypse-Cinema: 2012 and Other Ends of the World*. Translated by Will Bishop. New York: Fordham University Press.
Tarr, Carrie. 2005. *Reframing Difference*. New York: Manchester University Press.
Taylor, Makenzi. 2020. "ISIS Recruitment of Youth via Social Media." *Global Affairs Review* (February 2020). https://wp.nyu.edu/schoolofprofessionalstudies-ga_review/isis-recruitment-of-youth-via-social-media/.
Tyler, Imogen. 2013. *Revolting Subjects: Social Abjection and Resistance in Neoliberal Britain*. London: Zed Books.
Vincendeau, Ginette. 2005. *La Haine*. London: I. B.Tauris.
Virilio, Paul. 2009. *University of Disaster*. Cambridge, UK: Polity.
Vitali, Valentina, and Paul Willemen, eds. 2008. *Theorising National Cinema*. London: British Film Institute.
Wagner, Keith B. 2015. "Globalizing Discourses: Literature and Film in the Age of Google." *Globalizations* 12 (2): 229–43.
Wagner, Rachel. 2016. "Screening Belief: The Life of Pi, Computer Generated Imagery, and Religious Imagination." *Religions* 7 (8): 96.
Wang, Yanjie. 2015. "Violence, Wuxia, Migrants: Jia Zhangke's Cinematic Discontent in A Touch of Sin." *Journal of Chinese Cinemas* 9 (2): 159–72.
Wheatley, Catherine. 2009. *Michael Haneke's Cinema: The Ethic of the Image*. New York: Berghahn Books.
Whissel, Kristen. 2006. "Tales of Upward Mobility: The New Verticality and Digital Special Effects." *Film Quarterly* 59 (4): 23–34.
White, Thomas. 2018. "What Did Hannah Arendt Really Mean by the Banality of Evil?" Aeon. April 2018. https://aeon.co/ideas/what-did-hannah-arendt-really-mean-by-the-banality-of-evil.
Whyte, Jessica. 2013. *Catastrophe and Redemption: The Political Thought of Giorgio Agamben*. Albany: State University of New York Press.
Willemen, Paul. 1994. "The National." In *Looks and Frictions: Essays in Cultural Studies and Film Theory*, 206–19. Bloomington, IN: Indiana University Press.
Young, Robert. 2009. "The Violent State." In *Experiencs of Freedom in Postcolonial Literatures and Cultures*, edited by Annalisa Oboe and Shaul Bassi, 43–58. London: Routledge.

Žižek, Slavoj. 1993. "The White Issue: The 'Theft of Enjoyment.'" *Village Voice*, May 18: 30–31.
Žižek, Slavoj. 1995. "Woman Is One of the Names-of-the-Father: Or How Not to Misread Lacan's Formulas of Sexuation." *Lacanian Ink* 10: 24–39.
Žižek, Slavoj. 1997. "Multiculturalism, or, the Cultural Logic of Multinational Capitalism." *New Left Review*, no. 225: 28–51.
Žižek, Slavoj. 2002. *Welcome to the Desert of the Real! Five Essays on September 11 and Related Dates*. London: Verso.
Žižek, Slavoj. 2006. *The Parallax View*. Cambridge, MA: MIT Press.
Žižek, Slavoj. 2008a. "Nature and Its Discontents." *SubStance* 37 (3): 37–72.
Žižek, Slavoj. 2008b. *Violence: Six Sideways Reflections*. New York: Picador.
Žižek, Slavoj. 2009. *In Defense of Lost Causes*. London: Verso.
Žižek, Slavoj. 2010. *Living in the End Times*. London: Verso.
Žižek, Slavoj. 2012. "The Politics of Batman." *New Statesman*, August 2012. https://www.newstatesman.com/culture/culture/2012/08/slavoj-%C5%BEi%C5%BEek-politics-batman.
Žižek, Slavoj. 2013a. *Less Than Nothing: Hegel and the Shadow of Dialectical Materialism*. London: Verso.
Žižek, Slavoj. 2013b. "Neighbors and Other Monsters: A Plea for Ethical Violence." In *The Neighbor: Three Inquiries in Political Theology*, by Slavoj Žižek, Eric L. Santner, and Kenneth Reinhard, 134–90. Chicago: University of Chicago Press.
Žižek, Slavoj. 2013c. "The Act of Killing and the Modern Trend of 'Privatising Public Space.'" *New Statesman*, July 2013. https://www.newstatesman.com/culture/2013/07/slavoj-zizek-act-killing-and-modern-trend-privatising-public-space.
Žižek, Slavoj. 2014. "ISIS Is a Disgrace to True Fundamentalism." *New York Times*, September 3, 2014, sec. Opinion. https://opinionator.blogs.nytimes.com/2014/09/03/isis-is-a-disgrace-to-true-fundamentalism/.

Index

For the benefit of digital users, indexed terms that span two pages (e.g., 52–53) may, on occasion, appear on only one of those pages.

Tables and figures are indicated by *t* and *f* following the page number

9/11, 19, 28–29, 80–81, 87, 93–94, 105–6, 137–40, 171–77, 183–84, 253–54
12 Monkeys (1995), 137n.5, 164

abject / abjection, 9–12, 16–19, 20–22, 38–57, 58–74, 75–78, 79–82, 86–89, 92–94, 96–98, 106–7, 115–18, 120–21, 124–30, 139–41, 143–44, 152–53, 162–63, 176–77, 181, 202–8, 209–11, 213, 224–25, 227–30, 238–41, 245–49, 258–59, 270–71, 274–76, 278, 282–85, 289–90, 292–93, 295–96, 297, 300–2
   abject art, 39–40
   aesthetics of abjection, 245–48
   becoming-abject, 275–76, 278–79, 283–84
   self-abjection, 55–56, 60–61, 106–7, 187, 247–48, 276
action-image, 59–60, 135–36, 203
Act of Killing, The (2012), 116–20, 129
addiction, 155–57, 174–75
Agamben, Giorgio, 8–9, 109–10, 125–26, 220, 274
agent / agency, 9–11, 16–17, 43–44, 56–57, 61, 68, 69, 72–75, 80, 81–82, 98, 151–52, 176–77, 181–82, 183–84, 185–90, 205–6, 208, 248, 276, 284–85, 290–91
   abject agency, 9–10, 11–12, 16–17, 43–47, 65–66, 68, 70–71, 72–74, 77–78, 176–77, 183–84, 187, 227–29, 240–41, 245–46, 248, 258–59, 284–85, 290–91, 298–99
   floating agency, 205–9, 216
   performative agency, 56–57, 152–53, 183–87, 276–77

   sovereign agency, 56–57, 79–82, 98, 103–4, 105–6, 116–18, 129–30, 176–77, 185–90 (*see also* sovereignty)
amor fati, 166–67, 172–73, 296–98
anarchy, 11–12, 104–8, 122–23, 210–11
Anderson, Benedict, 1
Andrew, Dudley, 12–13, 13n.2
animality, 40–41, 68–69, 77–78, 102–4, 111–12, 245–48, 263–68, 264n.2
apocalypse / post-apocalypse, 136–37, 139–40, 170–71, 176
   (post-)apocalyptic cinema, 142–44, 152–54, 157–58, 161–62, 164
Arendt, Hannah, 37–38, 116–18, 117n.6
atopia, 11–12, 16, 18, 22, 71, 162–63, 176, 209–10, 224–25, 277–79, 284–85, 286–302, 296n.5, 300*t*
   See also atopian ethics
axis of evil, 4, 80, 107, 253–54

Babel (2006), 198–200, 213
Badiou, Alain, 43, 278
Balibar, Étienne, 36–38, 43
Banlieu 13 (2004), 44–45
Banlieu 13: Ultimatum (2009), 44–45
bare life. See *homo sacer*
Bataille, Georges, 41n.9, 293
Batman. *See* the *Dark Knight* trilogy
Baudrillard, Jean, 236–37
Bazin, André, 206–8, 229–30
Benjamin, Walter, 19–20, 77, 101–5, 109–13, 114–15, 120–23, 154, 254, 272–73
Binding of Isaac, 22, 269, 270–77, 282–83
   Abraham, 22, 269, 270–71, 272–74, 275–77, 282–83
   Isaac, 22, 269, 270–71, 273, 274, 275–77, 282–83

biopolitics, 2–3, 8–9, 37–38, 41–42, 79–80, 101, 102–3, 125–27, 141, 144, 146, 149–50, 163–64, 165–66, 200–1, 202–3, 209–10, 214–15, 216–17, 220–21, 245, 251–53, 278–79, 280–81, 286, 288
  biopower, 8–9, 37–38, 80, 125–26, 141, 143, 159–60, 200–1, 216, 217, 239–40
Birdman (2014), 208–9, 212–13
Bond series, The, 19, 72, 81–94, 97–98, 106, 182, 187
  See also *Skyfall*
Bordwell, David, 180, 195, 196–97, 203
Bourne Trilogy, The, 19, 93–98, 178–79, 182, 183–84, 185–86, 187
Brexit, 6–7, 82, 124

Camus, Albert, 222–23, 296–97
capitalism, 2–8, 25–27, 31–32, 65–66, 67–68, 72–75, 84, 108, 145–46, 153–54, 234–35, 237–38, 249, 287, 288
  cognitive capitalism, 71–72, 77, 88–89, 92, 93–94, 95
  disaster capitalism, 94–95, 132–33, 141, 148–49
  emotional capitalism, 76–77, 78
  financial capitalism, 74–75, 77, 108, 181–82, 230–31
  See also neoliberalism
catastrophe, 6, 11–12, 16–17, 20–21, 58–59, 108, 121, 124–27, 130–31, 133–35, 143, 144, 148–49, 162, 165–68, 171, 187, 204–5, 222, 245, 254–55, 256–57, 286, 289, 294, 295–96
  cinema of catastrophe, 20, 59–60, 101, 128–30, 131–33, 135–41, 153–54, 223–24
chora, 39, 42
Chungking Express (1994), 215–16, 234–35
Children of Men (2006), 289, 292–93, 296–97
Class, The (2008), 49–50
clearing / lighting, 255–57, 268, 293
climate change, 163–64
communism, 4–5, 25–29, 32–33, 105, 116–20, 154, 238–39, 248

community, 4–6, 8–12, 16, 21, 56–57, 60, 64, 67–68, 193–95, 197–99, 200–5, 209–13, 214–19, 232–37, 245, 262, 293, 298–99, 300*t*
  community-based narratives (*see* narratology)
  imagined community, 1, 13–14, 215–16
contingency, 11–12, 16, 70–71, 166–67, 172, 203, 215–16, 230–31, 248–49, 284, 286, 301–2
control, 2–3, 39–40, 147–48, 162–63, 181–83, 199–200, 210–11
  control society / societies of control, 181–82, 210–11, 239–40, 250
cosmopolitanism, 2, 12–13, 14–15, 41–42, 127, 129, 299–300
Crash (2004), 197–98, 203–4, 213
Crouching Tiger, Hidden Dragon (2000), 215–16, 231–34
cruel optimism, 147–48, 185–86, 239–40

Dark Knight Trilogy, The, 19–20, 103–9, 115–16, 240–41
  Batman Begins (2005), 106
  Dark Knight, The (2008), 103–4, 105–6
  The Dark Knight Rises (2012), 105–7, 115–16
death drive, 134, 155, 276, 288, 298–99
  See also drive
debt, 27, 74–75, 151–52, 250, 261, 275–76, 294–95
Deleuze, Gilles, 17, 59–60, 63, 162–63, 172–74, 181–82, 210–12, 214, 229–30, 239–40, 245–47
  and Félix Guattari, 10–11, 63, 210–11, 245–46
democracy, 3, 4–5, 7–8, 27, 32–33, 34–35, 90, 103–4, 126–27, 253–54
  liberal democracy, 4–5, 27, 32–33, 49, 84, 87, 124, 254
Derrida, Jacques, 104–5, 109–10, 111–12, 115, 173–74, 249–50, 254–55, 299–300
Desert Dream (2007), 66–67
desire, 11, 19, 60–61, 113, 118–19, 162, 201–2, 209, 276, 286–87
Dheepan (2015), 51–52
dialectic(s), 6, 36–37, 253

différance, 104–5, 284–85
disaster, 20, 124–25, 130–31, 138, 141, 148–49, 294
　disaster genre, 61, 130, 132–33, 135–39, 143–44, 168, 195, 263–65
dissensus, 4, 6, 7–8, 34–35, 298–99
Dogville (2003), 113–14, 248–49, 251–57, 262–63
Donnie Darko (2001), 168–76
Dooman River (2009), 66–68
double death, 16–17, 19, 58–59, 60, 61–64, 65–66, 81–82, 93–94, 135–36, 222, 258–59, 294–95
Double Life of Veronique, The (1991), 25, 26–27, 195–96
drive, 11, 37, 77–78, 113, 114, 148, 155–56, 162, 210–11, 287, 288, 298–99
dystopia, 88, 108, 132–33, 136–37, 142–45, 154, 213, 289–93, 298–99

ecology, 149–50, 152–53, 260–61, 263–64
Edge of Heaven, The (2007), 195–96, 270–71, 279–85
Edge of Tomorrow (2014), 188
Elsaesser, Thomas, 14–15, 26–27, 39–40, 43, 138–39, 165–66, 181–83, 189–90, 299–300
Elysium (2013), 2, 142–43
end of history, 3, 84–85, 155–57, 162–63, 287
ensemble plot, 195–96, 197–98, 208, 237–38
Esposito, Roberto, 200–1
eternal return, 172–73
ethics, 2–11, 31, 34–35, 50–53, 54–56, 122–23, 132, 168–70, 175–76, 250, 269–73, 276, 299–302
　alternative ethics, 11–12, 21–22, 245, 270–71, 297–98
　atopian ethics, 22, 284–85, 294, 297–302
　double ethics, 6, 11–12, 16, 34–35, 36–37, 44, 45–46, 52, 66, 108–9, 125–26, 204–5, 224–25, 245–46, 253–54, 269–70, 286, 288
　ethical turn, 4, 6, 7–8, 34–35, 36–37, 132, 134–35, 281

hard ethics, 4, 5–6, 8, 9, 16, 34–35, 36–37, 41, 45–46, 50–51, 54, 55–57, 60–61, 67–68, 80, 108–9, 122–23, 129, 204, 216–17, 225–26, 253–54, 261–62, 269–71, 274–75, 286
soft ethics, 4, 5–11, 14–15, 16, 18–19, 22, 34–37, 41, 42, 47, 50, 53, 56–57, 66–67, 108–9, 125–26, 129–30, 204, 216–17, 225–26, 229, 245, 253–54, 259–60, 261–62, 269–70, 274–76, 280–85, 286, 299–300
exclusion, 2–3, 4, 6–7, 8–9, 16, 28–29, 30–31, 33–35, 38, 43, 44, 109–10, 145–98, 199–200, 245, 286
　internal exclusion, 28–29, 37–41, 43–44
　symptoms of exclusion, 5–6, 8–9, 16, 61–63, 87, 124, 127
existentialism, 22, 222–23, 294–99

Failan (2001), 64–65
Fight Club (1999), 138–39, 165–66
flânerie, 205–6, 235
Foucault, Michel, 1–2, 37–38, 39, 181–82, 210–11, 290–91
free will, 111–12, 114–15, 134, 166–68, 170–73, 181, 189–90, 271, 273, 283–84, 288, 296–97
Freud, Sigmund, 120–22, 134–35, 160, 166, 201–2, 278–79
Fukuyama, Francis, 3
fundamentalism, 4, 5–6, 31–32, 55, 108–9, 122–23, 125–26, 159–60, 163–64, 202–3, 215–19, 288

Ghost in the Shell (2017), 188–89
gift, 11–12, 16–17, 18, 56–57, 66–67, 151–52, 199–200, 248–53, 254–57, 261–64, 266–68, 275–76, 283–85, 289–90, 296–97, 298–99
　ethics of the gift, 21–22, 251–52
　gift culture, 249, 251–52, 261, 262–63
　gift economy, 249, 250–51, 252–53, 266–67
　gift-giving, 16, 21–22, 66–68, 224–25, 248–49, 252, 255–57, 261–63, 279–80, 284–85, 289–91, 298–99
global frame, 16–17, 62–63, 84, 214–15, 297–98

globalization, 1–8, 16, 82–83, 124, 127, 199–200, 258
  global (non-)citizens, 270–71
  global community, 1–2, 4–5, 11, 195, 197–98, 204, 213, 236–37, 245
  global network, 10–11, 71, 87, 90, 94–95, 199–200, 203, 213, 215–16, 220–21, 237–38
  global village, 193, 215–16, 236–37
Goodbye, Lenin! (2003), 26, 27, 32–33, 248
Gran Torino (2008), 146–47, 254–55, 258–63, 289–90, 295–96
Grain in Ear (2005), 66, 67–68
guilt, 54–55, 97–98, 109–11, 219–20, 278

Hadewijch (2009), 55–57
Haine, La (1995), 18–19, 29–30, 35–37, 44–47, 50–51
Hardt, Michael and Antonio Negri, 7–8, 181–82
Harvey, David, 2–3, 28, 32–33
hate, 16, 35–38, 55–56
Heidegger, Martin, 104–5, 250, 255–56, 262–63, 293
heterotopia, 290–92
Hidden (2005), 52–53, 54
Himizu (2011), 141, 294–96, 297–98
Holy Motors (2012), 206–8, 211–13
homo sacer, 8, 60–61, 68–69, 77, 79–80, 94, 109–10, 113, 146–47, 159, 200–1, 219, 220, 252–53

identity, 2–3, 8, 11–12, 14, 15–16, 37–38, 40–41, 43–44, 197–98, 200–1, 209–10, 214, 259–60, 276
  identity politics, 4–5, 7–8, 14, 16–17, 33
ideology, 5–6, 30–31, 58–61, 187–90
inclusion, 2–3, 8, 10–11, 28–29, 44, 50, 125–26, 127, 199–200, 203–4, 269–70, 280–81, 286
  inclusive tolerance, 33–34
  systems of inclusion, 4–5, 16, 75–77, 87, 124, 127
infinite justice, 4, 34–35, 80, 107, 253–54
infinity, 11, 22, 116, 268, 271–72, 292–93
Intouchables, The (2011), 47–48
Islam, 5–6, 55–56, 215–25

Jameson, Fredric, 31–32, 153–54, 161, 196–97
Journals of Musan, The (2010), 73–74, 293

Kant, Immanuel, 11–12, 113–14, 132, 133–35, 136–37, 166–67, 273, 299–300
Kierkegaard, Søren, 114–15, 271, 273–74, 276–77, 282–83
Kristeva, Julia, 9, 38–42, 79–80, 245–46, 301

Lacan, Jacques, 11, 38, 53, 74–75, 113, 174, 201–2, 201f, 209–10, 245–46, 276, 283–84
Latour, Bruno, 211–12
law, 19–20, 31, 45–46, 101–5, 109–10, 112–13, 115, 116, 119–20, 216–17, 260
Levinas, Emmanuel, 22, 31, 97–98, 121–22, 159, 271–72, 274–75, 278–79, 282–83, 284–85
Life and Nothing More... (1992), 21, 141, 215–16, 223–24
Life of Pi (2012), 21–22, 141, 248–49, 263–68
Lives of Others, The (2006), 27, 248
Lyotard, Jean-François, 134–35

Mad Max series, 20, 143–44, 157–64
  Mad Max (1979), 158
  Mad Max 2: The Road Warrior (1981), 158
  Mad Max Beyond Thunderdome (1985), 159
  Mad Max: Fury Road (2015), 157, 159–60, 164
Magnolia (1999), 195, 197–98, 203–5
mapping, 12–13, 19, 72–73, 88–89, 93–94, 96–97, 178–79, 195, 206, 235, 286
master, 147, 212, 253, 265–66
  master-slave dialectic, 253
Matrix, The (1999), 147, 164
Mauss, Marcel, 249–50, 262–63
Mbembe, Achille, 37–38
McLuhan, Marshall, 193
Melancholia (2011), 139–40, 162
migration, 4–5, 14, 64, 124, 269–70
mind-game (film), 19, 20–21, 121, 165–68, 175–79, 180–82, 188, 190, 215–16
Minority Report (2002), 138, 166–67

modular narrative, 180, 196–97, 212
multiculturalism, 15–17, 30–33, 34–35, 44, 225–26, 233–34, 259–61
Mysterious Object at Noon (2000), 208–9, 212–13

Nancy, Jean-Luc, 200–1, 223–24, 293
narratology, 193–95, 212
　community-based narratives, 193–94, 203, 212
　modular narratives, 180, 196–97, 212
　network narratives; pure network narratives, 21, 193–95, 196–97, 198–99, 203–4, 206–8, 212–13, 216
national cinema, 13–14, 16
　national frame, 13–14, 93, 214
　nationalist cinema, 13–14
natural disaster, 124–25, 129
necrofuturism, 148–49
necropolitics, 37–38, 148–49
neighbor, 22, 209–11, 254–55, 278, 283–84, 292–93, 297–99, 300–1
neocolonialism, 14, 27, 28–30, 42
neoliberalism, 20–21, 42, 78, 83, 89–90, 94–95, 118–19, 124, 145, 148–49, 160, 182, 189–90, 237–38
network, 10–13, 19, 21–22, 62–64, 87, 193–213, 214–26, 231–32, 234, 236–190, 286, 292–93, 300*t*
　network narratives, 193–99, 203–4, 205, 208, 212–13, 216, 234, 237–38, 240–41 (*see also* narratology)
　totalized network, 11–12, 16, 197–98, 203, 204–5, 213, 216, 236–37, 240–41, 245
Nietzsche, Friedrich, 11, 114, 135–36, 154, 166–67, 172–73, 174–75, 273, 286–87, 288, 296–98
nihilism, 11–12, 16, 22, 88, 174–75, 286–88, 297–99, 300*t*
　active nihilism, 88, 175, 288, 289–90, 298–99
　negative nihilism, 286–87, 288, 298–99
　passive nihilism, 11, 174–75, 287, 288–91
　positive nihilism, 11–12, 22, 297–99
nomadism, 14, 69, 94, 143, 152–53, 157–58, 162, 206, 212, 215–16, 222, 230–31, 233–34, 270–71

non-place, 66, 96–97, 234–35, 236–37

objet petit a, 174, 176, 209–10
Occupy movement, 7–8, 106, 145
Oedipus, 39, 151, 218–19, 245–46, 278–79
ontology, 165–66, 245–46, 254–55, 262–63, 268, 293
big Other, the, 11, 55–56, 114–16, 154, 180–81, 202, 273, 282–83, 284–85, 297–98
Others, The (2001), 175–76, 253

performativity, 26–27, 40–41, 43–44, 56–57, 109–10, 118–19, 151–52, 156–57, 162–63, 181, 205, 206, 208–9, 248–49, 276–77, 284–85, 298–99
pharmakon, 199–200, 250
philosophy, 165–66, 194–95, 270–71, 301–2
　film-philosophy, 301–2
Playtime (1967), 205–6, 223–24
Poongsan (2011), 68–71, 72–74
post-Cold War, 27, 32–33, 68, 81–83, 93–94, 124
postmodernism, 20, 31–32, 36–37, 162–63, 176, 212, 235–36, 259–60
post-politics, 3–6, 7–8, 16, 22, 34–35, 141, 204, 230–31, 269–70, 286, 299–300
precarity, 11–12, 85–86, 88–89, 164, 204–5, 267, 269–70, 284–85, 290–91, 297–99
Promise, The (1996), 22, 269–71, 273–79, 282–83, 297–98
Prophet, A (2009), 51–52

Rancière, Jacques, 4, 7–8, 34–35, 43, 132, 134–35, 220–21, 253–54, 256–57, 281
Rang de Basanti (2006), 21, 215–16, 226–29, 230–31
Real, the, 26, 33–35, 38, 47–48, 53, 60–61, 118–19, 121–22, 130–31, 138–39, 174–76, 201–2, 209, 230–31, 245–46, 288
retroactive causality / retroaction, 20–21, 166–68, 171, 184–85, 188, 250–51, 273, 297
revelation, 18, 55–56, 113–14, 130–31, 142, 176–77
rhizome, 214, 300*t*

Roja (1992), 21, 215–16, 225–29, 230–31

sacrifice, 20–21, 60–61, 110–11, 186–87, 188, 219–20, 269, 281–82
   ritual sacrifice, 219–20
   sacrifice of sacrifice, 186
   self-sacrifice, 20–21, 162, 167–71, 175, 184, 185–86, 222, 286–87, 288, 298–99
sanctity of life, 11–12, 19–20, 21–22, 77, 111–13, 121–23, 151–52, 190, 215–16, 245, 292–93
Save the Green Planet! (2003), 139–40, 144
Serial (Bad) Weddings (2014), 48–49
sexuation, 201–3, 201f, 209, 278–79
Shoah (1985), 132
Shohat, Ella and Robert Stam, 7–8, 15–16, 33, 34–35
Short Cuts (1993), 196–98, 203–5
simulacra / simulation, 26, 28, 118, 131, 138–39, 205–6, 236–37, 268, 288
Sinnerbrink, Robert, 105, 111n.3, 254
Skyfall (2012), 19, 80–93, 95, 97–98
Sloterdijk, Peter, 1–3
Slumdog Millionaire (2008), 21, 215–16, 229–31
Snowpiercer (2013), 20, 143–57, 164
Source Code (2011), 20–21, 176–87
sovereignty / sovereign power, 8, 9–10, 19–20, 51–52, 60, 67–68, 69, 77, 79–82, 103–4, 106, 109–10, 120–21, 146, 148, 158, 159, 176–77, 181, 183–84, 185–90, 200–1, 202, 276, 283–84
   See also (sovereign) agency
spy genre, 19, 72, 80, 81–82, 84, 91–92, 93–94
state of exception, 8, 37–38, 51–52, 74–75, 76–77, 79–80, 85–86, 89, 94, 97–98, 105, 116–18, 119–20, 139–40, 146, 155–56, 158, 159, 187, 200–1, 252, 254–55, 264–65, 288
   state of emergency, 8–9, 45–46, 72, 80, 89, 95, 105, 107, 125–26
Still Life (2006), 28, 296n.5
subaltern, 8, 14–15, 37–38, 127
subject / subjectivity / subjectivation, 8–13, 38–39, 43–44, 56–57, 58, 61, 79–80, 82, 134–35, 200–1, 202, 205, 209–11, 245–46, 286–87, 292–93, 297
sublime, the, 11–12, 20, 132–41, 167–68, 172–73, 175–76
superheroes, 45–46, 88–89, 103–4, 106–7, 108, 168, 170–71, 182–83
Symbolic, the, 38–39, 60–61, 118–19, 201–2, 209, 245–46, 247–48, 262, 278, 286–87, 288, 294–95
   symbolic death, 19, 58–59, 60–61, 81–82, 86–87, 88, 93–94, 162, 294–95

Taste of Cherry (1997), 206–8, 215–17, 221–22, 296–97
Tazza: The High Rollers (2006), 74–77
territorialization, 16, 214
   deterritorialization, 10–11, 16, 36–37, 214, 216, 232, 245–46
   reterritorialization, 10–11, 16, 28–29, 44, 93–94, 218–19, 223–24
terrorism, 5–6, 44, 82–83, 85, 107, 116, 125–26, 213, 225
Terror Live, The (2013), 139–40, 144
Thieves, The (2012), 19, 72–75, 77, 195
Third Way, 4–6, 27
Thirst (2009), 19, 75–76, 77–78
Timbuktu (2014), 21, 202–3, 215–20
time travel / time loop, 20–21, 136–38, 164, 165–71, 172–73, 176–78, 183–85, 187–90
totality, 11–12, 200–1, 209–12, 292–93
Touch of Sin, A (2013), 21, 128–29, 213, 215–16, 237–41
transnational cinema, 14, 16, 62–63, 198–99, 214–15, 216
   transnational frame, 14, 15–16, 214–15
trauma, 20–21, 54–55, 94, 97–98, 120–22, 129–30, 134–35, 161–62, 166–67, 187, 268
Trumpism, 6–7, 124, 163–64
Tyler, Imogen, 10–11, 41–43, 54–55

utopia, 7–8, 16, 46–47, 153–54, 160, 209–10, 213, 277–78, 284–85, 290–93

video game logic, 96–97, 121–22, 178–79, 229–30

violence, 11–12, 19–20, 45–46, 101–7, 109–20, 122–23, 220, 227–29, 237–38, 240–41, 253–55
    divine violence, 11–12, 19–20, 46–47, 102, 104–6, 107, 109–11, 112–18, 119–20, 122–23, 142, 155–57, 240–41, 251–52, 253–54, 278–79
    lawmaking violence, 19–20, 45–46, 101–5, 109–10, 115, 116–18, 220, 254–55
    law-preserving violence, 45–46, 101–2, 103–5, 115, 216–17, 220
    pseudo-divine violence, 19–20, 115, 116, 119–20, 122–23, 129–30, 219, 220, 240–41, 254, 286–87

Waking Life (2001), 206–8, 212–13
Waltz with Bashir (2008), 121–22, 129–30
World, The (2004), 28, 195, 215–16, 236–38, 237n.4, 239–40
world cinema, 12–17, 21, 129, 214

Yellow Sea, The (2010), 19, 69–74

Žižek, Slavoj, 31–32, 33–34, 79–80, 113–16, 118–19, 122–23, 134, 152–53, 156–57, 166–67, 172–73, 174, 197, 217, 237–38, 249, 259–60, 260n.1, 261, 278, 282–83, 287, 289–90